Forbidden Words

Many words and expressions are viewed as 'taboo', such as those used to describe sex, our bodies and their functions, and those used to insult other people. This book provides a fascinating insight into taboo language and its role in everyday life. It looks at the ways we use language to be polite or impolite, politically correct or offensive, depending on whether we are 'sweet talking', 'straight talking' or being deliberately rude. Using a range of colourful examples, it shows how we use language playfully and figuratively in order to swear, to insult, and also to be politically correct, and what our motivations are for doing so. It goes on to examine the differences between institutionalized censorship and the ways individuals censor their own language. Lively and revealing, *Forbidden Words* will fascinate anyone who is interested in how and why we use and avoid taboos in daily conversation.

KEITH ALLAN is Reader in Linguistics and Convenor of the Linguistics Program at Monash University. His research interests focus mainly on aspects of meaning in language, with a second interest in the history and philosophy of linguistics. He has published in many books and journals, and is author of *Linguistic Meaning* (1986), *Euphemism and Dysphemism: Language Used as Shield and Weapon* (with Kate Burridge, 1991), *Natural Language Semantics* (2001) and *The Western Classical Tradition in Linguistics* (2007).

KATE BURRIDGE is Chair of Linguistics at Monash University. Her main research interests are on grammatical change in Germanic languages, Pennsylvania German, linguistic taboo, and the structure and history of English. She is a regular presenter of language segments on ABC radio. Her many published books include *Blooming English* (Cambridge, 2004) and *Weeds in the Garden of Words* (Cambridge, 2005).

Forbidden Words

Taboo and the Censoring of Language

Keith Allan and Kate Burridge

CAMBRIDGE
UNIVERSITY PRESS

CAMBRIDGE UNIVERSITY PRESS
Cambridge, New York, Melbourne, Madrid, Cape Town, Singapore, São Paulo, Delhi

Cambridge University Press
The Edinburgh Building, Cambridge CB2 8RU, UK

Published in the United States of America by Cambridge University Press, New York

www.cambridge.org
Information on this title: www.cambridge.org/9780521525640

First published 2006
Fourth printing 2009

Printed in the United Kingdom at the University Press, Cambridge

A catalogue record for this publication is available from the British Library

Library of Congress Cataloguing in Publication data

Allan, Keith, 1943–
Forbidden words: taboo and the censoring of language / Keith Allan and
Kate Burridge.
p. cm.
Includes bibliographical references and index.
ISBN 0-521-81960-1 (hardback)
ISBN 0-521-52564-0 (pbk.)
1. Taboo, Linguistic. 2. Censorship. 3. Politeness (Linguistics) 4. Jargon
(Terminology) 5. Swearing. 6. Euphemism. 7. Political correctness.
I. Burridge, Kate. II. Title.

P305.18.T33A43 2006
417'.2–dc22
2006003312

ISBN 978-0-521-81960-2 hardback
ISBN 978-0-521-52564-0 paperback

To our spice
Wendy Allen and Ross Weber

Contents

Figures

Acknowledgements

We owe gratitude to many people, none more than our superb research assistant Wendy Allen, who also offered valuable critical comment as the drafts developed. Many other friends and colleagues were generous with their help and we express our thanks to Ana Deumert, Andrew Markus, Arnold Zwicky, Bill Bright, Chen Yang, Hilary Chappell, Humphrey van Polanen Petel, Jae Song, Jane Faulkner, John Schiller, Jun Yano, Kerry Robinson, Lesley Lee-Wong, Marieke Brugman, Patrick Durell, Pedro Chamizo, Ross Weber, Sarah Cutfield, Tim Curnow and William Leap. We also thank Monash University for a small ARC Grant that paid for our Research Assistant and some incidental expenses.

We are grateful to George Chauncey and Basic Books for permission to reproduce the *Brevities* collage as Figure 7.1.

1   Taboos and their origins

This is a book about taboo and the way in which people censor the language that they speak and write. Taboo is a proscription of behaviour that affects everyday life. Taboos that we consider in the course of the book include

- bodies and their effluvia (sweat, snot, faeces, menstrual fluid, etc.);
- the organs and acts of sex, micturition and defecation;
- diseases, death and killing (including hunting and fishing);
- naming, addressing, touching and viewing persons and sacred beings, objects and places;
- food gathering, preparation and consumption.

Taboos arise out of social constraints on the individual's behaviour where it can cause discomfort, harm or injury. People are at metaphysical risk when dealing with sacred persons, objects and places; they are at physical risk from powerful earthly persons, dangerous creatures and disease. A person's soul or bodily effluvia may put him/her at metaphysical, moral or physical risk, and may contaminate others; a social act may breach constraints on polite behaviour. Infractions of taboos can lead to illness or death, as well as to the lesser penalties of corporal punishment, incarceration, social ostracism or mere disapproval. Even an unintended contravention of taboo risks condemnation and censure; generally, people can and do avoid tabooed behaviour unless they intend to violate a taboo.

People constantly censor the language they use (we differentiate this from the institutionalized imposition of censorship). We examine politeness and impoliteness as they interact with orthophemism (straight talking), euphemism (sweet talking) and dysphemism (speaking offensively). We discuss the motivations for and definitions of jargon, slang, insult, and polite and impolite uses of language when naming, addressing and speaking about others, about our bodies and their functions, nourishment, sexual activities, death and killing. Political correctness and linguistic prescription are described as aspects of tabooing behaviour. We show that society's perception of a 'dirty' word's tainted **denotatum** (what the word is normally used to refer to) contaminates the word itself; and we discuss how the saliency of obscenity and dysphemism makes the description *strong language* particularly appropriate. This is not a triumph of the offensive over the inoffensive, of dysphemism over euphemism, of impoliteness over politeness; in fact the tabooed, the offensive, the dysphemistic and the impolite only seem more powerful forces because each of them identifies the marked behaviour. By default we are polite, euphemistic, orthophemistic and inoffensive; and we censor our language use to eschew tabooed topics in pursuit of well-being for ourselves and for others.

Taboo and the consequent censoring of language motivate language change by promoting the creation of highly inventive and often playful new expressions, or new meanings for old expressions, causing existing vocabulary to be abandoned. There are basically two ways in which new expressions arise: by a changed form for the tabooed expression and by figurative language sparked by perceptions of and conceptions about the denotata (about faeces, menstrual blood, genitals, death and so on). We have shown elsewhere (e.g. Allan and Burridge 1991, Allan 2001) that the meanings and forms of some words can be traced back to several different sources; the paths from these sources converge and mutually strengthen one another as people seek a figure that is apt. In these ways taboos and the attendant censoring trigger word addition, word loss, sound change and semantic shift. They play havoc with the standard methods of historical linguistics by undermining the supposed arbitrary link between the meaning and form of words.

This book offers an interesting perspective on the human psyche, as we watch human beings react to the world around them by imposing taboos on behaviour, causing them to censor their language in order to talk about and around those taboos. Language is used as a shield against malign fate and the disapprobation of fellow human beings; it is used as a weapon against enemies and as a release valve when we are angry, frustrated or hurt. Throughout the book we are struck by the amazing poetic inventiveness of ordinary people, whose creations occasionally rival Shakespeare.

This first chapter makes a general survey of taboo before we scrutinize the nature of censorship and distinguish censoring from censorship.

The origins of our word *taboo*

The English word *taboo* derives from the Tongan *tabu*, which came to notice towards the end of the eighteenth century. According to Radcliffe-Brown:

In the languages of Polynesia the word means simply 'to forbid', 'forbidden', and can be applied to any sort of prohibition. A rule of etiquette, an order issued by a chief, an injunction to children not to meddle with the possessions of their elders, may all be expressed by the use of the word tabu. (Radcliffe-Brown 1939: 5f)

On his first voyage of 1768–71, Captain James Cook was sent to Tahiti to observe the transit of the planet Venus across the Sun. In his logbook he wrote of the Tahitians:

the women never upon any account eat with the men, but always by themselves. What can be the reason of so unusual a custom, 'tis hard to say, especially as they are a people, in every other instance, fond of Society, and much so of their Women. They were often Asked the reason, but they never gave no other Answer, but that they did it because it was right, and Express'd much dislike at the Custom of Men and Women Eating together of the same Victuals. We have often used all the intreatys we were Masters of to invite the Women to partake of our Victuals at our Tables, but there never was an instance of one of them doing it in publick, but they would Often goe 5 or 6 together into the Servants apartments, and there eat heartily of whatever they could find, nor were they in the least disturbed if any of us came in while they were dining; and it hath sometimes hapned that when a woman was alone in our company she would eat with us, but always took care that her own people should not know what she had donn, so that whatever may be the reasons for this custom, it certainly affects their outward manners more than their Principle. (Cook 1893: 91)

Cook does not name this custom either *taboo* or by the equivalent Tahitian term *raa*. It is in the log of his third voyage, 1776–9, that he first uses the term *tabu* in an entry for 15 June 1777 and then again, five days later:

When dinner came on table not one of my guests would sit down or eat a bit of any thing that was there. Every one was *Tabu*, a word of very comprehensive meaning but in general signifies forbidden.[1]

. . .

In this walk we met with about half a dozen Women in one place at supper, two of the Company were fed by the others, on our asking the reason, they said Tabu Mattee. On further enquiry, found that one of them had, two months before, washed the dead corps of a Chief, on which account she was not to handle Victuals for five Months, the other had done the same thing to a nother of inferior rank, and was under the same restriction but not for so long a time. (Cook 1967: 129, 135)

In the entry for 17 July 1777, Cook wrote:

Taboo as I have before observed is a word of extensive signification; Human Sacrifices are called *Tangata Taboo*, and when any thing is forbid to be eaten, or made use of they say such a thing is Taboo; they say that if the King should happen to go into a house belonging to a subject, that house would be Taboo and never more be inhabited by the owner; so that when ever he travels there are houses for his reception. (Cook 1967: 176)

In the journal entry for July 1777, the surgeon on the *Resolution*, William Anderson, wrote:

[taboo] is the common expression when any thing is not to be touch'd, unless the transgressor will risque some very severe punishment as appears from the great

apprehension they have of approaching any thing prohibited by it. In some cases it appears to resemble the Levitical law of purification, for we have seen several women who were not allow'd the use of their hands in eating but were fed by other people. On enquiring the reason of it at one time they said that one of the women had wash'd the dead body of the chief already mentioned who died at Tonga, and another who had assisted was in the same predicament, though then a month after the circumstance had happen'd. It also serves as a temporary law or edict of their chiefs, for sometimes certainly articles of food are laid under restriction, and there are other circumstances regulated in the same manner as trading &c when it is thought necessary to stop it. (Cook 1967: 948)

Tabooed objects may cease to be tabooed:

I now went and examined several Baskets which had been brought in, a thing I was not allowed to do before because every thing was then *Tabu*, but the ceremony being over they became simply what they really were, viz. empty baskets. (9 July 1777, Cook 1967: 153)

Cook and Anderson use *taboo* (or *tabu*) to describe the behaviour of Polynesians towards things that were not to be done, entered, seen or touched. Such taboos are, in some form, almost universal. For instance, there are food taboos in most societies. These are mostly religion-based: the vegetarianism of Hindus; the proscription of pork in Islam; the constraints on food preparation in Judaism; fasting among Jews at Passover and Muslims during Ramadan; the proscription of meat on Fridays among Roman Catholics – to mention just a few examples. Most human groups proscribe the eating of human flesh unless it is the flesh of a defeated enemy or, in rare cases, such as among the Aztecs, a religious ritual. Today, cannibalism is only excused as a survival mechanism as when, after an air crash in the Andes in 1972, surviving members of the Uruguayan rugby team ate the dead to stay alive. Assuming with Steiner[2] (among others) that the constraint against Tahitian women eating with men was regarded as a taboo on such behaviour, it appears comparable to the constraint against using your fingers instead of cutlery when dining in a restaurant. It is an example of a taboo on bad manners – one subject to the social sanction of severe disapproval, rather than putting the violator's life in danger, as some taboos do. However, we can look at this taboo in another way, as the function of a kind of caste system, in which women are a lower caste than men; this system is not dissimilar to the caste difference based on race that operated in the south of the United States of America until the later 1960s, where it was acceptable for an African American to prepare food for whites, but not to share it at table with them. This is the same caste system which permitted men to take blacks for mistresses but not marry them; a system found in colonial Africa and under the British Raj in India.

Fatal taboos

A nineteenth-century view, attributable directly to Wundt's[3] 'folk psychology', is a belief attributed to so-called 'primitive peoples' that there is a 'demonic' power within a tabooed object comparable with the dangerous power of a Polynesian chief or the Emperor of Japan or Satan himself. The effect on whomsoever comes into inappropriate – if not downright unlawful – contact with a tabooed person or thing is severely detrimental to the perpetrator.[4] This was the common (but not universal) interpretation of the term *taboo* among anthropologists. Mead, for instance, restricts the term *taboo* 'to describe prohibition against participation in any situation of such inherent danger that the very act of participation will recoil upon the violator of the taboo'.[5] It is as if the tabooed object were like a radioactive fuel rod, which will have dire effects on anyone who comes into direct contact with it unless they know how to protect themselves. 'Cases are on record in which persons who had unwittingly broken a taboo actually died of terror on discovering their fatal error', writes Frazer.[6] To violate a taboo can lead to the auto-da-fé of the perpetrator. In old Hawai'i, a commoner who had sex with his sister was put to death. A woman who commits adultery can be stoned to death under Sharia law in parts of northern Nigeria today. Under Governor George W. Bush, a convicted murderer was very likely to be executed in the US state of Texas. According to the Bible, God told Moses, 'You shall not permit a sorceress to live' (Exodus 22: 18); implementing scripture, hundreds of heretics and witches were burned in Europe when Christianity had more political power than it does today. Although most taboo violations do not result in capital punishment, there are plenty of other sanctions on behaviour prohibited under the law – whether this is law as conceived and promulgated in a modern nation state, or traditional lore in eighteenth-century Polynesia, or (under church law) the Spanish Inquisition. That which is illegal is *ipso facto* taboo by the very fact that it is prohibited behaviour. But, as we have already seen, there is more that falls under the heading of taboo.

Uncleanliness taboos

There are taboos in which notions of uncleanliness are the motivating factor. Many communities taboo physical contact with a menstruating woman, believing that it pollutes males in particular; some Orthodox New York Jews will avoid public transport, lest they sit where a menstruating woman has sat. Many places of worship in this world taboo menstruating women because they would defile holy sites. The Balinese used to prefer one-storey buildings so that unclean feet (and worse) would not pass above their heads; they still avoid walking under washing lines where garments that have been in contact with unclean parts of the body might pass over their heads. Many communities taboo contact with a corpse, such that no one who has touched the cadaver is permitted to handle food.

Violating taboo and getting away with it

In all these and similar cases, there is an assumption that both accidental breach and intentional defiance of the taboo will be followed by some kind of trouble to the offender, such as lack of success in hunting, fishing, or other business, and the sickness or the death of the offender or one of his/her relatives. In many communities, a person who meets with an accident or fails to achieve some goal will infer, as will others, that s/he has in some manner committed a breach of taboo.

Generally speaking, we do have the power to avoid tabooed behaviour. When a breach can be ascribed to 'bad karma', there remains a suspicion that the perpetrator is somehow responsible for having sinned in a former life. Even ascribing a breach to 'bad luck' is barely excusable: why is this person's luck bad? That question has a negative presupposition. The conclusion must be that any violation of taboo, however innocently committed, risks condemnation.[7]

Those who violate a taboo can often purify themselves or be purified by confessing their sin and submitting to a ritual. The *OED* (*Oxford English Dictionary* 1989) quotes from Cook's *Voyage to the Pacific* ii. xi (1785) I. 410: 'When the *taboo* is incurred, by paying obeisance to a great personage, it is thus easily washed off.' Hobley describes a Kikuyu ritual for legitimizing and purifying an incestuous relationship:

It sometimes happens, however, that a young man unwittingly marries a cousin; for instance, if a part of the family moves away to another locality a man might become acquainted with a girl and marry her before he discovered the relationship. In such a case the *thahu* [or *ngahu*, the result of the violation of the taboo] is removable, the elders take a sheep and place it on the woman's shoulders, and it is then killed, the intestines are taken out and the elders solemnly sever them with a sharp splinter of wood . . . and they announce that they are cutting the clan '*kutinyarurira*', by which they mean that they are severing the bond of blood relationship that exists between the pair. A medicine man then comes and purifies the couple. (Hobley 1910: 438)

In the Nguni societies of southern Africa who practise *hlonipha*, under which it is forbidden for a woman to use her father-in-law's name or even to utter words containing the syllables of his name (particularly in his presence), inadvertent violation of the taboo may be mitigated by spitting on the ground.[8] Christians confess their sins to a priest and are given absolution on behalf of God.[9]

Exploiting taboo

Taboos are open to beneficial exploitation. A person's body is, unless s/he is a slave, sacrosanct. By tradition, a Maori chief's body is taboo. Once upon a time, the chief might claim land by saying that the land is his backbone – which makes invading it taboo. Or he could claim possession by saying things like *Those two canoes are my two thighs.*[10] The taboos on a chief could be utilized by their minions: 'they gave the names of important chiefs to their pet animals and thus prevented others from killing them', wrote Steiner.[11] Samoans sometimes tabooed their plantation trees by placing certain signs close to them to warn off thieves.[12] One sign indicated that it would induce ulcerous sores; an afflicted thief could pay off the plantation owner who would supply a (supposed) remedy. Most dire was the death taboo, made by pouring oil into a small calabash buried near the tree; a mound of white sand marked the taboo, which was said to be very effective in keeping thieves at bay in old Samoa.

The genital organs of humans are always subject to some sort of taboo; those of women are usually more strongly tabooed than those of men, partly for social and economic reasons, but ultimately because they are the source of new human life. Few women today are aware of the supposed power of the exposed vulva (commonly referred to as 'vagina') to defeat evil. The great Greek-mythical warrior Bellerophon, who tamed Pegasus and the Amazons and slew the dragon-like Chimaera, called on Poseidon to inundate Xanthos; he was defeated by the women of Xanthos raising their skirts, driving back the waves, and frightening Pegasus. Images of a woman exposing her vulva are found above doors and gateways in Europe, Indonesia and South America; in many European countries such figures are also located in medieval castles and, surprisingly, many churches. They include the *Sheela-n-Gig* images (from Irish *Síle na gCíoch* or more likely *Síle in-a giob* 'Sheela on her haunches'), such as that in Figure 1.1 from L'église de Ste Radegonde, Poitiers, France. The display of the tabooed body part is a potent means of defeating evil.

One eighteenth-century engraving by Charles Eisen for an edition of the book *Fables* by Jean de la Fontaine depicts the ability of an exposed vagina to dispel evil forces beautifully . . . In this striking image, a young woman stands, confident and unafraid, confronting the devil. Her left hand rests lightly on a wall, while her right raises her skirt high, displaying her sexual centre for Satan to see. And in the face of her naked womanhood, the devil reels back in fear. (Blackledge 2003: 9)

Less serious taboos

Taboo is more than ritual prohibition and avoidance. We have seen that infractions of taboos can be dangerous to the individual and to his/her society; they can lead to illness or death. But there are also milder kinds of taboo, the

Figure 1.1. A woman exposing her vulva, L'église de Ste Radegonde.

violation of which results in the lesser penalties of corporal punishment, incarceration, social ostracism or mere disapproval. Humans are social beings and every human being is a member of at least a gender, a family, a generation and – normally – also friendship, recreational and occupational groups. An individual's behaviour is subject to sanction within these groups and by the larger community. Some groups, for example the family and sports-team supporters, have unwritten conventions governing behavioural standards; others, for example local or national government, have written regulations or laws. Groups with written regulations also have unwritten conventions governing appropriate behaviour. In all cases, sanctions on behaviour arise from beliefs supposedly held in common by a consensus of members of the community or from an authoritative body within the group. Although Freud[13] has claimed that 'Taboo prohibitions have no grounds and are of unknown origin', it seems obvious to us that taboos normally arise out of social constraints on the individual's behaviour. They arise in cases where the individual's acts can cause discomfort, harm or injury to him/herself and to others. The constraint on behaviour is imposed by someone or some physical or metaphysical force that the individual believes has authority or power over them – the law, the gods, the society in which one lives, even proprioceptions (as in the self-imposed proscription, *Chocolates are taboo for me, they give me migraine*).

There can be sound reasons for putting specific parts of our lives out of bounds. Rules against incest seem eminently sensible from an evolutionary point of view. Communities remain healthier if human waste is kept at arm's length. Many food prejudices have a rational origin. Avoidance speech styles help prevent conflict in relationships that are potentially volatile. Of course, once the taboo rituals are in place, the motives (sound or otherwise) usually become obscured. Original meaning gives way to symbolic idiom, although different stories may later suggest themselves. Take the taboo against spilling salt. Indispensable to life, vital to the preservation of food and a delicacy in cooking, salt was once the symbol of purity and incorruptibility. It was also expensive. Spilling such a precious commodity was calamitous; it may even have exposed the perpetrator to evil forces, because the devil is repulsed by salt. In this case, evil is averted quite simply by throwing a pinch of the spilt salt with the right hand over the left shoulder. The reason for 'left' and 'right' here stem from old associations: the left side is weak and bad while the right is strong and good. Those among us who still engage in this sort of irrational behaviour don't stop to think about the original motivations for the ritual. There's just a vague notion that the act of spilling salt somehow brings bad luck – and we don't tempt fate.

To an outsider, many prohibitions are perplexing and seem silly. But they are among the common values that link the people of a community together. What one group values, another scorns. Shared taboos are therefore a sign of social cohesion. Moreover, as part of a wider belief system, they provide the basis people need to function in an otherwise confused and hostile environment. The rites and rituals that accompany taboos give the feeling of control over situations where ordinary mortals have little or none – such as death, illness, bodily functions and even the weather in those communities that still practice rain ceremonies. Mary Douglas' anthropological study of ritual pollution offers insights here.[14] As she saw it, the distinction between cleanliness and filth stems from the basic human need to structure experience and render it understandable. That which is taboo threatens chaos and disorder.

There is no such thing as an absolute taboo

Nothing is taboo for all people, under all circumstances, for all time. There is an endless list of behaviours 'tabooed' yet nonetheless practised at some time in (pre)history by people for whom they are presumably not taboo. This raises a philosophical question: if Ed recognizes the existence of a taboo against patricide and then deliberately flouts it by murdering his father, is patricide not a taboo for Ed? Any answer to this is controversial; our position is that at the time the so-called taboo is flouted it does not function as a taboo for the perpetrator. This does not affect the status of patricide as a taboo in the community of which Ed is a member, nor the status of patricide as a taboo for Ed at other times in his life. Our view is that, although a taboo can be accidentally breached without the violator putting aside the taboo, when the violation is deliberate, the taboo is not merely ineffectual but inoperative.

Sometimes one community recognizes a taboo (e.g. late eighteenth-century Tahitian women not eating with men) which another (Captain Cook's men) does not. In seventeenth-century Europe, women from all social classes, among them King Charles I's wife Henrietta Maria, commonly exposed one or both breasts in public as a display of youth and beauty.[15] No European queen would do that today. Australian news services speak and write about the recently deceased and also show pictures, a practice which is taboo in many Australian Aboriginal communities. You may be squeamish about saying *fuck* when on a public stage, but lots of people are not. Today, no public building, let alone place of worship, would be allowed to incorporate a display of the vulva like that pictured above from L'église de Ste Radegonde. You may believe it taboo for an adult to have sex with a minor, but hundreds of thousands of people have not shared that taboo, or else they have put it aside. Incest is tabooed in most communities, but Pharaoh Ramses II (fl. 1279–1213 BCE) married several of his daughters. Voltaire (1694–1778) had an affair with his widowed niece Mme Marie Louise Denis (née Mignot, 1712–90), to whom he wrote passionately in terms such as:

My child, I shall adore you until I'm in my grave . . . I would like to be the only one to have had the happiness of fucking you, and I now wish I had slept with no-one but you, and had never come but with you. I have a hard on as I write to you and I kiss a thousand times your beautiful breasts and beautiful arse.[16]

Not your typical 'cher oncle'. It is tabooed in most jurisdictions to marry a sibling, but some of the Pharaohs did it; so did the Hawai'ian royal family, among others. Killing people is taboo in most societies; though from time to time and in various places, human sacrifice has been practised, usually to propitiate gods or natural forces that it is thought would otherwise harm the community. Killing enemies gets rewarded everywhere, and judicial execution of traitors and murderers is common. Some Islamists believe that blowing themselves up along with a few infidels leads to Paradise. The Christian God said to Moses, 'He that smiteth a man, so that he die, shall be surely put to death' (Exodus 21: 12). Yet in the Bible we find human sacrifice approved in the murder of an Israelite and a Midianite woman 'so [that] the plague was stayed from the children of Israel' (Numbers 25: 8). God had it in for the Midianites; he told Moses to 'vex . . . and smite them' (Numbers 25: 17). 'And [the Israelites] warred against the Midianites as the Lord commanded Moses; and they slew all the males', burned their cities, and looted their cattle and chattels (Numbers 31: 7–11). Then Moses sent the Israelites back to complete the Lord's work by killing all male children and women of child-bearing age, keeping other females 'for yourselves' (Numbers 31: 17–18). God's work or not, this is military behaviour that would be tabooed today and might lead to a war crimes trial. We are forced to conclude that every taboo must be specified for a particular community of people, for a specified context, at a given place and time. There is no such thing as an absolute taboo (one that holds for all worlds, times and contexts).

Taboo applies to behaviour

As originally used in the Pacific islands when first visited by Europeans, taboos prohibited certain people (particularly women), either permanently or temporarily, from certain actions, from contact with certain things and certain other people. A tabooed person was ostracized. The term *taboo* came to be used with reference to similar customs elsewhere in the world, especially where taboos arose from respect for, and fear of, metaphysical powers; it was extended to political and social affairs, and generalized to the interdiction of the use or practice of anything, especially an expression or topic, considered offensive and therefore avoided or prohibited by social custom.

Where something physical or metaphysical is said to be tabooed, what is in fact tabooed is its interaction with an individual, a specified group of persons or, perhaps, the whole community. In short, a taboo applies to behaviour.

Taboo refers to a proscription of behaviour for a specifiable community of one or more persons, at a specifiable time, in specifiable contexts.

In principle, any kind of behaviour can be tabooed. For behaviour to be proscribed, it must be perceived as in some way harmful to an individual or to his/her community; but the degree of harm can fall anywhere on a scale from a breach of etiquette to downright fatality.

In this book, we are largely concerned with language behaviour. One hears of people who would like to erase obscene terms like *cunt* and slurs like *idiot* and *nigger* from the English language; most people recognize after a few moments' reflection that this is a wish that is impossible to grant – not least because, under the conditions of their creation, these words will not be taboo. Such words are as much a part of English as all the other words in the *Oxford English Dictionary*. However, there is evidence that swear words occupy a different brain location from other vocabulary; people said never to have sworn earlier in their lifetime often lose other language but do swear as senile dementia sets in.[17] It is possible to taboo language behaviour in certain specified contexts; in fact it is often done. Some tabooed behaviours are prohibited by law; all are deprecated and lead to social, if not legal, sanction.

Censorship and censors

The 1791 First Amendment to the Constitution of the United States proclaims:

Congress shall make no law respecting an establishment of religion, or prohibiting the free exercise thereof; or abridging the freedom of speech, or of the press; or the right of the people peaceably to assemble, and to petition the Government for a redress of grievances.

We take this, and in particular the clauses referring to freedom of speech and freedom to publish, as succinctly describing the antithesis to the censorship of language.

The *censorship* was instituted in ancient Rome in 443 BCE and discontinued in 22 BCE. The *censor* was a magistrate with the original function of registering citizens and assessing their property for taxation. This sense lives on in our noun *census*. Our theme of taboo and the censoring of language can ignore as irrelevant the original link between censor and census, though there is a throwback to this sense when censors claim to reflect and act upon the consensus of right-thinking people in their community.

The work of a Roman censor expanded to include supervision of moral conduct, with the authority to *censure* and penalize offenders against public morality. For many centuries, in many cultures and jurisdictions, governments have exercised censorship as a means of regulating the moral and political life of their people. Thus, according to the *OED*, the censor was and is a person 'whose duty it is to inspect all books, journals, dramatic pieces, etc., before publication, to secure that they shall contain nothing immoral, heretical, or offensive to the government'.

The sentiment is to be found in Aristotle's *Politics* towards the end of Book VII, written *c*.350 BCE:

there is nothing that the legislator should be more careful to drive away than indecency of speech; for the light utterance of shameful words leads to shameful actions. The young especially should never be allowed to repeat or hear anything of that sort. A freeman if he be found saying or doing what is forbidden, if he be too young as yet to have the privilege of reclining at the public tables, should be disgraced and beaten, and an elder person degraded as his slavish conduct deserves. And since we do not allow improper language, clearly we should also banish pictures or speeches from the stage which are indecent. Let the rulers take care that there be no image or picture representing unseemly actions, except in the temples of those gods at whose festivals the law permits even ribaldry, and whom the law also permits to be worshipped by persons of mature age on behalf of themselves, their children, and their wives. But the legislators should not allow youth to be spectators of iambi [satire] or of comedy until they are of an age to sit at the public tables and to drink strong wine; by that time education will have armed them against the evil influences of such representations. (Aristotle 1984: 1336^{b}4–23)

Censorship is often extended to the control of news, propaganda and even would-be private correspondence of civil prisoners in times of hot and cold war or other perceived national emergency or external threat. Thus censors are thought police given to *censure*, given to presenting 'adverse judgement, unfavourable opinion, hostile criticism; blaming, finding fault with, or con- demning as wrong; expression of disapproval or condemnation', according to the *OED*.

Censors license for public distribution speeches, writings and other works of art, scholarship and reportage; but they are less celebrated for what they sanction than infamous for what they restrict and prohibit. These are the characteristics that affect our understanding of the words *censorship* and *censoring*.

Censorship in Tudor, Jacobean and Stuart England

The relevant definition of *censorship* for our purposes focuses on language:

Censorship is the suppression or prohibition of speech or writing that is condemned as subversive of the common good.

The problem lies in the interpretation of the phrase *subversive of the common good*. For instance, the censorship of incitement to (as well as actual) violence against any citizen supposedly guards against his/her physical harm. The censorship of profanity and blasphemy supposedly guards against his/her moral harm. The censorship of pornography supposedly guards against his/ her moral harm, and perhaps physical danger, by someone stimulated to rapine action by exposure to the excitement of pornography. A concern for the common good and for the protection of the citizenry from physical and moral jeopardy is expressed in the following preamble to a City of London Ordinance of 6 December 1574, regulating dramatic performances:

Whereas heartofore sondrye greate disorders and inconvenyences have been found to ensewe to this Cittie by the inordynate hauntynge of greate multitudes of people, speciallye youthe, to playes, enterludes and shewes; namelye occasyon of frayes and quarrelles, eavell practizes of incontinencye in greate Innes, havinge chambers and secrete places adjoyninge to their open stagies and gallyries, inveyglynge and alleurynge of maides, speciallye orphanes, and good cityzens children under age, to previe and unmete contractes, the publishinge of unchaste, uncomelye, and unshamefaste speeches and doynges, withdrawinge of the Quenes Majesties subjectes from dyvyne service on Soundaies & hollydayes, at which tymes such playes weare chefelye used, unthriftye waste of the moneye of the poore & fond persons, sondrye robberies by pyckinge and cuttinge of purses, utteringe of popular, busye and sedycious matters, and manie other corruptions of youthe, and other enormyties; besydes that allso soundrye slaughters and mayhemminges of the Quenes Subjectes have happened by ruines of Skaffoldes, Frames and Stagies, and by engynes, weapons and powder used in plaies. And whear in tyme of Goddes visitacion by the plaigue suche assemblies of the people in thronge and presse have benne verye daungerous for spreadinge of Infection. (Gildersleeve 1961: 156f)

In the view of Elizabethan London's aldermen, attendance at plays keeps the youth away from divine service and wastes their money while they – especially the maids, streetkids and underage children among them – are in moral jeopardy of being led astray by exposure to drink, seditious and indecent talk, and licentious behaviour. They are also in physical danger from affray, muggers, murderers, from the collapse of stages and stands, and from gunpowder and the like used in stage effects. Furthermore, the congregation of people risks spreading the deadly plague (which regularly killed about forty people a week in London, with occasional outbreaks that killed hundreds). Recognizable echoes of such concerns recur across the intervening centuries, although assessments of what constitutes protection of the common good varies; for instance, today we worry not about the plague but about SARS or HIV and AIDS.

The tradition of censorship in the English-speaking world arose from the religious troubles of the Reformation and the policies of Henry VIII in the 1530s. For many centuries, the focus was on suppressing heresy and anything likely to stir up political revolt; before the nineteenth century, it was rare to find the concern with indecency and licentiousness evident in the 1574 quotation above: 'inveyglynge and alleurynge of maides, speciallye orphanes, and good cityzens children under age, to previe and unmete contractes, the publishinge of unchaste, uncomelye, and unshamefaste speeches and doynges'. An Act for the Advancement of True Religion and for the Abolishment of the Contrary (Statute 34 and 35 Henry VIII cap. 1, 1543) orders suppression of anything conflicting with doctrines authorized by the King in sermons and 'prynted bokes, prynted balades, playes, rymes, songes, and other fantasies'.[18] Henry's daughter by Catherine of Aragon, Mary I (1553–8), reinstituted the Roman Catholic religion which was subsequently revoked by her half-sister Elizabeth I (1558–1603). Mary proclaimed on 18 August 1553:

And furthermore, forasmuche also as it is well knowen, that sedition and false rumours haue bene nouryshed and maynteyned in this realme, by the subteltye and malyce of some euell disposed persons, whiche take vpon them withoute sufficient auctoritie, to preache, and to interprete the worde of God, after theyr owne brayne, in churches and other places, both publique and pryuate. And also by playinge of Interludes and pryntynge false fonde bookes, ballettes, rymes, and other lewde treatises in the englyshe tonge, concernynge doctryne in matters now in question and controuersye, touchinge the hyghe poyntes and misteries of christen religion . . . Her highnes therfore strayghtly chargeth and commaundeth all and every her sayde subiectes . . . that none of them presume from henceforth to preache . . . or to interprete or teache any scriptures, or any maner poynts of doctryne concernynge religion. Neyther also to prynte any bookes, matter, ballet, ryme, interlude, processe or treatyse, nor to playe any interlude, except they haue her graces speciall licence in writynge for the same, vpon payne to incurre her highnesse indignation and displeasure. (Gildersleeve 1961: 10f)

Taking the Lord's name in vain[19] was frowned upon and eventually banned – which is mild retribution compared with what the Bible sanctions:

And he that blasphemeth the name of the LORD, he shall surely be put to death, and all the congregation shall certainly stone him: as well the stranger, as he that is born in the land, when he blasphemeth the name of the LORD, shall be put to death. (Leviticus 24: 16)

Elizabeth I is reputed to have favoured *God's wounds* as an oath,[20] but during her reign arose euphemisms like *'sblood* $\Rightarrow$ *'s'lood* $\Rightarrow$ *'slud*,[21] *'sbody*, *'sfoot*, *'slid* [eyelid], *'slight*, *'snails*, *'sprecious* [body] and *zounds*, a fore-clipping of *God*, sometimes also remodelled, e.g. *God's wounds* $\Rightarrow$ *'swounds* $\Rightarrow$ *zounds*, pronounced /zunz/ $\Rightarrow$ *zaunds*, pronounced /zaunz/. Henry Fielding's *The History of Tom Jones* of 1749[22] omits letters to euphemize, e.g. 'Z—ds and bl—d, sister' (XVI.4) and contains *'Sbodlikins* (X.5) and *Odsbud!* (XVI.7) as variants of *God's body*, along with *Odsooks!* (XII.7) and *Odzookers!* (XVIII.9) from *God's hooks* (nailing Christ to the cross) and *Odrabbet it!* (XVI.2) or *Od rabbit it* (XVII.3, XVIII.9) from *God rot it!* ('confound it'), which lives on in *drat it*. *I' fackins* (X.9) is a variant of *i' faith* and *Icod!* (XVIII.8) derives from either *in God's name* or *By God*.

How does remodelling work? The following explanation says something about misspellings, which one might look upon as accidental remodellings:

Aoccdrnig to a rsecherear at an Elingsh uinervtisy, it deosn't mttaer in waht oredr the ltteers in a wrod are, the olny iprmoatnt tihng is that frist and lsat ltteer are in the rghit pclae. The rset can be a toatl mses and you can sitll raed it wouthit porbelm. Tihs is bcuseae we do not raed ervey lteter by itslef but the wrod as a wlohe.

No fluent speaker of English has any trouble reading the above (which explains the power of the designer label FCUK).[23] Taking context into account, and working on a system of analysis-by-synthesis, we match misspelled words with their normal forms. A similar kind of constructive process is used in making sense of the following story of *Ladle Rat Rotten Hut*.

Wants pawn term dare worsted ladle gull hoe lift wetter murder inner ladle cordage honor itch offer lodge dock florist. Disc ladle gull orphan worry ladle cluck wetter putty ladle rat hut, end fur disc raisin pimple caulder Ladle Rat Rotten Hut. Wan moaning Rat Rotten Hut's murder colder inset: 'Ladle Rat Rotten Hut, heresy ladle basking winsome burden barter end shirker cockles. Tick disc ladle basking tudor cordage offer groin murder honor udder site offer florist. Shaker lake, dun stopper laundry wrote, end yonder nor sorghum stenches dun stopper torque wet strainers.' (Garner 1994: 1–2)

Here, normal English words are used, but not in normal contexts. Based on the assumption that the author intends to communicate something coherent, the reader makes the effort to construct meaning and finds a phonetic similarity to syntactically coherent sequences of words that tell the story of Little Red Riding Hood. The point of this digression is that when language is systematically remodelled with the intention of communicating, the fluent speaker doesn't normally have too much trouble recognizing the intended meaning. Thus the use of an expression like *Golly!* communicates as effectively as the profane use of the expletive *God!*

In 1606, the Act to Restraine Abuses of Players (3 Jac.I. cap.21) severely penalized profanity:

If . . . any person or persons doe or shall in any Stage play, Interlude, Shewe, Maygame or Pageant jestingly or prophanely speake or use the holy name of God or of Christ Jesus, or of the Holy Ghoste or of the Trinitie . . . [they] shall forfeite for every such Offence by him or theme committed Tenne pounds. (Quoted in Hughes 1991: 103)

In consequence, the 1616 folio of Ben Jonson's plays replaces *By Jesu* with *Believe me*. A 1634 edition of Beaumont and Fletcher's *Philaster* (first acted c.1608) had *Faith* either cut or replaced by *Indeed* or (somewhat strangely) by *Marry* – a remodelling of Christ's mother's name; *By Heaven* is remodelled to *By these hilts*; and *by the (just) Gods* is altered to *By my sword, By my life, By all that's good, By Nemesis, And I vow*, despite the original reference to pagan gods not being truly profane for a Christian.[24] Religious censorship remained in force until significantly weakened during the twentieth century. The fact that Andres Serrano's *Piss Christ* (a photograph of a cheap plastic crucifix in urine)[25] has been accused of being blasphemous demonstrates this. US Senator Alfonse D'Amato began an address to the Senate on 18 May 1989 with these words:

Mr President, several weeks ago, I began to receive a number of letters, phone calls, and postcards from constituents throughout the Senate concerning art work by Andres Serrano. They express a feeling of shock, of outrage, and anger. They said, 'How dare you spend our taxpayers' money on this trash.' They all objected to taxpayers' money being used for a piece of so-called art work which, to be quite candid, I am somewhat reluctant to utter its title. This so-called piece of art is a deplorable, despicable display of vulgarity. The art work in question is a photograph of the crucifix submerged in the artist's urine.[26]

When *Piss Christ* travelled to Australia in September 1997, Roman Catholic Archbishop (later cardinal) Dr George Pell said, in an affidavit before the court, 'Both the name and the image Piss Christ not only demean Christianity but also represent a grossly offensive, scurrilous and insulting treatment of Christianity's most sacred and holy symbol.' On 12 October 1997, the photograph was attacked with a hammer in the National Gallery of Victoria and immediately removed from exhibition.[27]

Restrictions on language and weapons have the same motivation

Criticism of monarchs, heads of state and other persons of rank is often severely censored, particularly in times of national instability. In sixteenth- and seventeenth-century Britain, remarks were censored if they were perceived to be hostile to the prevailing government ideology and powerful foreign allies, or likely to stir up discontent and create disorder. For instance, the deposition scene from Shakespeare's *Richard II* (Act IV.i) was expurgated from the first and second quartos (1597 and 1598), and it was alleged in early 1601 to have been a symbol of insurrection for supporters of the rebellion of Robert Devereux, second Earl of Essex, which led to his execution.[28] The correlation of words and actions was recognized in John Milton's *Areopagitica* of 1644:

I deny not, but that it is of greatest concernment in the Church and Commonwealth, to have a vigilant eye how Bookes demeane themselves as well as men; and thereafter to confine, imprison and do sharpest justice on them as malefactors: For books are not absolutely dead things, but doe contain a potencie of life in them to be as active as that soule was whose progeny they are; nay they do preserve as in a violl the purest efficacie and extraction of that living intellect that bred them. I know they are as lively, and as vigorously productive, as those fabulous Dragons teeth; and being sown up and down, may chance to spring up armed men. (Milton 1644: 4)

Milton suggests that books do purvey ideas; but they are no more likely to 'spring up armed men' than the dragons' teeth of fable. On the face of it, language censorship – like the restriction on gun ownership – is a reasonable constraint against abuses of social interaction amongst human beings. However, attitudes to restrictions on gun ownership in, say, Britain differ markedly from those of many citizens of the United States – especially from members of the politically powerful National Rifle Association. The NRA champions the right to bear arms in accordance with the Second Amendment of the US Constitution: 'A well-regulated Militia being necessary to the security of a free State, the right of the people to keep and bear arms shall not be infringed.' (Furthermore, forty-four states have constitutional provisions affirming the individual's right to keep and bear arms.) Some Americans, together with most people who live outside of the US, correlate the resulting very extensive gun-ownership in that country with the proportionately much higher incidence of gun-inflicted injury and death than in any otherwise comparable country (e.g. in 1993, 66 per million versus 1.4 per million in the UK).[29] Statistical evidence on the effects of widespread gun-ownership fails to influence the views of the NRA supporters – their belief in the rightness of their cause outweighs any rational counterargument. Compare this situation with what happens with respect to language censorship: certain beliefs are held by politically powerful members of the community on the ways that language can subvert the common good, and no amount of rational argument against their position will be accepted.

Milton against censorship

John Milton (1608–74) was not only the greatest epic poet in English (*Paradise Lost, Paradise Regained, Samson Agonistes*), but also a libertarian historian and pamphleteer on behalf of the Anglican Church, civil liberties and democratic values. *Areopagitica* became a classic, though it had very little effect in its own time. It argues against the censorship law of 14 June 1643, but applies to censorship of any kind at any period. The 1643 order was specifically a response to 'false . . . scandalous, seditious, and libellous [works published] . . . to the great defamation of Religion and government'. It was a time of social and political instability that, within a couple of years, led to civil war and the execution of King Charles I in January 1649. Since Henry VIII broke with Rome over a century earlier, there had been ideological conflict between the Protestant majority and papists who were widely suspected of sedition, especially after the Gunpowder Plot was thwarted in November 1605. Milton's principal argument against censorship is that it chokes access to knowledge ('Truth' and 'Wisdom'), stifles the pursuit of art and learning, and cripples human development and progress:

it will be primely to the discouragement of all learning and the stop of Truth, not only by disexercising and blunting our abilities in what we know already, but by hindring and cropping the discovery that may bee yet further made in religious and civill Wisdome.
. . . unlesse warinesse be us'd, as good almost kill a Man as kill a good Book; who kills a man kills a reasonable creature, Gods Image; but hee who destroyes a good Booke, kills reason it self, kills the Image of God, as it were in the eye. Many a man lives a burden to the Earth; but a good Booke is the pretious life-blood of a master spirit, imbalm'd and treasur'd up on purpose to a life beyond life. 'Tis true, no age can restore a life, whereof perhaps there is no great losse; and revolutions of ages doe not oft recover the losse of rejected truth, for the want of which whole Nations fare the worse.
. . .
Well knows he who uses to consider, that our faith and knowledge thrives by exercise, as well as our limbs and complexion. Truth is compar'd in Scripture to a streaming

fountain; if her waters flow not in a perpetuall progression, they sick'n into a muddy pool of conformity and tradition. (Milton 1644: 4, 26)

History shows that censorship empowers people who are by inclination illiberal and unlikely to be artistically creative or broadly schooled. The judgment of a censor is open to error, fashion, whim and corruption:[30]

the Councell of Trent, and the Spanish Inquisition engendring together brought forth, or perfeted those Catalogues and expurging Indexes, that rake through the entralls of many an old good Author, with a violation wors then any could be offer'd to his tomb. Nor did they stay in matters Hereticall, but any subject that was not to their palat, they either condemn'd in a prohibition, or had it strait into the new Purgatory of an Index.
. . .

The State shall be my governours, but not my criticks; they may be mistak'n in the choice of a licencer, as easily as this licenser may be mistak'n in an author: this is some common stuffe; and he might add from Sir *Francis Bacon*, That *such authoriz'd books are but the language of the times*. For though a licencer should happ'n to be judicious more then ordinary, which will be a great jeopardy of the next succession, yet his very office, and his commission enjoyns him to let passe nothing but what is vulgarly receiv'd already.
. . .

[In Italy in 1638] I found and visited the famous *Galileo*, grown old a prisner to the Inquisition, for thinking in Astronomy otherwise than the Franciscan and Dominican licencers thought. (Milton 1644: 7, 22, 24)

Here is an early twentieth-century view of censors:

CENSORSHIP in action has little to recommend it. Suppression is a sordid, unhappy sport. The legal chicanery brings out the worst in every one concerned . . . To act the rôle of censor develops a lack of honesty more anti-social than any amount of sexual excess. The perfect censor does not exist. (Ernst and Seagle 1928: 13)

Trust should be placed in the judgment of the individual person, and tolerance is the best policy:

suddenly a vision sent from God, it is his own Epistle that so averrs it, confirm'd him [Dionysius, Bishop of Alexandria *c*.190–265 CE] in these words: Read any books what ever come to thy hands, for thou art sufficient both to judge aright, and to examine each matter. To this revelation he assented the sooner, as he confesses, because it was answerable to that of the Apostle to the Thessalonians, Prove [= try] all things, hold fast that which is good.[31] And he might have added another remarkable saying of the same Author; To the pure all things are pure,[32] not only meats and drinks, but all kinde of knowledge whether of good or evill; the knowledge cannot defile, nor consequently the books, if the will and conscience be not defil'd.
. . .

Yet if all cannot be of one mind, as who looks they should be? this doubtless is more wholsome, more prudent, and more Christian that many be tolerated, rather than all compell'd. (Milton 1644: 11, 37)

Milton would have been thinking only of sophisticated, well-educated (male Protestant) individuals like himself; on behalf of such people he offers a strong argument against censorship. The counterargument from Big Brother is that censorship is necessary to protect the innocent, the inexperienced, the ignorant, the morally weak.[33] The alternative is an invitation to anarchy. Perhaps we can identify groups within a society who do manage to act without admitting any censorship, linguistic or otherwise, on their behaviour; but there exists no comprehensive society (constituted of humans of both sexes, all ages and in a full range of occupations) that does not censor some kinds of behaviour − by custom if not by law. The problem for any human society is how to constrain censorship in order to allow for maximum expression of personal freedoms without these subverting the common good.

Is censorship futile?

Censorship fails to prevent people intent on flouting it:

this Order avails nothing to the suppressing of scandalous, seditious, and libellous Books, which are mainly intended to be suppresst. (Milton 1644: 4)

Not that this infelicity has ever stopped the imposition of censorship.[34] A document emanating from the office of Master of the King's Revels less than nineteen years after Milton published these words (25 July 1663) suggests that previous ordinances must have been ineffective:

That the Master of his Maiesties office of the Revells, hath the power of Lycencing all playes whether Tragedies, or Comedies before they can bee acted, is without dispute and the designe is, that all prophaneness, oathes, ribaldry, and matters reflecting upon piety, and the present governement may bee obliterated, before there bee any action in a publique Theatre.

The like equitie there is, that all Ballads, songs and poems of that nature, should pass the same examinacion, being argued a Major ad Minus, and requiring the same antidote, because such things presently fly all over the Kingdom, to the Debauching and poisoning the younger sort of people, unles corrected, and regulated.

The like may bee said as to all Billes for Shewes, and stage playes, Mountebankes, Lotteries &c. (Gildersleeve 1961: 86)

Laws issued since then show that censorship is like whistling in the wind.

As well as engaging in sexual perversions with actresses, his wife and his sister-in-law, the Marquis de Sade[35] was able to exploit his position as a well-connected member of the *ancien régime* of pre-revolutionary France to commit sodomy, rape, whippings and mutilations of prostitutes; and to abduct and sexually abuse boys and girls. He also masturbated on a crucifix. For such behaviours he was imprisoned, executed in effigy, and only escaped the guillotine by chance. His fictional accounts of violent sexual behaviour were even more grotesque than what he practised; they glorify the abuse of power that enables a sociopath to exercise tyrannical whim over a powerless victim to the extent of debauching, enslaving, torturing, mutilating and murdering them. In Sade's writings,[36] virtue can never win. His dominant characters defend a 'philosophy' of selfishness, hedonism, debauchery, immorality, torture and general mayhem, such as celebrating the decapitation of a woman by her lover because she orgasmed;[37] or having the Pope not only bugger a woman while masturbating her, but claim, 'never do I retire for the night with unbloodied hands . . . Murder is one of [Nature's] laws . . . that . . . is no crime at all.'[38] Here is a description of a sadomasochistic orgy such as Sade himself might well have indulged in:

this fine lad's [the valet Augustin's] superb ass does preoccupy my mind . . . let me kiss it and caress it, oh! for a quarter of an hour. Hither, my love, come, that I may, in your lovely ass, render myself worthy of the flames with which Sodom sets me aglow. Ah, he has such beautiful buttocks . . . the whitest! I'd like to have Eugénie [age fifteen] on her knees; she will suck his prick while I advance; in this manner she will expose her ass to the Chevalier, who'll plunge into it, and Madame de Saint-Ange astride Augustin's back, will present her buttocks to me: I'll kiss them. Armed with the cat-o'-nine-tails, she might surely, it would seem to me, by bending a little, be able to flog the Chevalier who, thanks to this stimulating ritual, might resolve not to spare our student [Eugénie]. (Sade 1965: 346)

This is harmless pornography compared with what we read in *Juliette*. Noireceuil and Juliette celebrate their marriage by torturing, mutilating and dismembering several young women, as Noireceuil sodomizes them. In turn, he is buggered by his sons; then he buggers one of them while eating the boy's heart, which has been torn out by Juliette as she is being masturbated. While Juliette is fucked, front and back, by flunkeys, she accedes to Noireceuil having her young daughter Marianne held down – first to be anally, and then vaginally, raped. Then, as Juliette orgasms, she offers Marianne to him as a sacrifice. Sade has Juliette write:[39]

No sooner does he hear these words than he decunts, takes hold of the poor child in his two wicked hands, and hurls her, naked, into the roaring fire; I step forward and second him; I too pick up a poker and thwart the unhappy creature's natural efforts to escape, for she thrashes convulsively in the flames: we drive her back, I say; we are being frigged, both of us, then we are being sodomized. Marianne is being roasted alive; and we go off to spend the rest of the night in each other's arms, congratulating each other upon the scene whose episodes and circumstances complement a crime which, atrocious perhaps, is yet, in our shared opinion, too mild.

'So tell me now,' said Noireceuil, 'is there anything in the world to match the divine pleasures crime yields? . . .'

'No, my friend, not to my knowledge.' (Sade 1968: 1184–7)

Such vile deeds are not punished, virtue never prevails in Sade; instead he has the King appoint Noireceuil prime minister.

It is hardly surprising that Sade's writings were subject to censorship. Because of them, Napoleon condemned Sade to the insane asylum at Charenton for the last thirteen years of his life. Sade's son burned some of his manuscripts; others circulated underground or were on restricted access in the Bibliothèque Nationale until the twentieth century. By the 1960s, they were widely available to the general public. Shattuck suggests that because Sade's work was claimed in their trials to have influenced the 'Moors murderers' Ian Brady and Myra Hindley in 1965, and the serial killer Ted Bundy during the 1970s, there is a case for censoring at least some of Sade's texts.[40] The argument for censorship is that, although most readers will not be provoked to copy the violent sexual excesses of Sade's fictional characters (nor even of the man himself), there may be some benighted souls who are – with severe consequences for their victims and concomitant cost to the community. There is a parallel with the justification for restrictions on cigarette smoking, which is based on the cost in disease and death not only to the smokers themselves, but to the community as a whole. The difference is that, whereas cigarette smoking *causes* disease that may lead to death, there is no evidence that reading works such as *Juliette* has in fact caused debauchery or torture – although their enjoyments may be concomitant. As long as humankind has been in existence there has been sexual perversion, child abuse, rape, torture, mutilation and murder, mostly by people who had never heard of Sade, and certainly had not read him; a handful of examples from among thousands that are recorded (never mind what has gone unrecorded) include Caligula (Gaius Caesar Germanicus 12–41 CE) and the late fifteenth-century Vlad Die Tepes (the Impaler), known as Dracula. The sixteenth-century Hungarian countess Elizabeth Báthory reputedly humiliated, sexually mutilated and tortured to death 650 girls and women, on occasion feeding their flesh to soldiers and drinking (and perhaps bathing in) the blood of virgins. In 1728, the Keeper of Halsted Bridewell was convicted of whipping a woman eight months pregnant with his child until she miscarried; he then threw the foetus into a latrine. A few years later a ten-year-old boy was sentenced to life in the navy for torturing a five-year-old girl to death because she wet the bed they shared. In 1936, white American Albert Fish was executed after raping, torturing, murdering and eating at least fifteen mostly poor, black children; he consumed not only their flesh, but urine, blood and excrement, in order to experience immense sexual pleasure (or so he claimed). In Ecuador in 1980, Pedro Alonso Lopez was sentenced on fifty-seven counts of murdering young girls (he claimed more than 300 victims from Columbia, Ecuador and Peru); after raping them, he slowly strangled them for the sexual thrill of watching them die, and then sometimes acted out games with the dead bodies.

In 2001, three Serbs were convicted of systematic rape, torture and enslave-
ment of Muslim girls and women in Bosnia in 1992. In 1994, Hutus in the
Rwandan Interahamwe militia raped (sometimes with artefacts), enslaved,
tortured, and mutilated the genitals and breasts of Tutsi women, sometimes
forcing them to kill their own children. There were similar atrocities in Sierra
Leone during the ten years from 1991. It is impossible, or very unlikely, that
any of this small sample of horrific acts against defenceless victims were
committed by people inspired by the writings of the Marquis de Sade. It is
possible that exposure to Sade's work expands the imagination of anyone
predisposed to sadistic behaviour, such as those in the historical record; there
are reports of pornographic and violent movies being cited as evidence for the
normality of illegal acts (including murder) that have been committed; there
is little doubt that, today, those who act like Sade and his characters often do
possess quantities of violent, pornographic and sadomasochistic stimulatory
material in various media. Here we make no judgment on graphic media, but
limit ourselves to language: to censor Sade's written works is about as
effective as shooting the messenger for bringing bad news.[41]

There is another argument against censorship: as Publius Cornelius Tacitus
(56–120 CE) pointed out, banned writings are eagerly sought and read; once
the proscription is dropped, interest in them wanes.[42] To maintain authority
over dogma and biblical texts, the early Christian church proscribed texts
deemed heretical, such as the Gospel of Mary (Magdalen), certain works of
Aristotle and the Talmud. Existing heretical works were burned on the
recommendation of St Paul:

19 Many of them [Jews and Greeks dwelling at Ephesus] also which used curious arts
brought their books together, and burned them before all men: and they counted the
price of them, and found it fifty thousand pieces of silver. 20 So mightily grew the
word of God and prevailed. (Acts 19: 19–20)

Around 1350, Boccaccio's *Decameron* was allowed to be published after
offensive reference to ecclesiastics was removed: for instance, sexual adventures
were transferred from nuns and abbesses to nobles, from monks to conjurers.[43]
From 1467, the church in Europe required all books to be approved by the local
ordinary, usually a bishop, and in 1545, the first *Index Librorum Prohibitorum*
was published. This created new market opportunities for booksellers.

Indeed in 1589 the Church found it necessary to outlaw lay possession of copies of the
Index Librorum Haereticorum (a catalogue of proscribed titles prepared annually)
because book sellers were using it to locate titles which would be in greatest demand
on the illegal market in the coming year. Eventually Protestant publishers took full
advantage of the exploitive possibilities by listing the *Index*'s prohibition on the title
page below the printer's colophon – the location of the *imprimatur* on Catholic
publications. (Jansen 1991: 65f)

Censorship nearly always has such confounding effects. The prohibition on the manufacture and sale of alcohol in the United States between 1920 and 1933 was notoriously ineffective and counterproductive, in that it led to the establishment of organized crime syndicates. The experience has had little effect on today's law-makers, who insist on banning recreational drugs with similar results. Attempts by Senator Jesse Helms and others to ban a 1988 retrospective of photographer Robert Mapplethorpe's work led to its universal notoriety and a ten-fold increase in prices.[44]

Censorship versus censoring

For as much as all profane Swearing and Cursing is forbidden by the Word of GOD, be it therefore enacted, by the authority of the then Parliament, that no Person or Persons should from thenceforth profanely Swear or Curse, upon Penalty of forfeiting one Shilling to the use of the Poor for every Oath or Curse. (21 Jac. I. cap. 20, 1623; quoted in Hughes 1991: 105)

A distinction can be drawn between *censorship* – as in the quote above – and *censoring*. The former is typically an institutionalized practice carried out by someone with the job description of *censor*. We shall use the phrase *the censorship of language* only for institutional suppressions of language by powerful governing classes, supposedly acting for the common good by preserving stability and/or moral fibre in the nation.

The phrase *the censoring of language* encompasses both the institutionalized acts of the powerful and those of ordinary individuals: everyone *censors* his/her own or another's behaviour from time to time, and for such an occasion s/he can be justly described as a *censor*; but the title is temporary and contingent upon the occasional act of *censoring*. All kinds of tabooed behaviour are subject to *censoring*, but only certain kinds are subject to *censorship* – for instance, child pornography is subject to both *censorship* and *censoring*, but picking your nose in public is subject only to *censoring*. Shakespeare's work was subject to censoring (rather than censorship) by Dr Thomas Bowdler in 1818, who omitted 'those words . . . which cannot with propriety be read aloud in a family'. As with many censors in the twentieth and twenty-first centuries, he rejected what he perceived to be profane or sexual, but kept the violence. For instance, Bowdler expurgated the struck-through parts of Timon's diatribe:

> Obedience fail in children! Slaves and fools,
> Pluck the grave wrinkled senate from the bench,
> And minister in their steads! ~~To general filths~~
> ~~Covert, o'the instant, green virginity,~~
> ~~Do't in your parents' eyes!~~ Bankrupts, hold fast
> Rather than render back, out with your knives,

And cut your trusters' throats! Bound servants, steal!
Large-handed robbers your grave masters are,
And pill by law: ~~Maid, to they master's bed,~~
~~Thy mistress is o'the brothel!~~ Son of sixteen,
Pluck the lin'd crutch from thine old limping sire,
With it beat out his brains!

(Bowlderized Shakespeare,
Timon of Athens, IV.i.4–15)

Unlike most such sanctimonious busybodies, Bowdler was the inspiration for an eponymous neologism, *bowdlerize* 'to censor a work of art to make a travesty of it'.

To satisfy twenty-first-century 'sensitivity review guidelines', the New York State Education Department bowdlerized texts for use in an exam, supposedly to prevent students feeling ill at ease. Passages were sanitized of references to race, religion, ethnicity, sex, nudity, unusual (we dare not write *abnormal*) body size, alcohol and profanity. In an excerpt from the work of Jewish writer Isaac Bashevis Singer, all mention of Judaism was eliminated; thus a reference to 'Most Jewish women' became 'Most women', and even the tautologous truism 'Jews are Jews and Gentiles are Gentiles' was deleted. The phrase 'even the Polish schools were closed' was altered to 'even the schools were closed'. In a passage from Annie Dillard's *An American Child-hood*, whose point is to emphasize the understanding of racial differences, reference to race was edited out of a description of her childhood trips to a library in the black section of town, which had but few white visitors. Deleted from a speech by United Nations Secretary General Kofi Annan was a reference to the United States' unpaid debt to the UN. His praise of 'fine California wine and seafood' was reduced to praise for merely 'fine California seafood'. In Carol Saline's *Mothers and Daughters*, a girl who 'went out to a bar' with her mother simply 'went out' after the text was censored. In an excerpt from *Barrio Boy* by Ernesto Galarza, a 'gringo lady' becomes an 'American lady'; a boy described as 'skinny' became 'thin', while a 'fat' boy became 'heavy'. In a passage from Frank Conroy's *Stop-Time*, 'hell' was replaced by 'heck' and references to sex, religion and nudity were excised. From Anne Lamott's *Bird by Bird*, the sentence 'She's gay!' was deleted. According to a *New York Times* report (2 June 2002) authors, professors, students and the general public complained. One professor wrote: 'I implore you to put a stop to the scandalous practice of censoring literary texts, ostensibly in the interest of our students. It is dishonest. It is dangerous. It is an embarrassment. It is the practice of fools.' Someone else commented: 'The butchery of literary texts . . . is a fresh illustration of the fact that somewhere along the way, people got the ridiculous notion that they have a right "not to be offended". In fact, it should be obvious that such a right, if it existed, would cancel out all other rights.' Bowing to the storm of complaint, the New York Regents have reinstated the original uncensored versions of the texts to be read for examination.

In Australia in late 2004, there was a furore over a children's book (for ten- to thirteen-year-olds) called, revealingly, *The Bad Book*, in which Little Willy set fire to a cat, his penis, his bum and his head; while Little Betty wouldn't get out of bed because she was dead. It features such rhymes as:

> Bad Jack Horner
> Sat in a corner
> Pulling the wings off a fly.
> He swore at his mum
> Kicked his dad in the bum
> And said, 'Oh what a bad boy am I!'
>
> Bad diddle diddle
> The cat did a piddle
> The cow did a poo on the moon.
> The little dog barfed to see such fun
> And then ate it all up with a spoon.
>
> (Griffiths 2004)

Reputedly, children love the childish humour in the book but adults disapprove. A few schools, educational suppliers and bookshops have banned it for 'the undermining of commonly held values in our society . . . [It] gives children permission to speak and behave in a manner which is vulgar, violent and disrespectful.'[45]

Wowserism (puritanical fundamentalism) flourishes along with neo-conservative politics. The *Encarta World English Dictionary* censors words denoting mental or physical incapacity, and terms denoting sex, age or race; it is, of course, unable to distinguish humorous, ironic or affectionate uses from intended insults (*you silly bugger* can be affectionate or insulting, depending on tone and circumstance), so it tries to ban them all. Then there is software to sanitize DVDs: it uses filters sensitive to sex, drug use, some violence, profanity and 'crude language and bodily humor' to skip scenes. It is nationalistic and politically biased. As one reviewer of the DVD version of *Black Hawk Down* wrote:

When Americans are shot . . . the editors carefully omit the bullet's moment of impact. But when Somali gunmen are blown apart, you see the whole twitching, gruesome scene. (David Pogue, *The New York Times*, 27 May 2004)

This kind of censorship fits the taste, sensibilities, and political and religious beliefs of the software company and its (perceived) target market.

It's for like-minded adults, specifically those who are offended by bad language and sexual situations but don't mind brutality, destruction and suffering. (ibid.)

Censorship simply gives institutional clout to censoring; but it is no less subject to the current personal beliefs, preferences and whims of the censor.

We have defined what we mean by *taboo, censorship* and *censoring*. We now offer the following definition:

The **censoring of language** is the proscription of language expressions that are taboo for the censor at a given time, in contexts which are specified or specifiable because those proscribed language expressions are condemned for being subversive of the good of some specified, specifiable or contextually identifiable community.

Taboo and the censoring of language

We have seen that taboo is more than ritual prohibition and avoidance. Taboos normally arise out of social constraints on the individual's behaviour. They arise in cases where the individual's acts can cause discomfort, harm or injury to him- or herself and to others. Any behaviour that may be dangerous to an individual or his/her community is likely to be subject to taboo, whether this is in the domain of the sacred or the otherwise metaphysical, or touches on earthly persons of power, or concerns contact with dangerous creatures. A person's soul or bodily effluvia may put him/her at metaphysical, moral or physical risk, or may contaminate others. Finally (though these categories are obviously not discrete), a person's social behaviour may violate taboos on politeness. We have seen that infractions of taboos can lead to illness or death, as well as to the lesser penalties of corporal punishment, incarceration, social ostracism or mere disapproval. Even an unintended violation of taboo risks condemnation; but generally speaking, people can and do avoid tabooed behaviour, unless they intend a taboo violation.

A taboo is a proscription of behaviour for a specifiable community of people, for a specified context, at a given place and time. There is no such thing as an absolute taboo that holds for all worlds, times and contexts. We likened taboo to a radioactive fuel rod, which will have dire effects on anyone who comes into direct contact with it unless they know how to protect themselves. Being able to violate a taboo has shock value and displays the semblance of power, which is often effective. That is why the women of Xanthos overcame Bellerophon, why the church was powerful in medieval Europe, and why the Sex Pistols succeeded in having hit records in the 1970s.

Language is constantly subject to censoring: individuals who do not censor their language, and so normally say whatever first enters their heads without considering the circumstances of utterance, are deemed mentally unstable. To what extent should (language) censorship be imposed upon us by those in power? We have suggested that there should be minimal censorship of that kind; there is no evidence that it protects the society or does anything more than impose a repressive ideology that restricts behaviour needlessly.[46] This is a matter on which opinions will differ. Do we trust in the individual's sense of responsibility to the society as a whole, or do we instead favour the 'nanny state'?

In the pages that follow, we examine attitudes to the censoring of language and the consequences for language and its use. We shall focus upon attitudes to language expressions that are regarded as subversive of the common good, and therefore subject to taboo. We offer a rational explanation of the basis for such attitudes, and evaluate the effects on language and language behaviour.

2   Sweet talking and offensive language

Discussion of taboo and the censoring of language naturally leads to a consideration of politeness and impoliteness, and their interaction with euphemism (sweet talking), dysphemism (speaking offensively) and orthophemism (straight talking). The term *euphemism* (Greek *eu* 'good, well' and *phēmē* 'speaking') is well known; but its counterpart *dysphemism* (Greek *dys-* 'bad, unfavourable') rarely appears in ordinary language. *Orthophemism* (Greek *ortho-* 'proper, straight, normal', cf. *orthodox*) is a term we have coined in order to account for direct or neutral expressions that are not sweet-sounding, evasive or overly polite (euphemistic), nor harsh, blunt or offensive (dysphemistic). For convenience, we have also created the collective term *X-phemism* to refer to the union set of euphemisms, orthophemisms and dysphemisms.[1] Important to this discussion is the concept of **cross-varietal synonymy**, i.e. words that have the same meaning as other words used in different contexts. For instance, the X-phemisms *poo, shit* and *faeces* are cross-varietal synonyms because they denote the same thing but have different connotations, which mark different styles used in different circumstances. We also examine the criteria for words being labelled 'dirty' and explain why it is that, where a word has a taboo homonym, the polite sense is usually censored out. Although we focus on English, other languages behave in a similar way.

Politeness

Every polite tongue has its own rules. (Murray 1824: 174)

To broach the subject of polite terms for impolite topics we need to establish some ground rules on politeness. What counts as courteous behaviour varies between human groups; and, because the smallest group consists of just two people, the variation is boundless. Consequently, the way Ed and Jo address one another may strike them as polite but Sally as impolite. The manners regarded as polite in previous centuries sometimes seem ridiculously pedantic today and, if practised in the twenty-first century, would be inappropriate. For

29

instance, Fielding's *The History of Tom Jones* has the following interchange between aunt and niece:

> 'How, Miss Western,' said the aunt 'have you the assurance to speak of him in this manner, to own your affection for such a villain, to my face!' 'Sure, madam,' said Sophia. (Fielding 1749: XVII.8)

Such formality, at least towards older-generation family members, was common among English speakers until the early twentieth century (and perhaps later in some parts of the United States). Politeness is sensitive to social standing. In Fielding's novel, the two lady's maids of Sophia and her supposedly more sophisticated aunt have a tiff, which leads the latter to assert her superiority through being impolite:

> 'Creature! You are below my anger, saucy trollop; but, hussy, I must tell you your breeding shows the meanness of your birth as well as of your education, and both very properly qualify you to be the mean serving-woman of a country-girl.' (Fielding 1749: VII.8)

In her turn, Sophia's maid puts on airs, asserting her own superiority over the landlady of an inn who has boasted, 'Several people of the first quality are now in bed. Here's a great young squire, and many other great gentlefolks of quality.'

> 'Sure you people who keep inns imagine your betters are like yourselves . . . Don't tell me . . . of quality! I believe I know more of people of quality than such as you . . . Good woman, I must insist your first washing your hands [before you slice me some bacon]; for I am extremely nice and have been always used from my cradle to have everything in the most elegant manner.' The landlady . . . governed herself with much difficulty . . . 'I beg the kitchen may be kept clear, that I may not be surrounded with all the blackguards in town; as for you, sir,' says she to Partridge, 'you look somewhat like a gentleman, and may sit still if you please; I don't desire to disturb anybody but mob.' (Fielding 1749: X.4)

This behaviour translates much more directly into twenty-first-century terms. Nevertheless,

> Politeness is the ritual of society, as prayers are of the church; a school of manners, and a gentle blessing to the age in which it grew. (Emerson 1856: 325)

Whether or not language behaviour counts as good manners will depend on a number of factors. These include: the relationship between speakers, their audience, and anyone within earshot; the subject matter; the situation (setting); and whether a spoken or written medium is used. In other words: **politeness** is wedded to context, place and time. That which is polite is at least inoffensive and at best pleasing to an audience. That which is offensive is *impolite*.[2] Notice that impoliteness is more explicitly defined than politeness.

Although we may say that someone who is polite is *polished* (as the spelling suggests, the words *polish* and *polite* have a common ancestor), we refer to both language and behaviour as *polite* when it is not impolite. For instance, what we say in our definition of (im)politeness is itself polite, because the words used in the definition are not impolite.

Dysphemism, orthophemism and euphemism

Because impoliteness is more readily determined than politeness, we examine first the concept of **dysphemism**, followed by **orthophemism**, then **euphemism**. Roughly speaking, dysphemism is the opposite of euphemism and, by and large, it is tabooed. Like euphemism, it is sometimes motivated by fear and distaste, but also by hatred and contempt. Speakers resort to dysphemism to talk about people and things that frustrate and annoy them, that they disapprove of and wish to disparage, humiliate and degrade. Dysphemisms are therefore characteristic of political groups and cliques talking about their opponents; of feminists speaking about men; and also of male larrikins and macho types speaking of women and effete behaviours. Dysphemistic expressions include curses, name-calling, and any sort of derogatory comment directed towards others in order to insult or to wound them. Dysphemism is also a way to let off steam; for example, when exclamatory swear words alleviate frustration or anger. To be more technical: a **dysphemism** is a word or phrase with connotations that are offensive either about the denotatum and/or to people addressed or overhearing the utterance.

The denotatum of a language expression is the kind of thing that speakers refer to when using the language expression: denotation is the relation between language expressions and things or events in worlds – not just the world we live in, but any world and time (historical, fictional, imagined) that may be spoken of. The *connotations* of a word or longer expression are semantic effects (nuances of meaning) that arise from encyclopaedic knowledge about the word's denotation and also from experience, beliefs and prejudices about the contexts in which the word is typically used. Sets of words can have the same denotative meaning, but differ considerably in connotation. For example, *dog*, *dish-licker*, *bow-wow*, *cur*, *mutt*, *mongrel*, *whelp*, *hound* all denote a canine animal of either sex, but the expressions have quite different expressive or connotative meaning; each takes on distinctive connotations from the various contexts in which it is used. *Dish-licker* smacks of dog-racing jargon; and *bow-wow* either racing slang or baby-talk (compare *gee-gee*). *Cur* is pejorative along with *mutt*, *mongrel* and *whelp*, which have additional senses, as does *hound*, except that it connotes a noble animal. *Dog*, however, connotes nothing in particular, being the unmarked lexeme. A speaker could use *dog* to refer to an entity which is not a canine

Table 2.1. *Contrasting X-phemisms*

Orthophemism	Euphemism	Dysphemism
faeces	*poo*	*shit*
toilet	*loo*	*shithouse*
menstruate	*have a period*	*bleed*
my vagina	*my bits*	*my cunt*
Jesus	*Lord*	*Christ!* [blasphemy]

quadruped. If the referent were human, then the expression is dysphemistic: the speaker is accusing the male human referent of being worthless and despicable, or a woman of being ill-dressed and ugly. The affective meaning, social and expressive information about the speaker's feelings, is what is most significant. Connotations differ from context to context, from one community to another, and occasionally from one individual to another.

Because impolite behaviour is offensive, it is *dysphemistic*, and because polite behaviour is more or less the opposite of impolite behaviour, polite behaviour is **non-dysphemistic**. Once again, the classification is wedded to context, place and time. The context makes all the difference, as the following examples show. At moments of intimacy, lovers may pleasurably and inoffensively refer to tabooed body parts using terms that would be dysphemistic in a doctor's surgery. Among a group of male squaddies in a boozer (soldiers in a bar), the term *shithouse* would most likely be non-dysphemistic and if one of them used the euphemism *loo* instead (other than jokingly), he would probably be laughed at; the term could be regarded as dysphemistic because it would be as insulting to the others as addressing them using baby language.

Compare a small set of orthophemisms, euphemisms and dysphemisms in Table 2.1. The dysphemism is tabooed as the impolite choice, or in the case of *bleed* perhaps merely dispreferred; it is the expression most likely to be deemed offensive. What is the difference between orthophemisms and euphemisms? **Orthophemisms** and **euphemisms** are words or phrases used as an alternative to a dispreferred expression. They avoid possible loss of face by the speaker, and also the hearer or some third party. A *dispreferred* language expression is simply one that is not the preferred, desired or appropriate expression. For instance, under most circumstances the dispreferred response to an invitation is refusal; dispreferred responses to a greeting are a dismissal or a cold stare.[3] Dispreferred expressions might alternatively be dubbed *tabooed expressions*.

Our definition refers to *face*. This is extremely significant in any discussion of politeness. Social interaction is generally oriented towards maintaining (saving) face. Just as we look after our own face (self-respect), we are expected to be considerate of, and look after, the face-wants of others. Those who are skilled at this are said to have social *savoir faire*; they are said to be perceptive and diplomatic. In short, in Anglo communities, **face** is one's public self-image. That is, the way that one perceives one's self to be viewed in the eyes of others. In European communities until the mid twentieth century, a person's public self-image was largely determined by his/her family's place in society; even though wealth and education were then, as now, a social asset (this is explicit in the earlier quotes from Fielding's eighteenth-century novel *Tom Jones*). In some other communities, the notion of self is still sublimated in a similar way to the public image of the family, clan or religious community of which one is a member; but because we are focusing on language taboos in English, we will stick with face as 'public self-image'. Face has two aspects: the want of a person to have their attributes, achievements, ideas, possessions and goals well regarded by others; and the want of a person not to be imposed upon by others.[4] Face can be lost (affronted), gained (enhanced), or just maintained. In virtually every utterance, a speaker needs to take care that what is said will maintain, enhance or affront a hearer's face in just the way s/he intends, while at the same time maintaining or enhancing the speaker's own face (which can be achieved by being self-effacing). There is a general presumption that a speaker will be polite except when intending to affront the hearer.

The term *speaker* is to be interpreted as the person who utters the language under consideration; *speaker* is widely used by academic linguists to refer to writers as well as to producers of spoken language. Similarly, *hearer* makes abbreviated reference to the audience or readership – the person or persons addressed.

To return to the definition of orthophemisms and euphemisms, we conclude that both arise from conscious or unconscious self-censoring; they are used to avoid the speaker being embarrassed and/or ill thought of and, at the same time, to avoid embarrassing and/or offending the hearer or some third party. This coincides with the speaker being polite. Now to the difference between orthophemism and euphemism:

- An **orthophemism** is typically more formal and more direct (or literal) than the corresponding euphemism.
- A **euphemism** is typically more colloquial and figurative (or indirect) than the corresponding orthophemism.

Like euphemisms, dysphemisms are typically more colloquial and figurative than orthophemisms (but, for instance, to truthfully call someone *fat* is direct). We therefore suggest that X-phemisms (the union set of orthophemisms, euphemisms and dysphemisms) are related as shown in Figure 2.1.

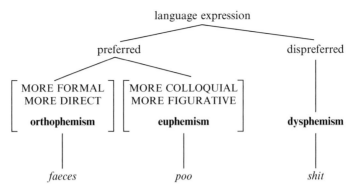

Figure 2.1. Distinguishing X-phemisms.

In the following extract from the sixteenth-century writer Aretino, Antonia is objecting that Nanna is using too many euphemisms when comparing the lifestyles of a nun, a wife and a courtesan; it is an appeal against the use of euphemism, but is it a call for orthophemism?

I meant to tell you and then I forgot: speak plainly and say 'ass' [*cul(o)*], 'prick' [*cazzo*], 'cunt' [*potta*] and 'fuck' [*fottere*] if you want anyone other than scholars from the Sapienza Capranica to understand you. You with your 'rope in the ring', 'obelisk in the Colosseum', 'leek in the garden', 'key in the lock', 'bolt in the door', 'pestle in the mortar', 'nightingale in the nest', 'tree in the ditch', 'syringe in the flap-valve', 'sword in the scabbard'; not to mention 'the stake', 'the crozier', 'the parsnip', 'the little monkey', 'her thing', 'his thing', 'the apples', 'leaves of the missal', 'the fact', 'the thanks-be-to-God', 'that thing', 'that affair', 'that big news', 'the handle', 'the arrow', 'the carrot', 'the root' and the shit that you don't want to say straight out, so you go tiptoeing round it. So say yes when you mean yes and no when you mean no; otherwise, keep it to yourself. (Pietro Aretino, 'Ragionamento della Nanna e della Antonia', 1534; quoted in Frantz 1989: 74f)

It depends on the context of use whether terms such as *arse/ass*, *prick*, *cunt* and *fuck* are orthophemistic or dysphemistic. A few people find the appearance of such terms in a scholarly piece of work to be dysphemistic; most do not. What is unspeakable for one is not necessarily inexcusable for another.

The middle-class politeness criterion (MCPC)

Despite the implication that particular expressions are not necessarily euphemistic or dysphemistic in all contexts, it would ignore reality to pretend that ordinary people do not treat them that way – for instance, as terms for a toilet, *loo* and *bathroom* are widely judged euphemistic, whereas *shithouse* is not. What seems to be in operation is a **middle-class politeness criterion** (MCPC):

- In order to be polite to a casual acquaintance of the opposite sex, in a formal situation, in a middle-class environment, one would normally be expected to use the euphemism or orthophemism rather than the dispreferred counterpart. The dispreferred counterpart would be a dysphemism.

We do not suggest that the middle-class politeness criterion fails to apply between, say, close acquaintances of the same sex; however, language exchange between casual acquaintances of different sexes offers the most probable default conditions for the MCPC. Let us suppose that, by the middle-class politeness criterion, *I'm going to the bathroom* is a euphemism for, and preferred to, *I'm going to urinate* – in which case the latter must be the dispreferred (tabooed) expression.

Our definition of the middle-class politeness criterion invites the question, what is a middle-class environment? It is a deliberately vague notion used to exclude, on the one hand, those so rich and/or so powerful that they can disregard social conventions observed by the mass of the community; on the other hand, it also excludes those so uneducated, poor and deprived that they are unaware of, or cannot afford to observe, the niceties of such social conventions. We use the description 'middle-class' to mean much the same as the apocryphal *man on the Clapham omnibus* or *the man who takes the magazines at home and in the evening pushes the lawn mower in his shirt sleeves* or *the man in the street* – all of which were intended to refer to very ordinary persons of either sex.[5] Dictionaries such as the *OED*, *Webster's* and the *Longman Advanced Learner's Dictionary* give meanings that we would say observe the middle-class politeness criterion. Of course, not everyone would agree. In 1976, the educational commissioner of Texas banned the four major American college dictionaries (among others) from schools; he objected to terms like *bed*, *clap*, *deflower*, *john*, *G-string*, *slut*, *bastard* and many others. Newspaper accounts of dictionaries being banned from the school libraries and classrooms of small-town USA are commonplace.[6]

Many hundreds of terms are now labeled as *disparaging, contemptuous* or *offensive* in dictionaries, often on the strength of dubious evidence but out of fear that they will be taken to be insensitive to some group. The *Encarta World English Dictionary* (*EWED*) has carried this trend to an extreme. *EWED* considers almost any word offensive that has to do with mental or physical incapacity, mental mistakes, sex, age, or race. It considers the word *madness* offensive, and one can't call someone a *nut* or *nutty* or a *nutcase* in its book without being offensive. *Weirdo* is off limits, and no one can be a *basket case* or a *vegetable* or *off his* (or *her*) *rocker, screwed up, schizoid,* or *handicapped. EWED* makes no distinction between words used humorously or affectionately and words used to insult. So among the words it labels *offensive* are *jerk, slob, schnook, klutz, loony,* and *crazy*. It views language as a fortified castle of virtue, and every battlement is equipped with a cannon loaded with warnings. (Lindau 2001: 234)

So, defining the boundaries of taste is controversial. Nevertheless, when we describe an expression as an orthophemism or euphemism or dysphemism without making reference to the context of its use, it is the middle-class politeness criterion (MCPC) that we have in mind.

By our definition of dysphemism, some of the language in the following quote would count as dysphemistic, i.e. offensive. Although the speaker was summonsed for using offensive language, the case was dismissed. The scene occurred outside the defendant's house at around 11.30 at night; police were at the scene.

'What the fuck are youse doing here. My fuckin' son had to get me out of bed. I can't believe youse are here. What the fuck are youse doing here?' (to the police).

'I fuckin' know what this is about. Its about that fuckin' gas bottle. They can get fucked, I'm not paying them fucking nothing. They can get me our fuckin' bottle back' (to the police about the neighbours).

'We never had any fuckin' trouble till youse fuckin' moved here. Youse have fuckin' caused this trouble and called the fuckin' police on me' (to the neighbours). (*Police* v. *Butler* (2003) NSWLC 2 before Heilpern J, 14 June 2002)

By the MCPC, the defendant did use offensive language – why is it not offensive in law?[7] The judgment in the case in question referred to another case, where a defendant was summonsed for saying to the police restraining him during a brawl:

Get fucked you cunts, I'm just trying to help my mates.

That case was dismissed on the following basis:

I [Justice Yeldham] determined by a consideration as best I could of community standards today and decisions on this kind of legislation over the last twenty years, that the words were not intrinsically 'offensive' in the requisite legal sense of that word.

In *Police* v. *Butler*, Justice Heilpern referred to several similar cases, and also to the extreme prevalence of words like *fuck* and *cunt* within the community, and their frequency on free-to-air television and other media:[8]

Channel 9 has recently broadcast a show (*Sex in the City*) that includes the words 'fuck off' and 'fucking' as well as 'cunt'. The word was used on '*The Panel*' and the station only received two complaints. Recently, the *Sydney Morning Herald* revealed that 'fuck' was used in the television program '*The Sopranos*' seventy-one times in one single episode (*SMH* April 29, 2000, 3s). *Big Brother* residents evidently cannot live without the word in every episode.

Justice Heilpern concluded that:

This is a classic example of conduct which offends against the standards of good taste or good manners, which is a breach of the rules of courtesy and runs contrary to accepted social rules – to use the words of Justice Kerr. It was ill-advised, rude, and improper conduct. Some people may be offended by such words, but I am not satisfied beyond a reasonable doubt that it is offensive within the meaning of the section. There is doubt in my mind that a reasonably tolerant and understanding and contemporary person in his or her reactions would be wounded or angered or outraged. Such a person would be more likely to view it as a regrettable but not uncommon part of living near people who drink to excess. I have no doubt that people would have been disturbed as a result of being awoken or distracted by the yelling and carry on, whatever the language used. I ask myself this question – what difference would it make to the reasonably tolerant person if swear words were used or not. I answer that there would be little difference indeed.

What is interesting about this legal decision is that it demonstrates that the MCPC is sensitive to offence against the standards of good taste or good manners, which is a breach of the rules of courtesy and runs contrary to accepted social rules. But the law imposes a much narrower taboo on behaviour. These judgments show that the law reflects the change in social attitudes: taboos on various kinds of profanity have been relaxed, but racist language is very likely to be found offensive in law.

It is surely relevant that behaviour which offends against the MCPC is often referred to as *coarse behaviour*; and language which offends the MCPC is *coarse language*. The adjective *coarse* is used in its primary sense of 'ordinary, common, mean (in the depreciatory sense of these epithets); base; of inferior quality or value; of little account', to quote the *OED*, which later adds 'unrefined; rough, rude, uncivil, vulgar . . . gross, indelicate . . . indecent, obscene'. Thus, *coarse language* is, by association, that of the vulgar classes, untrammelled by the middle-class politeness criterion.

X-phemisms and the use of language

The middle-class politeness criterion establishes a default condition for assessing the X-phemistic value of an expression. An innocuous word like *telephone* is normally an orthophemism but it may occur in an utterance that is made referentially dysphemistic by the addition of an expletive as in *He's on the bleeding telephone still* or *He keeps fucking telephoning me!* We have argued that it is the particular context of use which determines the true X-phemistic value of a given occurrence of a language expression. To address Jesus Christ in prayer makes orthophemistic use of *Jesus Christ*; the same words uttered when swearing are often dysphemistic and tabooed.

The picture in Figure 2.2 constitutes a visual euphemism according to the MCPC. It was found in a monthly catalogue, widely distributed to British households, that mostly offers household and personal appliances of one kind and another. The advert is for a 'flexible personal massager' which is positioned as if to massage the woman's neck; however, its phallic shape and

Melt Away Tension

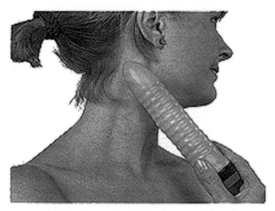

Help reduce pressure and stress in complete home
privacy and comfort, with this versatile,'soft touch',
flexible personal massager. The soothing, speed-
adjustable vibrations penetrate deeply to melt away
the tensions and frustrations of the day – bringing
blissful relaxation and total contentment. Length 18 cm
(7") approx. Uses 2 x AA type batteries (not supplied).

Massager
Code: 00000 £9.95

| DON'T FORGET! |
| Pack of 4 x AA Batteries |
| £0.95 Code:0000 |

Figure 2.2. Visual euphemism.

length, and the description, 'speed-adjustable vibrations [that] penetrate
deeply to melt away the tensions and frustrations of the day – [bring] blissful
relaxation and total contentment', leave no doubt that it is a vibrator, intended
for sexual stimulation. Similar euphemistic advertisements for vibrators have
been around since 1906.[9]

The MCPC does not operate when euphemisms are used in deference to or
to avoid conflict with spirits, gods and other metaphysical entities. Because it
was blasphemous to name the god of the Jews and his cohorts, the name was
written without vowels, *YHVH*, but read out either as *Ha Shem* 'The Name'
(sometimes written as simply the initial letter ה 'Heh') or as *Adonai* meaning
'Lord' – a euphemism that has carried over into Christianity, in both addressing and naming God and Jesus Christ. There is a euphemism for *Adonai* used
outside of formal religious service by devout Jews, *Adoshem* from *Ha Shem*;
very devout Jews will write *G–d* for *God* (as Christians used to do), just as
they would write *Yah*,[10] an acronym for the first two letters, Yod and Heh, of

יהוה (*YHVH*).[11] The names of dangerous animals are often not used in case the animal hears and feels called to attack. Hence the Ukrainian proverb *Pro vovka pomovka a vovk u khatu* 'One speaks of the wolf and it runs into the house' [lit. 'about wolf talk and wolf into house'] and the English proverb *Speak of the devil and he comes running*. Thus, in most Slavic languages the bear is euphemistically called something like 'the honey eater'; and the orthophemistic English word *bear* derives from the euphemistic '[the] brown one' (hence *Bruno the bear*, in which *bruno* is Italian for 'brown'). Among the Zia of south-eastern Papua New Guinea, fishermen avoid talking about (and even try to avoid thinking about) dangerous creatures like sharks, rays and saltwater crocodiles, for fear of inviting attack. If such creatures are seen, they are referred to using the class name *woo* 'fish' instead of *bawang* 'shark' or *beoto* 'ray'; likewise, the crocodile will not be called *ugama* but *emo meko* 'man bad'.

Euphemistic dysphemisms and **dysphemistic euphemisms** are expressions at odds with the intentions that lurk behind them. More formally, the locution (the form of words) is at variance with the reference and illocutionary point of the utterance (i.e. what the speaker is doing in making the utterance). The expressive exclamation *Shit!* typically expresses anger, frustration or anguish, and is ordinarily a dysphemism. Its remodelled forms *Sugar!*, *Shoot!*, *Shivers!* or *Shucks!* are euphemisms – they are linguistic fig leaves for a thought that can be castigated as dysphemistic. The act of swearing – using so-called 'four-letter words' – is conventionally perceived to be dysphemistic and therefore tabooed; but by using an expression that is not intrinsically offensive, a speaker's dysphemistic intention can be accomplished euphemistically. These are prime examples of the censoring of language for the purpose of taboo avoidance. A person may feel the inner urge to swear, but at the same time may not wish to appear overly coarse in their behaviour. Society recognizes the dilemma and provides a way out – a conventionalised euphemistic dysphemism like *Gosh!*, *Sugar!*, *Shoot!* or *Shivers!* Flippant terms like *doodle* 'penis', and rhyming slang like *jimmy-riddle* 'piddle' are also most often euphemistic dysphemisms. A euphemistic dysphemism exists to cause less face-loss or offence than an out-and-out dysphemism (although it will not always succeed in doing so).

Conversely, there are locutions which are dysphemistic while the illocutionary point is euphemistic. For example, apparent terms of opprobrium are used in good-humoured raillery to display friendship and affection to someone close to you. Calling a good mate an *old bastard* or *silly little dag* is to use dysphemistic euphemism. Other examples are flippant expressions for death like *call it quits*, *croak*, *check out*, *cock up one's toes*, *push up the daisies*, *buy the farm*, *bought it*, *kick the bucket*, *pop off*, *peg out*, *conk out* and *cark it*. Of course, for many occasions these would be straight dysphemisms. If a doctor were to inform close family that their loved one had *croaked* during the night, it would normally be inappropriate, insensitive, unprofessional and tabooed; in short, dysphemistic. Yet, given another context with a different set of interlocutors (e.g. among fatality inured hospital staff), the same expression could just as well be described as cheerfully euphemistic. The flippant connotations of these expressions distract from the sadness of the situation and can be preferred. Flippancy toward what is feared is a means of coming to terms with fear by downgrading it. Other examples of dysphemistic euphemisms are terms for menstruation such as *have the curse, woman's complaint, be feeling that way, off the roof, flying the red flag* and *surfing the red wave*. They are simple dysphemisms if a man is whingeing about the sexual unreceptiveness of his female partner, or perhaps when a woman is complaining about one or another incommoding effect of *riding the red rag*.[12] From another point of view, terms like *ride the red wave, have my rags* and *bleeding like a stuck pig* are dysphemistic to some because they are explicit and vulgar.

The dirt on dirty words

When you speak of the anus, you call it by a name ['ring'] that is not its own; why not rather call it by its own [viz. *culus*]? If it is indecent, do not use even the substituted name; if not, you had better call it by its own. (Cicero 1959, *Epistulae ad Familiares* IX, xxii)

Who ever stubbed his toe in the dark and cried out, 'Oh, faeces!'? (Adams 1985: 45)

The phrase *taboo language* commonly refers to language that is a breach of etiquette because it contains so-called 'dirty words'. But words are sounds heard, sequences of symbols on a page, abstract language constituents: how can they count as *dirty*? The description derives from a persistent belief that the form of an expression somehow communicates the essential nature of whatever is being referred to. As Frazer wrote, 'the link between a name and the person or thing denominated by it is not a mere arbitrary and ideal association, but a real and substantial bond which unites the two'.[13] This view persists among the wider community, despite it being generally accepted by most scholars since Aristotle (384–322 BCE)[14] that there is no causal relationship between the form of a word and its meaning. Otherwise, why is a canine animal called *dog* in English, *chien* in French, *Hund* in German, *pies* in Polish, *ájá* in Yoruba, *kare* in Hausa, *mbwa* in Swahili, and innumerable other names in yet other languages? There are no rational grounds to accept that a 'dirty word' like *shit* should be treated in the same way as we treat faecal matter. But we can admit that the connotations of taboo terms are contaminated by the taboo topics which they denote. We conclude that the sobriquet *dirty words* denotes people's attitudes toward the denotations and connotations of the words. The dysphemism *shit* is no more dirty than the word *faeces* nor the euphemism *poo*.

Epithets for taboo topics, and the words naming them, are *bad*, *dirty*, *filthy*, *foul*, *gross*, *grotty*, *impure*, *unclean*, *vile* and so forth; hence the parent's command to a child heard uttering a taboo term: *Wash your mouth out!* Tabooed and offensive behaviour is sometimes described as *off*, like rotting food. Tabooed language is referred to as *off-colour*,[15] again like rotting food or a sick person. The producer of off-colour language may be accused of having a *mind like a drain* or *a cess-pit* (a conduit or receptacle for foul effluent). There is an association between dirt, rotting organic material, and bodily effluvia like ear-wax, menstrual blood, piss, semen, shit, snot, spit, sweat and vomit. Social conventions (based in part on sound medical evidence) require us to 'wash our hands' after contact with the effluvium, before we handle food or shake hands with others. Thus *dirt* and other words within the same semantic field typically have dysphemistic connotations. Offensive (dysphemistic) behaviours are often described as *dirty*, e.g.: *act shitily*, *be a shit*, *be dirty* ('addicted to illicit drugs'), *dirty business*, *dirty deeds*, *dirty looks*, *do the dirty on*, *play dirty*, *foul play* and so on.

The noun *dirt* is in the same semantic field as *crud*, *evil*, *grot*, *grunge*, *gunge*, *impurity*, *insanitary*, *mess*, *muck*, *pollution*, *slops*, *stain*, *something the cat brought in*. Someone or something dirty may be described as *crude*, *evil*, *grotty*, *grubby*, *impure*, *insanitary*, *lewd*, *manky*, *mucky*, *scuzzy*, *seedy*, *sleazy*, *slovenly*, *sordid*, *squalid*, *unclean*.

One gets and gives *the dirt on* someone to *blacken* his/her name; rotting substances go black, and the verb *blacken* is associated with the darkness of night and hence the *black arts* of malevolent witchcraft too. A dysphemistic act is said to *be a rotten thing to do*, to *stink*, and so forth. Like dirt, diseases *contaminate* people, and a person without a sexually transmissible disease might describe him/herself to a prospective sexual partner as *clean*; so too might a person rehabilitated after addiction to hard drugs. People with *bad* characters (like *shysters*, *slatterns*, *slobs*, *sluts*) *contaminate* and *corrupt* others – perhaps, if they have *a mind like a cess-pit* – by using *dirty* words that *pollute* the atmosphere or by uttering *profanities* that *defile*.

That part of tabooed language constituted by *dirty words* consists of terms for:

- bodily organs concealed by bikinis and swimming trunks – because they are organs of sexual desire, stimulation and gratification and/or used for micturition and defecation;
- activities involving these SMD (sex, micturition, defecation) organs;
- bodily effluvia issuing from these SMD organs.

Dirty words have the power to *titillate*, that is, 'stimulate as by tickling, excite agreeably, gratify the senses or the imagination'. Alan Read, indulging in a little hyperbole, puts it this way:

The ordinary reaction to a display of filth and vulgarity should be a neutral one or else disgust; but the reaction to certain words connected with excrement and sex is neither of these, but a titillating thrill of scandalized perturbation. (Read 1977: 9)

Later we explore the scientific evidence supporting the view that taboo terms are the most emotionally evocative of all language expressions. This is something most native speakers know from experience: compared to other vocabulary, dirty words evoke stronger skin conductance responses (cause bigger goose-bumps), and we recognise them and recall them more readily.

[S]entences with profane and sexually suggestive language elicited responses quite different from those [without . . .] Sentences with off-color language [euphemism!] possess a memorability that is quite independent of their role in conversation. (MacWhinney et al. 1982: 315)

It is not surprising, therefore, that there is a general tendency for any derogatory or unfavourable denotation or connotation within a language expression to dominate the interpretation of its immediate context. As we see in the next section, this can be a potent trigger for word loss and meaning shift. It is this power of dirty words that leads to them being condemned and their users censured. However, there are contexts in which non-dysphemistic reference needs to be made to the denotata of dirty words, for instance for therapeutic or medical purposes. On such occasions the language provides polite words for impolite topics.

Homonymous dysphemisms win out because they are 'strong' language

KATHERINE: Ainsi dis-je d'elbow, de nick, et de sin. Comment appelez-vous le pied et la robe?
ALICE: De foot, madame; et de coun.
KATHERINE: De foot et de coun! O Seigneur Dieu! ce sont mots de son mauvais, corruptible, gros, et impudique, et non pour les dames d'honneur d'user: je ne voudrais prononcer ces mots devant les seigneurs de France pour tout le monde. Foh! le foot et le coun!
(Shakespeare, *Henry V*, III.iv.46–53)

[Katherine asks what you call a foot and a gown in English. In response to Alice telling her, she says, 'Oh Lord God, these words sound bad, corrupting, gross and impure, and not to be used by women of honour. I wouldn't like to utter these words in front of French gentlemen for all the world.' The reason for this outburst is that *foot* sounds to her like *foutre* 'fuck' and *coun* (i.e. *gown*) like *con*, which is etymologically linked to 'cunnie' and 'cunt'; however, *pussy* is probably a better translation here.]

Dysphemisms are contaminated by the taboo topics which they denote; but, by definition, the euphemisms are not (yet) contaminated. In fact, a euphemism often degenerates into a dysphemism through contamination by the taboo topic. Cicero observes (in 50 BCE) that Latin *penis* 'tail' had been a euphemism for *mentula* (itself a euphemism literally meaning 'sprig of mint'): 'At hodie *penis* est in obscenis' 'But nowadays *penis* is among the obscenities.'[16] English *undertaker* once referred to someone who undertakes to do things, i.e. an 'odd-job man'; it was used as a euphemism for the person taking care of funerals, a *funeral undertaker*. Like most ambiguous taboo terms, the meaning narrowed to the taboo sense alone, and is now replaced by the euphemism *funeral director* – though even that may by now be an orthophemism. Euphemisms like this often start off with a modifying word, 'funeral' in *funeral undertaker*, and then the modifier is dropped as the euphemism fades. Further examples are *mentally deranged* ⇒ *deranged, lunatic asylum* ⇒ *asylum* and *coarse/strong language* ⇒ *language* (advice about language used in a TV programme). Throughout the ages, country folk have been held in low esteem in most communities. Latin *urbanus* 'townsman' gives rise to *urbane* 'sophisticated, elegant, refined' versus *rusticus* 'rustic', with connotations of 'clownish, awkward, boorish'. *Boorish* means 'ill-mannered, loutish, uncouth' and derives from the noun *boor*, which existed in Old English and lives on in *neighbour*; however that seems to have faded and been reintroduced from the Dutch *boer* 'farmer'. A *villain* was 'a low born or base-minded rustic' but has long meant 'an unprincipled or depraved scoundrel; a man naturally disposed to base or criminal actions, or deeply involved in the commission of disgraceful crimes'.

The once euphemistic [*going to the*] *toilet* is fading from euphemism to orthophemism, and is being superseded by the euphemisms *bathroom* or *restroom* in American English and *loo* in spoken British and Australian English. Perhaps it will go the way of *necessary house*.[17] We know of no converse histories in which a taboo term has been elevated to a euphemism, with the possible exception of Greek *kakos* 'bad': it derives from the Indo-European root **kak(k)-* 'shit', which is the source for our *cacky* and its cognates in other Indo-European languages.[18] But perhaps Indo-European **kak(k)-* originally meant 'bad' and was euphemistically applied to shit and so became contaminated. There have been some euphemisms that degraded into taboo terms and later came back from the abyss, having lost their taboo sense. During the seventeenth and eighteenth centuries, the verb *occupy* meant 'copulate' (for reasons you can well imagine); at the same time, non-taboo senses lapsed. *Occupy* only re-entered the lexicon in its current sense of 'inhabit, take up' after it had ceased to be used dysphemistically. All this supports the view that taboo terms are classified as dysphemistic because of a belief, be it ever so vague, that their form reflects the essential nature of the taboo topics they denote. This is exactly why the terms themselves are often said to be unpleasant or ugly sounding; why the SMD words among them are miscalled 'dirty words'.

There is a wealth of evidence to suggest that where a language expression is ambiguous between a taboo sense and a non-taboo sense, its meaning will narrow to the taboo sense alone. This perhaps explains why dysphemistic language is often referred to as *strong language*. For instance, since the 1960s, the adjective *gay* has been used less and less in the sense 'bright, full of fun' (a sense dating back to the Middle Ages) because it also has the meaning 'homosexual'. Throughout the centuries, there have been many other examples of word senses narrowing to the taboo sense alone, and of innocent vocabulary items that have dropped by the wayside because of bogus associations with dirty words:

- Cicero pointed out that *ruta* 'rue' and *menta* 'mint' could be used without impropriety; the same was true for the diminutive of *ruta*, *rutula* but not of *menta*, because the resulting *mentula* meant 'penis'.[19]
- In late eighteenth-century England, *ass* was gradually replaced by *donkey*.[20] The motivation was exactly what Bloomfield[21] noted for the same change in American English: *ass* was being confused with *arse* and indeed has replaced it in American, with the meaning 'arse' or 'cunt'.
- The noun *accident* once meant 'that which happens, a chance event' (cf. *accidentally*, *by accident*), but, except in the phrase *happy accident*, its association with misfortune has narrowed the meaning to 'chance misfortune', as in *There was an accident* or *Little Harry had an accident in his new trousers on his fourth birthday*.
- Until the late nineteenth century, *coney* (rhymes with *honey*) was the word for 'rabbit'; it dropped out of use because of the taboo homonym meaning 'cunt'.
- Hock[22] believes that phonetic similarity to *fuck* led to the demise of the following words: *fuk* 'a sail'; *feck* (the stem for *feckless*); *feck* or *fack* 'one of the stomachs of a ruminant'; *fac*, an abbreviation for *factotum*; *fack(s)* 'fact(s)'. He may be right with respect to *fuk*, but the pronunciation /fæk(s)/ is still used freely as the common pronunciation of *facts*, of *fax* (end-clipped from *facsimile* [*machine*]), and of *FAQs*, the acronym for 'frequently asked questions'.
- The British still use *cock* to mean 'rooster'; but, because of the taboo homonym meaning 'penis', this sense of *cock* started to die out in America in the early nineteenth century; it is nowadays very rare in Australia. There has also been an effect on words containing *cock*: former Mayor Ed *Koch* of New York City gives his surname a spelling-pronunciation /kač/; the

family of Louisa May *Alcott* (author of *Little Women*) changed their name from *Alcox*; *cockroach* is often foreclipped to *roach* in American English; but on the other hand, *cockpit* and above all *cocktail* show no sign of being avoided; the same is true for those plumbing terms *ballcock* and *stopcock*. And although there were other factors at work too, the use of *haystack* in place of *haycock*, and the use of *weather-vane* as an alternative to *weather-cock*, were undoubtedly influenced by taboo avoidance.

- Among South Africans, for whom *kaffir* pronounced [ˈkafər] `black person' is a dysphemism, the same two syllables in *kaffir lime leaves* are euphemized with different stress and corresponding vowel difference to [kaˈfir] – a nice example of dissimilation as a form of self-censorship.[23]

There are two reasons why language abandons homonyms of taboo terms. First, there is the relative salience of taboo terms.[24] One possible explanation for the salience is that obscene vocabulary is stored and/or accessed differently in the brain from other vocabulary. Evidence comes from people with Tourette's syndrome, which is characterized by involuntary outbursts of coprolalia (foul language); and some people lose all other language ability: this could only be possible if the means of storage and/or access were separate from that of obscene vocabulary.[25] A second reason for abandoning the homonyms of taboo terms is that a speaker will not risk appearing to use a dysphemism when none was intended. For example, the Danish King of England from 1016 to 1035 was originally called *Cnut* (the English *C* in place of the Norse *K*); but because the letters are as readily transposed as those of today's clothing manufacturer FCUK, *Cnut* came to be spelled *Canute*. There are a few (older) English speakers who, if they catch themselves using the adjective *gay* in its former sense will, with mild embarrassment, explicitly draw attention to this intended meaning. Their nineteenth-century forbears, fearful of seeming impropriety, avoided the terms *leg* and *breast*, even when speaking of a cooked fowl, referring instead to *dark* or *red meat* and *white meat*. Grose (1811) lists *thingstable* used in place of *constable*, commenting that it reveals 'a ludicrous affectation of delicacy in avoiding the pronunciation of the first syllable in the title of that officer, which in sound has some similarity to an indecent monosyllable'. The United States Chief of Naval Operations is the *CNO*; the Department of Defense is the *DOD*; however the Secretary of Defense is not the *SOD*, but the *SecDef*. All these exemplify the censoring of language.

Sometimes, where there is little likelihood of being misunderstood, the homonyms of a taboo term will persist in the language. This is the case for instance with *queen* 'regina', which is under no threat from the homonym meaning 'gay male, male transvestite', simply because one denotatum is necessarily female, the other is necessarily male; the converse holds for the end-clipped American epithet *mother* 'motherfucker'. Similarly, some do not censor themselves saying *It's queer* but we generally avoid saying *He's queer* if we mean 'He's peculiar', preferring *He's eccentric* or *He's a bit odd*. More subtly, *bull* meaning 'bullshit' is dissimilated from *bull* 'male, typically bovine, animal' because it heads an uncountable noun phrase instead of a countable (pluralizable) one.

Nonetheless, dissimilarity does not always safeguard the innocent language expression. For instance, *regina* makes some people feel uncomfortable because of its phonetic similarity to the tabooed and therefore salient *vagina*; it is quite usual for speakers to avoid expressions which are phonetically similar to taboo terms. The linguistic infelicities of non-native speakers and the similarity of some foreign language item to a taboo term can have embarrassing effects that may result in amusement or censoring – as Shakespeare has French Princess Katherine tell us (quoted earlier). There is a (possibly apocryphal) tale of a poster in Japanese English in 1952, that read in part: *We play for MacArthur's erection* (MacArthur later withdrew from the US Presidential race). A true tale is of a presentation by a non-native male graduate student, in which he several times used the phrase 'my testees' to refer to 'those subjected to a test': the neologism provoked a good deal of barely suppressed mirth in part of the audience. Reportedly, bilingual Thais may get apprehensive about using the Thai words *fâg* 'sheath', *fág* 'to hatch' and *fuk* 'gourd, pumpkin' in the hearing of other Thais fluent in English. *Fuk* is used for the name of the main character in the award-winning Thai novel *Kham Phi Phaksa* (*The Judgement*) by Chart Kobjitti,[26] and there was much speculation about how the name would be transliterated when the novel was translated into English. The translator called him 'Fak'. Thai English-teachers experience some embarrassment, and their students some amusement, with the English word *yet* which is the equivalent of 'to fuck' in colloquial Thai. Farb[27] reports something similar: 'In the Nootka Indian language of Vancouver Island, British Columbia, the English word *such* so closely resembles the Nootka word meaning 'cunt' that teachers find it very difficult to convince their students to utter the English word in class.' Similar reports of cross-language effects have been reported elsewhere, too (e.g. Cicero).[28] Such is the power of taboo to motivate the censoring of language. We conclude with part of a letter from the British Ambassador Sir Archibald Clerk Kerr in war-torn Moscow to Lord Pembroke in England, on 6 April 1943. (Back in 1943, the racism in the final sentence would have been dysphemistic to a Turk; today it is dysphemistic to a much wider public.)

My dear Reggie:

In these dark days man tends to look for little shafts of light that spill from Heaven. My days are probably darker than yours, and I need, my God I do, all the light I can get. But I am a decent fellow, and I do not want to be mean and selfish about what little brightness is shed upon me from time to time. So I proposed to share with you a tiny flash that has illuminated my sombre life and tell you that God has given me a new Turkish colleague whose card tells me that he is called Mustapha Kunt.

We all feel that Reggie, now and then, especially when spring is upon us, but few of us would care to put it on our cards. It takes a Turk to do that.

Cross-varietal synonyms and X-phemisms

I know a dead parrot when I see one, and I'm looking at one right now . . . It's stone dead . . .'E's bleedin' demised! . . .'E's passed on! This parrot is no more! He has ceased to be! 'E's expired and gone to meet 'is maker! 'E's a stiff! Bereft of life, 'e rests in peace! If you hadn't nailed 'im to the perch 'e'd be pushing up the daisies! 'Is metabolic processes are now 'istory! 'E's off the twig! 'E's kicked the bucket, 'e's shuffled off 'is mortal coil, run down the curtain and joined the bleedin' choir invisible!! He's fuckin' snuffed it! . . . THIS IS AN EX-PARROT!! (Monty Python)

The notion that different varieties of a language use different terms, with the same or substantially the same denotation, has been called cross-varietal synonymy.

Therefore you clown, abandon – which is in the vulgar 'leave' – the society – which in the boorish is 'company' – of this female – which in the common is 'woman'. Which together is: abandon the society of this female, or, clown, thou perishest! Or, to thy better understanding, diest! Or, to wit, I kill thee! Make thee away! Translate thy life into death! (Touchstone in Shakespeare's *As You Like It*, V.i.52)

X-phemisms are cross-varietal synonyms because an X-phemism, such as *shit*, means the same as another expression, in this case the orthophemism *faeces* and the euphemism *poo*; the three are typically used in different contexts, perhaps in different varieties or dialects of the language. Cross-varietal synonyms share the same denotation but differ in connotation. The connotations arise from encyclopaedic knowledge about the denotation and also from experience, beliefs and prejudices about the contexts in which the expression is typically used.

For instance, the name *Bob Dylan* identifies the same person that bears the name *Robert Zimmerman*, but the names are used differently. To say *Robert Zimmerman wrote 'Blowin' in the wind'* is misleading because Robert

Zimmerman's name does not appear on the credits – Bob Dylan's does; to make the clause felicitous, it needs qualifying: *Robert Zimmerman wrote 'Blowin' in the wind' under his stage name of Bob Dylan*. In Britain or Australia one might say *I'll ring you tomorrow evening*, whereas in the USA one would say *I'll call you tomorrow evening*; the verb *ring* in two English dialects denotes the same as the verb *call* does in a third dialect, namely 'telephone'. The nouns *dandelion* and *Taraxacum densleonis* are also cross-varietal synonyms: they denote exactly the same species of plant, but because they have different connotations, they are typically used in different circumstances. It is one thing to like *dandelion wine*, but only a pedant or a comic could claim to drink *Taraxacum densleonis wine*. In medieval medical texts the dandelion is orthophemistically referred to as *pissabed* because of its diuretic effect. This term continued to be used until modern times, but as early as 1822 was described in a medical text as the dandelion's 'vulgar name' (*OED*). How many of us would seriously say *These flowers have passed away* rather than *These flowers have died*? People and pets may *pass away* but not flowers. The same female human being could be referred to using any of the nouns *girl*, *woman*, *lady*, *lass*, *broad*, *chick*, *sheila*, *hen* (and many more cross-varietal synonyms); the connotations of these words differ, and there are contexts in which one is appropriate while others would be dispreferred and even offensive, and therefore dysphemistic. Essentially, the reason that cross-varietal synonyms exist is to cover this kind of range of possibilities across varieties of the language. Because we define X-phemism in terms of choices between alternative expressions, we presuppose that each such expression has at least one synonym.

Normally, the choice between alternatives depends entirely on context. Take the choice between *menstruation* and *period*: in this book, we discuss the 'menstruation taboo'; to refer to this as the 'period taboo' seems inappropriate. The choice is not always so clear: in an article on the victims of bank hold-ups and the like in *Time Australia* (12 September 1988: 24) was the following:

'A lot of stress starts to happen for those who have been lying on the floor with a gun at their head,' says Michelle Mulvihill, a Sydney psychologist. 'Women lose their periods; people develop migraines, backaches and symptoms of real anxiety.'

In this context, Mulvihill could just as well have said *Women stop menstruating*, although it would have been marginally more formal than 'Women lose their periods.' The comparative informality of the latter is consistent with Mulvihill's style of spontaneous speech (as quoted). Furthermore, *period* seems to be the most commonly used noun among contemporary British, Australian and American women:[29] note, however, that this does not, in our view, make *menstruate* the dispreferred term. *Menstruation* is an abstract noun, whereas *period* is a concrete noun; hence one can more readily say

I had my last period two weeks ago than ?*I had my last menstruation two weeks ago*. Note also that there is an adjective *menstrual* which has no felicitous counterpart derived from *period*: *period* has adnominal function in *period pain*, which is matched by *menstrual discomfort*. These different characteristics are consistent with the greater formality of the orthophemism *menstruation*.

Alternative proper names are sometimes motivated for reasons similar to euphemism. Political change caused St Petersburg to be renamed Leningrad in 1924 and then return to its earlier name in 1991. The Gold Coast was renamed Ghana on independence in 1957. The name Papago was regarded as an outsider's term of abuse for Native Americans, who now call themselves the Tohono O'odham. Americans use *John Doe* and *Jane Doe* in courts to protect identity, where other jurisdictions use *Mr X*, *Ms Y*, etc. These practices are completely euphemistic. If one regards the base name as orthophemistic, then nicknames tend to be euphemistic when expressing solidarity and dysphemistic when disrespectful. Mary Ann Evans presumably thought she had a better chance of being taken seriously as a novelist if she adopted the male pseudo-nym George Eliot. Presumably, career advancement explains swapping Declan McManus for Elvis Costello, Reginald Dwight for Elton John, Bernard Schwartz for Tony Curtis and Frances Gumm for Judy Garland. On the other hand, presumably Caryn Johnson became Whoopi Goldberg for reasons similar to Vincent Furnier becoming Alice Cooper and John Ritchie becoming Sid Vicious – shock value, with a motive closer to dysphemism than euphemism.

Because cross-varietal synonyms have the same denotation, the denial of the denotatum of any one of a set of synonyms denies it for all of them (if *Max didn't urinate in the swimming pool* then *Max didn't piss in the swimming pool* and *Max didn't make a number 1 in the swimming pool* and *Max didn't relieve himself in the swimming pool*). However, it is quite possible to deny the applicability of one term while asserting what amounts to a preference for the appropriate connotations of its cross-varietal synonym, as in *He's not a lodger, he's a paying guest* or *They're not boobs, they're bosoms*, or *It wasn't Norma Jean Baker who starred in 'Gentlemen Prefer Blondes' – well, she sort of did but under the name of Marilyn Monroe*, or *He's not a liar, he's just careless with the truth*. The difference in variety may correspond to a difference in jargon, and some people sometimes find the use of jargon dysphemistic and think it should be censored.

Alternative points of view

Often a euphemism is linked with the speaker's point of view, dysphemism with some other view – it is an *us* versus *them* situation. For instance, consider the import of the parenthetical remark in the following:

I cross the swinging footbridge over Salt Creek pestered all the way by a couple of yellow cowflies (cattlemen call them deerflies). (Abbey 1968: 40)

Abbey's point is that, by calling these blood-sucking pests *deerflies*, cattlemen seek to avoid all responsibility for their numbers by associating them with feral beasts rather than their own multitudinous charges. Similarly, Australian honey-makers refer to *Echium vulgare* as *Salvation Jane*, while farmers call it *Paterson's curse*. Employees *take industrial action*, which their employers call a *strike*. Company officials *misappropriate* goods; burglars *steal* them. In comparisons of personal behaviour, like *I'm generous, but she's spendthrift* or *I'm thrifty, but he's mean*, the second clause is intentionally dysphemistic by comparison with the first; compare Russell's celebrated conjugation *I am firm; you are obstinate; he is a pig-headed fool.*[30]

During the Cold War of 1946–89,[31] NATO had a *deterrent* (euphemism) against the Russian *threat* (dysphemism). In the mid 1980s the USSR claimed to have been *invited* (euphemism) into Afghanistan; the Americans claimed that the Russians were *aggressors* (dysphemism) there. We get *invited in*; they are *aggressors*; the orthophemism is *take military action in a foreign land*. Dysphemism is indicated by the term *so-called*: e.g. *the so-called democracies of the eastern bloc* doesn't make a dysphemism out of 'democracies', but it does indicate disagreement with, and disapproval of, the presupposition that there are such things as democracies in the eastern bloc. The latter phrase, *eastern bloc*, is itself dysphemistic: note the totalitarian and obstructive connotations of *bloc* 'block' when contrasted with the free-among-equals connotations of *western alliance*. The spread of *glasnost* to central and eastern Europe, and the concomitant moves towards multiparty democracies in the 'eastern bloc' in the latter part of 1989, led to the abandonment of these dysphemisms. Instead there is the bogey of *international terrorism*, though the so-called terrorists think of themselves as *liberators*, or *freedom-fighters*, or *holy warriors*.

The different points of view are nicely described in the following extract, provoked by the invasion or liberation (as you prefer) of Iraq in 2003:

CNN was more irritating than the gleefully patriotic Fox News channel because CNN has a pretense of objectivity. It pretends to be run by journalists. And yet it dutifully uses all the language chosen by the special forces of media relations at the Pentagon: it describes newly occupied portions of Iraq as being 'liberated'; it describes anti-Saddam rebels as 'freedom fighters' (whereas the guerrillas fighting the invading forces using classic partisan tactics engaged in 'terrorism'); it describes the exploding of Iraqi soldiers in their bunkers as 'softening up'; it describes slaughtered Iraqi units as being 'degraded'; some announcers have even repeated the egregious Pentagon neologism 'attrited' (to mean 'we are slowly killing as many of them as we can'). I don't know if I'm more offended by the insidiousness of this euphemism or by the absurdity of its grammar.

The long faces and sombre tones at CNN when 'terrorist' tactics emerged were laughable. The terrorist tactics included wearing civilian clothes – something that French and Russian resistance fighters did when fighting Nazi occupation. We call them heroes. Hit-and-run tactics have been used by overwhelmed locals in every invasion. The United States itself has made heroes of the civilian militias (or 'paramilitary groups') who fought British troops in their own war of independence. And the gangs who killed British troops and committed acts of sabotage in British-occupied Palestine after the Second World War – groups whose tactics were terrorist by anyone's definition – later formed the state of Israel.[32]

In the Iraq of 2004, American *liberators/invaders* fought Iraqi *insurgents/ freedom-fighters*. In the extract, military heroes *disengage from the enemy* or make a *tactical withdrawal*; the enemy *retreats*. The troops cause *collateral damage* while they are *getting the job done*; the enemy commits *terrorist acts against civilians*. In both cases the orthophemism is *civilian deaths (that result from military action)*.

Like euphemism, dysphemism is not necessarily a property of the word itself, but of the way it is used. There is nothing intrinsically dysphemistic in the word *Asian*, but when they are in Australia, many people from Asia feel that being described as 'Asians' rather than more specifically as Chinese, Indian, Kampuchean or Thai, etc. is dysphemistic. The point is more vividly demonstrated by the use of the word *liberalism* in a racist tabloid: 'simply a manifestation of the sickness called liberalism which is carrying Western man swiftly toward his extinction'.[33] Here 'liberalism' is a dysphemism. Later we discuss some of the relabelling initiatives carried out in the name of political correctness: the PC battle is often over who has the power to name.

Like euphemisms, dysphemisms interact with style and therefore have the potential to produce stylistic discord; an example would be where someone at a formal dinner party publicly announces *I'm off to have a piss*, rather than saying something like *excuse me for a moment*. According to our definition, euphemisms and dysphemisms are deliberate. However, they may occur inadvertently, for instance, when someone commits a social gaffe like Eliza Doolittle does in Shaw's *Pygmalion*, Act III:

LIZA	[*nodding to the others*] Goodbye, all.
FREDDY	[*opening the door for her*] Are you walking across the Park, Miss Doolittle? If so –
LIZA	[*perfectly elegant diction*] Walk! Not bloody likely. [*Sensation.*] I am going in a taxi. [*She goes out.*] *Pickering gasps and sits down.*
MRS EYNSFORD HILL	[*suffering from shock*] Well, I really can't get used to the new ways.

(Shaw 1946: 78)

For a while, *bloody* was euphemized as 'the Shavian adjective'. Because of their offensive nature, inadvertent dysphemisms like Liza's will always draw attention to themselves in a way that inadvertent euphemisms do not.

It is generally accepted that *cunt* is the most tabooed word in English. But the same is not true of its cognates in other languages. Although French *con* and Spanish *coño* have the same origin and literal meaning as *cunt*, their extended uses are much less dysphemistic. French *vieux con* ('old cunt') is more likely to be jocular than insulting; *Fais pas le con* 'Don't be stupid' compares better with British English 'Don't be such a twat' or American English 'Don't be a jerk' than with the more severe 'Don't be a cunt'; and the exclamative comment *Quelle connerie!* means something like 'What (a load of) bollocks!'. Spaniards are nicknamed *coños* in Chile, Mexico and other parts of South America because, by reputation, they so frequently use the word. A delicious experience might be described as *como comerle el coño a bocaos* 'like eating cunt by the mouthful'; the back of beyond is *en el quinto coño* 'in the fifth cunt'; a response to an utterance that is very difficult to believe or patently false is *¡Y el coño de mi hermana!* 'and my sister's cunt!'; a pain in the arse is *pena pa mi coño* 'pain in my cunt'; *¿Dónde coño estás?* means roughly 'Where the hell/fuck are you?' and *¡Coño! ¿Dónde estás?* means something like 'Shit! Where are you?'. *Cunt* was already a well-established word in Early Middle English – so it presumably existed in Old English. Strangely, it turns up in medieval place names: e.g. there were a number of *Gropecuntlanes* in the thirteenth and fourteenth centuries[34] – a name suggesting a disreputable lovers' lane or red-light district. It is also found in people's names, e.g. *Godwin Clawecuncte* (1066), *Simon Sitbithecunte* (1167), *John Fillecunt* (1246), *Robert Clavecunte* (1302) and *Bele Wydecunthe* (1328);[35] these are the real-life counterparts to *Biggus Dickus* in *Monty Python's Life of Brian*.[36] However, such names almost certainly seem worse today than they sounded in the Middle Ages, because *cunt* does not appear to have been intrinsically dysphemistic then. Thus, it was used in *Lanfranc's Science of Cirurgie c.*1400 where *vagina* (or perhaps *urethra*) would be required today:

In wymmen þe necke of þe bladdre is schort, & is maad fast to the cunte. (*OED*)

There was a Cunte Street in Bristol, but that may well be because a *cunt* was a water channel. What in the eighteenth century was still sometimes called the River Cunnit by Wiltshire locals had become (as it now is) the River Kennet; adjacent to it was the Roman settlement Cunetio.[37] The terms *cundy*, *cundit*, *kundit*, *cundut* are all early variants of *conduit* found in the *OED*.

Although the term *cunt* may once have been orthophemistic, this does not guarantee that the use is orthophemistic. Between the thirteenth and the late nineteenth century, this body-part term was homophonous in some dialects with the adjective *quaint*, also spelled *queynte* (among other ways) by, for instance, Geoffrey Chaucer in the *Miller's Tale*:

And prively he [Nicholas] caughte hire [Alison] by the queynte (Chaucer 1396, *The Canterbury Tales*, line 3276)

It seems likely that the action of a young man stealthily grabbing a young woman's genitals would have provoked exactly the same frisson in the fourteenth century as it would today – whatever word is used to describe the body part in question.

One characteristic of euphemism is that it involves doublethink: in a given context, something tabooed can be acceptably spoken of using a cross-varietal synonym that avoids dysphemism by employing a euphemism. It is as if the denotatum were viewed from two opposing points of view. The ability of individual human beings to hold contradictory points of view on a common entity or phenomenon is something that upsets rationalists, and will be very difficult to incorporate into artificial intelligence. We guess that such double-think is necessary to permit an intelligent organism to pragmatically adapt to its environment. For instance, most human groups have forms of ritual ceremony symbolizing death, followed by resurrection or new birth, thus embodying the paradox that out of life comes death and out of death comes life. Tabooed substances are often attributed magical properties. This is mocked by Ben Jonson in his 1612 play *The Alchemist*,[38] where Subtle and Face are conning Sir Epicure Mammon into buying from them a 'Philosopher's Stone' that will enable him to make himself and anyone he chooses rich, young, and whatever else he fancies. The ingredients include:

> menstrues and materials,
> Of piss, and eggshells, women's terms, man's blood,
> Hair o' the head, burnt clouts, chalk, merds, and clay,
> Powder of bones, scalings of iron, glass,
> And worlds of other strange ingredtys.
>
> (Jonson, *The Alchemist*, Act II, scene i)

Out of bad things, good things grow!

Politeness and X-phemism

Consideration of the censoring of language in order to avoid violating taboo leads naturally to the examination of politeness and impoliteness as they interact with X-phemism: orthophemism (straight talking), euphemism (sweet talking) and dysphemism (speaking offensively). We defined politeness in terms of inoffensiveness, and described orthophemism and euphemism in much the same terms. Politeness and orthophemism or euphemism go together as do their negative counterparts impoliteness and dysphemism. (In)offensiveness is definable in terms of face which, anglocentrically, we described as 'public self-image'. All these categories of language and behaviour are wedded to context, time and place. They are therefore necessarily variable and malleable, such that no two groups, and perhaps no two individuals and even no single individual acting on different occasions or under dissimilar circumstances, will be certain to make the same judgments as to the offensiveness, politeness, or the X-phemism of a given language expression. The picture is further complicated by the existence of euphemistic dysphemisms and dysphemistic euphemisms, even though these occur in quite small numbers.

Although the X-phemistic value of language expressions is determined by the particular context in which they are uttered, many are perceived as (and marked in dictionaries as) intrinsically orthophemistic (*faeces*), euphemistic (*poo*) or dysphemistic (*shit*). Such default evaluations are motivated by the middle-class politeness criterion. The MCPC is determined by what would be considered the polite form when addressing a casual acquaintance of the opposite sex, in a formal situation, in a middle-class environment. Etiquette demands that a speaker addressing a public audience should automatically assume the MCPC; in other words, the language is carefully and consciously selected, with a respectable mixed-gender middle-class audience in mind.

We explained the meaning of the phrase *dirty words* and drew attention to the saliency of obscene terms – and of dysphemism more generally. This salience demonstrates the suitability of the descriptive euphemism *strong language*. We saw examples of pejorization; it usually results from society's perception of a word's tainted denotatum contaminating the word itself. The degree of contamination perceived in the denotatum ranges on a scale which has fear, abhorrence, loathing and contempt at one end, and nothing worse than low social esteem at the other. We reviewed many examples of taboo terms smothering non-taboo homonyms. This looks like a triumph of the offensive over the inoffensive, of dysphemism over euphemism, of impoliteness over politeness; but in fact the tabooed, the offensive, the dysphemistic and the impolite only seem more powerful forces because each of them identifies the marked behaviour. By default we are polite, euphemistic, orthophemistic and inoffensive; and we censor our language use to eschew tabooed topics. They are censored out as we pursue well-being for ourselves and for others.

Finally, we saw that one person's euphemism is another's dysphemism. There are alternative points of view in different communities and at different times; and perhaps occasionally within the mind of a single individual on different occasions.

3   Bad language? Jargon, slang, swearing and insult

Towards the end of Chapter 2, we remarked that the use of jargon is sometimes judged dysphemistic. This chapter reviews the reason for the denigration of jargon that leads some people to censor it; we seek to rehabilitate jargon. There are people for whom slang is taboo. We discuss the similarities and differences between jargon and slang, and X-phemistic evaluations of both. We also look at where swearing fits in the picture. Both slang and profane swearing are found only in colloquial styles – which leads us to the discussion of styles as varieties of English. From swearing and cursing, we proceed to insults and maledictions. Except for style, all these topics have at some time been referred to as 'bad' language.

Jargon

Readers of the previous chapter may well regard terms like *orthophemism* and *cross-varietal synonymy* as unwelcome jargon. Most people use the term *jargon* pejoratively, as does the author of the following quotation:

> At a conference of sociologists in America in 1977, love was defined as 'the cognitive-affective state characterized by intrusive and obsessive fantasizing concerning the reciprocity of amorant feelings by the object of the amorance'. That is jargon – the practice of never calling a spade a spade when you might instead call it a manual earth-restructuring implement. (Bryson 1984: 85)

So, should jargon be censored? Many people think it should. However, close examination of jargon shows that, although some of it is vacuous pretentiousness,[1] and therefore dysphemistic, its proper use is both necessary and unobjectionable. Our purpose here is to explain how jargon comes to be both dysphemistic on the one hand and euphemistic (as well as orthophemistic) on the other.

   The word *jargon* probably derives from the same source as *gargle*, namely Indo-European **garg-* meaning 'throat',[2] and it originally referred to any noise made in the throat. In Middle English, it was generally used to describe the chattering of birds, or human speech that sounded as meaningless as the chattering of birds (*OED* 1, 3). A French–English Dictionary of 1650 lists:

Jargon. Gibridge, fustian language, Peddlar's French; a barbarous jangling.
Jargonneur. A chatterer, gibridgemonger, counterfeit rogue that speaks fustian, or a language which either himself or his hearers understand not. (R. Cotgrave, *French–English Dictionary*. London: Whitaker 1650; quoted in Burke 1995: 2f)

And then there is Samuel Johnson's definition:

Jargon. unintelligible talk; gabble; gibberish. (Johnson 1755)

English *jargon* retains vestiges of such meanings even today. Both Daniel Defoe and Samuel Johnson referred to the trade language of the Mediter-ranean, Levant and Indian coasts as *jargon*. Chinook Jargon, a combination of Chinook, Nootka (and other Native American), English and French terms, was the trade language of the north-west coast of America; it was used from California to Alaska, after contact with American and British fur traders. In *Sense and Sensibility* (begun in 1795 and published in 1811), Jane Austen used the word *jargon* for what we would now call *cliché*:

'It's very true,' said Marianne, 'that admiration of landscape scenery is become a mere jargon. Everybody pretends to feel and tries to describe with the taste and elegance of him who first defined what picturesque beauty was. I detest jargon of every kind, and sometimes I have kept my feelings to myself, because I could find no language to describe them in but what was worn and hackneyed out of all sense and meaning.' (Austen 1983: 62)

For most people, *jargon* came to be 'applied contemptuously to any mode of speech abounding in unfamiliar terms, or peculiar to a particular set of persons, as the language of scholars or philosophers, the terminology of a science or art, or the cant of a class, sect, trade, or profession' (*OED* 6). According to the *Macquarie Dictionary*, for example, this has now become the primary sense. We define it as follows:

Jargon is the language peculiar to a trade, profession or other group; it is the language used in a body of spoken or written texts, dealing with a circumscribed domain in which speakers share a common specialized vocabulary, habits of word usage, and forms of expression.[3]

Jargons involve more than just lexical differences; they often differ from one another grammatically, and sometimes phonologically or typographically. This can be seen by comparing some of the requirements on the cricket field with the two-line excerpt from a knitting pattern, and with the wedding invitation below it, and by comparing all of these with the excerpt from a Wordsworth poem and a text message version of it (such as might be conveyed using the SMS (short message service) facility on a mobile phone):

A fast-medium right arm inswing bowler needs two or three slips, a deep third man, a gully, a deepish mid-off, a man at deep fine leg and another at wide mid-on.

Cast on 63 sts: Knit 6 rows plain knitting.

7th row: K4, wl. fwd. K2 tog to the last 3 sts. K3.

Earth has not anything to shew
  more fair:
Dull would he be of soul who
  could pass by
A sight so touching in its majesty.
(Wordsworth, *Upon Westminster
  Bridge*)

erth nt a thng so brill

hes dul v soul pssng by

sght of mjstic tch.
(Peter Finch, *N Wst Brdg*, a text message
  version of the Wordsworth lines)[4]

The texts above are just five examples of jargon from the many thousands
that exist. A jargon is identified by one or more of the following criteria (all
three manifest in the examples of jargon given above):

i. **Lexical markers**
   a. Vocabulary specialized for use in a particular domain (the subject
      matter of a jargon). The lexical relations among specialized vocabu-
      lary will reflect the accepted taxonomies within the domain (e.g.
      forms, varieties, species, genera, families, orders, classes in biology).

b. Idioms and abbreviations, e.g. in telecommunications, *DNA* 'does not answer', *MBC* 'major business customer', *HC&F* 'heat coil and fuse', *LIBFA* 'line bearer fault analysis'; in linguistics, *Noun Phrase* and NP; in logic, *if and only if* and *iff*; in biology, ♂ and ♀.

ii. **Syntactic markers** such as:
   a. imperatives in recipes and knitting patterns;
   b. large numbers of impersonal passives in reports of scientific experiments (e.g. *It was observed that . . .*);
   c. full noun phrases in place of pronouns in legal documents (e.g. *A term of a sale shall not be taken to exclude, restrict or modify the application of this Part unless the term* [not 'it'] *does so expressly or is inconsistent with that provision*).

iii. **Presentational markers**
   a. Prosodic (voice quality, amplitude, rhythm, etc.) and paralinguistic and/or kinesic (gaze, gesture, etc.) characteristics within a spoken medium; e.g. a hushed tone and minimal kinesic display is more frequently expected in 'funeralese' than in football commentary or anecdote.
   b. Typographical conventions within a written medium: e.g. in mathematics, {a,b}, <a,b> and (a,b) will normally have different and conventionally prescribed interpretations; in linguistics, language expressions that are mentioned rather than used are usually italicized.
   c. Format in which a text is presented; this is particularly evident in the written medium, as can be seen from the five examples above.

Jargons are often characterized solely in terms of their vocabularies for two reasons. First, novel words and words used in new ways are more conspicuous than are syntactic or phonological novelties. Second, the specialized vocabulary names those things which are the particular focus of the domain in which the jargon is used. However, jargon is manifested much more by the form and structure of birth and death notices, of parliamentary and legal documents, of recipes, of poems, of stock-market reports, and of football and cricket commentaries – among the boundless number of examples possible – than simply the vocabulary used.

Jargon has two functions:

1. to serve as a technical or specialist language for precise and economical communication;
2. to promote in-group solidarity, and to exclude as out-groupers those people who do not use the jargon.

To the initiated, jargon is efficient, economical and even crucial, in that it can capture distinctions not made in the ordinary language. A linguist would claim that ordinary non-specialist language cannot adequately capture all the precision that 'linguisticalese' (the jargon of linguistics) can. Outside the discipline of linguistics, there already exists an extensive non-technical vocabulary used by the lay public when talking about language; unfortunately, the terminology is often too imprecise to be of real use within the discipline of linguistics. Linguists are therefore faced with having to narrow and redefine everyday terms like *sentence*, *word*, *syllable* and *grammar*, as well as add a number of new terms to overcome imprecision and to distinguish things that non-linguists ignore and that, in consequence, ordinary language lacks terms for. For example, linguists find the term *word* insufficiently precise for all their purposes, and so occasionally need to distinguish between *grammatical*, *orthographic* and *phonological words*, as well as introducing new terms like *lex*, *lexeme*, *morph* and *morpheme* to capture additional distinctions. Because one mark of a linguist is control of linguisticalese, to achieve its purpose, the following quote has to use jargon (bolded):

Syntagmatic relations are characteristically based on the **co-occurrence of elements** in the **speech chain**, while **paradigmatic oppositions** only obtain within the total **system**, all elements of each **network of relations** but one being absent from the actual **string of phonemes** or words through which ***langue*** **manifests itself in** ***parole***. (Atkinson et al. 1988: 106)

The text (which is rendered incomprehensible to many readers by being taken out of context) can only be paraphrased for a non-specialist by extensive and discombobulating circumlocution involving a partial account of Saussure's linguistic theory.[5] If this were quantum mechanics and not linguistics, no one would question the right to furnish the discipline with a technical vocabulary all of its own. But to the non-linguist the jargon of linguistics is perceived as intellectual hocus-pocus, and all the more dysphemistic precisely because it seems to deal with a familiar domain.

Here is an early complaint about (French) legalese:

Why is it that our tongue, so simple for other purposes, becomes obscure and unintelligible in wills and contracts. (Montaigne 1948 [1580])

There are many distinguishing aspects of legal vocabulary. One is the preponderance of borrowings from Latin and French; e.g. *de novo* 'from the beginning, anew'; *ex aequo et bono* 'on the basis of what is fair and good'; *mens rea* 'guilty mind'; *chose in action* 'incorporeal personal property right enforceable in court of law'; *voir dire* 'to say truly'. Another is the practice of stringing together two or three synonyms as doublets or triplets: *act and deed*; *goods and chattels*; *in my stead and place*; *cease and desist*; *remise, release and forever discharge*; *rest, residue and remainder*.

These phrases derive from an early literary practice of conjoining one noun of Germanic origin with a synonym of Romance origin, as in the case of *false and untrue* and *will and testament*. But the most befuddling aspect of legalese to out-groupers is probably its grammatical structure. Long and extremely complex sentences can render a piece of legalese very difficult for the general reader to comprehend. Section 1 of Form S6/147 (Guarantee for Existing or New Advance), issued by the Australia and New Zealand Banking Group Limited, consists of one sentence of about 1,270 words long. The average length of a sentence in a legal document is 55 words, which is twice the number for scientific English texts and eight times the number found in dramatic texts.[6] In the quotation below, the subject 'a term of sale' is separated from its predicate 'is void' by a complex of embedded material containing as many as 11 propositions expressed in 88 words. Section 2 includes a string of negatives, 'not', 'exclude', 'restrict', 'unless', 'inconsistent', and this significantly complicates the comprehensibility of the passage.

1. A term of a sale (including a term that is not set out in the sale but is incorporated in the sale by another term of sale) that purports to exclude, restrict or modify or purports to have the effect of excluding, restricting or modifying –
    a. the application in relation to that sale of all or any of the provisions of this Part [of the act];
    b. the exercise of a right conferred by such a provision; or
    c. any liability of the seller for breach of a condition or warranty implied by such a provision –
        is void.
2. A term of a sale shall not be taken to exclude, restrict or modify the application of this Part unless the term does so expressly or is inconsistent with that provision. (Sales Act, State of Victoria, Australia)

It would be dysphemistic for a lawyer not to use jargon when creating a legal document: that is exactly what legalese is for. However, the combination of esoteric vocabulary, grammatical complexities like abnormally long sentences, large numbers of passives (e.g. 'A term of a sale shall not be taken to exclude'), nominalizations (e.g. 'the effect of excluding, restricting or modifying'), intrusive phrases (e.g. '(including a term that is not set out in the sale but is incorporated in the sale by another term of sale)'), multiple embeddings (e.g. most of section 1 in the quote above) and multiple negatives (e.g. in section 2 in the quote), as well as the unconventional presentation and maintenance of topics, typically leads the out-grouper to perceive a legal document as having a discourse structure that is hard to follow. So when the public are presented with documents written in legalese, they will often feel offended by the perception that the writer has required them to expend unreasonable effort in order to understand what the document means.[7] As a result, they may feel incapable of understanding the implications of what is said without help from a lawyer. At worst, they see legalese as a kind of secret language that conspires to maintain the exclusivity of the legal profession at their expense.[8]

EXPLANATORY NOTE
Regulation 3 of the Local Government (Allowances) Regulations 1974 ('the 1974 regulations') (S.I. 1974/447) made provision prescribing the amounts of attendance and financial loss allowance to members of local authorities. Regulation 3 of the Local Government (Allowances) (Amendment) Regulations 1981 ('the 1981 regulations') (S.I. 1981/180) substituted a new regulation for regulation 3 of the 1974 regulations. Regulation 3 of the Local Government (Allowances) (Amendment) Regulations 1982 ('the 1982 regulations') (S.I. 1982/125) further amends regulation 3 of the 1974 regulations, with effect from 8 March 1982, by increasing the maximum rates of attendance and financial loss allowances. [Etc.] (Quoted in Cutts and Maher 1984: 57)

Exasperation with jargon like this so-called 'Explanatory Note' has given rise to many social and political movements currently pushing for clear and simple English, particularly in laws, legal documents (like contracts) and government documents of all kinds. Similar movements have sprung up throughout Europe.[9] They have had considerable success in elucidating the language in insurance and other legal documents foisted onto members of the public. Nonetheless, problems still arise. Something like the laws of the imaginary country Brobdingnag, visited by Lemuel Gulliver, would be ideal:

No Law of that Country must exceed in Words the Number of Letters in their Alphabet; which consists only of two and twenty. But indeed, few of them extend even to that Length. They are expressed in the most plain and simple Terms, wherein those people are not Mercurial enough to discover above one Interpretation. And to write a Comment upon any Law, is a capital Crime. (Swift 1958[1735]: 104)

If only it were possible in our world.

For in-groupers (insiders) jargon is 'a kind of masonic glue between different members of the same profession'.[10] Yet it binds not only professionals, but members of any group who use a particular jargon. The way to show in-group membership is to use the appropriate jargon. This is why in the medical and legal professions, for which there is a long and difficult apprenticeship, there is a consequent feeling amongst in-groupers that they belong to an exclusive club. Prestige is awarded to those who command the jargon, which can be used as a form of display. For instance, patients have certain expectations of their physicians. Most would probably prefer the jargon expression *patellar tendon reflex* to everyday *knee-jerk*, *dysmenorrhoea* to *period pains*, and whereas *pityriasis rosea* sounds like an expert diagnosis, *rash* does not; indeed, after the latter diagnosis, a patient might well wonder why s/he has bothered to pay for a medical opinion at all! Full command of medical jargon is viewed as part of the competence of a medical expert. From another point of view, there are people who might prefer to say, euphemistically, they have *spirochaetal* or *luetic disease* rather than the orthophemistic *syphilis*, just as people may prefer to say *Excuse me a moment* or *I have to go to the loo* instead of *I have to urinate / have a piss*.

Some jargons seem to use highfalutin language for simple notions: uplift is another motivation for jargon. Official language describing poverty, for example, draws overwhelmingly from the Romance and Classical languages. It is characterized by the flourishing of terms like *indigent, impecunious, destitute* and *impoverished* that seek to upgrade alternative nomenclature. Poverty is an area of social taboo – an inevitable target for euphemism. Recent times have seen a rise in circumlocutions like *economically marginalised, negatively privileged, economically non-affluent, culturally deprived* or even *differently advantaged*. The hamburger industry's use of the term *autocondimentation* as opposed to *precondimentation* is an economical way of distinguishing a client's right to sauce his/her own hamburger. It is certainly not necessary to use *autocondimentation* in order to get the meaning across, so why use it? The answer is, of course, that it confers on the hamburger industry a certain dignity. The dignity comes from the Greek or Latin roots of the words used (*the Graeco-Latinate lexicon*), because they are reminiscent of such prestigious jargons as legalese and 'medicalese'.[11]

Jargons like 'bureaucratese' (the language of government and corporate offices) have two motivations. One, shared with criminal jargon and slang, is the exclusion of out-groupers. This exclusion is in part designed to intimidate the populace through mystification. The second motivation is shared with the hamburger industry. The matters with which bureaucrats deal are mostly mundane and can be fully described and discussed in sixth-grade English. In order to augment their self-image, therefore, bureaucrats create synonyms for existing vocabulary using a Graeco-Latinate lexicon, seeking to obfuscate the commonplace and endow it with gravity; this achieves a double-whammy by mystifying and intimidating the clientele. A notice to householders from the City of Fitzroy in Melbourne, Australia,[12] read:

Refuse and rubbish shall not be collected from the site or receptacles thereon before the hour of 8.00am or after the hour of 6.00pm of any day.

It contains some quintessential features of ponderous legalese: (1) the doublets *refuse and rubbish* and *the site or receptacles thereon*; (2) *shall* with a third person subject; (3) the negative proposition *refuse and rubbish shall not be collected*; (4) the archaic adverbial *thereon*; and (5) the redundant phrase *the hour of*. Householders would probably have found it easier to understand the more colloquial *We will collect your garbage between 8.00am and 6.00pm*. We rarely uncover such blatant lexical substitution as the following emendation to a traffic plan for a London borough:

Memorandum

To: *The Prime Minster* *14 November*

From: *The Secretary of the Cabinet* [Sir Humphrey Appleby]

Certain informal discussions have taken place, involving a full and frank exchange of views, out of which there arose a series of proposals which on examination proved to indicate certain promising lines of enquiry which when pursued led to the realization that the alternative courses of action might in fact, in certain circumstances, be susceptible of discreet modification, in one way or another, leading to reappraisal of the original areas of difference and pointing the way to encouraging possibilities of significant compromise and co-operation which if bilaterally implemented with appropriate give and take on both sides could if the climate were right have a reasonable possibility at the end of the day of leading, rightly or wrongly, to a mutually satisfactory conclusion.

I [the Prime Minister] stared at the sheet of paper, mesmerised. Finally, I looked up at Humphrey. 'Could you summarise this please?' I asked.

He thought hard for a moment. 'We did a deal,' he replied. (Lynn and Jay 1989: 402f)

Figure 3.1 Bureaucratese (from *Yes, Prime Minister*).

Delete 'Bottlenecks', insert 'Localised Capacity Deficiencies'. (Quoted in Cutts and Maher 1984: 45)

No wonder Charles Dickens referred to Whitehall as the Circumlocution Office. Bureaucratese is nicely mocked in the excerpt from *Yes, Prime Minister*, Figure 3.1.

In American English, the general term for bureaucratese is *gobbledygook*, whereas in British and Australian English the sense of this word has generalized to mean '(any type of) incomprehensible language'. The word was coined by Texas Congressman Maury Maverick[13] 'thinking of the old bearded turkey gobbler back in Texas, who was always gobbledy-gobbling and strutting with ludicrous pomposity. At the end of this gobble there was a sort of gook'.[14] In other words, *gobbledygook* is the mouthing of a turkey. Used of a person, cross-varietal synonyms of American English *turkey* include Australian English *dork*, *dill*, *galah* and British English *wally* and *prat*.

Demands for understandable 'plain language' have been heard throughout the history of English. It took many centuries for English to be accepted as a written language. Latin and Greek were the languages of religion and scholarship; like other vernacular languages, English was the language of the street. In Renaissance Europe, emerging literate groups from the middle classes struggled to understand the Latin documents in which their legal and professional rights were set out before they were rendered into the vernacular languages. It is hardly surprising that when scribes began writing in English they attempted to emulate what they considered to be the good classical style of Ancient Greece and Rome, and borrowed extensively from Greek and especially Latin. This gave rise to the arcane professional jargons that are now being popularized by reinterpretation in 'plain English' and the like. Participants in the *inkhorn controversy*, as it came to be known, protested against what they saw as the excessive borrowing of learned words, especially from Greek and Latin. The *inkhorn terms*, branded as *dark* ('obscure, not perspicuous'), led John Locke (in 1690) to write, 'Modern philosophers . . . have endeavored to throw off the Jargon of the Schools, and speak intelligibly.'[15]

In the seventeenth century, the language of pompous, prating, incomprehensible physicians was often mocked in plays. When the sister of a colonel wounded in a duel asks a surgeon about her brother's condition, he replies:

SURGEON: *Cava Vena*: I care but little for his wound i' th *orsophag*, not thus much trust mee, but when they come to *diaphragma* once, the small *intestines*, or the *Spynall medull*, or th rootes of the *emunctories* of the noble parts, then straight I feare a *syncope*; the flankes retyring towards the backe, the urine bloody, the excrements *purulent*, and the colour pricking or pungent.

SISTER: Alasse, I'me neer the better for this answer.

SURGEON: Now I must tell you his principal *Dolour* lies i' th region of the liver, and theres both inflammation and *turmefaction* fear'd marry, I made him a *quadrangular plumation*, where I used *sanguis draconis*, by my faith, with powders *incarnative*, which I temperd with oyle of *Hypericon*, and other liquors mundificative.

SISTER: Pox a your mundies figatives, I would they were all fired.

SURGEON: But I propose lady to make an other experiment at next dressing with a *sarcotrike*, *medicament*, made of *Iris* of Florence. Thus, (*masticke,*) *calaphena, apoponax, sacrocalla*.

SISTER: Sacro-halter, what comfort is i' this to a poore gentlewoman: pray tell me in plaine tearmes what you think of him.

(Thomas Middleton, *A Faire Quarrell*, IV; quoted in Porter 1995: 43; *sic*)

Is it much different today?

Family members look intently at the physician as he speaks. 'Scan . . . cytology . . . report . . . primary site . . . malignant tumor . . . adenocarcinoma . . . metastasis . . .' Brows furrow as the family continues to hear: 'excision . . . chemotherapy . . . contraindicated . . . radiotherapy . . . palliative . . . any questions?' 'Yes,' responds

the family member, 'Can you tell yet whether he has cancer and will he get well?'
(Cassileth and Hamilton 1979: 242)

Such obfuscating terminology unfortunately typifies exchanges between medical professionals and the bewildered public. In this case, it reflects the
professional's difficulty in communicating the realities of cancer to the lay
population.

There are times when bewildering jargon is quite deliberate. The linguistic
disguise of criminal jargon conceals the disreputable (see the discussion of
antilanguage below). There are Dutch fishermen who reverse syllables, and also
sometimes words, to disguise their speech so that other fishermen won't discover
their secrets. Trade jargons like Romani can work as a secret code to conceal
information from customers or any would-be competitors on the outside.[16]

Because it is founded on a common interest, the most remarkable characteristic of a jargon is (as mentioned) its specialized vocabulary and idiom.
While jargons facilitate communication among in-groupers on the one hand,
on the other, they erect communication barriers that keep out-groupers out. It
is, of course, out-groupers who find jargon 'abounding in uncommon or
unfamiliar words', and therefore 'unintelligible or meaningless talk or
writing; gibberish'.[17] If the out-grouper is sufficiently rancorous, s/he might
also conclude that the jargon is 'debased, outlandish or barbarous'.[18]

The linguistic features found in a jargon can start life with a very clear
function, but over time the original motivation becomes obscured and they
turn into self-perpetuating idiosyncrasies. Legalese avoids pronouns to ensure
clear unambiguous identification, as in *The Lessor hereby leases to the Lessee
and the Lessee hereby agrees to take from the Lessor the property*; but, of
course, there are many occasions where the use of a pronoun would be
completely unambiguous. With time, such features become ritual requirements of the professional style; mere skeuomorphs.[19]

Jargon is a variety of language used among people who have a common
work-related or recreational interest. Its principal function is to serve as an in-
group language that is an essential tool in precise and economical communication, using devices not found in other varieties of the language. This
primary function of jargon is far from dysphemistic to in-groupers. For some
jargons, such as legalese or linguisticalese, the in-group is fairly well defined.
For others, such as stock-market reports and games such as bridge, football
and cricket, there is barely an in-group at all, except among professionals. For
language dealing with death, birth notices and recipes, there is even less of a
non-professional in-group – though there is a special vocabulary, and there
are conventional patterns of expression for all of these. The facts are clear:
where in-groupers are associated with a particular trade or profession, they
constitute a well-defined group (sharing similar educational and professional

standards); they are somewhat less well defined by a common recreational interest; and the most ill-defined in-group are those defined merely by a temporary interest in the topic of the jargon – such as those members of the public who publish birth notices.

It follows that every text (discourse), including social chit-chat, is jargon of one kind or another, and that everybody uses at least one jargon. In fact, almost everybody controls several jargons, and often many. Readers of this chapter have already been exposed to a variety of jargons, and those still reading will have taken it in their stride. It is often the case that an expert in one domain (an in-grouper with respect to its jargon) needs to explain something within the domain – including, perhaps, jargon – to a novice outside the domain (an out-grouper), with minimal use of jargon. An example would be where a lawyer needs to explain some point of law to a client; or a doctor needs to explain a medical condition to a patient; and educationists almost all of the time. Any jargon is in constant contact with others, and it should be fairly obvious that jargons are not discrete from one another: all of them borrow from language that is common to other jargons. The following is an excerpt from a chat room interchange, replete with chat-room jargon such as *lol* (the acronym from 'laughing out loud' which is used here as a mark of empathy like a grin in *f2f* 'face to face' conversation), *j/k* 'just kidding', and emoticon smiles *:)*, *:-)* and wicked smile *>:)* ; there is also jargon appropriate to in-group discussion of computer hardware, but note the divergence into less esoteric matters than disk drives and controllers. This mixing of jargons is very common in regular conversational discourse.

<DARKMAN-X>	so wait becuz i have the onboard raid controller i could fit 2 hdd's on the raid controllers and 2 on the ide controllers?
<MARK>	RAID is just a standard of combining different drives.. you can make a raid out of scsi drives along side ide drives if you want
<MARK>	you could make a raid out of a hard drive and a ram drive
<MARK>	just forget about the raid stuff
<DARKMAN-X>	lol
<MARK>	and picture it as another ide controller
<MARK>	thats all it is unles syou setup the raid stuff
<DARKMAN-X>	so wait i can have 2 hdd's on the raid, 2 on teh primary ide and then 2 drives on the secondary ide?
<MARK>	i guess.. tried reading the manual?
<DARKMAN-X>	lol manual?
<MARK>	:)
<MARK>	didnt your motherboard come with any papers
<DARKMAN-X>	iz that that book that says A7V333 on it?
<[RAW]>	yes
<DARKMAN-X>	lol the one that i'm using to prop up my comp table?

<[RAW]>	probably
<DARKMAN-X>	whoops
<DARKMAN-X>	:-)
<DARKMAN-X>	j/k
<JOHN>	lol
<[RAW]>	yur supposed to use your school books for that dummy
<DARKMAN-X>	ummm no i dun wanna look at em
<DARKMAN-X>	they're evil
<[RAW]>	keep your motherboard manual close to your heart
<[RAW]>	>:)
<DARKMAN-X>	lol

(Logged 29 August 2002; *sic*)

A jargon cannot be precisely defined because the boundaries of any one particular jargon are impossible to draw non-arbitrarily.

Everyday language picks terms from jargons and expands their use. One example is the verb *to contact* which in the early nineteenth century was used only in its etymologically basic meaning of 'touch together'. A hundred years later, its semantic extension to the figurative 'to get in touch with someone' – described by the *OED* as 'orig[inally] US colloq[uial]' – was considered shocking jargon, and there was public condemnation, one person describing it as a 'lubricious barbarism'.[20] This sense of the verb *contact* undoubtedly fills a gap in our everyday vocabulary; it is more abstract than *call*, *see* or *speak to* and less clumsy than *get in contact with*. Furthermore, speakers are always on the lookout for newer, more exciting ways of saying something. *Epicentre* is a term from geology denoting 'the true centre of a seismic disturbance'; recently, the Australian Broadcasting Corporation reported the arrest of a person described as 'the epicentre of a drug ring'. The word 'epicentre' seems to have been chosen because it sounds more exciting or vivid than *centre*. Such novel usage attracts criticism. As Dwight Bolinger put it: 'Old vices are accepted, new ones viewed with horror – the familiar jargon is the alcohol of our verbal drug culture, the unfamiliar is its marijuana.'[21]

It is impossible to taboo jargon. Jargon cannot be translated into 'ordinary English' (or whatever language) because there is no such thing. Changing the jargon alters the message: a speaker simply cannot exchange *faeces* for *shit* or *terrorist* for *freedom-fighter*, or even *bottlenecks* for *localised capacity deficiencies*, without changing the connotations of the message s/he intends to convey. There is no convenient substitute for some jargon: to replace legalese *defendant* with *a person against whom civil proceedings are brought* is communicatively inefficient. Legal language is difficult because laws are complex, and not because lawyers try to obfuscate.[22] We would argue the same for linguisticalese in the earlier quote, repeated here for convenience:

Syntagmatic relations are characteristically based on the co-occurrence of elements in the speech chain, while paradigmatic oppositions only obtain within the total system, all elements of each network of relations but one being absent from the actual string of phonemes or words through which *langue* manifests itself in *parole*. (Atkinson et al. 1988: 106)

No linguistics student we have asked has yet succeeded in censoring the linguistic jargon from this text without hugely extending its length and communicative efficiency.

Nonetheless, we maintain that those who write for the general public have a duty to make their language as intelligible as possible. The insurance industry has shown that its incantations do not defy translation. Of course, this does not guarantee comprehension, as is clear from the *Annual Reviews* and *Updates* of the Insurance Enquiries and Complaints Scheme (of Australia). There has been considerable improvement in the layout and wording of policy documents, yet 'ambiguity remains despite attempts by insurers to produce Plain English contracts'.[23] Insurance policies are complex documents (which is probably why even the Plain English versions lie unread at the bottom of many people's drawers). Moreover, even the most plain and simple wording cannot guarantee that the interpretations of readers and the intentions of writers will be a perfect match.[24]

Like cross-varietal synonyms, jargons exist to facilitate communication among the in-groupers who use them. Cross-varietal synonyms differ from one another in their connotations, and it is dysphemistic connotations that lead out-groupers to try to censor a jargon. People need to step back and reflect on the fact that X-phemisms and jargon maintain the fecundity of language as spoken by living, breathing human beings.

Slang

The line of demarcation between jargon and slang is open to dispute because *slang* is sometimes defined in such a way as to overlap almost completely with the definition of *jargon*. The *OED* entry for *slang* includes the following:

The special vocabulary or phraseology of a particular calling or profession; the cant or jargon of a certain class or period.

An illustrative quote is:

1872 Geo. Eliot *Middlem.* xi. Correct English is the slang of prigs who write history and essays. And the strongest slang of all is the slang of poets.

The more familiar meaning of *slang* is better illustrated by quotations like:

1809 E. S. Barrett, *Setting Sun* I. 106. Such grossness of speech, and horrid oaths, as shewed them not to be unskilled in the slang or vulgar tongue of the lowest blackguards in the nation.

1824 Scott, *Redgauntlet*, ch. xiii. What did actually reach his ears was disguised . . . completely by the use of cant words, and the thieves-Latin called slang.
1868 Doran, *Saints & Sinners* I. 107. He [Latimer] occasionally employed some of the slang of the day to give force to his words.

The word *slang* first made its appearance some time during the eighteenth century, originally to refer to the patter of criminals. Its etymology is uncertain. Some lexicographers have tried to connect it with the Dutch word for 'snake', which seems unlikely. Eric Partridge suggests a connection with the verb *sling*, as in the expression *sling off at someone*, meaning 'give cheek, or abuse; engage in a slanging match'.[25] This source seems appropriate because *slang* originally referred to the sublanguage of the underworld. For us,

Slang is language of a highly colloquial and contemporary type, considered stylistically inferior to standard formal, and even polite informal, speech. It often uses metaphor and/or ellipsis, and often manifests verbal play in which current language is employed in some special sense and denotation; otherwise the vocabulary, and sometimes the grammar, is novel or only recently coined.

Both of the terms *argot* and *cant* appear in discussions of slang, and their relevant senses overlap completely with our definitions of *jargon* and *slang*. The *OED* has for *argot*: 'The jargon, slang, or peculiar phraseology of a class, *orig.* that of thieves and rogues.' The word was borrowed from French, where it is the usual translation for English *slang*. However, like English *jargon*, it often refers to the language of traditionally nomadic occupational groups such as actors, beggars, chimney-sweeps, gypsies, masons, sailors, soldiers and thieves.[26] For *cant* the *OED* has: 'The peculiar language or jargon of a class: **a.** The secret language or jargon used by gipsies, thieves, professional beggars, etc.; *transf.* any jargon used for the purpose of secrecy.' The term *cant* is probably cognate with *chant* (from French *chanter*, Latin *cantare*).

[It was] first applied to the tones and language of beggars, 'the canting crew': this, which according to Harman was introduced *c.*1540, may have come down from the religious mendicants; or the word may have been actually made from Lat[in] or Romanic in the rogues' jargon of the time. The subsequent development assumed in the arrangement of the verb is quite natural, though not actually established. Some have however conjectured that *cant* is the Irish and Gaelic *cainnt* (pronounced kaɲtj, or nearly kantʃj) 'language'. (*OED*)

So the term *cant* very possibly arises from Romance, from which its meaning was extended as a result of contact with the Celtic homonym, the two coming together in the meaning 'language of gipsies, thieves, and professional beggars' – who, so far as speakers of the standard language are concerned, were despised social (and actual) outlaws. We shall not make further use of the terms *argot* and *cant*, but assume that everything denoted by these terms falls under our terms *jargon* and *slang*.

In the eighteenth and nineteenth centuries, *slang* denoted the 'thieves-Latin', the 'vulgar tongue of the lowest blackguards in the nation'. So slang is, by association, 'bad language', such that any language disapproved of on moral grounds (as profanity, swearing, obscenity) will be branded *slang* and subjected to censoring.

The most significant characteristic of slang overlaps with a defining characteristic of jargon: slang is a marker of in-group solidarity, and so it is a correlate of human groups with shared experiences, such as being children at a certain school or of a certain age, or being a member of a certain socially definable group, such as hookers, junkies, jazz musicians or professional criminals. For example, *Polari* (aka *Parlare*, *Pa(r)lary*, *Parl(y)aree*, *Panarly*) is a slang used by British homosexuals in the twentieth century, which probably derived from slang used by actors, show-people and other mendicants, and overlaps with slang still widely used in the London area (and perhaps elsewhere). The use of slang within a definable group gives rise to the other overlap with jargon as sublanguage. Not only medicalese and legalese, but also street jargon/slang, druggie jargon/slang, 'criminalese', queer slang and the like, have many terms with synonyms in other jargons/ slangs – i.e. there are cross-varietal synonyms. The slangs serve as in-group recognition devices and purportedly disguise meanings from out-groupers – which is why Halliday described them as **antilanguage**, 'the language of the antisociety'.[27] Consider examples from several regions: *work* for 'work as a prostitute', *a trick* or *a john* for 'a prostitute's client'; *tea* or *grass* for 'marijuana', *shit* for 'cannabis resin', *speed* for 'amphetamines', *horse* or *brown sugar* for 'heroin', *snow* for 'cocaine', *the works* or *a fit* for a *mainliner*'s 'hypodermic syringe and spoon'; *a grass* for 'a police informer'; *doing porridge* or *at college* for 'being in prison'. To a greater extent than jargon, slang is 'antilanguage' because it is intended to dissimilate users from out-groupers. The language of those involved in unofficial or illegal activities needs to exclude regulators and law officers; it is reported that the language of drug addicts changes constantly and rapidly for this reason.[28] Out-groupers meet with severe problems when trying to learn and use the slang of a particular group. For example, teenagers today use 'inverted language': someone who is particularly attractive might be described as *scum*; words like *vicious*, *sick*, *rancid* and *putrid* describe things which are exceptionally good. Parents and teachers who try using this sort of slang to show empathy with the youngsters usually sound phoney; however, *wicked* 'exceptionally good' seems to have escaped into the wider community and is often heard in adverts. Perhaps *wicked* plays on the fact that excessive enjoyment is, like passionate sexual congress or oodles of Belgian chocolates, somehow unholy.

Like jargon, slang identifies activities, events and objects that have become routine for those involved, and it has an important function in creating rapport in the work or recreational environment. Indeed, many jargons have a colloquial or slang component. Australian 'hospitalese' includes slang 'diagnoses' like *FLK* 'funny looking kid, but it is not known what is wrong', *GOK* 'God only knows what is wrong', and *cactus* 'dead'. In American hospitals, there are the terms *beached whale* 'obese person', *crock* 'patient deteriorating rapidly', *gomer* 'derelict with poor personal hygiene' and *squirrel* 'fusspot who complains too much'.[29] *Cupid's measles* is slang for *treponemal disease* or *syphilis*.

Reduction of form is another feature that slang shares with jargon. For example, terms like *rents* ⇐ *parents*, *rad* ⇐ *radical*, *dis* ⇐ *disrespect*, *shot* ⇐ *good shot*, *sec* ⇐ *second*, *hellava* ⇐ *hell of a* 'very', *chill* ⇐ *chill out*, *later* ⇐ *see you(s) later*, *spaz* ⇐ *spastic* 'defective', *bro* ⇐ *brother*, *prob* ⇐ *probably*, *awes* ⇐ *awesome*, *dizz* ⇐ *dizzy*, *cuz* ⇐ *cousin* (as in Shakespeare), *stiff* ⇐ *stiff bikkies / shit* 'bad luck!', *stuff* ⇐ *good stuff*, *do the biz* ⇐ *do the business* 'suffice'. There are a number of reasons for these clippings. Frequent or everyday words will often crop up in casual settings where abbreviations are well tolerated, because there is a lot of common ground. In a class on historical linguistics, a student reduced the cumbersome linguistic term-of-art *grammaticalization* 'the creation of grammar' to *gramtion*, which became a buzz word for that particular group. Abbreviation is the result of the automation that follows from the repetition of articulatory movements.[30] Cognitively, words of high frequency are easier to access for speakers and hearers.

As we said, most jargon is linguistically conservative (fast changing domains like information technology are less conservative). Specialized content works something like formaldehyde, such that jargon expressions become embalmed, giving rise to skeuomorphy, and become the targets of censoring by verbal hygienists,[31] like those within the Plain English movement. One mark of slang that distinguishes it from jargon is that it dates much faster, the slang of schoolchildren having the fastest turnover of all. A study of student slang at the University of North Carolina Chapel Hill, showed that over a fifteen-year period fewer than 10 per cent of the expressions had survived.[32] That which is slang for one generation is either outdated for the next or becomes mainstream. *Cool* might have made a comeback, but the language of the 'beat' culture of the 1950s and 60s is now mostly passé – *far out* has been replaced by *awesome*, and who knows what new such words lurk in the wings. When slang does survive, it has ceased to be slang (which might be the case with *cool*). Just look in early dictionaries, particularly at the entries labelled unfit for general use. In Samuel Johnson's *Dictionary* of 1755, for example, we find the verb *to colour* described as 'a low word, used only in conversation' and *bamboozle* as 'a cant word not used in pure or in grave writings'. A lot of Johnson's entries were clearly contemporary slang. Outdated slang is readily recognizable in the seventeenth-century description of someone as a *shite-a-bed scoundrel*, a *turdy gut*, a *blockish gruntnol* and a *grouthead gnat-snapper*.[33] Leafing through Grose's late eighteenth-century *Dictionary of the Vulgar Tongue*,[34] a majority of the slang terms seem outdated. Some of this results from changes in technology: yesterday's *horse thief*, a *prigger of prancers* or a *prad* ['horse'] *napper* is today's *car thief*. A *star glazer* stole window glass, but there is no call for that today. Even when the topics for slang terms have hardly changed, the slang often has. In early nineteenth-century London and Australian slang,

A woman was a *bat*, a *crack*, a *bunter*, a *case fro, cattle,* a *mort*, a *burick*, or a *convenient*. If she had a regular man, she was his *natural* or *peculiar*. If married, she was an *autem* ['church'] *mott*; if blonde, a *bleached mott*; if a very young prostitute, almost a child, a *kinchin* ['child', cf. German *kindchen*] *mott*; if beautiful a *rum blowen*, a *ewe*, a *flash piece of mutton*. If she had gonorrhoea, she was a *queer mort*.[35] (Hughes 1987: 258)

Few of these terms are still in use. Eventually, slang expressions either stop being slang by intruding into neutral style and become standard usage, or they drop by the wayside.

A striking feature of slang is its playfulness. David Crystal demonstrates the ubiquity and creativity of language play among ordinary language users, and points out that 'when children arrive in school, their linguistic life has been one willingly given over to language play'.[36] It stays with people as they grow up. The playfulness of slang is a characteristic shared with many euphemisms and dysphemisms, but not with orthophemisms. Whether speakers are creating names for new concepts, or simply adding to the names of old concepts, metaphor, irony and sound symbolism are important forces behind the new expressions. Take colloquial terms for drunkenness, such as *sloshed, soused, smashed, sozzled, soaked, stinking, stewed* and other cooking terms like *steamed, boiled, cooked*. The imagery here is buttressed by sound association: most of these slang expressions for 'drunk' begin with *s*. *Inebriated* and *intoxicated* are two of the very few elevated terms for 'drunk'. Verbal play is not solely the prerogative of the skilled writer. Much slang demonstrates the poetic inventiveness of ordinary people: it reveals a folk culture that has been paid too little attention by lexicographers, linguists and literaticians, and, indeed, by the very folk who use them: you, me, our friends and relatives. Rhyme, quasi-reduplication, alliteration, pleasing rhythms and silly words give rise to euphemistic dysphemisms, or just plain dysphemisms.

Examples are *shit on a shingle* 'chipped beef on toast'; *over-shoulder boulder-holders* 'bra'; *Wham, bam, thank you ma'am!*; *hoddy-doddy (all arse and no body)* 'a short clumsy person' (archaic); *om–tiddly–om–pom* and *umpti–poo* 'toilet'; *tantadlin tart* 'turd'; *tallywags* or *twiddle-diddles* 'testicles' (both archaic); *doodle, diddle, dink, dong* 'penis'; *tuzzy-muzzy* 'vagina'; *rantum-scantum* 'copulate'; numerous terms for 'masturbate': *beat the bishop, beat the beaver, pull the pope, pull one's pud, crank the shank, jerkin' the gherkin, tweak one's twinkie, juice the sluice* and *stump-jump*.[37] Australian expressions for male urination are the alliteration *point Percy at the porcelain* and the rhyme *siphon the python*.

The advert for Miller beer, which reads *Wear the fox hat*, is a conceit based on the **rhyming slang** of ordinary working folk.[38] The following examples vary from the transparent to the opaque:

Would you Adam and Eve it?	'Would you believe it?'	
Get down to brass tacks	'Get to the facts'	
He was ducking and diving	'skiving, shirking'	
Use your loaf	'use your head; think; be smart'	[*loaf of bread*]
boat	'face'	[*boat race*][39]
barnet	'hair'	[*Barnet Fair*]
minces	'eyes'	[*mince pies*]
hampsteads	'teeth'	[*Hampstead Heath*][40]
bristols	'breasts'	[*Bristol city* = titty]
thrupnies	'breasts'	[*thrupnies* ⇐ *threepenny bits* = tits]
khyber	'arse'	[*Khyber Pass*]
aris	'arse'	[*aris* and [*lose one's*] *bottle* ⇐ *Aristotle* ⇒ *bottle and glass* = arse][41]
He lost his bottle	'he was scared'	
cobblers	'rubbish, nonsense'	[*cobblers awls* = balls]
rabbit on	'talk and talk'	[*rabbit and pork* = talk]

Slang interacts with X-phemism in much the same way as jargon does. The verses which follow use rhyming slang, which has been italicized for salience. One function of some of this (and other) rhyming slang is euphemism.

Key:

Her *scotches*, long and slender   scotch [pegs] 'legs';
Reached to her *kingdom come*,   kingdom come 'bum, fanny';
Her *hobsons*, low and husky   Hobson's [choice] 'voice';
Made my *newingtons* go numb.   Newington [Butts] 'guts';
I took her for some *Lillian Gish*   Lillian Gish 'fish';
Down at the chippy caff.
We squeezed into my *jam-jar*   jam-jar 'car'.
And drove back to my gaff.[42]

(Barker 1979: 21)

The primary function of most of the slang in 'Cockney's Lament', from which these verses are taken, is to amuse the reader, and very little of it is otherwise euphemistic; nor is it dysphemistic, except perhaps to an extremely strait-laced prude (the poem ends with her dropping her *early doors*). It is the rhyming slang that creates a minor work of art from a mundane seduction story.

Another distinguishing feature of slang is that it can usually be replaced by standard language without loss of communicative efficiency,[43] whereas the best jargon cannot. However, such a substitution will necessarily change the connotations of the utterance or text and, consequently, the communicative effect. You could describe someone as *pickled*, *pissed* or *plastered*, or you could simply say they are *drunk*. On the other hand, as we said earlier, many jargon expressions simply do not have viable alternatives – the art historian's *skeuomorphy*, the lawyer's *plaintiff* and the cricketer's *man at deep fine leg* all fill a gap. Of course when *drunk* replaces *pickled*, *pissed* or *plastered*, gone are the rhetorical effects conveyed by these slang expressions. Speakers can use slang to deliberately express irreverence, i.e. to deliberately flout social or linguistic conventions. Slang can also show familiarity with what is being referred to, or at least familiarity with the group that uses this term. To describe something as *awes* (= 'awesome') is more than saying this thing is good; it has connotations that the conventional language does not convey.

Swearing and cussing

Jargon does not *ipso facto* include swearing; although someone using jargon may well swear. Slang also does not necessarily include swearing, but as a matter of practice it often, and perhaps usually does. At least part of the reason is that both slang and (profane) swearing are highly colloquial varieties of language. Martin Joos identified five levels of formality.[44] In Figure 3.2,

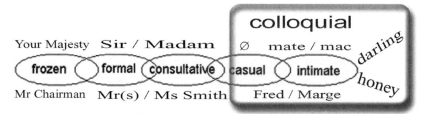

Figure 3.2. Styles in English.

the boundary between each pair of styles is shown as fuzzy, and the casual and intimate styles are bundled under the heading 'colloquial'; sample address forms are included for exemplification (the ∅ indicates avoidance of any term of address).

Jargon takes the full gamut of styles, but slang and (profane) swearing are restricted to colloquial styles; that is what makes exclamatives like those in (1) so impossible by comparison with (2).

1. *Oh faeces! *Copulate off! *What a fornicate up! *That's a load of testicles! *Testicles! *This nut's a real vagina to get off!
2. Oh shit! Fuck off! What a fuck up! That's a load of bollocks! Bollocks! This nut's a real cunt to get off!

Any one person's language may reflect a wide range between the extremes of frozen and intimate style. Touchstone is playing with just two styles (formal and colloquial) in the earlier quote from *As You Like It* (V.i.52):

Therefore you clown, abandon – which is in the vulgar 'leave' – the society – which in the boorish is 'company' – of this female – which in the common is 'woman'.

Style varies according to:

who we are and whom we are communicating with;
whether we are speaking or writing;
where we are and when the utterance takes place;
what we are talking about; and
how we feel about the whole situation.

If any one of these factors is changed, the style may well change accordingly. For any given utterance, there exists a wide variety of possible stylistic choices: not only lexical choices (although these are the most obvious), but also choices of grammar, pronunciation and paralinguistic features like gesture and facial expression. Usually, the speaker's stylistic choices are tuned to create just the impression s/he wants to create: where the speaker wants to avoid offence, s/he will be orthophemistic or euphemistic and choose a style appropriate to that end; where the speaker wants to be offensive, s/he will choose a style of language that is dysphemistic. Thus, X-phemism is intimately bound up with style and perlocutionary intent – that is, the effect that the speaker intends the utterance to have on the hearer.

The original meaning of the verb *swear* is 'to take an oath; make a solemn declaration, statement, affirmation, promise or undertaking; often in the eyes of God or in relation to some sacred object so that the swearer is, by implication, put in grave danger if found to be lying', e.g. *I swear by Almighty God to tell the truth, the whole truth, and nothing but the truth. So help me God.* The noun *oath* 'an act of swearing' is the nominal counterpart of the verb *swear*. These original meanings ('make a solemn declaration' etc.) still obtain, alongside those of **profane swearing** and **profane oaths**. At first, these would have been statements made with profane reference to the deity; they have been around at least since the Middle Ages,[45] and probably much longer. The extension of profanity from irreligious language to incorporate obscene language took swearing and (to a lesser extent) oaths with it. The dysphemistic senses of *swear* and *oath* became dominant in unmarked contexts; a result aided by the fact that situations favourable to orthophemistic attestation (*I swear by Almighty God . . .*) are infrequent compared to the number conducive to profane swearing and profane oaths. Profane swearing uses dysphemisms taken from the pool of dirty words as well as blasphemous and profane (i.e. irreligious) language. To *swear at someone or something* is to insult and deprecate the object of abuse, as well as to use other kinds of dysphemism.

Hayduke, under the hair and sunburned hide, appeared to be blushing. His grin was awkward. 'Well, shit,' he said. 'Fuck, I don't know, I guess . . . well, shit, if I can't swear I can't talk.' A pause. 'Can't hardly *think* if I can't swear.'
    'That's exactly what I thought,' said Bonnie. 'You're a verbal cripple. You use obscenities as a crutch. Obscenity is a crutch for crippled minds.' (Abbey 1975: 153f)

Judging from other parts of *The Monkey Wrench Gang*, Bonnie is probably not especially distraught by the obscenities themselves (though some people would be); what seems to motivate her here is that Hayduke's frequent use of obscenities distracts her from readily and easily understanding the rest of what he is saying. Hers is a fairly common reaction to the face affront she perceives to be inflicted upon her. Also, her view that 'Obscenity is a crutch for crippled minds' is a commonly held one; but there is no evidence whatsoever that it is correct.

The dysphemistic connotations of swearing lead to its being associated with *cursing* 'imprecating malevolent fate'. Although curses can hardly be literally profane, the term *Curses!* has certainly been used lightly as a euphemistic dysphemism for several centuries. Hence, we find in Matthew

26: 74 'Then began he [St Peter] to curse and to swear'.[46] Interestingly, the colloquial form of *curse*, *cuss*, is often used in *cussing and swearing*. The term *cuss word* is found from the nineteenth century as synonymous with *swear word*.

He didn't give a continental for *any*body. *Beg* your pardon, friend, for coming so near to saying a cuss-word. (Twain 1981: 341)

Mark Twain's 'continental' is end-clipped from *continental damn*, itself based on the worthlessness of *continental* money – American currency of around 1775. The phrase *continental dam* is modelled on phrases going back to Langland's *nouʒt worth a carse*, and more recently, *not give a tinker's cuss*. To be *cussing someone out* is to swear at and insult him/her. Also, from the late eighteenth century, the noun *cuss* is used as a mild insult, as in *He's an awkward cuss*. It is a euphemistic dysphemism, a milder version of *He's an awkward bastard*. Many languages invoke disfiguring, deadly diseases in maledictions. Current English no longer does so, though *A pox on/of you!* (principally smallpox) was used in early modern English; cf. Shakespeare's Falstaff exclaims:

A pox of this gout! or, a gout of this pox! for the one or the other plays the rogue with my great toe. (Shakespeare, *2 Henry IV*, I.ii.246)

With his usual aplomb, Shakespeare puns: the first 'pox' is 'smallpox', the latter 'venereal disease'. There is also his *a plague o' both your houses*[47] – invoking bubonic plague, with its blotchy red sores, pneumonic problems and death. In other languages we find cholera invoked, e.g. in the Polish expletive *Cholera!* which is roughly comparable in function to English *Shit!*

Swearing can act as an in-group solidarity marker within a shared colloquial style. Used when a higher style is expected, it is likely to cause offence and may be specifically used to offend, but in both cases it reflects discredit on the speaker. It is not only the style expected, but also the relative status of the interlocutors that affects the perceptions of profane swearing. Relative status derives from two sources: the relative power of the interlocutors and the social distance between them. The relative power is defined by social factors which obtain in the situation of utterance. The relative power of a physician and a highway patrolman is not given for every occasion, it depends on where they encounter one another: imagine how it will differ, depending on whether the highway patrolman is requiring a medical consultation at the doctor's office, or the doctor has been stopped on the highway for alleged dangerous driving. Social distance between interlocutors is determined by such parameters as their mutual (un)familiarity, comparative ages, genders and sociocultural backgrounds. The management of social status (power and social distance relations) involves the management of face, and consequently the management of X-phemisms. Swearing at someone of lower status is possible without loss of status, though it is generally assumed to demean the person swearing and can, in principle, be legally actionable. Swearing at someone of higher status is more likely to lead them to take umbrage and pursue sanctions against the low status perpetrator.

Most cussing is an emotive reaction to anger, frustration, or something unexpected and usually, but not necessarily, undesirable.

OLD LADY: I shouldn't cry if I were you, little man.
LITTLE BOY: Must do sumping; I bean't old enough to swear.
(*Punch* cartoon, 2 April 1913)

'Cursing intensifies emotional expressions in a manner that inoffensive words cannot achieve.'[48] Children of both sexes use swear words from as young as one year old, and swearing persists into old age, through senile dementia and Alzheimer's disease, even when other critical linguistic abilities have been lost. The language used varies across time[49] and between genders: males swear more often than females (about three times more frequently in one study) and they use stronger obscenities, e.g. among eight- to twelve-year-olds, 'males used words such as *shit, fuck* and *damn*, while females used words such as *god* or euphemisms *darn it* and *shucks*'.[50] Among adults, '[b]oth male and female speakers are more likely to swear in the company of same sex companions'.[51] Swearing and cussing, in what Erving Goffman[52] called 'response cries', is almost certainly a function of the right hemisphere of the brain for a majority of the population,[53] whereas normal language functions are carried out by and in the left brain. The right brain deals with emotions. Language functions, other than the ability to curse and swear, are often lost to people with damage to the left brain; right brain damage leaves linguistic ability intact but cuts the ability to swear. However, the left brain controls the impulse to swear and cuss: 'The control or inhibition of the offensive speech relies on the functions of the left hemisphere and prefrontal areas; when they are damaged, control over inappropriate cursing is lost.'[54] There is evidence that deeply religious individuals and those with high sexual anxiety are most likely to be offended by swearing; they restrain themselves and also attempt to prohibit others from swearing.[55]

We conclude that swearing and cussing is something that most people engage in from a very early age. To dismiss it as the act of an uneducated person or as linguistically inadequate performance is gross prejudice, with no basis in fact. One can swear in holophrases using the right brain; but more elaborate swearing and insulting makes recourse to the usual rules of grammar and language usage. It is well documented that even people with a reputation for not swearing know how to swear, an ability that they may come to demonstrate if they suffer some kind of brain decay or brain damage in later life.

Insults and maledictions

To insult someone verbally is to abuse them by assailing them with contemptuous, perhaps insolent, language that may include an element of bragging. It is often directly addressed to the target, as in:

B to A: You asshole, you're a fucking tight-assed cunt. Get fucked.

Verbal insults can occur in all styles of language. Insults are normally intended to wound the addressee or bring a third party into disrepute, or both. They are therefore intrinsically dysphemistic, and so typically tabooed and subject to censorship. Insults typically pick on and debase a person's physical appearance, mental ability, character, behaviour, beliefs and/or familial and social relations. Thus insults are sourced in the target's supposed ugliness, skin colour and/or complexion, over- or undersize (too small, too short, too tall, too fat, too thin), perceived physical defects (short-sight, squint, big nose, sagging breasts, small dick, deformed limb), slovenliness, dirtiness, smelliness, tartiness, stupidity, untruthfulness, unreliability, unpunctuality, incompetence, incontinence, greediness, meanness, sexual laxness or perversion, sexual persuasion, violence towards others (even self), ideological or religious persuasion, social or economic status, and social ineptitude. And additionally, supposed inadequacies on any of the grounds just listed among the target's family, friends and acquaintances. Dysphemistic terms of insult include all of the following.

Comparisons of people with animals that are conventionally ascribed certain behaviours, for example, calling someone a *bat, cat, fox, vixen, sow, pig, cow, bitch, cur, dog, mongrel, swine, louse, dove, hawk, coot, galah, chicken, turkey, mouse, rabbit, bull, ox, goat, ape, monkey, ass/donkey, mule, rat, snake*, etc. Names of female animals can normally be used only in naming or addressing women and male homosexuals: e.g. a *cat* is typically a 'vicious and/or scratchy woman', but *a pussy* is used (mostly in America) to insult a male for being 'effeminate, homosexual' and occasionally a female for having a 'weak character' (it is also slang for a *femme* 'lesbian who adopts the feminine role'); a *bitch* is a '(usually nasty) woman held in contempt';[56] a *vixen* is a 'cunning, perhaps sneaky, woman'; *cow* and *sow* don't differ much, generally denotes a 'woman disliked, who is typically doltish' – and there are connotations of being fat, too, cf. the commonly used *fat cow/sow*. (*Silly) old bat* would normally be used of a woman past middle age; *bat* in this sense does not occur unmodified. (The predicative *bats*, e.g. *You're bats*, is used of either sex, and probably derives from the figure *have bats in the belfry*, i.e. 'be mad, nuts'.) Some animal names are typically used of men: *mongrel, cur* or *swine* denotes a 'vicious, nasty fellow, held in contempt' (comparable with *cat* and *bitch* of women); a *fox* denotes a 'cunning man', compare *vixen* (*foxy lady* is a compliment to the sexiness of a woman); a *bull* is for a 'big, often rather clumsy, man'; a *goat* or *ram* can be used of a 'horny/randy man'. According to *Webster's New Collegiate Dictionary*, one sense of *dog* is 'worthless person'; *dog* and *bow-wow* are attested of a woman otherwise described as 'bone ugly'. A *louse* is 'someone unpleasant, irritating, that one wants to be rid of'; used of men, *louse* and *rat* usually denote 'unfaithful cad'. A *mouse* is more often applied to women than men, partly because it is not normally applied to big people; it denotes 'someone insignificant and timid'. *Coot, turkey* and *galah* are used of someone stupid, so too are *goat* and *ass* (or *donkey*); *donkey* and *mule* denote 'someone stubborn'; a *chicken* is a 'scaredy cat, coward', used mostly of men. A *pig* is 'someone rude, uncouth, slovenly', and for two centuries or more has been used to denote 'policeman, constable'. In some US dialects, *pig* and *oinker* are used of 'an over-dressed (or perhaps under-dressed) woman with too much make-up, who looks like a hooker'. An *ape* is 'someone uncouth', while a *monkey* is 'someone mischievous', usually a child – it is a tease rather than an insult. A *snake* is 'untrustworthy, sleazy, someone who will spread poison about other people'. *Worms* and *toads* have always been despised, even loathed, perhaps because of their association with dirt and decay, perhaps because they are unpleasant to touch. Applied to humans, the words *worm* and *toad* imply 'someone who is loathsome, who crawls, is sycophantic'; hence *toadyism*. Similar meaning attaches to *creep* and *crawler*, terms which derive from animal behaviour. An *insect* is 'someone insignificant, beneath contempt', a *parasite* is 'someone who lives on others', and *vermin* 'someone loathsome and contemptible'. Neither *dove* 'peace-worker, someone who is anti-war' nor its contrary *hawk* 'someone who favours the military' is intrinsically dysphemistic, but they are used dysphemistically by those of opposed ideology. Verbs based on animal nouns that have dysphemistic overtones are *ape, badger, bitch, dog, ferret, fox* and *outfox, weasel one's way in, whiteant* 'undermine', *wolf down food*. In summary, dysphemistic uses of animal names take some salient, unpleasant characteristic from the folk concepts about the appearance and/or behaviour of the animal, which is then metaphorically attributed to the human named or addressed. Because it is insulting behaviour, it is subject to taboo and censoring.

Epithets derived from tabooed bodily organs (e.g. *asshole, prick*), **bodily effluvia** (e.g. *shit*) **and sexual behaviours** (e.g. *fucker, poofter, arse-licker, dipshit, cock-sucker, wanker, whore, slut, slapper, slag*). Maledictions often utilize images of sexual violation, e.g. *I was stuffed; we got fucked/screwed; what a ball buster/breaker; he was just jerking us off.*[57] In English, only certain terms can function as epithets, expletives and terms of abuse; for instance, (3) shows that learned words for SMD organs and effluvia generally do not function in this way, but nor do certain mild obscenities and nursery terms such as those in (4).

3. *Defecate on you! *Urine off! *You anus! *You vagina! *You clitoris! *You penis! *You foreskin! *You faeces! *He's a real fornicating vagina!
4. *You poontang! *You quim![58] *You willie! *Wee-wee on you!

However, this constraint does not apply to all such terms in early modern English:

A horson filthie slaue, a dunge-worme, an excrement! (Jonson 1981, *Everyman in His Humour*, III.v.127)

Nor does it apply to terms of insult that comment on sexual persuasion, perversion or practice; presumably because the words used in the insult are intended to be taken literally instead of figuratively (even when this is known not to be the case in reality). Thus it is just as insulting to call someone a *penis-sucker* as a *cock-sucker* (even if the latter is the norm); the same is true of *masturbator* vs *wanker*, *behind-licker* vs *arse-licker*, *fornicator* vs *fucker*, *homosexual* vs *poofter*, and *prostitute* vs *whore*. It is true that the slang term is more vivid, and probably more effective, as an insult; but the alternative will also work well enough – especially as a euphemistic dysphemism that may appear to satisfy the middle-class politeness criterion. When terms like *wanker* and *fucker* are used figuratively (respectively 'despised and ineffectual' and 'despised, strongly condemned'), the more orthophemistic alternatives are inappropriate. Although attitudes to homosexuality have changed towards the positive in recent years, it is still an effective insult to accuse a man of sexual dalliance with other men. The ubiquitous North American malediction *it sucks* 'it is contemptible' is, in origin, a transference from the negativity in the homophobic jibe *he sucks (cock)*, that has lost the link with its past in most users' minds (rather like *have someone by the short and curlies*); as a result, both *he sucks* and *she sucks* can be used without fellatio coming to mind. (To accuse someone of being a *sucker* 'easily deceived, manipulated' is more innocently derived from the suckling of a neonate.)

Sadly, the long history of (men and women) insulting women by accusing them of promiscuity or prostitution seems to persist, despite a generation or two of feminism.

Dysphemistic epithets that pick on real physical characteristics that are treated as though they are abnormalities, like *Fatty!*, *Baldy!*, *Four-eyes!*, *Short-arse!*. Epithets like these merge into racist dysphemisms and dysphemistic epithets based on behaviours that the speaker disapproves of, such as homosexuality. Terms like *cripple, paraplegic*, etc. are normally ascribed to someone who has been physically inept in some way or another; similarly, with questions like *Are you blind?*, which can be dysphemistic about someone's visual perceptiveness; just as *Weakling!* can be dismissive of their physical prowess. Although we now say *Shit on you!* instead of *A pox on you!*, we still call someone *a poxy liar*; and also *pest*, a word derived from the French word for 'plague' (cf. English *pestilence*). The French formerly used *Peste!* as a swear word, the way the Poles say *Cholera!* The Dutch still use *Pestvent!* 'Pesky guy', or *Hij is een pest* 'He is a plague': these are fairly mild, not much stronger than the English *pest* (adjective *pesky*) with which they are cognate. Also, in current English we figuratively call someone a *leper*, meaning 'a person who is shunned'. The same disease is invoked in the somewhat archaic Korean insult *muntungisaykki* 'young of a leper', which has a force roughly comparable with American *son-of-a-bitch*. Thai invokes cholera in the imprecations *Tai hàa!* 'Die of cholera!', *Ai/Ii hàa* 'Cholera on you [male/female]'. These are matched by Yiddish *A kholerye af/oyf im!* 'May he get cholera!'. It is hardly surprising that the diseases utilized in curses are smallpox, bubonic plague, leprosy, cholera – all disfiguring and deadly, which brings to mind the exhortation to *Drop dead!*. Disease metaphors also turn up in racist insults, as we shall see.

There are many **imprecations and epithets invoking mental subnormality or derangement**: *Airhead!, Silly!, Retard!, Moron!, Idiot!, Cretin!, Kook!, Loony!, Loopy!, Nincompoop!, Ninny!, Fool!, Stupid!, Halfwit!, Nitwit!, Dickhead!, Fuckwit!, Fuckhead!, Shithead!*. The last three are doubly dysphemistic, in that they not only ascribe mental derangement but do so using a dysphemistic locution which unscrambles as 'your wits are (your head is) fucked (deranged)'. *Shithead!* has much the same meaning as *Shit for brains!* where the figure is made explicit.[59] All these insults reflect the stigma attached to mental subnormality, which requires euphemisms for the genuinely subnormal. *Cretin* began as a Swiss-French euphemism *crétin* 'Christian' (a charitable recognition in a Christian country that even the mentally subnormal are blessed, and therefore Christians); however *cretin* has sunk to dysphemism (a similar fate was suffered by the adjective *special* applied to someone with a mental or physical abnormality in the late twentieth century). Indeed, colloquial terms for the mentally subnormal regularly start out as euphemisms and degenerate; *mentally disabled* went the same route to dysphemism as its forerunners, being replaced by *mentally challenged*. It is notable that *silly* once meant 'blessed, blissful' (cf. modern German *selig*) and then changed to 'innocent, helpless, deserving of pity'; hence Chaucer's *sely wydwe* 'unfortunate widow'.[60] It is a short step from 'helpless, pitiable' to the current, only mildly dysphemistic meaning of silly. Expressions like

He's a jerk, *It's spaz/spastic*, *I was spastic* all suggest the jerky movements of true spastics, who until recently were all presumed to be mentally retarded, as well as physically abnormal; hence these expressions all mean 'no good, useless, stupid'.

The mental abnormality dysphemisms implicit in insults like *maniac*, *crazy* and *nutter* have been usurped as terms of praise among certain macho hooligans: their antisocial behaviour is decried by society in general, but they adopt such epithets as badges of honour in consequence of their revolt against the social norm.[61]

Sexist, racist, speciesist, classist, ageist and other **-IST dysphemisms** function as insults. One's proper name is closely associated with one's identity, and children (but rarely adults) deform proper names to insult or tease, e.g. Burridge becomes *porridge*, 'Zinkewitz becomes *Stinkyshits*, Potash becomes *Potass*, and Tina Fritz turns into *Freena Tits*.'[62] This is an early kind of -IST dysphemism. Turning to racist dysphemisms to exemplify -IST dysphemisms in general: all human groups, it seems, have available in their language a derogatory term for at least one other group with which they have contact (we will not subclassify racists into nationalists versus ethnicists, etc.). Among the racist dysphemisms of English are: *mick* and *paddy* for an Irish person, *frog* (Cockney *jiggle and jog*) for a French person, *kraut* and *hun* for a German, *chink* (Cockney *widow's wink*) for a Chinese, *jap* or *nip* (Cockney *orange pip*) for a Japanese, *paki* for a Pakistani, *polak* for a Pole, *wop* (Cockney *grocer's shop*) and *eyetie* for an Italian, *ayrab*, *towel head*, *dune coon* and *camel jockey* for an Arab, *kike* or *yid* (Cockney *dustbin lid* and *four-by-two*) for a Jew, *chief*, *Hiawatha* and *Geronimo* for male Native Americans and *squaw* for their womenfolk, and so forth. English whites tend use the adjective *swarthy* dysphemistically, and likewise *inscrutable* of Orientals. They may use *black*, *nigger*, *nignog*, *wog* (Cockney *spotty dog*), *coon* (Cockney *silvery moon*), etc. for people of African ethnicity and for other people with similar skin colour to Africans, such as Australian Aborigines and south Indians. In return, African Americans talk about *grays* and *honkeys*. In Australia, we hear *skip* 'Anglo-Celtic Australian' (from a television series *Skippy the Bush Kangaroo*); *boong* and *abo* for Aborigines; *gin* for an Aboriginal woman; and for people from east and south-east Asia, *slants/slanties*, *slopes*, *gooks*, *RGBs* (rice gobbling bastards), *UFOs* (ugly fucking orientals), *kanardles* (spelling uncertain) from *can hardly see*. Afrikaners once used *skepsel* 'creature' when referring to blacks and coloureds; in Nazi German, Jews were described as *kriechend* 'crawling, servile'; Nazis described the marriage of an 'Aryan' to a 'non-Aryan' as *Blutschande* 'blood disgrace' or *Blutvergiftung* 'blood poisoning, tetanus'.[63]

Racist terms are not intrinsically dysphemistic, and can be used without prejudice: for instance, *blacks* is not necessarily any more dysphemistic than *whites*; and in Australia, *boong* and *gin* are not invariably dysphemistic, no more so in fact than are *lebo* 'Lebanese', *wog* 'Caucasian Australian who is not Anglo-Celtic' and *skip(py)* 'Anglo-Celtic Australian'. Practically all these 'racist' terms can be used without irony in orthophemistic illocutionary acts. Consider the term *nigger*. African American law professor Randall Kennedy's book *Nigger: The Strange Career of a Troublesome Word* provoked a storm of protest from blacks and whites when it first appeared.

Patricia Williams, an African-American professor at Columbia Law School, objected to the title: 'That word is a bit like fire – you can warm your hands with the kind of upside-down camaraderie that it gives, or you can burn a cross with it. But in any case it depends on the context and the users' intention, and seeing it floating abstractly on a book shelf in a world that is still as polarized as ours makes me cringe.' (*New York Times*, 1 December 2001)

Used among African Americans, *nigger* is often a badge of identity and solidarity (when it is often spelled *nigga*):

nigger Form of address and identification among blacks (can connote affection, playful derision, genuine anger, or mere identification of another black person; often used emphatically in conversation). (Folb 1980: 248)

Something comparable holds true for almost all racist terms – indeed, all -IST terms. Nonetheless, the lexicon entries for the racist terms exemplified above will need to mark the degree to which they are dysphemistic: e.g. *black* should probably be marked as orthophemistic, whereas *nigger* should probably be marked as typically dysphemistic, with exceptional contexts identified. Privileged use of terms like *nigger* (and other -IST dysphemisms) may be extended to outsiders under certain circumstances. The problem is that side-participants and overhearers may not recognize this special dispensation. Randall Kennedy[64] cites the case of a white university basketball coach whose mostly black team gave him dispensation to use *nigger* as they did; both administrators and students at his university protested, and he lost his job for violating their taboos.

As the result of an automobile accident, John Callahan is a wheelchair-bound quadriplegic; this gives him licence to create the rambunctious, scatological, irreligious and very non-PC cartoon *Quads*. The main character, Reilly O'Reilly, who is also a wheelchair-bound quadriplegic, lives in Maimed Manor (bought with the settlement from his accident) along with the rest of the Magnificent Severed, who include Blazer (a head on a trolley), Lefty who has scythes in place of hands, and Fontaine the blind African American. *Quads* would be severely censured, and possibly censored from free-to-air broadcasting services, were it not created by a quadriplegic who, being one himself, is in a position to poke fun at the disabled.

Then there are terms of insult or disrespect, which invoke **slurs on the target's character**, such as *arsehole/asshole, bag, bastard, battle-axe, biddy, codger, crank, crone, cunt, dag, dick, dork, drip, dweeb, faggot, fogy, fuddy-duddy, fuss-budget, galoot, geezer, grommet, grot, grump, hag, nerd, pansy, perv(ert), poof(ter), prick, queer, schmuck, scumbag, shirtlifter, sissy, slag, slob, slut, SOB / son of a bitch, tramp, twat, wanker, wimp* and *witch*. Many of these derive from tabooed bodily organs, effluvia and sexual behaviours, of course. The ascription *He's a devil* is ambiguous between the dysphemism 'He's wicked', and a term of approbation: 'He's a dare-devil'. Note that *He's a little devil/demon* is an affectionate description for, e.g. a naughty boy, with only very slight disapprobation. There is an association with *dare-devil*, and perhaps *devil-may-care*, both of which are essentially orthophemistic. The phrase *silly old NOUN* is ageist and dysphemistic, and the insult is increased if 'NOUN' is a taboo term; thus *Cedric's a silly old fart* implies that 'Cedric talks a lot of hot air', i.e. the content of what he says is insubstantial and inconsequential. One is reminded of the putdowns like *He's about as effective as a fart in a windstorm!*

Ritual insults such as occur in **flyting** and its successor, **playing the dozens** seem to utilize the same categories as the kind of insults to outgroupers (or people cast as outgroupers) that we have been discussing. The term *flyting* has been around since before *Beowulf*, in the early tenth century. A Scandinavian counterpart is the thirteenth-century *Lokasenna*, a poem in which the trickster-god Loki taunts other gods and their wives. Scots poets engaged in mutual flyting during the sixteenth century. Late nineteenth-century American cowboys engaged in *cussing contests*, where a saddle would be awarded to the most abusive participant. *The dozens* is the term used of the same behaviour among African Americans today. In the nineteenth century, black field hands used the verbal assault of *the dozens* against house slaves in lieu of physical attack.[65] The name became attached to the practice of vilifying the target and his/her relatives after an uncopyrighted and unpublished scatological blues called *The Dirty Dozen*, which perhaps had twelve verses, each referring to a different sex act. There are a number of conjectures on the source of the term *dozens*: inferior slaves were sold in lots of twelve, so that the number twelve came to connote 'wretched, inferior'; a throw of unlucky twelve in craps; a corruption of *doesn't* as in *at least my mother doesn't*; or from the old verb *dozen* 'make doze, stun, stupefy, daze'. The dozens is also called *bagging, capping, chopping, cracking, cutting, dissing, hiking, joning, joan-*

ing, joining, ranking, ribbing, serving, signifying, slipping, sounding and *snapping*. Essentially, flyting and the dozens are (at best) a confrontation of wit, insight and upmanship, in which people try to outdo each other in the richness of their rhetorical scorn by taunting another person with insults about them or their family in front of an audience. For instance in *Lokasenna*, as they sit at a feast, Loki accuses the gods variously of being lazy, cowardly, a weakling, effeminate, homosexual, and one as being an incestuous pervert who likes 'golden showers'. Goddesses are drab and dirty, or whores, or nymphomaniacs who stoop to sleeping with servants, or they are incestuous. Such ritual insults for men and women sound familiar today; the difference from the dozens is that insults are basically restricted to the addressee, rather than being directed at the addressee's (presumed) loved ones. Here are some of the dozens:[66]

> You were so ugly at birth, your parents named you Shit Happens.
> You're so dumb, if you spoke your mind you'd be speechless.
> Your breath smells so bad, people on the phone hang up.
> I heard you were getting sex all the time until your wrist got arthritis.
> Your girlfriend is so stupid, the first time she used a vibrator she cracked her two front teeth.
> The only difference between your girlfriend and a subway is that everybody hasn't ridden a subway.
> Your sister is so stupid, she went to the baker for a yeast infection.
> Your father is like cement – it takes him two days to get hard.
> Your mother is so old, she was a waitress at the Last Supper.
> Your mother has so many crabs she walks sideways.
> Willie mother stink; she be over here on 128th Street between Seventh 'n' Eighth, waving her white handkerchief: [falsetto] 'C'mon, baby, only a nickel.'
> Iron is iron, and steel don't rust, but your mama got a pussy like a Greyhound bus.
> I hate to talk about your mother, she's a good old soul; she got a ten-ton pussy and a rubber asshole.

How widespread ritual insults are in gay communities, we don't know. The only celebrated example is the following, which 'took place at a large Thanksgiving dinner in a Canadian city':

B : Your ass is so stretched you should put in a draw-string.
A : Word is you've had your dirt-shute mack-tacked.
B : And you wall-papered your womb.
A : Where do you find tricks who'll rim your colostomy?
B : You douche with Janitor in a Drum.
A : Slam your clam.
B : Slam it, cram it, ram it, oooo, but don't jam it [demonstrating].
A : Cross your legs, you're showing your hemorrhoids.

B: You need to strap yours forward so you'll have a basket [genitalia].
A: Better than back-combing my pubies, like you do. Preparation H is a great lubricant.
B: [Pointing to A] This girl's hung like an animal – a tse tse fly.
A: Four bull dogs couldn't chew off this monster [pointing to his penis].
B: I don't think even a bulldog would want that in its mouth. Besides, I've seen chubbier clits.
A: Peeking under the door in the washroom again? . . .

(Murray 1979: 216; *sic*)

Many youngsters engage in ritual insults. Here are a couple of examples from Australia:

[*Two urban working-class Australian Aboriginal girls*]

A: If I had a pussy like yours I'd take it to the cats' home and have it put down . . .
B: If I had brains like yours I'd ask for a refund . . .
A: Well, if I had tits like yours I'd sell them off for basket balls . . .

[*Two working-class urban Australian Aboriginal males*]

A: Have you got a match?
B: Yeah, your prick and a jelly bean.
(Allen 1987: 62, 66)

Ritual insult is a competitive game, a kind of teasing; it is not an attack on an enemy or someone who is an outsider, despised or disparaged; it is an expression of group solidarity. This clearly comes out in a *celebrity roast* 'unmerciful mockery of a celebrity in his/her presence'. As a display of upmanship, the dozens uses insults based on people's supposed sexual practices, age, appearance (body and clothes), smell, and domestic arrangements. Exactly these categories are also found in true insults, intended to wound, humiliate and belittle. Thus, true insults are subject to taboo and censoring.

If we make the solidarity function of ritual insult the criterion which distinguishes it from true insult, then we have to class what is sometimes called **friendly banter** as ritual insult. It is marked by the use of normally abusive address forms or epithets which are uttered without animosity, which can be reciprocated without animus and which typically indicate a bond of friendship.

FIRST YOUTH: Hullo congenital idiot!
SECOND YOUTH: Hullo, you priceless old ass!
DAMSEL: I'd no idea you two knew each other so well!
(*Punch* cartoon; quoted in Stern 1965: 323)

We saw a recent example in the chat room interchange quoted earlier. Here is another:

[Two urban working-class Australian Aboriginal girls]

A: Gimme the smoke if you want it lit Eggbert.
B: Here shit-for-brains. [*Passes the cigarette*]
A: Geez you're a fuckin' sook. I swear to God.
B: Shut up fucker.

(Allen 1987: 63)

Jargon, slang, swearing, insult and X-phemism

Jargon is the language peculiar to a trade, profession or other group; the language used in a body of spoken or written texts dealing with a circumscribed domain, in which speakers share a common specialized vocabulary, habits of word usage and forms of expression. Slang is language of a highly colloquial and contemporary type, considered stylistically inferior to standard formal, and even polite informal, speech. It often uses metaphor and/or ellipsis, and manifests verbal play in which current language is employed in some special sense and denotation; otherwise the vocabulary and sometimes the grammar is novel or only recently coined. Whereas efficiency of communication is the primary function of a jargon, the primary motivation for slang is to operate as a device for dissimilation and even as a secret sublanguage, an anti-language, with respect to out-groupers. One consequence of this need for secrecy is a rapid turnover in slang; by contrast, jargon tends to be conservative. Everyone uses more than one jargon; it is probable that most people also use slang. It is less likely that people have command of several slangs.

The style used when speaking or writing partly determines the set of X-phemisms that are conventional within it and which therefore help to define and maintain it. For example, euphemistic circumlocution and metaphor characterize high style, both in polite society and in allegorical literature; orthophemisms and learned terms are used in formal styles and professional jargons like medicalese, whereas remodelling is common in colloquial styles.

Profane swearing, like slang, is restricted to colloquial (informal and intimate) styles; it includes religion-based profanity and blasphemy, as well as a wealth of obscenities taken from the pool of 'dirty words'. It is co-extensive with cussing/cursing. It is behaviour that is found among very young children, whose home circumstances will never protect them from learning how to do it. Unlike most linguistic expression, which is (for most people) generated in the left hemisphere of the brain, swearing in response to frustration, pain and anger is an emotive response cry generated in the right brain. It is, however, subject to suppression from activity in the prefrontal area of the normal undamaged left brain.

Verbal insults occur in all styles of language. An insult assails the target with contemptuous, perhaps insolent, language intended to wound or disparage. People may be likened to, and ascribed behaviour pertaining to, animals, SMD body parts and effluvia, sexual perversions, physical and mental abnormalities, character deficiencies, or attacked with -IST dysphemisms. All these are found in both true and ritual insults. 'One positive aspect of cursing is that it replaces more primitive physical aggression. Most would agree that it is better to yell at people than to hit them on the head.'[67]

In certain contexts, all of jargon, slang, swearing and insult may be dysphemistic, inappropriate and subject to taboo and censoring. In others, each may be a sign of solidarity among in-groupers. However, there are the following differences: it is **the use** (or non-use) of swearing that marks the in-group; it is this plus the **forms** of jargon and slang, specialist terms and lots of abbreviation to increase the efficiency of communication that do so. The idea that swearing and malediction is largely male behaviour eschewed by girls and women[68] has been shown to be false by research in America (Risch 1987), South Africa (De Klerk 1992) and the UK (Hughes 1992). A speaker is more likely to use 'off-colour language' in the company of members of the same gender. Even so, men and women used dirty words differently:

the word *ass* was used by females to denote either a social deviation or a body part; it was used mainly as a body part by males. *Cock, cunt,* and *dick* appeared as body parts in males' data but were not recorded for females. Similarly, neither *tits* nor *pussy* were used by females. For males, *tits* was a body part and *pussy* referred to a social deviation. *Piss* referred to anger for females but was more likely to mean a process for males. *Balls, fuck, shit,* and *suck* were used more or less the same by both males and females. (Jay 1992: 139)

There probably are people who don't swear;[69] but you can bet they have passive knowledge of almost all swear words. Everyone knows how to insult. With insulting, the in-group is defined by the use of ritual insults. It is insecure outsiders who taboo and would censor jargon, slang, swearing and even ritual insult.

4   The language of political correctness

What is it exactly that people mean when they say something is 'politically correct'? Noam Chomsky once described it as a 'healthy expansion of moral concern'.[1] Michael Barnard viewed it as a 'new strain of ideological virus'.[2] For Morris Dickstein, it was a 'dictatorship of the well-meaning and pure of heart' and for Eugene Goodheart a 'doctrine of opportunism'.[3] Perhaps the whole thing has been an illusion, as Ruth Perry put it, a 'will-o'-the-wisp on the murky path of history'.[4] Sometimes political correctness seems more like an urban myth, with stories of *the differently hirsute* ('hairy'), *the specially non-tall* ('short') and *the chronologically gifted* ('old') reminiscent of those widely circulated anecdotes about batter-fried rats, poodles in microwaves, spiders in hairdos and alligators in the sewers of New York. The term is hopelessly inexact and with so much polemical baggage on board, its meaning seems to change every time it makes an appearance.

We consider political correctness as a brainwashing programme and as simple good manners; and we examine the interaction of PC-inspired relabelling initiatives with notions of taboo and censoring. Because it is politically driven, political correctness will obviously attract more attention, and certainly more hostility, than most acts of linguistic censoring. We assume that PC language reflects, and also seeks to enforce, social change. Nonetheless, speakers typically dislike being told to change their linguistic habits, which they see as an attempt to manipulate their thinking. And yet political correctness has been extremely successful in getting people to change their linguistic behaviour. Even many of the deliberate efforts to shift the meanings and connotations of words have come up roses.

There is much more to political correctness than language use; but linguistic behaviour is the most conspicuous expression of the political correctness ethos, and language issues are key players in the PC arena. We emphasize from the start that the phrases *political correctness* and *politically correct*, and their abbreviated forms *PC* or *p.c.*, refer to a set of linguistic behaviours with no implied criticism, ridicule or abuse.

Political correctness – the early years

political correctness *noun* conformity to current beliefs about correctness in language and behaviour with regard to policies on sexism, racism, ageism etc. – **politically correct**, *adj.* (*Macquarie Dictionary* 2003)

In the 1990s, it seemed that just about wherever you looked there was something to read on the political correctness debate – 'Cliché of the Decade', 'University Faces Struggle in Political Correctness Debate', 'It's a Sexist, Racist, Fatist, Ageist World', 'Correct Thinking on Campus', 'No Free Speech Please, We're Students', 'Will Political Correctness Kill Free Speech Here Too?', 'Gay and Jew Get New Deaf Signs in NZ', etc. The expressions *political correctness*, *politically correct*, *PC* or *p.c.* became buzz words. For some time, the blend *polcor* also enjoyed some popularity, at least in Australia, but the term never really took off. Like *PC*, it turned into a media sneer phrase. Robin Lakoff's search of these terms in news databases in America throughout the 1980s and 1990s confirms that their use peaked between 1991 and 1995; by the late 1990s, media attention had died down.[5] Nonetheless, the PC controversies continue to bubble away, and every now and again familiar stories reappear.

Many people would have first encountered the term *political correctness* in the early 1980s, in the context of affirmative action hiring policies, curriculum revision, speech codes and general guidelines for non-discriminatory language. In Britain and Australia, *politically correct* quietly took over from the earlier expression *ideologically sound*. How did something that appeared to be so good, something supportive of equal opportunity, tolerance, sensitivity, open-mindedness, courtesy and decency, become so disparaged?

The practice of labelling certain behaviours and certain attitudes as either *correct* or *incorrect* has been around for a long time.[6] The phrase *politically correct* is not as recent as the media makes out. An early appearance is the 1793 US Supreme Court decision *Chisholm* v. *Georgia*. In the following extract, Justice James Wilson argues that, because it is the people who hold the true authority in the United States and not the state legislatures, a toast given 'to the United States' is literally 'not politically correct':[7]

The States, rather than the People, for whose sakes the States exist, are frequently the objects which attract and arrest our principal attention . . . sentiments and expressions of this inaccurate kind prevail in our common, even in our convivial, language. Is a toast asked? 'The United States,' instead of the 'People of the United States,' is the toast given. This is not politically correct.

Despite a few early appearances, the expression did not really take off until the emergence of the American New Left in the later 1960s. English translations of Maoist literature seem to have been the main influence. It is supposed that the description *politically correct* became a kind of in-house joke, to mock extreme toers of the party line: someone PC was a self-righteous ideological bigot.[8] It was intended as a kind of self-mocking irony in *Is that fruit salad politically correct, or has the fruit been picked by exploited non-unionized labour?* But the term was soon co-opted by conservatives, who stripped it of its ironical element and turned the meaning on its head, thereby creating a sneer (or snarl) phrase to rubbish left-wing activities such as affirmative action.

From that time, political correctness started to develop an image problem. As commentators are quick to point out, the public discourse on what political correctness means was initiated by sources categorically opposed to it. The shift from stamp of approval to slogan of opprobrium was striking; but perhaps also inevitable, given that the term *politically correct* would always have had a double edge. Certainly, there would have been some who used it as a straightforward statement of correctness or ideological commitment, without any sense of irony. However, bearing in mind most people's dislike of extremes and the usual cynicism that any stiff orthodoxy arouses, it is understandable that the term would eventually evolve in this way. You could compare the shift in meaning of the word *orthodoxy*, which is often a sneer term for the beliefs of others. The effect of this double edge became a dynamic double-whammy, with political correctness managing to offend members of both the right and the left.

The average person, not directly involved in any political subculture, encountered the term in the popular press. And for the press, which thrives on steady supplies of sensations and crises, a 'PC scare' was most welcome. It is a fact that the assault on PC-dom was largely media fed. During the 1990s, hyperboles such as the following were typical of the press coverage:

In an atmosphere fuelled by political correctness, you can now be hanged for uttering the wrong word. The resulting fear and suspicion engenders an intellectual paralysis and a drying out of male/female relationships. (*The Age*, Good Weekend, 11 February 1995)

And so hostility to political correctness grew, fuelled by endless reporting and re-reporting of stories of over-the-top speech codes, and banning of books and visual images. It is hard to believe that what speakers of English call the openings in sewers was ever really of consequence, but there they were, often in the news as *manholes, femholes, person holes, maintenance hatches, utility holes* and *personnel access structures.*[9] In 1995, the child-care centre at La Trobe University (Australia) banned the use of about twenty words which were considered to be offensive (including, curiously, terms such as *girl, boy* and even *shhhhhh*). An offender was made to pay a fine into a kind of swear box for using 'dirty words'. This is a true story; but many stories that appeared in print were, we suspect, invented. Real or invented, the most absurd and extreme positions were depicted as mainstream political correctness. They pressed the moral panic button to resonate with existing anxieties within the community:[10] if it is reported that a Dobermann pinscher mauled a person in Port Hedland, Western Australia, suddenly dog attacks are reported from all round the country, giving the appearance of a collective canine onslaught on humanity. Press-fed hysteria has apocryphal bands of stony-faced abusers and corrupters of the language ('PC-niks') at the forefront of an assault on free speech and common sense.

It was an Orwellian view of euphemism that came to dominate public discussion, with parallels drawn between political correctness and the fictional language Newspeak in *Nineteen Eighty-four*. The aim of Newspeak was to reduce the number of words in the English language to eliminate ideas deemed dangerous to Big Brother and the Party; if there were no words available, 'thoughtcrime' (subversion) would be impossible. 1990s castigations of political correctness include terms like 'evil', 'fascist', 'totalitarianism', 'a witch-hunt', 'the Plague', 'Stalinism', 'McCarthyism', 'thought police', 'a few goose-steps shy of Nazism', and, of course, 'Big Brother'. On the one hand, political correctness was being described as responsible for corruption of our language 'on a truly Orwellian scale';[11] and on the other, it was criticized for trivializing important issues precisely because it focused on insignificant language matters, and not on important political ones. It is puzzling how something can be seen as so egregiously bad and yet at the same time so very piffling; but when it comes to opinions about language, speakers have a remarkable ability to hold contradictory points of view, especially with respect to prescriptive observations.

There are always people with a vested interest in keeping controversy whipped up. Assorted right-wing critics were quick to take advantage of the more wacky PC-inspired coinages in order to discredit liberal initiatives, possibly even coining some of the more outrageous examples themselves. It is doubtful whether expressions like *person with hard to meet needs* ('serial killers') or *the differently pleasured* ('sado-masochists') were ever more than satirical inventions. And it all made great lampooning fodder for comedians, too. Cleft-palate afflicted comedian Wendy Harmer, for example, confronted her own 'unthinking lookism' and called for an 'Appearance Vilification Bill' and affirmative action within the modelling industry, so that within five years, 20 per cent of all models were to have big noses and flabby stomachs.[12] Many people will remember James Finn Garner's two books of politically correct bedtime stories for more enlightened times:

There once was a young person named Red Riding Hood who lived with her mother on the edge of a large wood. One day her mother asked her to take a basket of fresh fruit and mineral water to her grandmother's house – not because this was womyn's work, mind you, but because the deed was generous and helped engender a feeling of community. Furthermore, her grandmother was *not* sick, but rather was in full physical and mental health and was fully capable of taking care of herself as a mature adult.

So Red Riding Hood set off with her basket through the woods. Many people believed that the forest was a foreboding and dangerous place and never set foot in it. Red Riding Hood, however, was confident enough in her own budding sexuality that such obvious Freudian imagery did not intimidate her.

On the way to Grandma's house, Red Riding Hood was accosted by a wolf, who asked her what was in her basket. She replied, 'Some healthful snacks for my grandmother, who is certainly capable of taking care of herself as a mature adult.'

The wolf said, 'You know, my dear, it isn't safe for a little girl to walk through these woods alone.'

Red Riding Hood said, 'I find your sexist remark offensive in the extreme, but I will ignore it because of your traditional status as an outcast from society, the stress of which has caused you to develop your own, entirely valid, worldview. Now, if you'll excuse me, I must be on my way.' (Gamer 1994: 1–2)

The end result of all this was that the label *political correctness* had turned into a powerful rhetorical stick to beat your political opponents with; a way of bringing contumely on someone you didn't like; an effective strategy to short-circuit serious debate. No wonder the diverse group of 'alternative' organizations and individuals involved in PC initiatives denied that any such movement existed. Their denial made political correctness appear all the more menacing; PC-dom started to smack more strongly of Big Brother. It became 'so-called political correctness'; a political movement which no one actually appeared to endorse.[13]

Political correctness – from politics to etiquette

etiquette *noun* **1.** conventional requirements as to social behaviour; proprieties of conduct as established in any class or community or for any occasion. (*Macquarie Dictionary* 2003)

Specialist terms often get taken up by the mass media and introduced into everyday parlance. When this happens, meanings usually shift away from their original precision as the words appear in more and more contexts. Nowadays, *political correctness* typically refers to behaviour, especially verbal behaviour, rather than to a political position. Moreover, the emphasis has now moved to civil gentility. This shift was already apparent in 1995, when journalist Jefferson Morley wrote, 'the moral seriousness of politically correct people has become part of what is regarded as decorous behaviour'.[14] This is not a surprising change; the term was already one of ridicule, and 'correctness' had shifted out of the political arena. In a 1997 article in *The Big Issue* magazine, a computer programmer referred to the new virtual pet, Tamagotchi:

'I know it's not very politically correct these days,' says Rae, unintentionally wringing the very last drop of life out of that stupid phrase, 'but to be honest I wouldn't recommend one.'

Now, what on earth is PC about the world of Tamagotchi? The derived adjective *politically correct* has shifted meaning. This is political correctness as good manners; not legally enforceable fairness or tolerance, but discourse wiping its feet before it enters the public domain and leaving before it breaks wind. While there is the same intention not to offend any person or group, reference to a political position has disappeared, along with sympathetic concern for members of minority groups – indeed, mention of any current social issue.

The following quotes were gathered by contributors to the electronic mailing list *Linguist List*.[15] None was intended as ironical. The image is no longer one of Big Brother but of June Dally-Watkins, Barbara Murray-Smith, or Emily Post. This is political correctness 'doing the polite thing'; incorrect behaviour is little more than a social gaffe.

It is not politically correct to let your dinner hosts wash all the dishes themselves.

Sending a[n email] memo to the CEO of your company is as easy as sending one to the mail clerk, if not always politically correct.

Then there's Markoff's role. As Littman tells it, The Times reporter was obsessed with the hacker. 'I've thought about trying to catch Mitnick,' he allegedly told Littman on two occasions. 'But I guess that wouldn't be politically correct.'

. . . your code simply needs to trap the WM_NOTIFY:TTN_NEEDTEXT message, fill out the structure, and then return any value (although returning =DB is politically correct).

It's not politically correct to refer to someone as being 'overweight'.

Much of the PC activity . . . on our campus comes from the Student Activities Office. The housing folks have long been into euphemism/revisionism. We can't call the dorms anything but 'residence halls'.

[Of resale shops] Now, the politically correct term for such stores is consignment shops and owners say business is brisk.

[On Arnold Schwarzenegger's movie, *Eraser*] There's a rush to set up the buffet line as some background actors (the politically correct term for extras) begin trickling into the film's designated holding area.

Many of these examples involve prescriptive relabelling, to be sure, but in no sense can they be seen as political – except that body image has been politicized by feminists, so that referring to someone as *overweight* is politically incorrect. In the last three quotes, people are searching for 'politically

correct' terms for student residences, resale shops and actors. *Residence halls,*
consignment shops and *background actors* are a long way from the original
world of political correctness. These are certainly preferred (or 'correct')
terms, but not out of any commitment to a body of liberal or radical opinion
on social issues. They are simply chosen by speakers as felicitous expressions
for these concepts; the dispreferred terms – *student residences, resale*
(second-hand) shops and *extra actors* – could hardly be construed as discriminatory or pejorative. The phrase *politically correct* is now completely en-
tangled with euphemism and jargon.

Euphemism is driven by many different things: euphemistic expressions
can of course be motivated by a desire not to offend, but they are also
motivated by the wish to display in-group identity markers, the wish to
upgrade whatever they denote, and even the display of wit. Euphemism can
have a more sinister motivation too: to blur reality, not so much to avoid
offence, but to deceive. In the next example, the epithet 'euphemistic' could
easily substitute for 'politically correct' to describe the sort of relabelling
exercise illustrated here:

Companies continue to be fascinated by – pick your own politically correct term –
downsizing/rightsizing/RIF (reduction in force).

Politically correct has been extended well beyond its original sphere of use.
We shall see how it became confused with euphemism.

PC language – euphemism with attitude?

It is contentious to say that PC-inspired terminology is euphemistic, and there
are many people who will disagree with us, some vehemently. In fact, the
quarrel stems from different understandings of what constitutes euphemism.

Modern dictionaries of euphemism like Neaman and Silver (1983) and
Ayto (1993) include PC expressions among their entries. Yet contemporary
handbooks of non-discriminatory language[16] go out of their way to deny that
their guidelines are euphemistic; they put forward the view that PC usage
calls for a more precise and accurate use of language. For instance, since
women can chair meetings, *chairperson* is not euphemistic, it is simply
accurate. Moreover, they reflect social change: many handbooks stress that
political correctness is a matter of calling groups by the names they prefer.
There are numerous examples. In many places, the terms *married* and *de facto*
spouse only include those relationships sanctioned by law. A term such as
partner sidesteps that issue, and is therefore representative of relationships
other than heterosexual. The term *queer*, and more recently the umbrella
alphabetism GLBTIQ,[17] are preferred by non-heterosexuals because they
include groups which the terms *gay* and *lesbian* do not.

Secondly, there is the emphasis on the role of PC language as a form of public action. By drawing attention to form, it forces us to sit up and take notice. The use of 'generic' *she*, for example, is meant to jar – and succeeds. Some people intend the use of *he/she* and *him/her* to be deliberately clumsy. The dysphemism of a distracting style can be an effective way of getting a message across. PC language deliberately throws down the gauntlet, and challenges us to go beyond the content of the message and acknowledge the assumptions on which our language is operating. As Bolinger neatly put it (although not in a PC context), the double pronoun 'refuses to take the back seat that all languages reserve for pure anaphora'.[18] Moreover, politic-ally correct terms also deliberately highlight certain aspects of a group's identity. When members of the black community campaigned to be called *African Americans*, it was to emphasize not genetics or colour, but the historical roots of a group that forms part of the USA, thus bringing the name into line with those of other ethnic minorities, such as Japanese Americans and Italian Americans. There is a lot more involved than simply 'civility' and 'sensitivity'.[19]

In addition to their political ramifications, these accounts of PC-motivated language change fall well within the realm of euphemism. The use of in-appropriate styles for naming and addressing is dysphemistic and likely to affront the hearer's face. If political correctness has to do with extending to others the common courtesy of naming them as they would prefer to be named, then this is euphemistic or orthophemistic behaviour. But there is more involved than simple politeness. Certainly, euphemisms are motivated by the desire not to be offensive, and so they have positive connotations (at the least they seek to avoid too many negative connotations). But euphemisms are not simply 'linguistic fig-leaves'; many artful euphemisms conceal only as little as to be all the more titillating. In the mouth or pen of a political satirist, euphemisms can be deliberately provoking. George Orwell's *Animal Farm* is at one level a children's story and, at another, a blistering political satire.[20] Such writers exploit euphemism to publically expound taboo topics. Even euphemisms for death often do more than cover up abhorrent reality; they invoke points of view like death as a journey (*pass away*), or the consolation of death as the beginning of new life (*go to a better place*).

PC-inspired euphemism is not so very different: it aims not to disguise or conceal unpleasant reality, but to help remove the stigma of negative social stereotypes by compelling its audience to go beyond the simple content of the message and challenge prejudices embodied in language. Many people probably remain oblivious to the political message. It is more a case of mouthing the right-sounding words, consistent with the political correctness ethos. But this is the usual fate of taboos. Over time, original meaning gives way to unthinking ritual; fear and respect become lost in social convention.

For many, the political correctness protocol is the dessicated remnant of old knowledge and opinion.

The reluctance to view PC initiatives as euphemism may arise from deprecation of the term *euphemism* itself. For instance, some feminists reject the word *lady* as euphemistically implying some negative quality inherent in *woman*, their term of preference. For many people, euphemism is a pejorative label attaching to any deodorizing language; the sort of doublespeak that turns *dying* into *terminal living*, *killing* into *the unlawful deprivation of life* and *potholes* into *pavement deficiencies*. They believe such euphemism to be value-laden, deliberately obfuscatory jargon intended to befuddle the hearer. Understandably, if euphemism is seen in this light, those promoting PC-inspired relabelling disown it.

The decline of the word *euphemism* mirrors the deterioration of the labels *political correctness* and *politically correct*. These are not surprising developments. As we have seen in Chapter 2, negative connotations inevitably dominate the meaning of a language expression. The terms *euphemism* and *political correctness* are now so mired in pejorative connotations that they seem always to imply criticism. In this way the label 'euphemism' has become a double-edged sword, used by both supporters and critics of PC language to back their respective positions. For example, one handbook for non-discriminatory language states: 'responding to others with care and sensitivity involves describing people accurately, from an informed position. Euphemisms, or unnecessarily vague terms patronise people'.[21] Meanwhile in the other camp, critics of political correctness such as Robert Hughes, impatient with what they see as a pretence that sweeter words produce a sweeter world, scorn political correctness precisely because they argue it *is* just euphemism.[22]

The dysphemistic worm in the euphemistic bud

Among the general public there seems to be an implicit assumption that language is a monolith, with a fixed set of approved meanings and values. Our discussion of the middle-class politeness criterion in Chapter 2 shows that this is too simplistic. Orthophemism, euphemism and dysphemism are primarily determined by evaluating an expression within the particular context in which is it uttered. What determines them is a set of social attitudes or conventions that vary considerably between groups and individuals. Both critics and supporters of political correctness are apt to forget that there can be no such thing as 'Everyman's euphemism' or 'Everyman's dysphemism'. Word meanings and their associations vary continuously in response to the relationship between speaker and audience, the setting, and the subject matter; change any one factor, and the language may also have to change.

Apparent expressions of opprobrium like *you little shit* can be used in a jocular, even affectionate, fashion; and it has always been that way. Dysphemism or offensiveness is never an intrinsic quality of the word. Even apparently blunt expressions like *cark it* and *croak* can be cheerfully euphemistic between certain individuals. Their flippancy detracts from the seriousness of death; jocularity in the face of death is offensive only if it can be expected that the hearer would regard it as such.

The language of political correctness will be both euphemistic and dysphemistic, all the more because of its overtly political nature. When Aidspeak campaigners fought for labels such as *People with AIDS / PWAs*, and more recently *People Living with AIDS / PLAs*, it was to emphasise the fact of survival and play down the defeat and passivity implicit in terms like *victim* and *patient*. Nonetheless, *victim* is still the preferred term by the media, health care workers, and politicians battling for *victims' rights*. *Gay* is an in-group label, but is avoided by some who don't wish to politicize their sexual affinity; others refuse to use it of people with whom they cannot identify.[23] *Deaf* is preferable to *hearing-impaired* for those who identify with *Deaf Pride*. Some heterosexual males feel uncomfortable using the term *partner* of a wife, because it might be understood to refer to a male. Some women feel affronted and wrongfully excluded by compounds like *chairman*; others are quite happy to remain *Madam Chair* or *Madam Chairman* because they understand *chairman* to be an idiom denoting the office of chairperson. Australian Aborigines reportedly show no strong aversion to using terms such as *blackfella*, *Abo* and *boong* among themselves.[24] For some time, the term *wog* 'Caucasian Australian who is not Anglo-Celtic' has had positive in-group uses: as one told us, 'It's cool to be wog.' And it is now very much out there in the public, as evident in the success of movies such as *Wogs out of Work* and *Wog Boys* and the recipe collection *The Wog Cookbook*. These are examples of -IST dysphemisms, adopted as markers of group identity and badges of pride by people without malign motives. Of course, this does not mean that all who have 'natural cover'[25] are happy to use such labels; for some, they are too polemical or appalling. Here is a mechanism for reclaiming what, in the mouths of outsiders, is highly offensive pejorative language. This is one of the reasons it is so difficult to legislate against 'words that wound'. Language is not a perfect, logical, consistent and transparent linguistic system, one that matches thinking and dittoes reality. It is full of vagueness, indeterminacy, variability and ambiguity, and this fuzziness will always make prescriptive speech codes difficult to enforce.

Many euphemisms are short-lived: they degenerate into dysphemisms through contamination by the taboo topic and they are then replaced. PC language tramps the same treadmill. Many terms are subject to precisely the same narrowing and deterioration that accompanies any taboo term. During the controversy surrounding British Mencap's refusal to change the name *mental handicap*, their director of marketing observed: 'It is only a matter of time before even the most right-on expression becomes a term of abuse. It has been the same since people talked about village idiots, and "learning difficulties" is no exception. Children are already calling each other LDs as an insult.'[26]

Consider ways of referring to poor countries. One of the earliest expressions was *backward*, a word whose euphemistic sheen is so badly tarnished by connotations of mental illness and lack of civilization that it is difficult to ever imagine it as euphemism. In the late 1940s, it was substituted by *underdeveloped*, which was then replaced in the 1950s by *less developed*, or better still, *lesser developed* – the use of the comparative is a subtle euphemistic practice, ensuring the description is always a little fuzzy around the edges. The more positive *developing* appeared in the 1960s, followed closely by *emerging* or *emergent*. But the smack of colonialism soon rendered all these taboo, and as Ayto points out,[27] nowadays we tend to retreat to the safe territory suggested by geographical labels like *Third World*, and more recently *The South* – or else an acronym like HIPCs (highly indebted poor countries).[28]

Censorship and repression, whether manifest in full-blown sanctions or merely social niceties, always seem to provide fertile ground for the taboos they exist to control. During the Renaissance period, linguistic censorship in England coincided with a flourishing of linguistic subterfuge in the form of 'dismembering oaths' like *zounds* or *sfoot*.[29] Sex went underground during the Victorian era, but erotic literature flourished and sexual promiscuity was rife. Today, we see the same mix of exuberance and restraint: next to public PC etiquette there is a flourishing lexicon of bigotry. Green's collection of largely racial slurs highlights a brand new litany of abuse. Ironically, the United States of America, the land of immigrants and aliens, tops the list of abusers; American coinages make up the largest proportion of dysphemistic language in his book.[30] Like some kind of dysphemistic worm in the euphemistic bud, offensive language always seems to thrive on social sweetness.

Political correctness and self-censorship

PC-driven language is politically motivated, and so attracts more attention and resistance than most euphemism. PC euphemism is perceived to arise directly out of linguistic intervention. Except for slang (or at least their own slang), people generally dislike linguistic change, especially change that smacks of deliberate manipulation. Peggy Noonan, a journalist and former speech writer for Ronald Reagan, spent much of a piece on political correctness lamenting the loss of words she claims to have been hijacked and reinterpreted: 'I wish we could rescue them', she writes, 'and return them to their true meanings.'[31] She describes, for instance, *gay* as once being 'a good word because it sounded like what it meant – "merry and bright"'. As an aside, the etymology of *gay* can be traced back to one of two Old High German words – one with the meaning 'good, beautiful', the other 'impetuous, swift'. Presumably, neither of these is the 'true meaning' Peggy Noonan had in mind: 'merry, bright' is what she grew up with and feels comfortable with, and it is this meaning she believes is the true meaning that she wants to revive.

Like Noonan, many people complain about losing what they see as their freedom to call things by their 'right names' – as if there were something natural and correct about their own linguistic preferences; but perhaps this is what most of us feel. Linguistic changes, whether or not PC-motivated, are seen by many as the thin end of a wedge that will fragment society into factional interest groups. Such hostility is fuelled by media hyperbole and misrepresentation. Journalist Peter Jeans accuses the 'apostles of political correctness' of attempting to brainwash; slightly tongue-in-cheek, Jeans expresses his resentment at Big Brother's attempts to manipulate his thinking.[32]

And yet, political correctness has been remarkably effective in getting people to change their linguistic habits, far more effective than other kinds of linguistic prescriptions and proscriptions. Pauwels cites a handful of studies on gender and language reforms in Australia:

Considering the recent nature of non-sexist language planning, the changes observed so far are quite remarkable, especially in written language. (Pauwels 1993: 115)

Given that political correctness seems to have offended both sides of the political spectrum and is not actually a movement that anyone appears to endorse, the successful implementation of non-sexist guidelines is all the more striking. It is difficult to assess the degree to which change is the direct consequence of recommendations made by linguistic authorities and style guides because change comes from people's personal decisions to alter their language. There have been legal restrictions imposed in many countries to make race discrimination and vilification an offence. Formal speech codes have been imposed on some US campuses and by some publishers prohibiting expressions deemed sexist, racist, homophobic and anti-Semitic. There have been a few celebrated cases of people being sent to sensitivity workshops. But this is not a world where people 'can be hanged for uttering the wrong word' (as was suggested in the newspaper article quoted earlier). Speech codes have to be vague to allow for different contexts, making them virtually unenforceable.[33]

Societal shifts will always have linguistic repercussions, especially for the lexicon, and PC-driven changes are partly a form of natural linguistic evolution in the face of more general social change. What political correctness has done is create a climate of tacit censorship.[34] One reason for hostility towards political correctness is that a breach of PC protocol can quickly become an inquiry into a miscreant's character. When people without natural cover express themselves in an 'incorrect' way, there is always the danger that their audience will judge them on what is known about the character of others who have spoken in a similar way: true racists, true homophobes, true misogynists – in other words, real bigots, whose motives *are* malevolent. People are always mindful of what an expression might sound like (the MCPC comes into play). If, for example, advocates of diversity insist that Australian Aborigines be referred to as Kooris, then the safest thing is to adopt the PC-approved terminology. Of course, if the group itself wants this label, using it is a matter of simple civility. However, the term *Koori* is controversial because not all Aboriginal groups wish to go by that name.

All taboos are controversial, whether they involve sanctions against bodily effluvia, death, disease or dangerous animals. Any derogatory or unfavourable denotation or connotation within language expressions will dominate the interpretation of their immediate context.[35] Speakers will not risk appearing to use a taboo term when none was intended; therefore they are quick to drop the homonyms of taboo terms. Just as our nineteenth-century forbears used *dark meat* and *white meat* in place of *leg* and *breast* when speaking of a cooked fowl, some modern-day speakers prefer *coffee with* (or *without*) *milk* in place of *white* (or *black*) *coffee*. In the case of a failure to follow a PC regime, there is much more at stake. Just look at the now shocking nature of those flippant references to *niggers* and *chinks*, which were once second nature to writers like Rudyard Kipling. Use non-PC terms now, and doubts are raised about your basic moral commitments; the safest course to steer is one which carries the PC stamp of approval. The manufacturers of Darkie Toothpaste apparently had this in mind when they changed the English tradename of their product to Darlie Toothpaste, see Figure 4.1. Note how the human image changes from stereotypical black minstrel (left) to a racially indeterminate black and white face (right).

Even words and phrases that are similar to non-PC terms are avoided. In 1999, there was a controversy sparked by the use of the word *niggardly* by an employee in the Washington, DC, mayoral office. David Howard told his staff that, in light of cutbacks, he would have to be 'niggardly' with funds. Many connected this word with the taboo word *nigger* and the uproar that followed resulted in his resignation. In the blog 'American political correctness and the word "niggardly"', Anders Jacobsen describes another incident in September 2002, where Stephanie Bell, a fourth grade teacher at Williams Elementary School (Wilmington, IN), taught the word *niggardly* to her students and at least one parent wanted her fired.[36] In links to Jacobsen's posting, a number

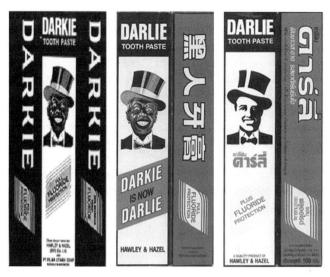

Figure 4.1. Darkie Toothpaste becomes Darlie Toothpaste.

of similar incidents are recounted. And in a reaction to this piece, George from CARM describes how he also avoids the term *reneged* and *reneger* – 'I have noticed myself using a different way to convey my message when I am around black people'. In his variety of English, the verb *renege* 'deny, renounce' is pronounced /rɪˈnɪg/.

In May 2002, the London *Telegraph* reported that a British government minister had been severely criticized for his use of the phrase *nitty-gritty* at a police conference because of its supposed racist overtones. He had told his audience that it was high time to 'get down to the nitty-gritty' in training officers. It was reported that in the modern British police service, the expression 'nitty-gritty' is prohibited because it is thought to have originally been used in reference to those in the lowest reaches of slave ships. This etymology appears to be spurious. We can find nothing to link this word *nitty-gritty* with the early slave trade.

Two other expressions on the police hit list of dirty words were *egg and spoon* and *a good egg*. Now, the police are in fact correct in their history of *egg and spoon*. Along with *harvest moon* and *silvery spoon*, it was originally nineteenth-century Cockney rhyming slang for *coon*. Its use has always been racist. It would seem from the report that this expression must have also contaminated other 'egg' expressions, such as *a good egg* 'a good chap' (as opposed to *a bad egg* 'a disreputable person; a stinker'). Do we also ban all other egg expressions? We might grant that *egghead* is offensive to bald people – and also to academics – but the *curate's egg*, the *egg on one's face*, *egging someone on*, *over-egging the pudding*, *putting all one's eggs into one basket* and of course *telling your grandmother to suck eggs*, should these go too?

Another forbidden word on the police list was *pikey*, a close relative of Australian English *piker* and its verb correlate *pike out* 'opt out, go walk-about'. *Pikey* was a piece of slang from the eighteenth century (originally from *turnpike*) used in reference to vagabonds and beggars. And here again is the problem with banning words: language is never a matter of one-size-fits-all. Ban *pikey* and *piker*, and you should most certainly also ban *rogue*, *rascal*, *ratbag* and American *bum*, not to mention those other shocking words *scoundrel* and *scallywag*. These were all once highly contemptuous terms used in reference to vagrants and vagabonds, but exaggerated use has caused them to shed their worst connotations. The words *bum*, *piker*, *rogue*, *rascal*, *ratbag*, *scoundrel* and *scallywag* are now quite playful, in some contexts almost terms of endearment. Quite simply, offensiveness is never an intrinsic quality of a word, and the choice between alternative expressions will always depend on context.

Some reactions to Jacobsen's 'niggardly' posting reveal that appearances have to be taken into account. For example, Mike Pugh writes (4 September 2002):

> I've always had a problem with the term 'niggardly'. It's always been my least favorite word in the English language. Yes, it's not technically a racial slang, but I do think that people with cultural sensitivity and taste avoid using the term.

Another respondent, Douglas, writes on the same day (note the possibly deliberate misspelling of 'niggardly' here):

> . . . There are just some things that you should not do in order to make sure that you are not misunderstood by someone as being rude and inconsiderate. I doubt that anyone can argue that there is no way that someone might feel that the speaker said 'niggerdly' meaning in the manner of a nigger. Are you really so short on words that you have to use this word? It does not mean anything negative but there are undoubtedly more prudent options in an intelligent person's vocabulary.

As is so often the case in issues to do with language, it doesn't matter what the linguistic facts suggest. The reality that *niggardly* has absolutely no etymological connections with *nigger* is of no consequence. What really matters is how speakers perceive their language to be, and if people do start connecting words such as *nitty-gritty* and *niggardly* with the N-word, then this will be the kiss of death for these words. Is it non-PC to have *niggling doubts* about this trend? *Fuk* 'sail' and *feck* 'purpose' had absolutely nothing to do with *fuck*, but that did not save them. And although *country* shows no sign of falling to the power of the C-word, *coney* 'rabbit' has bitten the dust.

A response to taboo?

Societies differ with respect to the degree of tolerance shown towards any sort of taboo-defying behaviour. Tolerance depends on their current values and belief systems. The topics placed under taboo will change over the centuries, too. Contemporary English-speaking society has evolved new taboos on gender, sexuality, disability, religion, race and ethnicity. No longer is the race or ethnicity of criminals reported in the press. When this taboo was recently violated in reporting the 'Sydney gang rapes', there was an uproar. There is a new apprehensiveness and shunning of anything that may be interpreted as discriminatory or pejorative. The push for equal opportunity has given rise to legally enforceable rights to fairness, sensitivity and tolerance. Laws against profanity, blasphemy and (sexual) obscenity have relaxed and been replaced in heinousness by sanctions against -IST language.

Robert Hughes described PC language as a 'linguistic Lourdes, where evil and misfortune are dispelled by a dip in the waters of euphemism'.[37] Is that all it is? Political correctness gets us to focus on the claims of different groups; it prescribes and proscribes public language for ethnicity, race, gender, sexual preference, appearance, religion, (dis)ability and so on. It supposedly ensures a fair go for all; but mixed in with it is a twist of fear and anxiety. The practical problems of maintaining dialogue in today's diverse democratic societies have given language a new volatility. One of the most dramatic outcomes of globalization is the massive flow of business travellers, tourists, refugees and migrants. This has produced an intermingling of people and cultures on an unprecedented scale that exposes us to other people's parochialisms and expectations of civility and religion, which can differ strikingly from our own. How do you engage everyone equally in discussion when you don't have a clue about their culture or their views on life? Especially when we are not entitled to expect that the people we insult and demean will pretend not to be insulted and demeaned.[38] Social commentator Phillip Adams is right when he says we live in times of increasing need for niceness.[39] In the west, diversity is sacrosanct, but often at odds with our responses to difference and non-conformity. Sometimes, difference is distasteful; it makes us angry, fearful, insecure and vulnerable. What most people want, it seems, is the comfort of the familiar.

Difference is also a scapegoat when polity and economics go wrong. There is no doubt, we are living in times of high anxiety and there is a lot for people to be frightened about. There is a compendium of scientific and technological horrors: weapons of mass destruction, holes in the ozone layer, vicious viruses, global warming, intrusive surveillance by employers and governments, diminishing sperm counts, etc. Globalization, rationalization, privatization, and reorganization go on around us, typically for the benefit of a handful of the rich and powerful. These activities have left people resentful, hurting and looking for someone to blame. French linguist Appignanesi gives an interesting illustration. In an anti-racism demonstration in France in the early 1990s, one placard read, *Un raciste c'est quelqu'un qui se trompe de colère*. The slogan contains a pun that derives from the closeness of the French words *colère* 'anger' and *couleur* 'colour' – 'a racist is someone who has found a mistaken object for anger' versus 'a racist is someone who's made a mistake about colour'.[40] In Australia, the years during which right-wing politician Pauline Hanson enjoyed her greatest popularity provide a glimpse of the horrible consequences of society's free-floating anxieties coming to rest on negative feelings towards migrants and Aborigines: 'they' displace 'us' from jobs; 'they' pervert 'our' culture; 'they' bring in vice, immorality and terrorism. Disgust with this sort of bigotry produces the need for a euphemistic vocabulary to create a kind of working tolerance, so that we can engage each other and discuss sensitive topics.

A large segment of contemporary western society is riven with guilt and shame for subjugating, enslaving, marginalizing and, in some cases, extinguishing other peoples. In Australia, as in other countries where aboriginal peoples were displaced by European immigrants, there is each year a semi-official 'National Sorry Day' where nationals[41] apologize for the treatment of Aboriginal people, in particular the forced removal of thousands of children from their families between the 1880s and 1960s. There are no conventionalized strategies for repentance; no twenty-first-century cutty stools for contrition, no hairshirts, no armies of chanting flagellants. Instead, we adopt politically correct attitudes to negotiate the linguistic minefield.

Evidence of evolving taboos

[I]f you were driving in your car, somebody cuts you up in your car, if they shout and call you a f-ing idiot, or a bloody idiot or whatever, fair enough. If they start putting your racial background into that, it's unacceptable. (Interview in Millwood-Hargrave 2000: 20)

The changing nature of taboo will always be reflected in shifts among preferred terms of opprobrium. The history of foul language in English, for example, has seen the sweeping transition from religious to secular swearing. Blasphemy, religious profanity and religious insults have lost their punch; and the potency of profanity relating to sexual and bodily functions has more recently diminished.[42] Television programmes frequently include the words *fuck, fuck off* and *fucking*, as well as *cunt* (although always with a warning).

In the genre of 'reality TV' like *Big Brother*, sitcoms like *Sex in the City* and dramas like *The Sopranos*, such words are commonplace. The designer label FCUK appears prominently on billboards and clothing everywhere. 'Foul language' regularly turns up in movies rated PG (parental guidance), and is no longer confined by the censors to more restrictive categories (MA, R, XXX). In Australia, such words are frequently encountered in the public arena and there is wide acceptance of it. In an April 1999 radio interview, Premier Jeff Kennett of Victoria described people who flouted the temporary restrictions on gas usage as *pricks*; there was barely a ripple. The same year, the Australia Institute's executive director, Dr Clive Hamilton, said *fuck* during an interview on the ABC's well-respected current affairs programme, *Four Corners*; it was the third occurrence of the word on the programme that year. About the same time appeared a highly successful TV advertisement using the expletive *Bugger!* to sell a Toyota utility truck. This followed a West Australian Lotteries advertisement, in which a winner says *Bullshit!*. Newspapers, which would once have resorted to coy abbreviations when reporting such events, now use the words explicitly without warning. In 1991, the Press Council of Australia ruled on a complaint against 'vile obscene language' in a press interview with actor Bryan Brown:

News Ltd responded at some length to Mr Purvey's objections, saying in essence that the use of expletives had gained wide acceptance and such profanities were no longer confined to the factory floor or dockside. It supported its argument with a Telegraph-Mirror article quoting a university language expert as saying that four-letter profanities were now widely used by both men and women. The Council believes, in this case, that the use of the word in full was justified.[43]

Since the 1980s, obscene language charges from around Australia have been dismissed, with courts ruling that words such as *fuck*, *shit* and *cunt* are no longer 'offensive within the meaning of the Act'.[44]

There are two reasons why SMD words have lost their former power. First, terms of abuse lose their sting with frequent use. Second, sex and bodily functions are no longer tabooed as they were in the nineteenth and early twentieth centuries. While some people still complain about hearing such words in the public arena, what is now perceived as truly obscene are racial and ethnic slurs, the use of which may provoke legal consequences. For instance, sports players are occasionally 'sin-binned' but never charged for foul language on the field, unless the complaint involves race discrimination or vilification. When a footballer was disciplined for calling Aboriginal player Michael Long 'black cunt' during an Australian Rules match, the reports and re-reports of the incident made no reference to the use of *cunt*. It was the racial abuse that triggered the uproar, and the incident gave rise to a new code of conduct against racial vilification both on and off the sporting oval.[45]

A recent British report provides qualitative and quantitative evidence for the linguistic fall-out from the new taboos.[46] Research carried out jointly by the Advertising Standards Authority, the British Broadcasting Corporation, the Broadcasting Standards Commission and the Independent Television Commission tested people's attitudes to swearing and offensive language. In the first part of the study, participants were asked to respond to the perceived 'strength' of swear words with no context suggested. Though there were gender and age biases, participants were clear about the relative severity of these twenty-eight words. Least offensive was verbal play, such as 'baby-talk' *poo* and *bum* or rhyming slang like *berk* (which almost no one links to *cunt*).[47] Ranked slightly more offensive were such profanities as *God* and *Jesus Christ*, followed by SMD expressions: expletives such as *shit* and *fucking hell* and sexual references such as *shag* and *pussy*. Towards the top of the scale of severity was derogatory language towards minority groups, including people with disabilities, those from different religious faiths, homosexual men and women, and ethnic minorities. Most severe of all was racial abuse. Evaluating the same twenty-eight swear words in the context of television programming more than 50% of respondents rated slurs such as *nigger*, *paki*, *spastic* and *Jew* with *cunt* and *motherfucker* as in-appropriate for transmission at any time. *Nigger* was at the top of the severity scale at 53%; by comparison, only 38% felt *fuck* should never be broadcast. Interestingly, a number of people felt *cunt*, *motherfucker* and *fuck* could be broadcast after 11.00pm (28%, 30% and 36% respectively,) but the figures were considerably smaller for words such as *Jew* (15%), *nigger* (14%), *paki* (13%) and *spastic* (12%). Changed rankings on the severity scale demonstrate a developing tendency already seen in a similar study, carried out two years earlier.

The evolving nature of taboo is also revealed in changes to lexicographical conventions. While dictionaries used to include religious and racial swear words but omit sexually obscene words, the late twentieth century saw mounting pressure on editors to alter, or even omit altogether, political and racial definitions of words. Robert Burchfield recounts the fierce debates in the early 1970s, while he was editor of the *OED*, over the inclusion in the dictionary of opprobrious senses of the word *Jew*.[48] In 1997, there was a dispute between the publishers of the *Merriam-Webster's Collegiate Dictionary* (tenth edition) and members of the African American community over the definition of *nigger*. The dictionary had indicated the offensive connotations of the term but only after the initial definition of *nigger* as 'black person'. Those disputing the definition wanted the word listed primarily as a 'slur', with the derogatory sense as part of the principal denotation.[49] In response to these sorts of pressures, some dictionary makers have been much more regulative in their policy. The practice in the most recent edition of the

Woordeboek van die Afrikaanse Taal ('Dictionary of the Afrikaans language') is to simply list racist terms (*Kaffir*, *Franse siekte* 'French disease, syphilis', etc.) and label them as 'racist', but leave them undefined with no supporting examples. Sexist terms and lexical items referring to 'deviations', handicaps and stigmatized diseases are explained, labelled and given a 'sensitive handling' in the dictionary's metalanguage. Readers may be referred to an orthophemistic synonym, for example, from *hoer* to *prostituut*, but there is no cross-reference from the orthophemism to the offensive synonym. The *Encarta World English Dictionary*, which made its appearance in 1999, has been described by reviewers as 'extremely sensitive to political correctness'.[50] The dictionary recognizes three degrees of offensiveness: insulting, offensive and taboo.

[*Encarta*'s] notes about terms that may be considered rude are the oddest thing about the new dictionary. They're PC in the extreme, often censorious and sometimes missing linguistic shifts that are taking place. It waggles its schoolmarmish finger even at *crone* (hardly a word most people employ these days), saying that it 'deliberately insults a woman's age, appearance, and temperament', but it doesn't flag that some feminists have now reclaimed it and use it in a positive sense. *Queer* gets similar treatment, but likewise it misses the way it is now used by gays themselves (as for example, in *queercore*, the next entry on the page, which wouldn't exist but for this shift). *Nigger* provokes a solemn sermonette: after warning about its offensiveness, it says 'Those who persist in using it, should remember that their use of the word reflects directly upon them, the users'. Every rude word is spattered with 'offensive term', repeated for every compound or derivative, often in the definition as well as the heading; the entry for *fuck*, for example, contains the warning 28 times in four column inches, plus seven instances of 'taboo offensive', just in case we don't get the point. (Quinion 1999)

Equally revealing of changing taboos is the behaviour of those guardians of linguistic goodness such as Dr Thomas Bowdler, Mrs Mary Whitehouse and the imaginary Mrs Grundy (see Chapter 1). In the early nineteenth century, Bowdler and his sister set out to expurgate Shakespeare. They produced the so-called 'Family Shakespeare' – from which, as he announced on the title page, 'those words and expressions are omitted which cannot with propriety be read aloud in a family'. *Bowdlerism*, as it came to be known, targeted profanity and sexual explicitness. There was subsequent bowdlerizing of a range of works, including the Bible. Perrin presents a history of expurgated works in both Britain and America, with a chapter on the targets of contemporary bowdlerism, notably dictionaries and literature classics. Perrin shows that, though censoring on religious and sexual grounds has diminished, the increase in racial and ethnic expurgation has been striking.[51] Earlier, we described a case of bowdlerization of English literary texts by the New York State Eduction Department, who censored references to race, religion, ethnicity, sex, nudity, alcohol, profanity and 'just about anything that might offend someone for some reason'. Diane Ravitch documents this and similar cases of linguistic censorship imposed on editors, writers and illustrators in the USA. Her glossary of forbidden usage details words, topics and illustrations collated from the bias guidelines of textbook publishers, state testing agencies and various other professional bodies. These laundering operations began with the intention of excluding any conscious or implicit statements of bias against racial or ethnic minorities and females; but there is now a broad and increasingly bizarre policy of censorship that extends far beyond its original scope.

> Publishers of tests and textbooks today routinely engage . . . panels of bias and sensitivity experts to screen their products. This is a process that effectively removes everything from tests and textbooks that might be offensive to any group or individual. It is designed to strip away words and ideas that offend anyone. Bias and sensitivity review has evolved into an elaborate and widely accepted code of censorship that is implemented routinely but hidden from public sight. (Ravitch 2004: 18)

The definition of 'dirt' has changed for today's bowdlerites, but the cleaning-up activities remain the same.

PC language

Verbal taboos are imposed by social conventions; they strengthen social cohesion and serve human interests by censoring out bald mention of things which threaten danger, distress and offence. Practical problems of maintaining dialogue make attention to face saving critical if we are to negotiate a way through the tensions and differences that must arise between disparate individuals and groups of people. The language of political correctness is no more a threat to freedom of speech than other types of verbal taboo. Certain restrictions must be observed for everyone to have the freedom to speak. We are rarely at liberty to say exactly what is in our minds in the plainest and most explicit terms, so it would be naïve to assume that everything said can be taken at face value. Any interaction with other people imposes on them and must take account of their needs and wants. It may seem that orthophemism and euphemism attend to the wants of others, while dysphemism satisfies the speaker's wants and needs. But the reality is far more complex; for instance, a speaker's own self-image and future needs may also be better satisfied by orthophemism and euphemism, because what goes around comes around. PC language is motivated by the same drive to be polite and inoffensive as orthophemism and euphemism; so, much PC language is euphemistic. But in this emotive discourse, words get politicized and used as ideological bludgeons. Whereas we generally use euphemism for the sake of social etiquette, in the political correctness arena it becomes a political gesture – in-your-face euphemism with an attitude. Like any X-phemism, the speaker's decision to use PC language and the hearer's response to PC language will depend on the context of its use. What is PC in one context may be non-PC in another, just as what is euphemistic in one context may be dysphemistic in another.

Despite the public hankering for a kind of 'no-frills', euphemism-free language, sanitized from politically correct jargon, humankind would have to be reinvented for this to come about. We need a way of talking about taboo topics. We need strategies for speaking to and about others, particularly others perceived to be disadvantaged, oppressed and different from ourselves; people who may be overly suspicious of our motives and overly sensitive to what we say, finding slights where none was intended. PC language was often consciously devised to ease the difficulties that arise in this volatile area of interpersonal relations. Disfavoured terms were proscribed, and preferred alternatives prescribed. And yet the censorship has always been more between the lines than overt. The PC restrictions on speech are mostly self-imposed, with speakers unwilling to run the risk of being judged to violate the accepted code for their context of utterance.

5   Linguistic purism and verbal hygiene

In this chapter we explore popular perceptions of language, in particular linguistic prescription. Speakers' concerns for the well-being of their language lead to puristic activities and linguistic censoring. Puristic attitudes are driven by an ideology of *the standard language*, so we devote a good part of our discussion to the concept of language standardization and aspects of the creation and cultivation of Standard English. We focus not on formal acts of censorship such as might be carried out by a language academy, but on the attitudes and activities of ordinary people, in letters to newspapers or comments on talkback radio.[1] In these contexts, ordinary language users act as self-appointed censors and take it upon themselves to condemn language that they feel does not measure up to the standards they perceive should hold sway. We argue that the struggle to define 'the boundless chaos of a living speech' (as Samuel Johnson wrote in the Preface to his dictionary)[2] and force it into the neat classificatory systems of a standard is part of the human struggle to control unruly nature.

Setting the scene

Like other tabooing practices, language purism seeks to constrain the linguistic behaviour of individuals by identifying certain elements in a language as 'bad'. Typically, these are words and word usage that are believed to threaten the identity of the culture in question – what eighteenth-century grammarians referred to as the 'genius' of the language.[3] Authenticity has two faces: one is the struggle to arrest linguistic change and to retain the language in its perceived traditional form; the other is to rid the language of unwanted elements and to protect it from foreign influences. But, as Deborah Cameron claims, the prescriptive endeavours of speakers are more complex and diverse than this. She prefers the expression 'verbal hygiene' over 'prescription' or 'purism' for exactly this reason. According to Cameron, a sense of linguistic values makes verbal hygiene part of every speaker's linguistic competence, as basic to language as vowels and consonants.[4] The 2004 'Runaway number 1

British Bestseller', *Eats, Shoots and Leaves: the Zero Tolerance Approach to Punctuation*, is evidence of this.[5] This amusing punctuation guide has been met by prayers of thanks by verbal hygienists[6] the world over. They are the people found in those language associations formed to promote causes as diverse as Plain English, simplified spelling, Esperanto, Klingon, assertiveness and effective communication – even something as esoteric as the preservation of Old English strong verbs (such as *thrive, throve, thriven*).[7] Verbal hygienists also enjoy thinking and arguing about words, correcting the writing of others and looking things up in dictionaries and usage guides. These activities are born of the urge to improve and clean up the language. As is so often the case when aspects of human behaviour are proscribed, it is what other people do that ends up on the blacklist.

Take an example from Australian English and its relationship with a powerful relative, American English. One consequence of the rise of mass media in the global village is that native Englishes are much more open to worldwide influences. There is a pervasive American dimension to much of what is global; indeed, a clear distinction between globalization and American cultural imperialism is difficult to draw. Given the dominance of the United States, and the loosening of ties between Britain and its former colonies, it is not surprising to find a good deal of linguistic steamrolling going on. The 'Americanization' of English has been a hot topic in Australia and New Zealand as it has increased since the Second World War. There are identifiable influences on teenage slang and, more generally, on teenage culture.[8] Many reactions from older folk are hostile. Newspaper headlines, such as 'Facing an American Invasion', go on to 'condemn this insidious, but apparently virile, infection from the USA'. In letters to the editor and talkback calls on the radio, speakers rail against 'ugly Americanisms' – many of which, in fact, are not Americanisms at all.[9] When, in 1969, the Australian State of Victoria advocated spellings such as *color* and *honor* in place of *colour* and *honour*, writers ignored the edict: 'why should our spelling be changed to follow the American pattern', one writer complained.[10] Public pressure persuaded *The Age* newspaper to return to the *-our* spelling in 2001. Even though many prestigious British publications, including the London *Times*, various editions of Daniel Jones' *English Pronouncing Dictionary*[11] and the *OED*, promote the *-ize* spelling on words such as *legalize*; most Australians reject it outright because it smacks too much of a deference to America. Such lay concerns about language usage are not based on genuine linguistic worries, but reflect deeper and more general social judgments. Hostility towards American usage is born of linguistic insecurity in the face of a cultural, political and economic superpower; American English usage poses a threat to authentic 'downunder English' and is tabooed.

The making of the standard

That the weather clerk really makes the weather probably none but infants believe, but that language is made by compilers of dictionaries and grammars is a conception not confined to the young or ignorant. (Hans von Jagemann 1899; cited in Wardhaugh 1999: 9)

In general, standard languages represent a kind of linguistic 'best practice' – a set of behaviours that claims to excel all others. Correctness, precision, purity and elegance are the qualities of the perceived standard. It is the measure of excellence – the benchmark against which all other varieties of the language are gauged.

best practice *noun* the set of operations achieving world-class results in quality and customer service, flexibility, timeliness, innovations, cost, and competitiveness, especially from the cooperation of management and employees in all key processes of the business.

benchmark *noun* **1.** *Surveying* a point of known elevation, usually a mark cut into some durable material, as stone or a concrete post with a bronze plate, to serve as a reference point in running a line of levels for the determination of elevations. **2.** A point of reference from which quality or excellence is measured. (*Macquarie Dictionary* 2003)

In the case of English, the standard language has been artificially created over many years, not by any English Language Academy, but by a patchwork of different groups, including writers of style guides and usage manuals, dictionary makers, editors, teachers, newspaper columnists and the like. Their activities have amassed an arsenal of prescriptive texts that promote and seek to legitimize a single fixed and approved variety: dictionaries, grammars and handbooks that record, regulate, tidy up and iron out the language.[12] Their neat lists, elegant definitions and fine-spun paradigms necessarily ignore the richness, diversity and variability that is found in any language system. So do histories of the language: with occasional lip service to regional differences, historical accounts of English have focused overwhelmingly on the making of the present-day standard; the story of one variety has become the story of our language.[13]

Standard English is the written variety that is promoted in schools and used in law courts and government institutions: students are expected to use it in essays, and ESL instructors teach it to foreign learners of English. Writers are supposed to acquire the standard rules, and those who do not are in danger of being regarded as recalcitrant, lazy and incompetent; they are said to have poor grammar – or, worse, no grammar at all. It should properly be referred to as the *standard dialect*; but since dialects are held to be substandard varieties of a language, the label is oxymoronic. For many people, Standard English *is* English. What they think of as the rules of English grammar are the rules of this one variety. There is a perception that words are not 'real words' until they appear in a dictionary. Speakers will, illogically, often ask linguists whether something they have heard, or even used themselves, is really a word or not. For the public, wide usage is not enough for a language expression to meet the standard. As Hans von Jagemann put it in his presidential address to the Modern Language Association, dictionary makers and grammarians are believed to build the language.

There is no standard spoken English: people reading speeches in parliament or scripts in broadcasts use Standard English in the written text, but the spoken delivery uses many accents. Once the most favoured accent was spoken at (the Royal) Court; then, it was the speech of the well-educated upper class ('received pronunciation'), the model for BBC English. Elsewhere in the world there were different accepted spoken varieties, such as General American. Although there are a few regional variations in written Standard English, regional variation in spoken English is extensive and far more obvious.

The earliest English grammars of the eighteenth century were negatively prescriptive, and the effects have persisted. The grammarians were 'mainly clergymen, retired gentlemen, and amateur philosophers'.[14] One wrote for the '*Female Teacher* in the British Dominions',[15] some wrote for the improvement of persons in trade or manufacturing; but 'the majority of writers seems to have felt that they were writing for the edification and use of gentlemen, to warn them against inadvertent contamination with the language of the vulgar'.[16] The prevailing attitude of the eighteenth century was put forward by Jonathan Swift, in *A Proposal for Correcting, Improving, and Ascertaining the English tongue*:

I do here, in the Name of all the Learned and polite Persons of the Nation, complain . . . that our Language is extremely imperfect; that its daily Improvements are by no means in proportion to its daily Corruptions, that the Pretenders to polish and refine it, have chiefly multiplied Abuses and Absurdities, and that in many instances, it offends against every part of Grammar. (Swift 1712: 8)

Forty years later, Dr Samuel Johnson wrote in the Preface to his *Dictionary*: 'I found our speech copious without order, and energetic without rules.'[17] These views led to an outflow of prescription for what was proper in English. Acrimony was common because what was correct to one writer was incorrect to another; and much of the argument was concerned with what should properly be regarded as stylistic variations. Lip service was paid to the norm of everyday usage; but it was generally ignored or transmuted to mean the usage of a select few, namely, the individual scholar and, at best, his circle (they were all men). As with any act of censoring, these eighteenth-century prescriptive practices were tied firmly to the censors' own personal beliefs and preferences. It was conduct that nineteenth-century and early twentieth-century linguistics castigated as unscientific: it gave so-called 'traditional grammar' a bad name.

In his *Essay on Human Understanding*, John Locke[18] argued that to understand thinking and knowledge, one must understand language as the means of thought and communication because linguistic forms represent the ideas of things and not the things themselves. The final chapters of the *Essay* deal with the imperfections of language and with avoidable abuses. Locke claimed that words only mean what they are understood to mean; consequently, usage must be the sole arbiter. Quintilian was more prestigious than Locke, and had said much the same sort of thing *c*.88 CE; for instance, the following observations were generally approved:

> Usage, however, is the surest pilot in speaking, and we should treat language as currency minted with the public stamp.
> [W]e must make up our minds what we mean by usage. If it be defined merely as the practice of the majority, we shall have a very dangerous rule affecting not merely style in language but life as well, a far more serious matter. For where is so much good to be found that what is right should please the majority? . . . I will therefore define usage in speech as the agreed practice of the educated. (Quintilian 1920–2, *Institutes* I.vi.3, 43, 45),

Eighteenth-century grammarians would doubtless claim to be presenting a 'consensus of the educated' in their works, but in reality there seems to have been very little consensus on what constitutes good usage; each grammarian presented his own judgments, which often disagreed with those of his fellow grammarians.

Any appeal to *good usage* ought to describe what is meant by such a phrase, and the better grammarians did so. For instance, in *The Philosophy of Rhetoric*,[19] George Campbell identified it as 'reputable, national, and present'. By 'reputable', he means the Court and authors of 'reputation' – presumably by consensus of the educated. By 'national', he means neither provincial nor foreign. By 'present', he means within the previous century, though he apparently excludes examples of good usage from living authors. His canons of good usage include:

- unambiguous expression;
- regular rather than irregular forms;
- simplicity rather than complexity;
- euphony;
- conformity with Latin or Ancient Greek syntax;
- avoiding solecisms (syntactic errors) and barbarisms (phonological errors).[20]

Appealing to reputable literary authorities was a problem. The classical English authors were all criticized for solecisms by one grammarian or another. Shakespeare, because of Ben Jonson's evaluation of his 'little learning', was expected to use vulgarisms. The 'wrong' use of prepositions was employed:

> even by Swift, Temple, Addison, and other writers of the highest reputation; some of them, indeed, with such shameful impropriety as one must think must shock every English ear, and almost induce the reader to suppose the writers to be foreigners. (Baker 1779: 109)

Archbishop Robert Lowth[21] and American-born Lindley Murray[22] later reported much the same. Of the classical languages, Greek was elevated to the highest position, followed by Latin – 'a Species of *Greek* somewhat debased' according to James Harris.[23] Romance languages were vulgar corruptions of Latin; Saxon was generally regarded as barbaric, along with other Germanic languages. Where necessary, authority lay with Latin grammar, and this could always be appealed to as the objective arbiter. Thus James Buchanan is unable to forgive the solecisms of Swift, Addison and Pope: 'Had they not the Rules of Latin Syntax to direct them?'[24] Dryden claimed to turn any doubtful phrase into Latin: thus *most highest*, used in the Old Vulgate translation of the Psalms, was regarded as illogical; and although some would allow it, perhaps as suitable for God alone, others rejected it because *maximus altissimus* was inconceivable in Latin (at least to them). Noah Webster was modern in espousing the norm of everyday usage: 'grammar is formed on language, and not language on grammar' (1784). Nevertheless, he often relied on analogy, reason and true or fanciful etymology; and he appealed to Latin when discussing whether or not the preposition should accompany the interrogative pronoun in *wh-* questions, and what form the *wh-* word should take (cf. *Who were you speaking to? To whom were you speaking?*).[25]

Prescriptive grammarians seeking to establish the Standard often failed to conform to their own prescriptions. Archbishop Lowth's *Short Introduction to English Grammar*[26] states that strong verbs, like *write* and *ride*, should distinguish between past tense and past participle forms. Lowth provided lists of what he described as common mistakes committed, even by 'some of our best Writers':[27]

> *He begun*, for *he began*; *he run*, for *he ran*; *he drunk*, for *he drank*: The Participle being used instead of the Past Time. And much more frequently the Past Time instead of the Participle: as, *I had wrote, it was wrote*, for *I had written, it was written*; *I have drank*, for *I have drunk*; *bore*, for *born*; *chose*, for *chosen*; *bid*, for *bidden*; *got* for *gotten* &c. This abuse has been long growing upon us, and is continually making further incroachments.

In his own private correspondence, however, Robert Lowth constantly flouted this grammatical rule. In a letter to his wife, he stated: 'My Last was wrote in a great hurry', and later in the same letter 'whose faces and names I have forgot'.[28] Lowth's preferred epistolary practice was clearly not best practice, so what was he thinking of? People have confused past tense and past participle forms of strong verbs since the beginning of the medieval period.[29] Lowth (and other codifiers) condemned the confusion and regulated it by fiat. The standardization process necessarily involves removing variation. There is no room for linguistic options. Lowth's grammatical rule makes it possible to put a tick or a cross beside any strong verb form: speakers cannot vacillate between *begun* and *began* – only one choice has the stamp of approval. In reality, language usage is not an absolute matter of assigning a tick or a cross. It is much more complicated and far more interesting, as Lowth's own practice shows. It was probably not deliberate hypocrisy: we cannot know why in his letters to his wife he violated his own theoretical prescriptions; it is possible that they were too formal for his intimate correspondence, but most likely that he simply did not notice that what he wrote in private correspondence contradicted his public pontificating. Language is not amenable to being forced into a standard mould, and anyone who attempts to do so will find themselves bemired in contradiction.

Speech communities are complex, and language has to cover a huge range of social behaviour. Yet variability and mutability – qualities intrinsic to any linguistic system – do not sit happily within the classifications of a 'pure' and consistent standard variety. The label 'standard' entails not only 'best practice', but also 'uniform practice'. This is only practical in the context of the written language, more especially formal written language. The conscious self-censorship that accompanies the writing process has a straitjacket effect that safeguards the language, to some extent, from the flux and variance that is found in the spoken language. Publishers and editors who supposedly value linguistic uniformity follow different guidelines from one another in their editing practices; they maintain different standards, and will continue to do so to because the social aspects of language work against homogeneity. What one group condemns, another cherishes; so there is unlikely ever to be a uniform set of publishing conventions. This is because Standard English is a myth, an abstraction or, more exactly, an ideal to strive for.

The arbiters of linguistic goodness

Another factor that energetically works against uniformity is language change. As soon as he had produced his dictionary, Samuel Johnson recognized the futility of his original aim; namely, to 'ascertain' or 'embalm' the language – an expectation which, as he put it, 'neither reason nor experience can justify'.

When we see men grow old and die at a certain time one after another, from century to century, we laugh at the elixir that promises to prolong life to a thousand years; and with equal justice may the lexicographer be derided, who being able to produce no example of a nation that has preserved their words and phrases from mutability, shall imagine that his dictionary can embalm his language, and secure it from corruption and decay, that it is in his power to change sublunary nature, or clear the world at once from folly, vanity, and affectation. (Johnson 1755: Preface)

Centuries later, an editor of the *OED* also wrote of the impossibility of stopping continuity and change in language: 'No form of linguistic engineering and no amount of linguistic legislation will prevent the cycles of change that lie ahead.'[30] Vocabulary is particularly unstable and dictionary compilers constantly have to redraw the boundary for marginal vocabulary items. *Yeah-no* is a new discourse marker in English[31] – when will it start to appear in our dictionaries? Even more of a headache for lexicographers are meanings. Modern dictionaries now acknowledge the 'inaccurate' use of many specialist expressions in ordinary language, such as *to go ballistic* – when missiles go ballistic they don't explode, but coast; *to push the envelope* – an aeronautical expression referring to the gas or air container of a balloon or airship; and *quantum leap* – technically the transition of atoms or electrons from one energy state to another. So when will they accept that the meaning of *epicentre* has moved beyond the safe confines of geology – where it denotes the source-point whence seismic waves go out – to the more general sense of 'middle; core'? All aspects of the linguistic system are constantly on the move, and most dictionaries and handbooks do not allow for this. Dictionaries that fail to update cease to be used.[32] And yet if the dictionary makers and handbook writers do acknowledge current usage, there are howls about declining educational standards – a fine illustration of the human capacity for doublethink.

If a sentry forsakes his post and places an army in danger, the penalty is severe. If a guardian ceases to guard and neglects his duty to children, there are few who would not condemn. If a great dictionary forsakes its post as the guardian of our language, how can one avoid disappointment? (Reverend Richard S. Emrich, 1962, Episcopal Bishop of Michigan; cited in Preston 2002: 149)

These fiery words were prompted by the release of Webster's *Third New International Dictionary* in 1961; Emrich lamented, 'the greatest of all American dictionaries has been corrupted at center. The greatest language on earth has lost a guardian.'

Thus, in addition to the formally acknowledged guardians, English has many self-appointed protectors, like Emrich; arbiters of linguistic goodness who engage in random acts of censoring by writing to newspapers and university linguistics departments, phoning in to radio stations or joining associations for spelling reform. These vexatious activists regularly publish lists of linguistic misdemeanours – mispronunciations, misplaced apostrophes, incorrect words, crimes of grammar under headings such as 'Lamentable Language', 'Descent into Linguistic Slobdom', 'Linguistic Junk'. Such acts are typically provoked by the fact that a celebrity, so-called 'expert' or sizeable portion of the speech community uses a shibboleth. Take, for instance, the current collision in Antipodean English of the two verbs *bring* and *buy*. Increasingly *bought* is appearing as the past of *bring*, as in 'Mr Eric Grant of Glen Iris bought in a couple of his 1975 Bin 389 [bottle of wine] for evaluation.' The fact that *bought* now commonly appears in print as the past of *bring* suggests the change is already entrenched. Many people are upset by this state of affairs. Yet most are truly fascinated by word origins and the stories that lie behind the structures in their language. Why, then, are they squeamish when they encounter changes happening within their lifetime? One of the main thrusts of verbal hygiene is conservatism; keeping the language 'pure' means maintaining it unchanged. People find it interesting that *go* stole its past tense *went* from *wend*, and that *to be* is a linguistic mongrel comprising verb forms from three or even four other verbs; but for *bring* to do likewise is calamitous. Change is fine only if it remains a historical curiosity. No matter what the verbal hygienists may wish for, Standard English may soon embrace the mixed pedigree of *bring* as it did earlier suppletions.

The Standard English that developed from the eighteenth-century prescriptivists is a linguistic fantasy – an ossified paragon of linguistic virtue that would be more accurately called the 'Superstandard', to acknowledge its otherworldliness.[33] Even Archbishop Lowth was aware that the rules he was laying down belonged to something not-of-this-world, but to a more abstract level of language to be distinguished from 'common discourse'. In his Preface, he wrote: 'It is not owing then to any peculiar irregularity or difficulty of our Language, but that the general practice both of speaking and writing it is chargeable with inaccuracy. It is not the Language, but the practice, that is in fault.'[34] Yet, many speakers of English believe in the Superstandard. They believe in, if not the existence, then the possibility of a single correct language system. Such beliefs are powerful – as anyone who has tried to meddle with the cherished standard knows. Speakers want their reference books to tell them what is and what is not 'correct' because they wish to appear well educated and to eloquently maintain 'correct usage'. Dictionaries and handbooks that acknowledge change are abrogating their responsibility. So too are the style manuals that recognize options. Language professionals are in a difficult position, as the shamans who stand between the object of worship and ordinary mortals.

In the eyes of the wider speech community, linguists are seen as supporters of a permissive ethos encouraging the supposed decline and continued abuse of Standard English. Some time back Kate Burridge suggested that English might be better off if it abandoned the hyphen in certain contexts and retained it only for other more useful functions.[35] This sparked fierce attack (as did her suggestion to abolish the possessive apostrophe). The following is but one of the many angry emails received:

Subject: Grammar
Just read an article regarding your strange ideas that you have just published in the weed book or something.

I'm 25, tattooed ex con, so not in the habit of sending emails like this (or ever actually).

Although there is one thing that REALLY annoys me. People that want to take away from the English language.

If you want to become more American in your use (or non-use) as the case maybe, then so be it.

Did you note the hyphen ;-)

But language makes us what we are, i's our common ground.

Already there are far too many illiterate people in the world. You seem to want to make a dumb world even dumber.

Good one. (e-mail from 'The Weatherman', 22 June 2005)

The gap between linguists and the wider community is considerable. The feeling between the two camps is one of mutual distrust; linguistic experts fail to address lay concerns and lay activists show no interest in heeding linguists.[36] In 1992, a newspaper article appeared which vividly conveyed the views of many in the wider community towards professional linguists: Laurence Urdang, editor of *Verbatim*, described linguists as 'categorically the dullest people on the face of the earth . . . rather than trying to present and explain information, they seem to be going in the opposite direction. They try to shield people from knowing anything useful about the language.'[37] For linguists, language is a natural (even if social) phenomenon, something that evolves and adapts and can be studied objectively. This stance is resoundingly rejected by others, for whom language is an art form, something to be cherished, revered and preserved. Linguists find such popular perceptions of language ill-informed and narrow-minded.

The public discourse on language and value is often ferociously passionate and confident, but, as many linguists complain, it also lacks the norms expected of debate on other topics. 'Many educated people know more about space and time, uncertainty, and quantum effects than they do about nouns and verbs.'[38] People are experts in English simply because they speak it, and native English speakers feel free to voice an opinion. They see a very clear common sense distinction between what is 'right' and what is 'wrong', from which no amount of well-argued rational linguistic evidence can dissuade them. In an opinion piece in *The Age*, David Campbell outlines the various functions that have been identified for the new discourse particle *yeah-no* in Australian English; he then dismisses these on the ground that he 'knows' that *yeah-no* is 'yet another example of speech junk – unnecessary words that clutter up our language'.[39]

Like other tabooing behaviour, linguistic purism has to do with the solidarity and separating function of language. It is about social status, too. Speakers constantly make negative judgments about others who use vocabulary, grammar and accent that they view as *bad English*, castigating such people as 'uneducated', even 'stupid'. The behaviour seems extraordinary in an era that is so obsessed with equality for all and the desire not to offend. The basic human right of respect is understood to mean that people can no longer speak of or to others in terms that are considered insulting and demeaning; yet, this behaviour does not extend to the way people talk about the language skills of others. Linguistic prejudices are usually accepted without challenge. Despite the profession of egalitarianism, conscious and unconscious discrimination against speakers of non-standard dialects and low-status accents is rampant.

Individual speakers justify their concerns about language by appealing to rational explanations, such as the need for intelligibility. As expressed in the words of a passionate supporter of the possessive apostrophe, 'we shall have no formal structure of our language: it will become unteachable, unintelligible, and eventually, useless as an accurate means of communication'.[40] It seems to be more than simply a breakdown in communication that people fear; there is more at stake. In many people's minds, there is also a link between linguistic decline and moral decline:

If you allow standards to slip to the stage where good English is no better than bad English, where people turn up filthy at school . . . all these things tend to cause people to have no standards at all, and once you lose standards then there's no imperative to stay out of crime. (Norman Tebbit MP, BBC Radio 4, 1985; quoted in Cameron 1995: 94)

As with other acts of censorship, Tebbit mouths concern for the common good. Protecting the language against perceived abuse guards against moral harm, perhaps even physical harm, because of the link made between bad language and bad behaviour. If you have no regard for the nice points of grammar, then you will probably have no regard for the law! Rules of grammar, like other rules in a society, are necessary for the health of that society.

Matter out of place

We can recognise in our own notions of dirt that we are using a kind of omnibus compendium which includes all the rejected elements of ordered systems. It is a relative idea. Shoes are not dirty in themselves, but it is dirty to place them on the dining-table; food is not dirty in itself, but it is dirty to leave cooking utensils in the bedroom, or food bespattered on clothing; similarly, bathroom equipment in the drawing room; clothing laying on chairs; out-door things in-doors; upstairs things downstairs; under-clothing appearing where over-clothing should be, and so on. In short, our pollution behaviour is the reaction which condemns any object or idea likely to confuse or contradict cherished classifications. (Douglas 1966: 48)

Mary Douglas' theory of pollution and taboo offers interesting insights into the relationship between taboo and linguistic purism. As Douglas sees it, the distinction between cleanliness and filth stems from the basic human need for categorization – our need to structure the chaotic environment around us and render it understandable. That which is dirty is that which does not fit in with our 'cherished classifications'; dirt is matter 'out of place'.[41] The standard-ization process forces languages into tidy classificatory systems. The neat lists and elegant paradigms inside the dictionary and handbook provide the perfect counterpart to the 'boundless chaos of the living speech' that lies outside. Grey areas are banished by imposed boundaries for what is and what is not acceptable. The language is defined by condemnation and proscription of certain words and constructions deemed impure or not belonging. The infiltration of linguistic innovations, lexical exotics and non-standard features is a transgression of the defining boundaries and poses a threat to the language – as well as to the society of which the language is a manifestation and a symbol. Accordingly, they are tabooed.

Acts that are committed in the name of verbal hygiene show traces of the same insecurities that lie behind many other taboos – the need to feel in control. Human beings are fearful when they feel they have lost or are losing control of their destinies. These fears are as acute today as they have been in the past. Endeavours to intervene in language are just more attempts to take charge and control nature; language standardization tries to impose order on a natural phenomenon. There have been individuals who have gone to extreme lengths to engineer logical, consistent and transparent languages that perfectly match the thinking of their speakers and ditto reality. If one such language could somehow become the first language of speakers, it would inevitably be struck with precisely the same linguistic infirmities as natural languages: the same vagueness, indeterminacy, variability, anomaly and inconsistency. Mary Douglas concludes her comments on pollution thus: 'The moral of all this is that the facts of existence are a chaotic jumble.'[42] Then so too is the language that describes these facts; a regular and homogeneous communication system would be dysfunctional. A standard language can never be a finished product. To create such a work of art is to enter into a partnership with natural processes; prescription would soon render the work sterile and inadequate. And here lies a paradox: puristic endeavours necessarily involve a degree of mental dishonesty that comes from the inevitable contradiction between the actual linguistic behaviour of language users and the views they hold about their language. Bad language can be proscribed and set apart, just like those other aspects of life that make people feel uncomfortable because they are dangerous or distasteful; they can be banned from being heard, seen or touched. But not only will they not go away, they are also essential to the continuation of life, living and language.

Linguistic prescription – an example of taboo

Standard language is an ideal that speakers have, and which everyday usage never quite matches up to – not even in the performances of 'good' speakers and writers. Editors, dictionary makers and handbook writers, who help to establish and maintain this object of worship, are the ones with the specialized knowledge. They possess the shamanic powers to control the events, to diagnose and to cure. Some may even create rituals of prohibition and avoidance – after all, it is the activities of language professionals that advertise violations of codes and draw people's attention to ill-chosen words, grammatical errors and infelicities of style. Once condemned by those in authority, these features quickly fall from grace.

Dictionaries and handbooks offer proponents of linguistic purification a public arena; yet linguistic purism is not simply the by-product of codification. For as long as records go back, people have complained about the degeneration of the language used in their own time. Feelings about what is 'clean' and what is 'dirty' in language are universal, and humankind would have to change beyond all recognition before these urges to control and clean up the language disappeared. An integral part of the language behaviour of every human group is the desire to constrain and manage language, and to purge it of unwanted elements: bad grammar, sloppy pronunciation, newfangled words, vulgar colloquialisms, unwanted jargon and, of course, foreign items. Next to the shamans are the self-appointed arbiters of linguistic goodness: ordinary language users who follow the ritual, and taboo those words and constructions they see as 'unorderly' and outside the boundaries of what is good and proper.

6   Taboo, naming and addressing

One's name is an inalienable part of one's identity; it is the essence of self and it is a means by which one is known to one's fellows. An assault on one's name is treated as comparable with, or even worse than, an assault on one's body. So names are tabooed in many communities. Calling a name risks malevolence falling on the name-bearer and the caller. Proper names are chosen with care and many communities have constraints on giving names, such that they render the individual identifiable with the community. Consequently, a person is stigmatized by their name, a fact that has both positive and negative consequences. We discuss styles of naming and addressing as they are affected by the speaker's attitude and by the perceived role and status, within the context of the talk exchange, of the speaker and the person addressed or named. Inappropriate naming, name-calling and addressing is subject to censoring and censorship.

Why names are tabooed

Personal names are (or have been) taboo among some peoples on all the inhabited continents, and on many of the islands between them. The taboo on names is a fear-based taboo. In the same way that malevolent magic can be wrought with one's person, bodily effluvia or shadow, so can it be wrought when another person is in possession of one's true name. 'The name of a person . . . is associated with the "essence" (*to ʔofungana*) of that person.'[1] In languages which distinguish alienable from inalienable possession, a name, like a body part, is inalienable. For instance, in the Australian language Pitjantjatjara, inalienable possession is marked with an accusative (ACC) case suffix, but alienable possession with a possessive (POSS) suffix.

*ngayu-**nya***	*mara*	
1SG-ACC	hand	'my hand'
*ngayu-**nya***	*ini*	
1SG-ACC	name	'my name'
*ngayu-**ku***	*karli*	
1SG-POSS	boomerang	'my boomerang'

In the early twentieth century, Frazer wrote (in terms that would no longer be acceptable):

> Unable to discriminate clearly between words and things, the savage commonly fancies that the link between a name and the person or thing denominated by it is not a mere arbitrary and ideal association, but a real and substantial bond which unites the two in such a way that magic may be wrought on a man just as easily through his name as through his hair, his nails, or any other material part of his person. In fact, primitive man regards his name as a vital portion of himself and takes care of it accordingly. (Frazer 1911: 318)

Personal names may be used by a few intimates, but are not given out to the general public. This is true even today for the Gullah-speaking African Americans who live on the Sea Islands, off the coast of South Carolina, USA.[2] In parts of Papua New Guinea,

> [t]o say a tabooed name is to assault the owner of the name, and requires sanctions to be brought against the offender. Punishment for violation of a taboo can be in the form of religious propitiation of an offended spirit, payment of goods to an offended party, exchange of goods to restore harmony between the guilty and the injured. Breaking the taboo can lead to death by murder, or suicide due to shame. An old man in Waritsian village in the Amari dialect area of Adzera told me that his father had broken a very strong name taboo in front of his father-in-law. The shame caused him to run off into the mountains where enemy groups lived; he deliberately put himself in their way and was killed. (Holzknecht 1988: 45)

As we have said, the name was often believed to capture the very essence of a person, so that 'he who possessed the true name possessed the very being of god or man, and could force even a deity to obey him as a slave obeys his master'.[3] In ancient Egyptian mythology, Isis gained power over the sun god Re (or Ra) because she persuaded him to divulge his name. In the European folktales about the evil Rumpelstiltskin,[4] the discovery of the villain's name destroyed his power. In some societies, it is acceptable to know a personal name provided the name is never spoken (perhaps for fear of evil spirits overhearing). In others, the name can never be uttered by its bearer, but is freely used by others. In many Austronesian societies, the names of affines and some cross-kin may not be used.[5] In some, no two people may bear the same name: 'I know one example of a child's name that had to be changed because an old woman came down from the mountains to a refugee settlement and this child had the same name as hers.'[6] Not only are personal names tabooed; for the same reasons, in some societies, the names of communities were not divulged to strangers.

What applies to the names and naming of ordinary folk applies *a fortiori* to rulers and to gods, because any threat to their power endangers the entire society they dominate. Taboos on the names of gods seek to avoid metaphysical malevolence by counteracting possible blasphemies and profanities that arouse their terrible wrath:

A *mantra* [hymn] recited with incorrect intonation and 'careless', arrangement of *varna* (letters) [reacts] like a thunderbolt and gets the reciter destroyed by God Indra. (Kachru 1984: 178; *sic*)

Despite secularization during the twentieth century, there are plenty of constraints on the names of our god(s) and their acolytes. Ritualized superstition is revealed in our response of *Bless you* when someone sneezes (note the euphemistic omission of *God* as the actor subject of *bless you*); the blessing was to prevent the devil from entering the body momentarily emptied of its soul by the sneeze. Many people make the old pagan appeal *touch wood* or *knock on wood* to guard against misfortune; some believe in lucky and unlucky numbers; thespians taboo the name of *the Scottish play*[7] in the theatre and do not wish their fellows *Good luck!* but instead *Break a leg!* But, you might say, nobody really believes in these taboos; we are different from all those 'primitive' souls. Are we? They may be just as sceptical in fact:

Once when a band of !Kung Bushmen had performed their rain rituals, a small cloud appeared on the horizon, grew and darkened. Then rain fell. But the anthropologists who asked if the Bushmen reckoned the rite had produced the rain, were laughed out of court (Marshall 1957). How naive can we get about the beliefs of others? (Douglas 1966: 73)

Nevertheless, name taboos seem remarkably robust everywhere.

In many societies, names of the dead are (or were until recently) taboo:

People on Misima [Island, Papua New Guinea] have several names, at least three, but one of these is their 'real' name, and this name is strictly tabooed by everyone in the area when they die (essentially, in their home village which may consist of 200–500 people). The penalty for breaking the taboo is to pay valuables to the offended relatives. Close relatives in the same clan are allowed to say the name of the deceased, but seldom do. (Simons 1982: 203)

In some societies (Misima among them), anyone bearing the same name as a deceased person must use another. In Tiwi (Australia), the ban is even more severe than this, for it extends even to those personal names which the dead person may have given to others.[8] Violations of such taboos are believed to cause misfortune, sickness and death;[9] often they cause offence to living descendants, too. Although native English-speaking communities do not have such taboos, there is a host of euphemisms for the topic of death and the dead. In many societies in which personal names derive from common words, when the name is taboo, the word – and even phonetically similar words – are tabooed too. This can mean that nearly 50 per cent of the vocabulary is potentially taboo for some people.[10] Euphemisms are created by circumlocution, phonological modification, extending the meaning of a near-synonym (thus reintroducing rarely used words into the basic vocabulary), borrowing from another language, or even by coining a new word. When newly introduced, a speaker will check for comprehension of the novel term before proceeding. The result is that the vocabularies of such languages undergo considerable and extremely rapid change, even in core items which normally resist change in other languages. For instance, on the death of a man named *Ngayunya*, some dialects of the Western Desert Language replaced the pronoun *ngayu* 'I/me' with *ngankyu*. Subsequently, this term was itself tabooed and replaced either by English *mi*, or by *ngayu*, borrowed back into the language from dialects where it had never been tabooed – which shows that the taboo on a word may cease after some years have passed, allowing it to come back into use. This recycling is one of the few ways in which a tabooed item can become an orthophemism.

Comparable tabooistic distortions have affected many languages. Women among the Nguni peoples of southern Africa practise *hlonipha* – respect expressed through avoidance of personal names of a husband's father and lineal males in his ascending generations.[11] Personal names of chiefs are tabooed for everyone, along with similar-sounding words. Children do not pronounce the names of their parents or their parents' siblings; the personal names of siblings are avoided after puberty; a wife avoids her husband's name and this is often reciprocated. Why is the naming taboo practised by wives and, principally (though not universally), pre-menopausal wives? Marriage in Nguni societies is patrilocal: the wife moves into the new husband's father's homestead, and is said to 'go on a long journey' towards integration – at death – into the husband's family. She is, therefore, an outsider rendered regularly impure by menstruation. A wife must not appear bare-headed and bare-breasted before her parents-in-law, or look them in the eye or point at them; she does not enter the father-in-law's hut, nor speak to him directly, nor eat his leftovers; nor can she enter the cattle kraal (i.e. mess with the homestead's wealth).[12] All senior male affines are treated the same way as the father-in-law; so there is a large number of personal names and similar-sounding words that the wife must not utter. Her predicament is made more difficult by the fact that Nguni personal names are often taken directly from general vocabulary, e.g. *Mandala* 'strength', *Siqandulo* 'grindstone', *Lange-lihle* 'nice day'. Unless the name-bearer is present, a new wife may be merely reprimanded for not practising *hlonipha*; but frequent breaches of the taboo have her returned to her father, and she can only go back to the husband's homestead with apologies and a goat or two to sacrifice to his ancestors. Violations of *hlonipha* are sacrilegious: they risk sickness, madness or some worse tragedy being visited on the homestead. *Hlonipha* is not practised by a son-in-law, although there are constraints on touching or eating together with his mother-in-law; she, however, must cover her head and breasts in the presence of her son-in-law. It is women who bear the weight of restrictive practice under *hlonipha*.

What explains the practice of *hlonipha*? Basically, it risks putting the name-bearer in harm's way; we will try to explain how. Note that it is the sound of the name, and of all syllables within it, that must be avoided. This is because calling a name draws attention to the name-bearer, and also to the caller. To use a male in-law's name draws attention to the name-bearer and puts him at risk. A name is not called after dark, lest it draw the attention of a ghost or a witch – or perhaps it is one of these which is calling. The names of dread diseases and dangerous animals are not spoken for similar reasons. Also, for a wife to utter her father-in-law's name belittles him. A wife has low status within the homestead and may even be ordered about by her husband's younger brothers. She will not be addressed by her personal name, but as the daughter of her father or of her clan; once she has a child, she is addressed as mother of that child. All this marks her as an outsider. Any behaviour that focuses attention on her is disallowed: a wife is not permitted to talk loudly or to call out (to a child, for instance; she has to get another child to do this). The wife must avoid drawing attention to herself. Because she retains allegiance to her birth group and their ancestors, she is an outsider. Outsiders are possible aggressors and may practise witchcraft; a wife is statistically the most likely person in a household to be accused of witchcraft. So, if a wife inadvertently violates *hlonipha*, she spits on the ground and denies she is calling her father-in-law's (or other male in-law's) name. The wife's practice of *hlonipha*, therefore, is a display of deference to the husband's family and of concern for their well-being.

Naming practices

For the name-bearer, the most important function of his or her name is to mark identity. For others, the most important function of names is to distinguish different referents. The typical proper name refers to an individual, but also named are collections whose members share some common property, real and imaginary people, pets, newly discovered and cultivated biological specimens, places and topological features, buildings, institutions, businesses, radio stations, pop groups, orchestras, acting companies, events like wars and epidemics, computer files, books, newspapers, films, TV shows, manufactured products of all kinds. A name's reference can be fixed in more than one way. The reference of the measurement name *metre* was fixed in 1875 as the length between marks on a platinum iridium bar at normal atmospheric pressure at 0°C. A *metre* is also defined as 1,553,164.13 wave lengths of red cadmium light, and as 1.093614 of a yard. For the average person, it is a length identified by whatever ruler or tape measure is to hand. All these are some of the many ways of fixing the reference of *metre*. Similarly, the reference of the personal name *Aristotle* will have been fixed initially by some kind of naming ceremony (which, following Kripke, we may loosely call a *baptism*).[13] Later, its reference is fixed by means such as identifying Aristotle as the pupil of Plato, the teacher of Alexander the Great, the philosopher born in Stagira, etc. Plato could have fixed the reference of *Aristotle* for, say, Eudoxus by pointing out Aristotle and telling Eudoxus the equivalent of *That's Aristotle*. Not everyone will fix reference in the same way, but the name holds for everyone for whom it identifies the same referent.[14] This is so even when a person's encyclopaedic information is minimal, such that the reference of, say, *Aristotle* is merely 'a historical personage'. If that person has only this information about *Plato*, too, all that keeps Aristotle distinct from Plato is the form of the name.

Many people have nicknames or familiar names in addition to their official name. *Michael* alternates with *Mike* in different, though overlapping, sets of contexts. A jazz buff will know that *Bird* refers to the same person as *Charley Parker*. The stage name *Bob Dylan* identifies the same person as bears the name *Robert Zimmerman*, and *Marilyn Monroe* the same person as bore the name *Norma Jean Baker*; the alternative names are mostly used in different contexts. Judgments about the appropriateness of names are judgments of semantic and pragmatic acceptability arising from the connotations of the names. For example, *Mike* and *Michael* can have the same reference but different connotations.

In every community, most personal names distinguish first the sex then the gender of the name-bearer; transsexuals almost invariably change their name to fit their target gender. Life would be tough for a boy named *Sue*; it was tough for the American who had his name changed to *One Zero Six Nine* – he had to go to four courts in two states before he found a sympathetic judge; and even then he was required to spell the numbers and not use numerals.[15] Across different cultures, certain naming practices can be seen to differentiate between girls and boys. Girls get flower names like *Rose, Violet*, and in Mongolian *Narantsetseg* 'sunflower', *Odval* 'chrysanthemum'; boys don't. Instead, they get names like *Dirk*, and in Mongolian *Bat* 'strong', *Sukh* 'axe'.[16] Chinese boys may be named 明 *ming³* 'bright, brilliant, light', 強 *qiang* 'strong, powerful' or 力 *li⁴* 'strength', and their sister 丽 *li* 'beautiful', 月 *yue⁴* 'moon, month', 美 *mei²* 'beautiful', 梅 *mei²* 'plum blossom', 玫 *mei* 'rose'.[17] And just as *John* is an unsuitable name for your new-born daughter, so is *Springtime in Paris* an inappropriate name for a 1200cc Harley-Davidson motorbike or an auto-repair shop. *Wheels and Deals* might be a good name for a used car mart, but not for a new strain of corn, nor for a maternity boutique. People are well aware of these facts: the proper names of car models, rock bands, beauty salons, streets and university buildings show that namings are mostly systematic, and each genre develops its own themes and styles based on connotation.[18]

In the United States, place names containing *squaw* are numerous, and they are controversial because the term is regarded as dysphemistic by Native Americans and used derogatorily by a large number of whites. There have been a number of actions to have such place names as Squaw Peak (Arizona) and Squaw Lake (Minnesota) changed, generally without success. The origin of the word *squaw* is disputed; it is widely thought to derive from Mohawk *otsískwaʔ* 'vagina', which fuels anger, especially among women. However, Mohawks disagree. It is more likely to have been borrowed in the early seventeenth century from the Massachussett word for 'young woman'.[19] Native Americans view the use of *squaw* much the same way as African Americans view the use of *nigger*. This renders the main argument against the use of *squaw* in place names, and more generally, a matter of discourtesy to Native Americans.

Names can be descriptive, picking up on a salient characteristic perceived in, wanted for, or (sometimes ironically) imputed to the referent. The original motivation for such names is description; yet once the referent is named, the name is rigidly and persistently associated with its name-bearer. Examples are the topographical names *Green River*, *Black Mountain*, *Shiprock*; Ghanaian day names such as *Akua* (woman born on Wednesday), *Kofi* (man born on Friday);[20] the Puritan Christian name *If-Christ-Had-Not-Died-For-You-You-Had-Been-Damned*; the characteristics Shakespeare imputed to *Doll Tear-sheet*, *Pistol*, *Justice Shallow*; the implications of nicknames like *Shorty* and *Four-eyes* (and nicknames given to schoolteachers), adopted names like *Sid Vicious* (John Ritchie) and *Judy Garland* (Frances Gumm), or family names like *Baker* and *Smith*. In many communities, children are named after celebrated (and admired) religious and public figures: *Jesus*, the saints, *Lenin*, *Winston*, *Diana*. Many Chinese names include 福 *fu²* 'lucky, prosperous'. Other names are chosen to confuse evil spirits, e.g. Mongolian *Muunokhoi* 'vicious dog', *Nergui* 'no name', *Enebish* 'not this one'.[21] Sometimes, a sick Jewish child was given a false name so that an evil spirit could not find it; and sometimes, the child got a new name to renew its health.[22] This is comparable to a new name being given on initiation into adulthood, or a religious order, or marriage – a new identity for a new role. It all harks back to the notion that names somehow encapsulate the essence of the name-bearer; the very fact which motivates taboos on naming. Our own community's attitudes are reflected by Iago:

> Good name in man and woman, dear my lord,
> Is the immediate jewel of their souls.
> Who steals my purse steals trash; 'tis something, nothing;
> 'Twas mine, 'tis his, and has been slave to thousands;

But he that filches from me my good name
Robs me of that which not enriches him,
And makes me poor indeed.
(Shakespeare, *Othello*, III.iii.155)

When we say of John Dolittle's son, Dick, that *Dick's a real Dolittle*, we are speaking as if the surname itself carries the genes that make Dick 'a chip off the old block'. The same is true for phrases like *make a name for oneself, have a good name, bring one's name into disrepute, clear one's name*, and so forth. Even in our Anglo-society we speak and act as if the name carries the properties of the name-bearer. And names do in fact have some such force: that is why proper names enter the general lexicon, not only in direct reference to an original celebrated name-bearer, as in the case of *He's a little Hitler* (spoken of, for instance, Dick Dolittle), but also in the case of words like *boycott, lynch, xerox, biro, hoover, kleenex* and *tampax*. A name encapsulates the identity of a person or type of product. Perhaps that is why a foetus is very rarely named in any community (though it is sometimes given a temporary nickname); it is not yet a person. For the same reason, among some peoples (such as the Kayan, a Bahau group in Borneo) a child is not named for several weeks after birth and is not yet counted one of the family; and if it dies within this time it is given the same funeral rites as a stillborn child. Even in English, a child can often be referred to using the inanimate pronoun *it* because it is not yet fully identified as a person.

Native speakers of English readily recognize some names as Scottish, or Welsh, or Cornish, or Jewish; and immigrants to an English-speaking country who wish to assimilate sometimes Anglicize their names: e.g. *Piekarsky* becomes *Parkes*, *Klein* becomes *Clyne*. Personal names have semantic properties: *Papadopoulos* is tagged as originally a Greek name, *Pavarotti* Italian, and *Sanchez* Spanish. This property may be a matter for pride, but it can also be the stigma of an outsider. In the centuries before 1945, German anti-Semitism characterized Jews as disparaged outsiders at best and vermin at worst. Traditionally, Jews had no surnames, although *Joseph* might be known as *Joseph ben* ['son of'] *Nathan*. In 1812, Jews were 'emancipated' on condition that they adopted a fixed surname and German dress codes, and kept their account books in German.[23] Many Jews attempted to assimilate by exchanging their Hebrew names for German names, e.g. *Moses* was changed to *Moser, Moritz* or *Martin, Kohn*[24] to *Körner*. Unsympathetic officials favoured names of origin (*Berliner*), patronymics (*Davidsohn*), attributive names (*Perlmann*), and arbitrary names which might be as mild as *Goldberg, Goldstein, Rosenthal, Rosenblum, Rosengarten*, as quirky as *Hyanzinthenduft* 'hyacinth scent', or *Violensaft* 'violet sap', or as dysphemistic as *Nachtsweiss* 'nightsweat', *Totenkopf* 'death's head' or *Fick* 'fuck'. Animal names such as *Fuchs* 'fox', *Hähnelein* 'chicken', *Hirsch* 'stag', *Lamm* 'lamb', *Loewe* 'lion', *Reh* 'deer', *Taube* 'dove' and *Wolf* were almost all borne by Jews. Why were many German Jews so keen to abandon the names which labelled their heritage? Because Jewish names were publicly mocked. Not only were the name-bearers degraded by this; potential employers found Jewish names offensive. One female teacher was refused employment because the headmaster 'feared that the surname Itzig [a name subject to particular derision and abuse] could be exploited as a nickname by the children' and all hell would break loose in the school.[25] Thus, a name potentially provokes a very negative attitude toward the name-bearer based on racist (ethnicist) stereotyping of character, religion, morality, etc. by out-groupers. Less noticeably, it will evoke positive attitudes from in-groupers from the same onomastic community.

Styles of naming and addressing

Appropriate addressing or naming of someone depends on the role the speaker perceives the person addressed or named – henceforth 'hearer-or-named' – to have adopted relative to the speaker in the situation of utterance.[26] This role may change in different situations. For instance, Freddie and Eddie might be on first-name terms while having lunch together before a board meeting; but when conducting official business in the boardroom, where Freddie is Chairman of the Board, Eddie will probably address Freddie as *Mr Chairman* and name him *the chairman* in accordance with his role. However, in an unofficial aside Eddie can quite properly revert to using *Freddie*, even in the boardroom. It is not the physical situation of the speaker and the hearer-or-named that is relevant, but the hearer-or-named's perceived role relative to the speaker within that situation. High social status is not a right, but a prerequisite of those who can either make or persuade other people to recognize such status.

The relative status of the speaker and the hearer-or-named derives from two sources: their relative power, and the social distance between them. The relative power of the speaker and the hearer-or-named is defined by social factors which obtain in the situation of utterance. As we said in Chapter 2, the relative power of a physician and a highway patrolman is not given for every occasion, it depends on how they encounter one another: whether the highway patrolman is requiring a medical consultation at the doctor's office, or the doctor has been stopped on the highway for alleged dangerous driving. The social distance between the speaker and the hearer-or-named is determined by such parameters as their comparative ages, genders and socio-cultural backgrounds. The management of social status – of power and social distance relations – involves the management of face, and consequently the management of language choice. Hence the style and variety of language that the speaker uses will depend on two things:

- the role the speaker perceives the hearer-or-named to have adopted relative to the speaker in the current situation of utterance or, if need be, on some prior occasion;
- the speaker's communicative purpose on this present occasion; in particular, whether s/he intends to be insulting or not.

We discussed strategies for dysphemism in Chapters 2 and 3; here we discuss the speaker's use of addressing or naming forms which seek to either enhance the hearer-or-named's face or, in the least, to avoid loss of face by any party.

The harm that kings and chiefs can do ensures that they are nearly always surrounded by taboos, most of which were originally instituted to protect the stability of the community by protecting the ruler against malevolent spiritual, physical or political acts. Consequently, special language is often used, both when communicating with rulers and when talking about them. Perhaps as an antidote to downgrading a ruler, naming or addressing him/her often involves extreme pomp and circumstance, beset with euphemism. In *Gulliver's Travels*, Jonathan Swift mocked the splendiferous titles given to contemporary princes in the following address to the Emperor of Lilliput – a man slightly taller than Gulliver's middle finger was long:

GOLBASTO MOMAREN EVLAME GURDILLO SHEFIN MULLY ULLY GUE, most Mighty Emperor of *Lilliput*, Delight and Terror of the Universe, whose Dominions extend five Thousand Blustrugs, (about twelve Miles in Circumference) to the Extremities of the Globe: Monarch of all Monarchs: Taller than the Sons of Men; whose Feet press down to the Center, and whose Head strikes against the Sun: At whose Nod the Princes of the Earth shake their Knees; pleasant as the Spring, comfortable as the Summer, fruitful as Autumn, dreadful as Winter. His most sublime Majesty proposeth to the *Man-Mountain* [= Gulliver], lately arrived at our Celestial Dominions, the following Articles . . . (Swift 1958: 24)

This mode of addressing or naming exaggerates the importance of the hearer-or-named by magnifying his/her perceived or pretended higher social status. Today, it is often those in the lower ranks who get the longest titles, e.g. *the Personal Assistant to the Secretary (Special Activities)* for 'cook'. This exaggeration is a kind of euphemism. Now that we have constitutional monarchs and democratically elected presidents, the terror which our rulers once inspired has been replaced by a notional respect, while terror has become the mark of the petty dictator and terrorist. Yet the language used to rulers has remained much the same, even if it is no longer so very different from the respectful deference extended to other hearer-or-named persons of superior power to the speaker. At the March 1989 coronation of Prince Mangkubumi in Yogyakarta, Indonesia, the new Sultan was given the following title: *Ngarso dalem kanjeng ratu inkang sinuhan sri sultan hamengku buwono adipati ingalogo ngabdurahman sayidin panoto gomo kalifatullah kaping X*, which translates along the following lines: 'His Exalted Majesty, whose Honour Shines Bright, Sultan of all the world, Commander in Chief, Servant of God, Protector of Religion, Assistant to God, the tenth.' Some of the accolades to the Emperor of Lilliput and to the Sultan of Yogyakarta are blatantly false; for example, the latter is not truthfully 'Sultan of all the world'. It is the connotations of courtesy and honour that are important.

Where the speaker is inferior to the hearer-or-named, s/he will use unreciprocated (or conventionally unreciprocable) deferential forms such as *Your/her Majesty*, *Your/his Highness*, *Your Lordship*, *Mr President*, *Madam Chair*, etc., all of which are frozen or formal style.[27] These titles do not include names, but identify roles or social positions; so, to some extent, they impersonalize. So do terms like *Sir*, *Madam*, *this lady*, *the gentleman*, etc. which may be formal or consultative (and much less likely, frozen). Children addressing adults sometimes use the titles *Mr* or *Mrs* alone, which is reminiscent of consultative style. Even within that style, these – but not *Miss*! – would be dysphemistic from an adult speaker, although this may not be true for all dialects. In rather stilted English, the hearer can be addressed in the third person. We have done it ourselves, as *the astute reader* (you) will doubtless have noticed. Occasionally, one encounters similar forms in the more expensive shops, e.g. *If Madam so desires, she could have our tailor alter the waistband just a touch.* Then there is the use of *we* as an address form, particularly in questions. This is commonly used to children, *Ooh, we're not a happy little person, are we? Shall we drink up our milk?* and to adults by those offering a service: *How are we today?* (doctor to patient), *What would we like to drink?* (waitperson to diners).

The impersonalizing manner of naming and addressing that we have just been discussing might be compared with the regular use in some languages of third person address forms to the hearer. For example, the deferential Polish question in (1), using third person, contrasts with the familiar version in (2), which uses second person and roughly corresponds to the colloquial style[28] of English:

(1)	*Co*	*mama*	*robi?*		(2)	*Co*	*robisz,*	*mama?*
	what	mother	3.SG.do			what	2.SG.do	mum
	'What are you doing mother?'					'Wotcha doin', mum?'		

In the canonical speech situation where the speaker and the hearer are in face to face conversation, there is a greater psycho-social distance, and often a greater physical distance, between the speaker and a third person than between the speaker and the hearer (second person). This difference in relative distance is captured in the ordinals of the terms *first*, *second* and *third* persons. Third person is intrinsically more distant from the speaker than second person is; hence its use to the hearer exaggerates the social distance between the speaker and the hearer. Such exaggeration is a widely used euphemistic strategy for indicating deference.

Another way for the speaker to indicate deference is to address or name not the individual hearer-or-named, but to include the hearer-or-named among a number of people spoken of. For example, in French, the speaker uses the second person plural as a deferential mode for addressing a singular hearer in (3), the colloquial form in (4):

(3) *Vous êtes très gentille, madame.*
    2PL are very kind madam
    'You are very kind, madam.'

(4) *T'es   très   gentille, maman.*
    2SG.are very kind mummy
    'You're very kind, mummy.'

These address modes go back to Latin, and perhaps further. From the Middle Ages until the eighteenth century, the use of *thou* and *ye/you* in English was somewhat comparable to French *tu* and *vous*: to oversimplify, *thou* was used to God, for in-group solidarity, in contempt, to social inferiors and to animals; *you* was a mark of respect.[29] Spanish has *tú* and *vos*, used much like their French counterparts; and also *Usted* as a more distant polite form derived from *vuestra merced* 'your grace' (hence the abbreviation *Vd*), in which *vuestra* is the possessive of *vos*. However, *Usted* is third person singular (there is a plural *Ustedes*). The deferential address form in German uses the third person plural form, though *Sie* 'you' is orthographically marked by an initial capital letter. Compare:

(5) *Sie   sehen   gut   aus*
    3PL/2SG 3PL.see good out
    'They/You look good.'

(6) *Du   siehst   gut   aus, Mutti.*
    2SG 2SG.see good out, mum
    'You look good, mum.'

Spoken Tamil shows respect by using a third-person plural form when naming a third-person singular – *avaanka* and *pooranka* for *motal mantiri* in (7), which is from a radio commentary on an unfolding event.

(7) *motal mantiri avaanka mantikal koota pooranka*
    first minister 3PL.POSS ministers together.with 3PL.going
    'the prime minister is going, accompanied by his ministers'

In examples (3), (5) and (7), the speaker acts on the normal presumption that any individual is representative of a group, and derives social standing accordingly. Because there is safety in numbers, the hearer-or-named is less vulnerable as a member of a group than if s/he were alone – any threat to the hearer-or-named may be perceived as a threat to the whole group. Thus, the speaker will pretend to greater respect for the hearer-or-named than if the hearer-or-named were a lone individual. We can look upon this strategy as exaggerating the relative power of the hearer-or-named. And, as we have shown, the vehicle for this is a plural form instead of the singular form for a single hearer-or-named. This strategy is somewhat less impersonalizing than the use of third person in place of second person.

The strategies we have been discussing can be ranked on an impersonalizing scale for naming or addressing single individuals:

most personalized 2SG – 2PL – 3SG – 3PL least personalized

But we know of no language that employs more than three of these (e.g. Spanish and eighteenth-century German have three). Rather than conflating the two strategies for marking deference on one personalizing scale correlating with relative status, it is more appropriate to recognize two distinct systems motivated by the components of social status: namely, social distance and power.[30] We have already done this in discussion, and we sum it up as follows:

- The **distance strategy** is used when deference to the hearer is marked by exaggerating the social distance between the speaker and hearer, e.g. by using third person to Hearer.
- The **power strategy** is used when deference to the hearer-or-named can be marked by exaggerating his/her power relative to the speaker, e.g. by using plural number for a single referent.

Languages like Japanese[31] and Korean have respect and humility markers in verbs, e.g.:

(8) *Watasi ga   iku.*
     I   NOM   go.CASUAL
(9) *Watasi ga   ikimas.*
                    go.POLITE
(10) *Watasi ga   mairimas.*
                    go.HUMBLE.POLITE
         'I'm going.'

The conventions of a particular language severely constrain the choices available to an individual speaker. In every language, the speaker may register a change in attitude towards the hearer-or-named by changing the style of naming or addressing from that which s/he has been using in prior discourse, or which s/he normally uses.

Consider occasions where the speaker wishes to display anger by using a linguistic form which distances him/her from the hearer-or-named in an abnormal way. For instance, a speaker who normally uses an intimate or casual style with a hearer-or-named will typically shift to a more formal style; the speaker may switch from given-name only (*Homer*) to given-name⌒surname, title⌒surname or surname alone (*Homer Simpson* or *Mr Simpson* or just *Simpson*). In some other languages, such as French or Japanese, the speaker can display anger by substituting out-group forms for normal in-group forms: using *vous* in place of *tu* in French. In Japanese, a section manager is normally addressed by the title *kachoo* and not by the pronoun *anata* 'you' (originally '(person) over there'); but during a staff protest s/he might be addressed by *anata* or even the colloquial *anta*:

(11) *Kachoo   ga   soo ossyaimasita.*
     section.manager NOM SO   say.HONOR.POLITE.PAST

(12) *Anata   ga   soo iimasita.*
     you   SO   say.POLITE.PAST
     'You said so.'

Social-distance marking in forms used for naming and especially addressing can be achieved in many languages through sarcastic use of intimate terms. In English, the angry speaker who is inferior in status to the hearer-or-named may use title alone (*Mr*) or an inappropriately familiar term (*bud*, *mate*). In French or Japanese, a speaker can insult a socially distant (out-group) hearer by using an in-group address form (such as French *tu*); in Japanese, a socially distant third person can be insulted in a similar way by the speaker using an in-group pronoun or verb form, e.g. *Ano yaroo ga soo iiyagatta* 'That guy said so [impolite form]'. Undisguised sarcasm in naming and addressing is of course dysphemistic, whatever style the speaker adopts: it is just as offensive to address a superior hearer with a sarcastic *Sir*, as it is to address someone of similar status with a sarcastic *Dear*. All languages have conventional strategies of one kind or another that allow a speaker to display antipathy by varying the normal mode of address or naming.

The hearer-or-named's self-image depends in part on the perception of his/her own status relative to the speaker, and of the social distance between them at the time of utterance. If the hearer-or-named perceives that either the social distance or the relative status is significantly distorted by the speaker, there will be an effect on his/her positive face. The kind of effect we are concerned with here is a detrimental one, in which the hearer-or-named's positive face is affronted. The following, taken from a letter to the editor of a German-Swiss journal *Der Schweizerische Beobachter*,[32] reports just such an affront:

In fact, we have a little problem. Recently my wife and I offered the fiancé of our daughter to say 'Du' to him. He then asked how he should address us. We explained he could address us just as he liked; we thought he would say either 'Mutter' and 'Vater' or 'Mama' and 'Papa'. However, we are greatly surprised to see that the young man calls us now by our first names. Whilst our daughter thinks this is all right, modern and colloquial, we ourselves find this world hostile and confounded. Being both about fifty years old, are we already hopelessly antiquated? (Adler 1978: 202)

In Germany, *du* is used to deities and saints (and also the deceased person at a funeral); it is used to children and used by them to peers up to their twenties. However, a child may expect strangers to use *Sie* from about fifteen; indeed, there is a law in many Länder that requires teachers to use *Sie* to students in the final few years of secondary school. According to Raymond Hickey, if they first meet on neutral ground (e.g. as next-door neighbours), speakers over thirty use *Sie* when they first meet, and unless a suitable occasion arises to switch to *du*, continue to use *Sie* for ever.[33] However, the choice of initial address form really depends on the character of the speaker, the semiotics of dress and appearance of the addressee, and the context of encounter.[34] Some bosses resist accepting *du* in the belief that control will be lost if criticism or a reprimand is warranted; others insist on *du* to create the impression of equality. The move from *Sie* to *du* involves an offer from the more powerful member of the dyad, and is rarely without ceremony. One initial move is to say something like *Sie können mich doch Hans nennen* 'you can call me Hans', where *Hans* is (an abbreviated) first name; but the use of *du* doesn't necessarily follow. Reverting from *du* to *Sie* is usually the result of some irreparable rift.[35]

Returning to the use of naming and addressing with the consultative style in English: the speaker will employ consultative style to address or name using *title⌒surname* for the task, e.g. *Mr Smith*, (a) where the speaker is superior in status to, but of friendly disposition towards, the hearer-or-named or (b) where the speaker and hearer-or-named are of similar social status but there is considerable social distance between them. If the speaker is superior in status to the hearer-or-named, s/he can choose either to maintain the status difference or to be less formal and show solidarity by using in-group markers; these demonstrate a concern to enhance the hearer-or-named's positive face,[36] by seeking to make the hearer-or-named feel good about themselves. Where the speaker and the hearer-or-named are of similar social status and there is little social distance between them, the informal in-group language found in colloquial styles is the regular mark of solidarity. These styles are marked by contractions, ellipsis, diminutives, colloquialisms, and perhaps slang and swearing.[37] Among adults, address forms in colloquial style include given name or nickname, perhaps with the surname; also American English *bud(dy)*, Australian and southern British English *mate*, northern British

(Geordie and Cumbrian) *marra*, southern British *old boy* (possibly archaic), and *brother* or *sister* in various American, Australian and British sociolects. These forms of address are also used in intimate style, and where we also find such terms as *auntie, babe, baby, daddy, darling, dear, duckie, ducks, fella(s), gorgeous, grandad, guys, handsome, honey, hunk, love (luv), lover, mac, momma, sexy, sis, sugar, sweetheart*, and a whole lot more.

In many English-speaking families, it remains dysphemistic to address or name consanguineal kin of an ascending generation by their given names. Instead, speakers use kin titles such as *Dad, Nan, Grandpa*, etc. for lineal kin; and for lateral kin, a kin title like *Auntie*, or *kin title⌢given name*, e.g. *Aunt Jemima*. If lineal kin of the second and higher ascending generations need to be distinguished from a collateral with the same title, *kin title⌢surname* is the usual form used, e.g. *Grandma Robinson* versus *Grandma Carter*. The social taboo against omitting the kin title is weakest with kin from the first ascending generation who are about the same age as the speaker, particularly collateral kin and step-kin; it is strongest with kin of the second and higher ascending generations. These are, of course, asymmetric conventions: given name only is the norm when the hearer-or-named is close kin of a descending generation; though more distant affinal kin from a descending generation may warrant *title⌢surname*.[38] Amongst the religious groups of Old Order Amish and Old Order Mennonites in Pennsylvania, USA and Ontario, Canada, everyone gives and receives first names only, regardless of relative familiarity, status, age and sex. These practices manifest the doctrine of humility. There exist no titles and no honorifics; even for use on public occasions like a church service or during any of the rites of passage. Furthermore, first names are derived only from the Old Testament, and there is a limited number of family names; in the small Mennonite town of St Jacobs in Waterloo County, Ontario, there were at one time twenty-seven David Martins registered at the local post office! So, most people have a distinguishing nickname (often gently mocking) that can be used to refer to some absent person.

Many Aboriginal Australians, Austronesians and Papuans traditionally taboo names for some kinsfolk, especially affines and, to a lesser extent, cross-consanguineal kin – in particular, siblings of the other sex, cross-cousins and 'clan brothers and sisters'.[39] In many societies, e.g. among the Zia, a non-Austronesian people who live in Morobe Province in south-eastern Papua New Guinea, personal names are not used among spouses, siblings, and often not to descending generations. Instead, speakers use kin titles and the translation equivalents of terms like *person, man, woman, boy, girl*. Other societies use public names, nicknames, clan names and kin descriptions like *mother of X*. Because relationships with in-laws are notoriously difficult in all societies, the so-called 'mother-in-law' languages[40] (*hlonipha* among the Nguni), and all similar taboos on naming and addressing kinsfolk are perhaps grounded in the desire to maintain social harmony.

Where the speaker should conventionally defer to the hearer-or-named because there is considerable social distance between them, or because of the latter's superior status, it is dysphemistic for the speaker to employ the naming or addressing forms from a lower style than convention warrants; such behaviour will affront the hearer-or-named's positive face – the person's wish, that s/he and things dear to him/her, be valued by others. And it is not only the person of superior status who can be affronted in this way: if the leering middle-aged male manager addresses a young female office worker as *sweetheart*, she might well object that the social distance between them requires at least the casual level of formality, and so find this intimate style offensive. Today, this particular affront would often be classed as 'sexist', which is not necessarily strictly accurate: it is the inappropriate intimate style which is the basic source of the problem here. (We won't guarantee that this nicety would sway the court if the office worker brought a sexual harassment charge against her manager.)

The last example is interesting: one might imagine that if the speaker is superior in status to the hearer-or-named and chooses nevertheless to adopt a casual or intimate style, then the hearer-or-named should be flattered – that is, experience positive face enhancement. However, in practice this is the result only when the superior's behaviour is welcome. It will be recalled from Chapter 2 that face is grounded in a person's wants; and, despite there being conventional beliefs about what a person might be expected to want, ultimately a person's wants are idiosyncratic. There are people (of no matter what status and social distance from oneself) whom one is pleased to (be seen to) come close to, and to have that closeness marked by the use of casual or intimate style; and there are other people whom one wishes to maintain a social distance from, a distance that is demonstrable through linguistic marking.

Throughout this book, we have sought to maintain *gender-neutral* language; for example, referring to the speaker and hearer as *s/he* and *him/her*, and the like. While this probably offends some among our readership, we believe it should offend the smallest number of people overall; consequently, it is nowadays our own preferred habit. In the late 1960s, the feminist movement began to make itself heard, objecting to a community attitude that downgraded women by comparison with men. People in the movement perceived this depreciating attitude to be reflected in language, and sought to change at least public language so that it should become less dysphemistic to women. They held, and continue to hold, the view that revising habits of language use will change community attitudes. Since the 1970s, a large number of guidelines for non-sexist language usage in private and public institutions, government offices, etc. have been issued.[41] Speakers and writers are advised to choose a gender neutral alternative to the generic use of *man* when referring to *human beings* in general, to prefer *chair* or *chairperson* to *chairman*, *supervisor* to *foreman*, etc. Obviously, the *-man* locutions are not dysphemistic when used of a male denotatum, and the neutral locution is primarily intended to name the office (job) itself, so as to acknowledge that women may hold such an office. It might be thought that terms suffixed *-ess*, and others such as *lady/woman doctor*, should be acceptable to a female referent; but it is widely perceived that women referred to using such terms are less highly valued than their male counterparts, therefore the terms are dysphemistic and the neutral alternatives are preferred for a female referent. There is a lot of experimental evidence that generic masculines (as in *As for the man in the street, he is rarely a spokesman for anybody* or *Every schoolchild should do his homework regularly if he wants to do well in life*) do in fact favour male reference and male images over females – both for male and female language users; this bias disappears when gender neutral terms are used. Unbiased generics also improve females' recall of texts they have read.[42] It is worth mentioning that individuals differ greatly in their attitudes to the terms listed as dysphemistic; a number of women are quite happy to be *Madam Chairman*, because they understand the word *chairman* as an idiom denoting the office of chairperson: on this view it should no more be decomposed into 'chair' and 'man' than either of *moonshine* meaning 'illegal liquor', or *fathead* meaning 'idiot, fool', should be decomposed into a semantically transparent pair of morphemes.

It is recommended in guides to non-sexist usage that address forms for women should be comparable with the address forms for men used in the same context. In the absence of knowing anything about the particular preferences of the individuals concerned, introducing a couple as e.g. *Dr and Mrs John Dolittle* might not cause offence to the lady thus named, but there is a growing number of women who have no wish to be named as if they are an appendage to their husband – which is one of the motivations for women not adopting their husband's surname. Moreover, John Dolittle's wife might well be due the title *Dr* herself;[43] we know of several occasions when offence has been caused by an insensitive introduction of this nature. Even worse, of course, are occasions where the superior title due to a wife or other female companion is wrongly transferred to her male partner because of entrenched expectations of differing relative achievements of men and women. Because a new convention is slowly replacing the old one, the speaker (particularly the male speaker) needs to be wary.

Taboos in naming and addressing

A personal name is an inalienable part of one's identity; it is the essence of self and it is a means by which one is known to one's fellows. Prisoners are often required to self-refer using a number, as a means of dehumanizing and degrading them. Rites of passage (and going into showbusiness) are often marked by the adoption of a new name to match the new identity. It is this correlation between name and self that leads to taboos on names. Knowing a person's name is felt to be similar to having possession of the name-bearer's soul. This is why, in many communities, a person has a secret name that captures his/her true identity and is known only to very few intimates, and a public name which can be put off like an article of clothing. Calling a name can be harmful to the name-bearer and the caller: it may be that the attention of a malevolent force is drawn to the name-bearer; the caller too is put at risk of malevolence falling upon him/her. All kinds of malevolent forces may strike: humans, devils, deities, ghosts, dangerous animals, sickness, death. In our society, *a good name* is jealously preserved and may be defended in a court of law. This is evidence of the strong taboo against *bringing someone's name into disrepute*.

Proper names are subject to censoring behaviour and are therefore usually chosen with care. Many communities have constraints on naming and most have some names peculiar to the community. Part of any individual's identity is shared with the clan, tribe, nation or religion. Consequently, a person is stigmatized by his/her name, a fact that may have either positive consequences among in-groupers, or negative consequences as a result of -IST stereotyping of the individual. -IST dysphemisms have the common property that they fail to demonstrate respect for some personal characteristic which is important to the hearer-or-named's self-image and his/her public image, too. Very few names are truly unique, though there are often constraints against two people holding the same name within a given community. In all human communities, most personal names distinguish males from females. And whereas common names differ greatly from one language to another (unless these are related), proper names tend to be transferred between languages, though phonological and morphological standardization is usual; for example *London* is French *Londres*, Tohono O'odham *Cuk Ṣon* was the basis for *Tucson*, *Kirinyaga* was the basis for (Mount) *Kenya*, the plural suffix in *Athēnai* gets picked up in *Athens*, αριστοτέλης is anglicized to *Aristotle*.

We discussed styles of naming and addressing, as affected by the perceived role and status within the context of the talk exchange of the speaker and the person addressed or named. We discussed ways in which the speaker demonstrates disaffection, disdain or anger with the hearer-or-named by using a style at the opposite pole of formality from the one normally required to mark the proper social distance between the hearer-or-named and the speaker. Because this will affront the hearer-or-named's self-image, such behaviour is dysphemistic. Normally, though, politeness is preserved by appropriate use (i.e. censoring) of names and forms of address.

7   Sex and bodily effluvia

This chapter examines the language for sex, gender, sexuality, sexual behaviours, tabooed bodily functions and effluvia from the organs of sex, micturition and defecation (SMD organs). Sexual activity is tabooed as a topic for public display and severely constrained as a topic for discussion. The language of sexual pleasuring and copulation gives rise to a great deal of verbal play and figurative language. Rather curiously for something that is indulged in for fun, as we saw in Chapter 3, it is also a source for terms of heinous insult; this is presumably a hangover from a time when all sex was unholy, except as necessary for procreative purposes between married couples. Our discussion of the language of bodily functions and effluvia makes a special study of the menstruation taboo.

Sex, gender and sexuality

It behoves us to define a few of the categorical terms we use. **Sex** is anatomical, and most people are born to one or the other sex (though a few are born sexually ambiguous and must be surgically altered to one of the sexes if they are not to remain that way). A person's **gender** is his/her identity as a certain kind of social being; gender normally coincides with sex, but it does not necessarily do so. People whose gender does not match their sex may choose to become transsexual and be chemically and/or surgically changed. All possible combinations of female, male, masculine and feminine occur; for instance, female-to-male transsexuals who prefer relationships with gay males! This last is an expression of **sexuality**: having certain kinds of sexual desires.[1] The two classic orientations are *heterosexuality* and *homosexuality*; these terms came into use in the mid nineteenth century, although the practices have been with humankind since the beginning. At first, *heterosexual sex* was any kind of non-procreative male–female sex, including oral sex. Today, it is used of any kind of sexual intercourse between male and female. Homosexuality is a degree of sexual intercourse between individuals of the same sex. However, as we shall see, the true picture of sexual relations among human beings is nothing like so cut and dried.

All sex is subject to taboos and censoring, but the taboos on male homo-sexuality and 'unfaithful' wives have been strongest. Indeed, they have been much the same as taboos on the much rarer phenomenon of sexual intercourse between human and animal: *bestiality*. In most cultures, the strongest taboos have been against non-procreative sex and sexual intercourse outside of a family unit sanctioned by religion and lore or legislation. Although these strictures have been relaxed in modern Anglo societies, their hold has not completely loosened.

Masturbation: taboo and therapy

> Frigging in the rigging,
> Wanking in the planking,
> Masturbating in the grating,
> There was fuck all else to do.
> (The Sex Pistols, *Friggin' in the riggin'*, chorus)

Masturbation is stimulation of the genitals for sexual satisfaction that is not achieved through penetrative intercourse or oral sex. It is typically carried out by individuals themselves, but masturbation by a heterosexual or same-sex partner is common, and for many centuries was a therapy for 'hysteria'. Masturbation begins, for both sexes, not at puberty but in the womb, from when the foetus is thirty-two weeks.[2] It is generally agreed that males masturbate more than females.[3]

Masturbation has been tabooed for at least four reasons:

- Masturbation involves stimulation of the genitals, not for procreation but for pure pleasure – it is seen by some as an unnatural act because it goes against God's plan for procreation.[4]
- Masturbation is supposedly addictive.
- Masturbation typically involves manipulation of the genital organs (hence the Latin term *manustuprationum*), giving rise to the emission of effluvium.
- It was long believed that seminal fluid and its counterpart in women, vaginal secretion, was refined blood that bore generative seed; wasting such precious fluid was supposedly even more debilitating than loss of blood.[5]

These four characteristics provide the principal rationale for the church to castigate masturbation as a mortal sin, akin to suicide. The church took its cue from God's treatment of Onan in Genesis 38: 6–10:

6 And Judah took a wife for Er his first born, whose name was Tamar. 7 And Er, Judah's firstborn, was wicked in the sight of the LORD; and the LORD slew him. 8 And Judah said unto Onan, Go unto thy brother's wife, and marry her, and raise up seed to

thy brother. 9 And Onan knew that the seed should not be his; and it came to pass when he went in unto his brother's wife, that he spilled it on the ground, lest that he should give seed to his brother. 10 And the thing he did displeased the LORD: wherefore he slew him also.

By not impregnating his dead brother's wife and naming their firstborn Er, Onan was violating custom; it is not clear whether God slew him for this or for spilling his seed on the ground, or perhaps both. The church focused on the spilling of semen on the ground and interpreted it as achieved through the sin of masturbation, though it was occasionally interpreted as the less sinful *coitus interruptus* (an orthophemism poorly matched by euphemisms *pull out* and *withdraw*). It is tempting to see the church fathers' abomination of masturbation as partly motivated by their own guilty consciences in recalling their personal experiences of *the horrible act, infamous practice, odious action, the crime, the solitary/secret/destructive vice, vile sin, beastliness*[6] *of self-pleasuring, self-defilement, self-abuse, self-pollution, touching oneself, playing/fiddling/twiddling with oneself.*

Although masturbation was always thought to lead to weakening of the mind and body, this view was ramped into hysteria by the anonymous publication in 1715 of *Onania or the heinous sin of self-pollution, and all its frightful consequences in both sexes considered, with spiritual and physical advice to those who have already injured themselves by this abominable practice*. There were many editions (at least twenty-two by 1778) and it grew from a few pages to over 300, incorporating many letters supposedly from victims of the vice. The apocryphal author is a Dr Bekkers, but there is no evidence that a person of that name existed; it is certain that the author was a quack and a clever one.[7] It was in a response to this pamphlet that the term *onanism* was coined as a euphemism for *masturbation*. From the eighteenth until the early twentieth century, the medical fraternity throughout Europe followed *Onania*'s lead in attributing to masturbation a mind-boggling range of afflictions:

> genital and urinary problems (including impotence and infertility),
> digestive problems,
> respiratory diseases,
> blindness,
> muscle degenerations of all kinds,
> physical deformities of many kinds,
> mental deficiency,
> madness, and
> a pain-wracked path to early death.

Needless to say, parents, teachers, guardians and a concerned society sought to protect children and young adults from the disastrous effects of masturbation, mostly with threats of incarceration in hell and in asylums for the blind, the mad or the infirm; the self-righteous guardians beat their charges, tied hands to bed posts, made children wear special restrictive garments, placed camphor and other noxious powders in underwear, had them infibulated or threatened with castration and clitoridectomy. From the late nineteenth century, it came to be recognized by the medical profession that:

masturbation does neither more nor less harm than sexual intercourse practised with the same frequency in the same conditions of general health and age and circumstance . . . I have seen as numerous and as great evils consequent on excessive sexual intercourse as on excessive masturbation: but I have not seen or heard anything to make me believe that occasional masturbation has any other effects on one who practices it than has occasional sexual intercourse, nor anything justifying the dread which sexual hypochondriacs regard the having occasionally practised it. I wish I could say something worse of so nasty a practice; an uncleanliness, a filthiness forbidden by God, and unmanliness despised by men. (Paget 1879: 291f)

Paget was Queen Victoria's physician and a distinguished academic. Why masturbation had for centuries been thought so much more dangerous to one's health than copulation was never satisfactorily explained. Such explanation as there was hinged on the belief that masturbation is an unnatural vice but copulation is natural, and so all the vital juices that are lost in 'self-abuse' are somehow passed back to oneself during copulation; perhaps it was believed that some went into the creation of new life, but we haven't found this mentioned. (Masturbation by a lover was not discussed and perhaps not even considered.) Although the medical profession now recognizes that there are probably no ill effects from masturbation, in folk memory the masturbator still risks being unable to engage in successful copulation, going blind, becoming mentally and physically feeble, and dying early. In both sexes, orgasm is thought to weaken a person, but particularly males; and it is part of sports folklore that celibacy should be observed before participating in a major sporting event.

Masturbate is an orthophemism. There are many slang expressions like *rodwalloping* – one of many words compounded with a stem verb, with the sense 'strike with the hand'; others are *beat the bishop/beaver, pull the pope, pull one's pud, crank one's shank, jerkin' the gherkin, spank the monkey, tweak one's twinkie, juice the sluice, stump-jump*;[8] and for women *finger, diddle* (from Old English *dyderian* 'cheat, deceive'),[9] *fishfinger* and the archaic *firkytoodle* are dysphemistic euphemisms. So too are expressions applicable to both sexes: *frig* (which has the same root as *friction*), *wank (off)* (*wank* is etymologically related to *wench*, curiously enough; the Germanic verb meant something like 'shake, waver', hence perhaps the misogynistic 'be inconsistent like a woman is'), *five finger exercise, finger fucking, make love to one's fist, pull one's pud* (⇐ *pudendum*), *jerk/jack*[10]*/jay/j- off,* *whack off, get off, come off, beat off, bring off, toss off* (which Grose glosses as 'Manual pollution'). Note the common occurrence of the particle *off* in phrasal verbs of masturbating: this particle captures the release from pent-up desire which motivates masturbation. In Australia (and Britain too), a nice extension of the figurative meaning of *wank* has developed, such that *a wank* is 'a self-indulgence' and *a wanker* is 'a charlatan, a humbug, a prick'. Both nouns are readily quoted in newspapers from the utterings of public figures – which indicates that they are not strongly tabooed; they are, however, dysphemistic.

By tradition, masturbation will lead to the physical and mental degradation of the masturbator:

'And will it not take time to work out our Church dogma that masturbation will render the Catholic lad blind, hairy-palmed, insane, doomed, and with the leg bones bent like an orphan with the rickets?' ([Boston-Irish policeman] Shem 1978: 395)

Male masturbation is mostly self-administered and not normally under medical instruction. There is a different story for female masturbation. According to the seventeenth-century physician Thomas Sydenham, the most common of all diseases except fevers was 'hysteria'.[11] The symptoms of *praefocatio matricis* 'suffocation of the mother' or *suffocatio ex semine retento* 'suffocation because of retained seed [not semen but the vaginal secretion that results from sexual arousal]' were anxiety, sleeplessness, irritability, nervousness, erotic fantasy, sensations of heaviness in the abdomen, lower pelvic oedema and vaginal lubrication. The standard treatment from the time of Hippocrates (470–377 BCE) until the 1920s was:

When these symptoms indicate, we think it necessary to ask a midwife to assist, so that she can massage the genitalia with one finger inside, using oil of lilies, musk root, crocus, or similar. And in this way the afflicted woman can be aroused to the paroxysm. This kind of stimulation with the finger is recommended by Galen and Avicenna, among others, most especially for widows, those who live chaste lives, and female religious, as Gradus proposes; it is less often recommended for very young women, public women, or married women, for whom it is a better remedy to engage in intercourse with their spouses. (Forestus 1653 III, 28; quoted in Maines 1999: 1)

When the patient was single, a widow, unhappily married, or a nun, the cure was effected by vigorous horseback exercise, by movement of the pelvis in a swing, rocking chair, or carriage, or by massage of the vulva by a physician or midwife . . . Single women of marriageable age who experienced hysterical symptoms were usually urged to marry and, as Ambroise Paré [1517–90] expressed it in the sixteenth century, 'bee strongly encountered by their husbands'. (Maines 1999: 8f)

Over the centuries it was practised, vaginal or vulval massage to orgasm became just another skill that male physicians and midwives must perfect for the benefit of their patients. (Blackledge 2003: 258)

Part of society believed that orgasm is essential to female health, and another part that female orgasm was somehow bestial. It is a fact that orgasm relieves such symptoms as pelvic hyperaemia, sleeplessness, anxiety, headaches and nervousness. Massage was often delegated to midwives, and eventually machines (manual and other) at ancient, medieval and modern bath houses or spas – venues that have been associated with sexual activity since antiquity. Roman baths were noted venues for prostitution, and the spas at Bath in England also had a scandalous reputation. Mechanical devices were quickly favoured because they accomplished within five minutes what the physician took an hour to achieve by manual stimulation.[12] Before vibrators came on the market, 'hysterical' women were encouraged to use jets of water, take up horseback riding, use treadle sewing machines, ride bicycles and even travel on trains (!). Mortimer Granville invented a portable battery powered vibrator in 1893 for the purpose of massage, though he did not approve of it being used for masturbation. However, vibrator ads appeared in the *Companion* as early as 1906 'for equipment strongly resembling the devices now sold to women as masturbation aids'.[13]

The first home appliance to be electrified was the sewing machine in 1889, followed in the next ten years by the fan, the teakettle, the toaster, and the vibrator. The last preceded the electric vacuum cleaner by some nine years, the electric iron by ten, and the electric frying pan by more than a decade, possibly reflecting consumer priorities. (Maines 1999: 100)

From first decade of twentieth century until the 1920s, the vibrator was

marketed as a home appliance through advertising in such periodicals as *Needlecraft*, *Home Needlework Journal*, *Modern Women*, *Hearst's*, *McClure's*, *Woman's Home Companion*, and *Modern Priscilla*. The device was marketed mainly to women as a health and relaxation aid, in ambiguous phrases such as 'all the pleasures of youth . . . will throb within you'. (Maines 1999: 19)

As we saw in Figure 2.2, the advertising patter has not changed. The American Vibrator advertised in *Woman's Home Companion* of April 1906, p. 42, '**can be used by yourself** in the privacy of dressing room or boudoir, and furnishes every woman with the very essence of perpetual youth' [*sic*]. The Bebout Vibrator sold for five dollars; the ad for it in *National Home Journal* of 1908 reads, 'Gentle, soothing, invigorating and refreshing. Invented by a woman who knows a woman's needs. All nature pulsates and vibrates with life.' In *Modern Priscilla* of April 1913, an ad promised 'a machine that gives 30,000 thrilling, invigorating, penetrating, revitalizing vibrations per minute'. The *Sears, Roebuck Catalogue* of 1918, p. 4, lists vibrators as 'Aids That Every Woman Appreciates'. Clearly, vibrators were being marketed to women for private use as frequently as they desired; and doubtless the more daring would involve their partners, too. The vibrator as a home and professional medical instrument was dropped by the retail catalogues when it began to be featured in porn films like *Widow's Delight* during the 1920s. When the vibrator reappeared in the mid 1960s, it was marketed as a *sex aid* and *personal care appliance*. Vibrators were always available in the United States in the between years, and presumably in other countries as well.[14]

When oral sex is not having sexual relations

There are no true euphemisms for oral sex; *give me oral pleasure* (used by a woman in the film *Pulp Fiction*) is possibly one. For oral–genital sex, the most orthophemistic terms are *fellatio* and *cunnilingus*, whose colloquial counterparts (which may count as orthophemisms in the sex industry) are *give head*; *give French*; *sit on someone's face*; *get/go down on*; *eat (out)*; *give/ do a blow job*; *soixante-neuf/sixty-nine* ('Wine me, dine me, sixty-nine me'); *suck off*; *tongue*, etc. There is also *anilingus* ('oral–anal sex'), probably more common among homosexual males than other pairings. The colloquial counterparts are *rim job* and *rimming*. Oral sex may be included in foreplay or replace copulation; it is subject to similar taboos. If Kinsey's figures are anything to go by, there is less of a taboo on fellatio than there used to be: he found that 29 per cent of wives born before 1900 practised it, compared to 57 per cent of women born in the 1920s.[15] Among male homosexuals, it is normal for *trade* – who normally regard themselves as straight – to offer their cock for sucking (as they would say). Of course, other queers engage in oral sex, just as heterosexuals do.

On 26 January 1998, US President Bill Clinton famously said 'I did not have sexual relations with that woman, Miss Lewinsky' despite the fact that he did finger her genitals and she fellated him. In his autobiography, Clinton writes:

> the definition [of *sexual relations*] covered most intimate contact beyond kissing by the person being asked the question, if it was done for gratification or arousal. It seemed to require both a specific act and a certain state of mind on my part, and did not include any act by another person. (Clinton 2004: 773)

The definition Clinton refers to was the one offered by Paula Jones' legal team and accepted by Judge Susan Webber Wright:[16]

> For the purposes of this deposition, a person engages in 'sexual relations' when the person knowingly engages in or causes –
>
> 1. contact with the genitalia, anus, groin, breast, inner thigh, or buttocks of any person with an intent to arouse or gratify the sexual desire of any person;
> 2. contact between any part of the person's body or an object and the genitals or anus of another person; or

3. contact between the genitals or anus of the person and any part of another person's body. 'Contact' means intentional touching, either directly or through clothing. (http://www. washingtonpost.com/wp-srv/politics/special/clinton/stories/clintondep031398.htm. Accessed October 2004)

In a 1991 survey, 60% of 599 undergraduates at a midwestern university in the United States would have agreed with Clinton's assessment. Stephanie Sanders and Julie Reinsich[17] found that what counts as *having sex* is penile–vaginal intercourse for 99.5% of this population, penile–anal intercourse for 80% of them, oral sex for 40%, genital fondling for 15%, and breast/nipple fondling only 3%.

Speaking of orgasm

The purpose of masturbation, oral sex and, of course, copulation is usually to achieve *orgasm* (orthophemism). Orgasm was once viewed as the shaking forth of seed (for both sexes) and is now perceived as the climax to a journey, hence *Are you there?* The alternatives are *climax, spend oneself, the big O* (euphemisms), *coming, seminal discharge, come* or *cum* – the latter two being nouns for *the vaginal secretion of a sexually excited woman*, as well as *a man's ejaculate* or *seminal fluid* (orthophemism), his *seed* (euphemism) or (the dysphemisms) *spunk, spoof* and *gis(su)m/giz(zu)m*.[18] This sense of the term *spunk* possibly arises from the sense 'man of spirit, mettle' (*mettle* is an archaic term for seminal fluid), which has now been extended to 'sexually attractive man or woman' as in *s/he is a spunk*. A man may also *spit white, get his rocks off, spend himself, drop his load* and *shoot*; the latter links the action with the weapon metaphor for *penis*. Hyperboles like *die, explode*, etc. describe the effect of orgasm. Men occasionally fake orgasm to save face and women frequently do it to please their partner.[19] It is well known that women can out-orgasm men:

[T]he highest number of female orgasms recorded [during one hour] in a laboratory setting was 134, whereas the top score for men in the same length of time was sixteen. (Blackledge 2003: 275)

Such feats put quite a gloss on the orthophemistic phrase *multiple orgasms*. The comparative inadequacy of the poor male is nicely captured in Rochester's long poem *The Imperfect Enjoyment*, which recounts a mutually successful first love-making, then

> Smiling, she chides in a kind murmuring noise,
> And from her body wipes the clammy joys,
> When, with a thousand kisses wandering o'er
> My panting bosom, 'Is there then no more?'
> She cries. 'All this love and rapture's due;
> Must we not pay a debt to pleasure too?'

> But I, the most forlorn, lost man alive,
> To show my wished obedience vainly strive:
> I sigh, alas! and kiss, but cannot swive.
> Eager desires confound my first intent,
> Succeeding shame does more success prevent,
> And rage at last confirms me impotent.
> Ev'n her fair hand, which might bid heat return
> To frozen age, and make cold hermits burn,
> Applied to my dead cinder, warms no more
> Than fire to ashes could past flames restore.
> Trembling, confused, despairing, limber, dry,
> A wishing, weak, unmoving lump I lie.
> This dart of love . . .
> Now languid lies in this unhappy hour,
> Shrunk up, and sapless like a withered flower.
> [He continues by cursing 'the base deserter of my flame']
> (Rochester 1968, *The Imperfect Enjoyment*, lines 19–45)

Some of the poetic figures Rochester uses would be found in the language of almost anyone who set about describing the situation.

Insults concerning orgasm typically refer to premature ejaculation by the male and frigidity on the part of the female partner.

Homosexuality and other queer behaviour

In the Bible, God decrees to Moses that for adultery, cross-generational incest and bestiality, the penalty was death. So too for male homosexuality:

If a man also lie with mankind, as he lieth with a woman, both of them have committed an abomination: they shall surely be put to death; their blood shall be upon them. (Leviticus 20: 13; see also Leviticus 18: 22)

Though female bestiality is damned in Leviticus 20: 16, female homosexuality is overlooked in the Old Testament,[20] but condemned along with male homosexuality by St Paul in verse 26 of Romans 1:

24 Wherefore God also gave them [Gentiles] up to uncleanness through the lusts of their own hearts, to dishonour their own bodies between themselves: 25 Who changed the truth of God into a lie, and worshipped and served the creature more than the Creator, who is blessed for ever. Amen. 26 For this cause God gave them up unto vile affections: for even their women did change the natural use into that which is against nature: 27 And likewise also the men, leaving the natural use of the woman, burned in their lust toward one another; men with men working that which is unseemly, and receiving in themselves that recompense of their error which was meet. (Romans 1: 24–6)

Medieval theologians recognized that verse 26 speaks of *lesbians* (though the term did not then exist) and that they were subject to the same laws as *sodomites*[21] because they all engage in 'unnatural sin'.[22] However, it is male homosexuals who have drawn most attention; England's 1533 statute against buggery applied only to men.[23] This is, first, because men are more sexually predatory than women; second, because the flamboyance of *flaming queens* among male homosexuals renders them more noticeably different from their *straight* peers than *butch dykes* in comparison with their straight sisters. (Furthermore, butch dykes are a relatively recent phenomenon – we are not speaking here of cross-dressers or transsexuals.) Third, some *queens* (effeminate male homosexuals) adopt *camp* mannerisms (e.g. are *limp-wristed*) and use *the voice*;[24] for these, there is no real counterpart among lesbians. Nonetheless, in Britain in 1994, a lesbian primary school principal who refused cheap tickets for *Romeo and Juliet* on grounds that the play is 'entirely about heterosexual love'[25] was described as follows:

With her short hair, heavy coat and workman style boots, she seemed to fit every stereotype of political correctness. Even her sullen, plainly unrepentant, expression seemed to match. (*Guardian*, 27 January 1994, p. 2)

Here, 'political correctness' seems to be a euphemism for *butch dyke*. Throughout the twentieth century, the euphemism for a homosexual man was *confirmed bachelor*.

In 1895 Oscar Wilde, wit,[26] poet, dramatist and poseur, was tried under the Criminal Law Amendment Act of 1885. Ellmann summarizes the Act:

Any male person who, in public or in private, commits, or is a party to the commission of, or procures or attempts to procure the commission by any person of, any act of gross indecency with another male person, shall be guilty of a misdemeanour, and, being convicted thereof, shall be liable, at the discretion of the Court, to be imprisoned for any term not exceeding two years with or without hard labour. When it was pointed out to Queen Victoria that women were not mentioned, she is reported to have said, 'No woman would do that.' (Ellmann 1988: 386)

In many of Wilde's works, a secret sin or indiscretion is exposed and disgrace ensues. Wilde was a man who 'could resist everything except temptation'[27] and who once said that life imitates art;[28] his did. Wilde, who was bisexual but exhibited many characteristics of a flaming queen, was partial to what would now be called *rent boys*, as well as to more aristocratic *tricks* (casual sex partners); he was blackmailed by the *rough trade* and mercilessly exploited by the beautiful, spoiled, spendthrift, reckless, vindictive Lord Alfred Douglas, known as 'Bosie'. Bosie was constantly at war with his father, the nineth Marquess of Queensbury, an obnoxious, adulterous bully. Wilde's demise was, indirectly and in part, collateral damage. Queensbury was smarting from the annulment of his second marriage and the suicide of his eldest son Drumlanrig over homosexual relations with Lord Roseberry, and he was infuriated at Bosie's love affair with Wilde. When Queensbury left his card at Wilde's club (The Albemarle) addressed 'To Oscar Wilde posing Somdomite [*sic*]', Wilde prosecuted him for libel. The action failed, and instead Wilde was tried and convicted with fellow queer Alfred Taylor, under the 1885 Act. Wilde was universally condemned before being convicted; the press mocked him, his books were withdrawn from sale and his name was removed from playbills and theatre programmes, even though *The Importance of Being Earnest* was playing to full houses at the time. Justice Sir Alfred Wills summed up:

That you, Taylor, kept a kind of male brothel it is impossible to doubt. And that you, Wilde, have been the centre of a circle of extensive corruption of the most hideous kind among young men, it is equally impossible to doubt. (Ellmann 1988: 448)

A sentence of two years hard labour all but killed Wilde. He was released in May 1897 and died in exile in November 1900, at the age of forty-six. His mortification is expressed in *De Profundis* and the *Ballad of Reading Gaol*. The biography of Oscar Wilde is a tragic story, and many less celebrated homosexual men have suffered almost as much.

Buggery is 'penile–anal intercourse'. In Middle English, *bugger* originally meant 'heretic', after a *Bulgar* sect (*bugger* ⇐ *bulgar*). *Buggery*, colloquially *browning*, is a heretical practice because, in the eyes of the church and state, it is an abomination. The last man to be hanged for buggery in Britain died in 1835; but until the second half of the twentieth century, homosexuality was very secretive. Like Oscar Wilde, many middle- and upper-class male homosexuals had affairs with people of their own class, but also engaged in casual encounters with rough trade. It was a way for the lower classes to earn a bob or two and experience some of the benefits of a richer life. In 1967, homosexual acts in private between consenting men were decriminalized in the UK. Nonetheless, the numerous convictions for *gross indecency* (which excludes *buggery*) have barely dropped off. Entrapment is common for gays *cruising* for trade on streets and in *cottages* 'public toilets'.[29] Men accused of *soliciting* in bars and theatres may merely have been chatting someone up, and introducing one gay person to another has been construed as *procuring*. Section 28 of Local Government Act 1988 explicitly forbids promoting homosexuality or presenting it as an established family relationship; this has led to the banning of books, plays, school discussions and gay/lesbian youth groups.[30] The 1988 Act also mentions *spread of disease*, apparently a euphemism for concerns about the spread of HIV/AIDS. Themes of indecency, corruption, buggery and a phobic threat to the *sanctity of family values* – based on a heterosexual family – put *queers* under a cloud in the eyes of government agents. Queers are thoughtlessly and wrongfully assumed to be paedophiles with a preference for rape, and it is felt that society should protect young people rather than champion abstract liberties.[31]

The same confusion is found in Australia. In early June 2004, a furore arose when the Australian Broadcasting Corporation's *Play School* programme for young children, in a segment that explores families from minority ethnic, social and religious backgrounds, aired a brief episode in which an eight-year-old girl says, over images of two girls with two women smiling and waving, 'I'm Brenna. That's me in the blue. My mums are taking me and my friend Meryn to an amusement park.' There was no mention of lesbians, gays or homosexuality – just *mums*; but several government ministers, the prime minister and the leader of the opposition condemned the ABC for not censoring such 'inappropriate' display of same-sex parenting. Many callers to talk-back radio equated same-sex parenting with child abuse and paedophilia. On the other hand, many members of the general public were strongly supportive of the educative aims of the broadcast programme and critical of the calls for censorship.

In New York, laws against sodomy were exercised irregularly until the 1940s, when prosecutions rose from fewer than a hundred a year to more than 3,000. There was the 1923 Penal Law 722, which identified 'degenerate disorderly conduct' as 'frequent[ing] or loiter[ing] about any public place soliciting men for the purpose of committing a crime against nature or other lewdness'.[32] In those days, homosexuals were referred to by such euphemisms as *long-haired men and short-haired women*; *lisping boys and deep-voiced girls*. A man flaunting his homosexuality was said to be *letting his hair down*: in the 1930s, 'typical markers of a fairy: bleached hair, tweezed eyebrows, rouged cheeks, and red tie'.[33] In 1920s New York, the Hamilton Lodge Ball in Harlem was widely known as the Faggots' Ball, and in 1930, the Pansy Club opened in Times Square. In 1927, Mae West was to put on Broadway *The Drag*, a play she had written about a closet married gay and the deception such behaviour as his wreaks on women; the dialogue included a lot of gay slang, and the openly gay theme proved too radical for the times. Under pressure from the religious right, a theatre censorship law was passed and the play never opened. This censorship was followed by a Hollywood film code prohibiting the representation of *sexual perversion*, and by the banning of female impersonation right across America. Gays and lesbians were now at much greater risk of prosecution. More discreet individuals would recognize one another using what is now called *gaydar* (*gay+radar*): they spoke of *dropping* (*hair*) *pins* ('dropping hints'). Most gays led a double life to avoid revealing their homosexuality to straights, for instance appearing with a *fag hag/fruitfly* as *a beard* (i.e. disguised as heterosexual). In-group solidarity bound gays to honour other men's decisions to keep their homosexuality a secret.[34] Until the 1960s, homosexuality was generally regarded as a pathological condition.

By the time of the 1969 Stonewall riot in New York,[35] homosexuality was beginning to be recognized as a social identity. From the 1970s, gays and lesbians identified themselves as oppressed minorities and there was a drive to *come out* (like debutantes) and declare their homosexuality in public. During the same period, HIV/AIDS began to take its toll and the euphemism *PWA* 'person with aids' was coined. By the 1990s, there was a growth of *queer theory*, with the claim that identity is a function of semiotic practices.

The term *queer* has come to subsume *gays, lesbians, bisexuals, third sexers* (including *chicks with dicks, guys with cunts*), *transsexuals* and *cross-dressers/transvestites* and those into *gender fuck* (e.g. a man displaying a hairy chest above a frock). Originally a dysphemism, *queer* has been re-claimed as orthophemistic jargon; the TV makeover show *Queer Eye for the Straight Guy*, featuring five gay fashionistas, has been a runaway success in the USA and Australia; nonetheless, *queer* is still often used as a dysphem-ism within the *straight* community. Queers are sometimes known generically by the euphemistic alphabetism *LGBT* (or *GLBT*) for *lesbians, gays, bisex-uals, transsexuals* – which is an orthophemism.[36] *Lesbian* is an orthophe-mism; *dyke* is a reclaimed former dysphemism among groups such as *dykes on bikes* and *diesel dykes*, but is still used dysphemistically by many straights. Lesbians come in two or three types: *fem(me)* (in 1930s New York *cunt*),[37] the more feminine *lipstick lesbian*, and the more masculine *butch* or *bull dagger* (a description that would be rejected by some feminist dykes). There was a term *bluff*, coined from *butch+fluff*, for a woman who refused one of the *femme* or *butch* roles.

We have already discussed the word *gay*. It was originally used of female prostitutes and adopted, along with terms like *trick*, for homosexual clients or casual partners; similarly *trade*. The use of *gay* was probably enforced by the roles assumed by *pansies, queens* (especially *flaming queens*), *nellies* and other *fairies, faggots, fruits* and *friends of dorothy*.[38] All these were, and still may be, dysphemistic terms of derision when used by straights, but adopted as in-group solidarity markers by queers. Terms like *sissy, buttercup, dinge-queen* (white who prefers blacks), *rice-queen* (white who prefers east Asians), *nance, nancy boy, homo, puff/poof, poofter, chi-chi man, batty boy, invert, pervert, degenerate, sod, shirt-lifter, arse-bandit* remain for the most part used by straights as dysphemisms.

Top looking for bottoms, weekday afternoons only. NameNumber@hotmail.com
(Scribbled on the wall of men's toilet, Melbourne 2001)

The *top* or active partner is a *wolf, butch, stud* – types who advertise themselves as *straight-acting, masculine, athletic*.[39] The *bottom*, or passive, partner was once a *Mary-Ann* (nineteenth century) or *pogue* (early twentieth century), later a *punk, queen, faggot, pansy, fairy, she-man*.

I'm a total bottom. I don't even like to get sucked. But I love giving good head for hours and I love getting fucked. (Leap 1996: 152)

Gay language was replete with verbal play, as can be seen in the headlines from the long-defunct New York tabloid *Brevities*, reproduced in Figure 7.1. The headlines warrant scrutiny for the verbal plays on the following words and/or their denotations: *balls, bean, camp, cods, cops on the lam, cruise, cunnilingus, daisies, degeneracy, drag, fag, fairies, flaunt, gay, hot chatter, lavenderish, lesbians, making love, navy yard, pansies, plague, pussy, queers, run afoul of, Sapphic sisters, sensational, sissies, sod, sucker, third sex, tool.*

Gay men are wont to refer to one another (certainly to queens) using female names,[40] feminine pronouns and feminine address forms, such as *sister, aunty, sweetheart, dearie, darling, bitch*, etc. In straight US, a man may be addressed as *Mac* or *Joe*; in gay US, he'll get *Mary*. Women are referred to as *fish* (from the characteristic smell of a vagina).[41]

'I adore seafood. Gorge myself whenever the fleet's in. But I can't stand fish,' [a gay man] might say, and any gay man would instantly know that the speaker was turned on by sailors and turned off by women, while the puzzled Mr and Mrs Readers Digest, listening in, would assume this was a discussion about food preferences. (Vining 1986: 55; quoted by Chauncey 1994: 286)

Gay ritual insults reported by Stephen Murray[42] have a lot in common with flyting and playing the dozens (see Chapter 3), e.g.:

A: Cross your legs you're showing your hemorrhoids.
B: You need to strap yours forward so you'll have a basket.

A gay person who gives themselves tickets is known as *Miss Thang*; the alphabetism YMCA is said to mean 'Why I'm so gay'; New York's Central Park near Columbus Circle, once a haunt for gays, had a *Fruited Plain, Vaseline Alley* and *Bitches' Walk*. In 1970s San Francisco, gays with facial hair wearing nuns' habits established a now worldwide order of Sisters of Perpetual Indulgence, in light-hearted mockery of Roman Catholic persecution of gays. Verbal play is found in other gay slang such as *bear* 'hefty hairy man', *twink* 'cute young man', *chicken* 'young boy', *chickenhawk* 'older man who prefers chickens', *datette* (with the common diminutive suffix *-ette*) 'brief date that involves no overnight stay', almost the same as *the three gets* 'get home, get off, get out', *tearoom/t-room* 'public toilet'.

Rape and the meaning of 'No'

Consensual sexual intercourse is constrained by taboos: it may not freely take place in public, and each party must have the power to refuse the other, thus

Figure 7.1. Banner headlines from *Broadway Brevities*, 1931–2 (from Chauncey 1994: 300).

neither party can be a minor. Non-consensual sex is either sexual assault or rape. The definition of *rape* differs among jurisdictions. At a minimum, it is non-consensual penile penetration of the vagina. Until fairly recently, there was no rape in marriage and homosexual rape was dealt with under sodomy laws. In Australia, rape is the penetration of a person via the vagina, anus or mouth, with any object (penis, finger, tongue, dildo or other foreign object) which violates the body and psychological person. In the UK, rape is restricted to wilful penile penetration of a bodily orifice, when there is no evidence that the rapist could reasonably believe the penetration is consensual. Penetration by objects other than a penis would be *sexual assault*. Rape is necessarily inflicted by a person more powerful than the victim.[43] In most cases of rape, and most especially *stranger rape*, the victim is humiliated not only by the physical act of assault and the feeling of degradation, but usually by insulting language as well. It is a product of hate rather than love, or even disinterested lust; rape is a common concomitant of war just because of these characteristics. However, most rape is committed by husbands, lovers and dates.

It is unfortunate that:

'No' often subsequently means 'Yes'. (Justice Bland in a rape case, *R* v. *Donald*, Morwell County Court, 15 April 1993, pp. 34–5; quoted in Moses 1993: 291)

The sense (i.e. the decontextualized meaning) of the one-word sentence *No* is uncontroversially negative; yet Justice Bland opined that, when a woman says *No* to sexual advances, she often means 'yes'. If you think that the judge's claim is absurd, it is because you believe that the woman's utterance meaning is the same as the sense of the sentence. For Justice Bland, the utterance meaning is 'yes', on the ground that the speaker is presumed to be teasing; consequently, the sentence sense 'no' is not to be understood literally. Detaching sentence meaning from speaker meaning is not always inappropriate: for instance, many people have said *It killed me* and have immediately been recognized as speaking non-literally. Is there any truth in Justice Bland's assumption? A questionnaire on this very topic, distributed to 610 undergraduate women at a university in Texas, found that:

39.3% of the women had engaged in token resistance at least once. Their reasons fell into three categories: practical [e.g. risk of being disturbed], inhibition-related [e.g. did not wish to appear promiscuous], and manipulative reasons [e.g. wanted the male to beg]. (Muehlenhard and Hollabaugh 1988: 872)

The figure of 39.3 per cent represents a very large minority of cases, and the problem for the male partner is to differentiate sincere rejections from the teases (cf. Zilbergeld 1978: 32). If the woman means no and the man persists, it is a legally tricky case of *date rape*. The difficulty arises because one party (almost invariably the male) will claim that sexual intercourse was consensual, and the other party will cry rape. A man who (after kissing and cuddling) inserted his fingers into the vagina of a Canadian student in her room in a dormitory, and whom she fellated for twenty minutes (and who voluntarily went on a date with him the following night), was acquitted of rape partly because the woman did not scream: she explained, 'I was afraid. I was ashamed I had lost control of the situation. I was embarrassed and above that I honestly can't tell you why I didn't scream.'[44] We don't doubt her sincerity, but do find her behaviour ambivalent and extremely foolish. The woman in such cases is liable to complaints of *provocation* and assailed by insults such as *cock-teaser*, *slut* and *whore*.

Rape in marriage is at least as problematic as date rape. Until recently, the words of St Paul (and therefore God) rendered rape in marriage impossible:

22 Wives submit yourselves unto your own husbands, as unto the Lord. 23 For the husband is the head of the wife, even as Christ is the head of the church: and he is the saviour of the body. 24 Therefore as the church is subject unto Christ, so let the wives be to their own husbands in everything. (Ephesians 5: 22–4)

If a husband wished to have sexual intercourse with his wife, by God's law she had to submit. The hold of religion has given way to a more humanitarian, socially aware view that has done away with one sense of *conjugal rights*. One partner no longer has any *right* of pleasure from, or access to, the other partner's body.

In *sadomasochistic* (*SM*, *S&M*) relationships, *No* and *Stop* are part of the game; so instead, the *bottom* (playing the *victim*) must agree on alternatives when the *dominator/dominatrix*, *master/mistress* applies too much pain: terms like *pickle*, *yellow*, *red* are used instead;[45] we guess the motivations may lie with *I'm in a pickle*, *I'm scared (yellow)* and the red of a stop light.

Incest and paedophilia

The terms *incest*, *paedophilia* and *pederasty* are orthophemisms. The press, the public and the law generally ignore incest, except when practised as paedophilia. And paedophiles, whether incestuous or not, are the bugaboos of today and (rightly) no longer ignored.[46] An Australian dysphemism for a *paedophile* is *rock spider*. The *age of consent*, which differentiates *statutory rape of a minor* from *consensual sexual intercourse*, has varied across communities and times. If there are euphemisms in English for paedophilia (including pederasty), they are to be found in expressions such as *child molestation* or *the sexual abuse of children*, where the nouns (derived from the intrinsically dysphemistic verbs *molest* and *abuse*) characterize society's abhorrence for the adult perpetrator. There is no conventional euphemism for incest between consenting adults, though the slang metaphor *roll your own* and the dysphemism *in-bred* exist, and there are -IST slurs like *hillbillies* and *Tasmanians*.

It is sometimes thought that the incest taboo is a motivation for naming taboos and avoidance languages, like the so-called 'mother-in-law' languages.[47] However, this seems to be wrong. For instance, in Bauro (Solomon Islands), there is a strong taboo on cross-sibling names and, in some parts, on cross-cousins too; but there is also an exactly similar taboo on a boy using his elder brother's name.[48] What alternative explanations can there be? We note, firstly, that there are no reports of verbal strategies as extreme as the use of 'mother-in-law languages' for use between consanguineal kin of opposite sexes. Since consanguineal incest is not as rare as hens' teeth, it seems unlikely that cross-affinal incest should lead to the development of avoidance languages, when consanguineal incest does not.[49] Secondly, we note that relationships with in-laws are notoriously difficult in all societies, and conclude that the so-called 'mother-in-law' languages, and all similar taboos on naming and addressing kinsfolk, are grounded in the desire to maintain social harmony in what all human communities recognize to be the most difficult area of intra-human relationships.

Constraints on mentioning bodily effluvia

In the folk magic of many cultures, there are spells that make use of bodily effluvia and detritus: faeces, urine, semen, spittle, menstrual blood, nail-pairings, (head) hair, pubic hair and the amniotic sac of babies. Lest you think such things are primitive superstitions, type the words *magic* and *effluvia* into your computer's search engine. You will find that the practice of using bodily effluvia in spell-casting is widespread in the twenty-first century, and in some places is still routinely passed from family member to family member. According to the instructions given in one URL, adding menstrual blood or urine to a man's tea or coffee is an effective way for a woman to obtain his sexual attention, by getting her scent 'into the beloved's sphere of consciousness'.[50] To avoid entrapment, men are taught to steer clear of anything, especially dark-coloured food and beverages, served to them by an unmarried woman. This may be what Blind Lemon Jefferson is referring to in *Dry Southern Blues*:[51]

> I can't drink coffee and the woman won't make no tea.
> I can't drink coffee and the woman won't make no tea.
> I believe to my soul sweet mama gonna hoodoo me.

Sexual spells are fairly benign, but the magic wrought with a person's effluvia can also be malevolent, and in many communities there are taboos on SMD organs and their effluvia to protect an individual from danger.[52] In Greece, from ancient times through to modern times, a target's bodily effluvia were cursed and then buried or drowned, together with a tablet on which the curse was inscribed; hundreds of such tablets have been discovered.[53] In our culture, the taboos on SMD organs and their effluvia no longer derive from fear of witchcraft. Reticence is motivated by distaste and concerns about pollution. We seem to find the bodily effluvia of almost anyone, especially any non-intimate, revolting. A stranger's dirty underwear, socks, cast-off condoms and the like are so much more revolting than our own: a sentiment captured in the German proverb *Eigener Dreck stinkt nicht* 'your own shit doesn't stink'. Of course, there are sound health reasons for keeping human waste at a distance. Yet, we know that it is not an instinctive repulsion that these substances arouse in us. Children and animals do not find them odious; the repulsion is something we learn.

In a questionnaire we distributed among staff and students at universities in Melbourne, Australia, in 1989,[54] subjects were asked to rank the bodily effluvia produced by an adult stranger on a five-point scale of decreasing revoltingness as RRR, RR, R, ½R, Not-R, in which R is the revolting median, the RRR-rating is worse than RR, and so on. Our summary findings are reproduced in Table 7.1. It is notable that other people's shit and vomit top the list of revoltingness, while 94 per cent of our subjects ranked tears not revolting. Tears hold this position because they are not waste produces; and unlike blood from a wound, tears do not stain and their flow cannot lead to death. The most interesting, yet hardly surprising, finding was the sexual dichotomy in attitudes to menstrual blood: 80% of men rate it either RR or RRR, whereas only 47% of women did so; moreover, whereas 17% of women found menstrual blood not-revolting (Not-R), not a single man did so. The comparative figures for blood from a wound are much closer to parity between the sexes: women 11% > R and 63% Not-R; men 11% > R and 47% Not-R.

The menstruation taboo

In most societies, menstruating women are or have been taboo. This may be in part because of the magical coincidence between a woman's ovulatory cycle and the lunar month.

In an amazing coincidence, if it is that, 29.5 days, a woman's optimal fertility cycle length, is the moon's periodicity too – the time it takes the moon to shift from new to full and back again. Even more curiously, women tend to bleed in concert with the full moon and ovulate with the new when enjoying the company of men. In contrast, celibacy, or being predominantly in the company of women, leaves menstruation tending to coincide with the new moon, and ovulation, if it occurs at all, with the full . . . Curiously, in gardening lore, the advice over centuries has been to sow seed when the moon is new. (Blackledge 2003: 242f)

Table 7.1. *Summary findings on revoltingness ratings (from Allan and Burridge 1991: 74)*

shit, vomit	RRR	84% > R	61% > RR
urine, semen/sperm	RRR	58% > R	
menstrual blood	RRR	55% > R	36% > RR
(MEN		80% > R, 0% Not-R)	
(WOMEN		47% > R, 17% Not-R)	
fart, snot	RR	70% > R	72% < RRR, 11% < R
pus	RR	67% > R	
spit	RR	56% > R	
belched breath	R	78% ≥ R	51% < RR, 49% ≥ RR
skin parings	R	64% ≤ R	
sweat	½R	58% <R	19% ≥ RR
nail parings	Not-R	65% < R	
breath	Not-R	71% < R	
blood from a wound	Not-R	79% < R	
hair clippings	Not-R	84% < R	
breast milk	Not-R	86% < R	
tears	Not-R	94% < R	0% > R

All subjects: N=86. The ranking scale is RRR, RR, R, ½R, Not-R, hence R is the median. In the table > means 'greater than', ≥ means 'greater than or equal to'; < means 'less than', and ≤ means 'less than or equal to'.

There is no other human cycle which matches that of a celestial body in this manner. It links women to the moon and the tides in a way that men simply cannot measure up to.

The menstruation taboo in our Judeo-Christian tradition is written into the Bible:

1 The LORD spake unto Moses and Aaron, saying . . . 19 And if a woman have an issue, and her issue in flesh be blood, she shall be put apart seven days: and whosoever toucheth her shall be unclean until the even. 20 And everything that she lieth upon in her separation shall be unclean: everything also that she sitteth upon shall be unclean. 21 And whosoever toucheth her bed shall wash his clothes, and bathe himself in water, and be unclean until the even. 22 And whosoever toucheth any thing that she sat upon shall wash his clothes, and bathe himself in water, and be unclean until the even. 23 And if it be on her bed, or any thing whereon she sitteth, when he toucheth it, he shall be unclean until the even. 24 And if any man lie with her at all, and her flowers be upon him, he shall be unclean seven days; and all the bed whereon he lieth shall be unclean. (Leviticus 15:1, 19–24)

Note the euphemisms *have an issue* and *flowers* for menstrual fluid (*flowers* is discussed shortly). Also noteworthy is the fact that the menstruating woman is 'unclean'. Traditionally, the menstruation taboo is based on a fear of contagion because catamenia is seen as purging or purifying, a cleansing away of ill humours – hence the Middle Dutch terms *purgacy* and *reynicheit*. In the Middle Ages, menstrual blood was believed to contain defiled spirits, and many of the most feared diseases, like leprosy and syphilis, were thought to be transmitted through menstruating women. So, because of the danger she posed, a menstruating woman was usually prevented from mingling freely in the community. Perhaps because men can only experience catamenia as the effluvium of a woman, menstrual blood is especially tabooed by men. In Manhattan, the Hasidic Jews who work in the diamond district have a private bus to take them to and from Brooklyn where they live, so as to avoid contamination from menstruating women on public transportation. In some societies, men will not even walk where a menstruating woman might have passed above;[55] and in many more, men are forbidden to have sexual intercourse with a menstruating woman.

Also thou shalt not approach unto a woman to uncover her nakedness, as long as she is put apart for her uncleanness. (Leviticus 18: 19)

And if a man shall lie with a woman having her sickness, and shall uncover her nakedness; he hath discovered her fountain, and she hath uncovered the fountain of her blood: and both of them shall be cut off from among their people. (Leviticus 20: 18)

In these passages *her nakedness* is apparently a euphemism for 'vagina' and *fountain* has the sense 'source'. We see that the menstruating woman is not only 'unclean' but that menstruation is a 'sickness'. So menstruation is seen as a polluting discharge that weakens the woman; the pollution and weakening can be transferred to a male partner and, at worst, may lead to the man's death.

In most communities, the malefactions of menstruation are not fatal. Navajo people frequently attribute severe arthritis, rheumatism and becoming hunchbacked or similarly deformed to inappropriate contact with menstrual blood.[56] Women are required to be very careful to cleanse themselves, and contaminated clothing and sheets have to be washed separately lest the pollution spread to other linen. The odour of menstrual fluid reputedly causes headaches. However, a girl's first and second periods have healing properties; they are *kinaalda* or *kinaaldsti*, whereas later cycles are *chooyin*. This is because the girl is pure and cannot yet conceive, but the *kinaalda* is an indication of her reproductive potential. By the third month, she is ready to be married. When menstruating, Navajo women cannot go into a sweathouse, a cornfield, or to ceremonies; they cannot weave baskets, butcher meat, ride horses, or sleep with either husband or children. These constraints often require that others in the community know when a woman is menstruating.

At this time too, the husband is forbidden to engage in ceremonies or, of course, have sexual relations with his wife. The management of taboos on menstruation has similarities with the management of other taboos among the Navajos; for instance, a man must also practise sexual abstinence when hunting. Blood and hair from a butchered deer (but not domesticated sheep or cattle) have to be carefully handled and disposed of well outside the dwelling, and all traces washed off the butcher, or the effects on the mind and body can be disastrous – giving rise to madness and cancer.

Restrictions on a woman's normal behaviour while she is menstruating are common across communities. Tabooed behaviour includes: sexual relations with a man, preparing food for a man (though perhaps females and boys may be cooked for), and entering sacred places or touching sacred and revered objects. Hence the Akan euphemisms for menstruation *ɔabu ne nsa* 'she has broken her hand', *ɔnkɔ gya ho* 'she does not go to the kitchen', *ɔnwe bosom so nam* 'she does not eat meat from the shrine', *ɔnkɔ ahemfie* 'she does not go to the palace'. One of the commonest Akan euphemisms is *ne nsa kɔ n'akyi* 'her hand has gone to her back';[57] this may not only reflect the manual constraints imposed upon her, but also the response to backache that is a common experience. One of the least explicable restrictions is that forty years ago, in Australia, girls were advised not to wash their hair when menstruating.

To some contemporary feminists, the menstruation taboo seems an outrageous denigration of womanhood:

menstruation [would] have been the locus for glorification had it been the experience of men. (Spender 1984: 200)

The only peculiarly male effluvium is male ejaculate which – when it is someone else's – women find less revolting than men do.[58] It is not too difficult to guess why menstrual blood and male ejaculate are regarded so differently today, as they were among the ancient Israelites. According to the Bible, a woman who comes in contact with semen is only unclean till evening, but the man who comes in contact with menstrual blood is unclean for seven days.

16 And if any man's seed of copulation go out from him, then he shall wash all his flesh in water, and be unclean until the even. 17 And every garment, and every skin, whereon is the seed of copulation, shall be washed with water, and be unclean until the even. 18 The woman also with whom man shall lie with seed of copulation, they shall both bathe themselves in water, and be unclean until the even. (Leviticus 15: 16–18)

It is naive to dismiss men's reaction to menstrual blood as simple gynophobia, and leave it at that. The taboos often inconvenience men as well as women (if not as much). Most likely, a menstruating woman is set apart for a combination of some or all of the following reasons:

- in a very real sense, catamenia is the discharge of decaying matter. Although menstruation may occur during anovulatory cycles and during pregnancy, it is typically induced by hormonal changes associated with an unfertilized ovum; these changes lead to the break down of the endometrium, in which blood soaked regions of it crumble away and are discharged, along with mucous and cellular debris that includes the unfertilized ovum.[59]
- There is the pollution taboo of any discharge through the vagina.[60]
- Menstrual discharge renders the vagina comparatively messy, and it smells and tastes unpleasant – consequently a menstruous woman is regarded as unclean (hence the German terms *Schweinerei* and *Sauerei*).
- Loss of blood is generally correlated with injury and loss of strength.
- Unlike other blood, menstrual blood does not coagulate.
- In many women, menstruation is sometimes accompanied by cramps or similar discomfort (dysmenorrhoea).
- Some women have reduced libido during the first days of menstruation.
- Some women suffer a brief period of premenstrual tension that may cause headaches, and often results in otherwise uncharacteristic irritability.

> Oh! menstruating woman, thou'rt a fiend
> From whom all nature should be closely screened.
> (Crawley 1960: 77)

- On a few occasions, menstruation is counterevidence to a desired pregnancy. It is reported that 'Maoris regard menstrual blood as a sort of human being *manqué*.'[61]

There are several characteristics of menstruation that make it appropriate for a woman to excuse herself for *being unwell*. Mabel Loomis Todd, the lover of poet Emily Dickinson's brother, kept a explicit diary of her sex life, her orgasms (including those induced by masturbation) and her menstrual cycle, which she referred to as 'my illness'.[62] If we put together all the characteristics of menstruation, we get a composite of the menstruating woman which typically puts her below her best in temper, in sense of well-being, in sexual receptivity and in sexual attractiveness. Furthermore, in some contexts, she will be disparaged for having failed to achieve pregnancy. So it is hardly surprising that one synonym for menstruation is *the curse*.[63] None of the listed disadvantages of catamenia is shared by male ejaculate; at worst, ejaculation is perceived to lead to the temporary weakening of the man.

Many X-phemisms for menstruation are based on the salient colour RED: *the Red Sea's in*; *it's a red letter day*; *riding the red rag*; *flying the red flag* (cf. Russian *krasnyi flag* and *pervomaiskie prazdniki* 'May Day celebration' because, in Soviet times, people marched with red flags);[64] *surfing the red wave*; *snatch box decorated with red roses*. Much more poetic and figurative is *her cherry is in sherry*;[65] as also was the red rose on the prostitute's dress that once indicated that *the shop was closed to business*. Australian English *I've got my P-plates* is truly euphemistic verbal play: 'P' presumably for 'period', but P[rovisional driver]-plates have red P on a white background. Because of the British military's pre-twentieth-century predilection for red coats, *the cavalry's here*, *entertaining the general* and French *j'ai mon anglais* all refer to having a period. The army's association with bloody deeds is not irrelevant, either. Blood gets direct mention in *bloody Mary*, and indirect implication in *the gal's at the stockyards*. Other X-phemisms characterize indisposition, antipathy, periodicity and visitation. INDISPOSITION: *indisposed, under the weather, unwell, sick; have stomach ache, the cramps*. ANTIPATHY (generally dysphemistic expressions or, at best, dysphemistic euphemisms): *the jinx, the pain, the foe, the plague, the curse, the drip, cramps, be off the roof*. PERIODICITY: Latin *mensis* 'month' is the source for the *menses*[66] of medical jargon, and the basis for Latin *menstruare*, whence English *menstruate*. *I've got* / *I'm having* / *it's my period*; *I've got my regular*; *It's that time* (*of the month*); *It's my time*; *It's the wrong time of the month*; *I've got the monthlies*; *It looks like a wet weekend*; *It's blood week*. When the Australian magazine *Woman's Weekly* came to be published monthly, the name was specifically not changed to *Woman's Monthly* to avoid direct association with menstruation. SANITARY PROTECTION: *on the (red) rag (OTR)*; *riding the cotton pony*; *on the saddle blanket*; *riding the horse*. VISITOR: *little sister's here*; *the girl friend*; *my buddy/friend/foe's here*; *Fred's here*; *George has come*; *I've got Fred/George/Jack*; *little Willie/Aunt Susie is here*; *Aunt Flo is coming from Redfield/taking the slow train to Redlands*; *Kit has come*. The notion of a visitor (which is not unique to speakers of English, cf. Russian *gosti prišli* 'guests have come', *tetka prišla* 'aunty is visiting', Akan *ɔahuri asi* 'he has jumped and landed', *akoa no abɛduru* 'the man has arrived')[67] is presumably motivated by the temporary nature of a period and the added trouble it brings. On the face of it, the adoption of male names is surprising; perhaps it arises from the (dysphemistic) idea that the default resident of a woman's sexual organs is a troublesome male.

The euphemism *I've got my flowers* is an old expression that has almost died out, except in Irish English (though it is listed as contemporary in Ernster 1975). Yet it seems to linger on in folk memory. In 1988, Ruby Wallace described her reasons for having her left shoulder-blade tattooed:

From the age of 15 onwards my periods stopped [because she was severely anorexic] . . . when my periods restarted, so many years later . . . [they] were a sign of health, of recovery, and to me they were a sign of womanhood that I welcomed and had in fact longed for.
    When I felt secure that I was fully 'well' and had learned to cherish my female body and femaleness, I wanted to celebrate. I performed what amounted to a menstrual rite.

I had myself tattooed. ('An urge deeper than the skin', *The Age* (Melbourne), 17 September 1988, Saturday Extra, p. 5)

And the tattoo? Flowers: scarlet blossoms! We cannot know whether this is folk memory, a symbol for spring, or pure accident; in any case, it demonstrates the powerful association between flowers and menstruation.

The expression *flowers*, or *monthly flowers*, and its translation equivalents in other languages, may have a variety of sources. The most likely one is the plant growth metaphor of *seed* for 'ovum; semen', *sap* for 'seminal fluid', *flower* or *bloom* for 'menstruation, i.e. prima facie evidence of fertility',[68] *fruit* for 'children'.

FRUITFUL VINE. A woman's private parts, i.e. that has *flowers* every month, and bears fruit in nine months. (Grose 1811; *sic*)

The metaphor is found in Middle Dutch medical texts, where the most frequent term for menstruation is *bloeme* 'flowers', along with the verb *bloyen* 'bloom'.[69] The word *dracht*, which usually denotes a yield of fruit or the fruit itself, was also used to mean 'foetus', and more often 'pregnancy'. The child was referred to as *vrucht* 'fruit':

'for just as trees without flowers [*bloemen*] will bear no fruit, so too will women be bereft of their pregnancy [literally 'yield'], if they are without [this] purging.' (Daems 1967:180)

It has been suggested[70] that *flowers* derives by either remodelling or folk etymology[71] from Latin *fluere* 'flow' via French *flueurs* (a medical term for 'discharge' from the sixteenth century),[72] which was either remodelled as, or in England misinterpreted as, *fleurs* 'flowers'. Enright suggests the origin of *flowers* is *flow* (cf. the archaic *a woman in her courses*). Tampons are graded for *heavy* or *light flow days*; and *flow* is used nowadays among North American female students (if not elsewhere, too), along with *flushing*.[73] Middle Dutch *vloet* 'flow' was an occasional alternative to *bloeme*. While such etymological speculations are suggestive, they will not account for the archaic German euphemism *Blumen* or Dutch *bloeme*, unless these are presumed to be loan translations of English *flowers* – which is most unlikely. The plant growth metaphor provides the most likely source for archaic *flowers* 'menstruation'. Yet there is plenty of evidence that X-phemistic popular terms for taboo topics often have multiple sources, each reinforcing the others.[74] Supposing that *flowers* 'menstruation' was indeed based on a plant growth metaphor, it may well have been reinforced by an association with the notion of 'flow'.

We should remember that virginity was held to be *the flower of maidenhood*, and it was lost on *deflowering* (a nicer expression than *popping her cherry*). In *Memoirs of a Woman of Pleasure*, Fanny Hill writes of her own 'virgin flower' and of another girl's 'richest flower' being 'cropped',[75] and gives graphic descriptions of the bloody result. In the thirteenth-century French allegory *Le Roman de la Rose*, the 'rose' is the maiden's hymen. Thus, there is a well established figurative link between flowers and blood issuing from the vaginal orifice, whether catamenic or the result of a ruptured hymen. The supposed fragility of virginity is captured in figures like *she has cracked her pitcher/pipkin/tea-cup* and the like.[76]

Yet another category of euphemism for menstruation is revealed in the following Middle Dutch recommendation for the daily dose of a special preparation: *es goet . . . den vrouwen haer dinch wel te doen comene* 'is good . . . to cause women's thing to come'. A euphemism like *a woman's thing* can be used for any number of delicate topics, leaving the context to determine which. John Wilmot, Second Earl of Rochester,[77] not a man noted for being bashful, writes of a mother taking her daughter to the waters at Tunbridge Wells, which were reputedly good for 'female complaints'.[78] The mother says to another woman that her daughter

> 'Is full sixteen, and never yet had *those*.'
> She soon replied, 'Get her a husband, madam:
> I married at that age, and ne'er had had 'em;
> Was just like her. Steel waters let alone:
> A back of steel[79] will bring 'em better down.'
> (Rochester 1968, *Tunbridge Wells*, lines 132-6; *sic*)

The intended meaning of '*those*' (italic in the original) and the two occurrences of '[th]em' is plain enough, but this topic is described euphemistically whereas, about ten lines later in the poem, a layabout is baldly described as 'With brawny back and legs and potent prick'.

Menstruation is a chronic recurrence in the first-hand experience of most women and the second-hand experience of many men; and, although there are some occasions on which its onset is welcome, the vocabulary for it reveals that menstruation is usually an unpleasing experience. All common experiential aspects of menstruation turn up in the lexicon: it is viewed like an illness and a troublesome source of discomfort; there is reference to its periodicity, to the flow or drip and the means and effects of stanching it, to the blood and the salient red colour. The most picturesque euphemism for menstruation is the archaic metaphor of blooms and flowers – which is perhaps a coalescence of influences from the colour red, the notion of flow, and, centrally, the plant growth metaphor. This metaphor is the most positive in the vocabulary for menstruation; it may have declined in concert with the social attitude which nowadays places less overall emphasis on the ability to conceive than on preventing conception.

Menstruation is managed using *personal hygiene* products (orthophemism), and more especially *feminine hygiene* products or *sanitary protection* (euphemism); and note the implication of cleanliness and health implicit in the words *hygiene* and *sanitary*. In the days of *sanitary towels* there was the euphemistic abbreviation *STs*; but towels have given way to *sanitary pad/napkin* – orthophemisms from which the omission of 'sanitary' creates a euphemism. These are also euphemistically referred to as *mouse-beds*. And there is another figure in 'I'm out of white bread, and George is calling tonight.'[80] Then there are *panty liners* (euphemistic and not intended for the full flood of menstruation, but rather for *spotting* and other leaks – 'Discreet protection for everyday freshness, minor discharge, light flow days and tampon back-up'). The use of *napkin* for 'sanitary napkin' is leading to the demise of the term used in the sense 'table napkin', which is replaced by *serviette* in Australia, Britain and New Zealand; this is not the case in America, where the trade name *kotex* has generalized to function as a euphemism. In Britain and Australia, the trade name *tampax* often generalizes to 'tampon'; in Australia, *meds* does the same. In television adverts for such products, discrete protection from wetness and from embarrassment seem to be the focus; though, strangely (and notoriously), absorbency is always demonstrated using blue fluid – a visual euphemism. There are many dysphemisms or dysphemistic euphemisms: *on the rag/jamrag*; *wearing the rag*; *riding the cotton bicycle*; *the hammock is swinging*, etc. Reference to *the rag* shows that language lags a generation or two behind contemporary means for sanitary protection. There is also a tasteless joke about an imaginary western, 'Blood on the Saddle', starring the Kotex Kid. Other metaphors include *covering the waterfront*; *wearing the manhole cover*; *closed for repairs*; *plugged up*; *too wet to plough*, etc. which mostly indicate sexual unavailability. A 1962 advert for 'Tampax internal sanitary protection' vaunts it as 'neat, discreet, easy to use and unfelt in place. It prevents odour, ends disposal problems, does away with belts, pins, pads. It lets you bathe, shower, do anything you'd normally do. Deciding to use Tampax is a sign you're not going to compromise with discomfort any longer'.[81] This advert implies much about the adversities of managing menstruation, at a time when *tampons* (orthophemism) were beginning to be widely used.

Menstrual blood and other pollutants as curative agents

> menstrues and materials,
> Of piss, and eggshells, women's terms, man's blood,
> Hair o' the head, burnt clouts, chalk, merds, and clay,
> Powder of bones, scalings of iron, glass,
> And worlds of other strange ingredients.
> (Jonson 1981, *The Alchemist*, Act II, scene i)

As we said in Chapter 2, out of bad things good things grow; and there is one curious aspect to the concepts of pollution and taboo that we need to address. This is the overlap that exists between filth on the one hand and purity and healthiness on the other. Bodily effluvia are not simply impure, odious and devitalizing substances. They (and certain parts of the human body) are also believed to have important health-promoting aspects which, over the years, have been used in official pharmacy, and also witchcraft and folk remedies, in many different societies. Urea is still an important ingredient of many skin lotions and creams (albeit artificially constructed rather collected from natural sources). Mares' urine is also a source of oestrogen for post-menopausal hormone replacement therapy. Many of the most polluting of substances (subject to the most severe taboos) have the greatest healing and amuletic powers of all. Any unified account of the existing linguistic taboos and prohibitions must also account for this apparent anomaly.

Many ancient Greek and Roman physicians recommended human excrement and urine as cures for headaches, insomnia, madness, melancholy, gout, eye inflammations, cataracts, nasal infections, tooth infections, syphilis and sterility. 'The medication was so widespread that Aristophanes called physicians *scatophagous*, excrement eaters.'[82] During medieval times, ashes of the bones of the dead, particularly the remains of those who had died a violent death (for example, executed criminals), were attributed special medicinal properties. Extract of human cranium was reputed to be efficacious against epilepsy; teeth and hair against gout. Virtually any bodily emission could be turned into a curative agent, and one of the most powerful of these was faeces, both human and animal. Dung-based health programmes abounded in Anglo-Saxon times.[83] Blood featured strongly in remedies against ailments of all description, especially in the treatment of serious diseases like leprosy.[84] Menstrual blood was particularly potent, and since it was generally believed that pollution from an 'unclean' person (such as a menstruating woman) could cause illness, menstrual blood provided both the cure and the source for diseases. Vaccination and homeopathic medicines are the modern counterpart. Symbols of polluting–curative substances were also endowed with special powers; for example, the colour red was sometimes attributed the same curative power as menstrual blood.

But pollutants are not only found in the fantastical remedies of our forbears. In China, bread soaked in the blood of an executed criminal is a traditional cure for tuberculosis. In many places, menstrual blood has been used for healing. Native Americans, native people from Guinea, Australia, Siberia, South Vietnam, India, Patagonia and Tibet all found it beneficial to eat faeces on certain occasions.

The Zuni Indians of New Mexico, for instance, after participating in a traditional dance, greedily drank urine out of a pot. When this same dance was performed in a large plaza, it was considered honorable to eat man's and dog's excrements as well . . . [T]he Parsi of ancient Persia . . . believed that upon delivering a baby, Parsi women should drink urine; and so too should children at the time of being dressed in the symbols of their faith. (Arango 1989: 45)

Anthropologist Anna Meigs describes at length the positive powers attributed to polluting substances among the Hua of New Guinea.[85] For Australian Aborigines, faeces has always been regarded as having protective and curative powers; one traditional practice was to smear the faces of new born babies with excrement.[86] Knowing this, it is no surprise to learn that our own practice of throwing rice and confetti at newly weds has its origins in the throwing of excrement.

It is puzzling that something can be both polluting and purifying. How can it reduce health, but at the same time promote it? Surely, it is not simply a matter that the cure has to be worse than the complaint? Meigs offers a perspective of the pollution theory to account for what she finds among the Hua. She points out the strong association between these substances and organic decay:

Body emissions are classified as polluting because they are perceived as decaying, rotting, dying, and anything which is so perceived is held to be polluting provided that it is threatening to gain access to the body. (Meigs 1978: 316f)

In decay there is death, and the anxiety inspired by pollutants is surely closely connected to the fear of death. Yet, it is also out of decay that new life is nourished; that which dies is the compost for future generations. Things which rot attract worms and vermin. Medieval belief held that such creatures thrive in the putrescent walking 'dung-heap', the *sterquilinium* that is the human body. Here is St Bernard's graphic comment:

Man is nothing but stinking sperm, a sack of excrement and food for worms. After man comes the worm, stench and horror. And thus is every man's fate. (St Bernard, *Meditationes*; cited in Camporesi 1988: 78)

Just as dung (under the euphemism *manure*) and rotting compost will enrich soil and promote growth in the garden, so too do bodily effluvia have special regenerative, curative and protective powers. Pulverized worm was the prime ingredient in many medieval remedies. Because the womb is the harbinger of life, a woman was believed to be fuller of vermin than a man; hence the 'dark, smelly, explicitly rotting interiors attributed to females' bodies' by the Hua,[87] and Aristotle's view of the nutritious residue from menses that combines with semen to grow an embryo.[88] A woman's power to give birth should have afforded her a dominating position in society, revered as divine; instead, women have often been regarded as dangerously polluting creatures, sometimes tabooed in the same way as corpses.

Language for the taboos on sex and bodily effluvia

But Love has pitched his mansion in
The place of excrement . . .
(Yeats 1965, *Crazy Jane talks with the Bishop*, lines 15f)

The birth canal from which we emerge lies between the uretha and the rectum; hence, as St Augustine wrote, *Inter faeces et urinam nascimur*. Perhaps this helps to account for the importance we attach to SMD organs and the bodily effluvia that issue from them.

We have reviewed some of the language of sex, gender, sexuality, sexual pleasure and sexual reproduction. We did not try to cover the whole field; almost completely missing is contraception, as well as discussion of humankind's oldest profession, female prostitution. Censorship, embodied in legislation, constrains not only sexual behaviour but the language for talking about such behaviour.

Human bodies need to expel the by-products of a living organism; and although we no longer worry that such effluvia will be used to perform black magic on us, they are normally obnoxious to the public – which makes them a potential source of embarrassment to the person from whom they issue. Failure to satisfy community expectations provokes malediction and verbal insult, often created from terms that name faeces and, to a lesser extent, urine (perhaps because faeces is solid, more resistant to dispersal and smells more strongly). *Spunk* is most unusual in being both a kind of effluvium and a term of praise, applicable to both genders. Because of its sexual specificity and significance to reproduction, menstruation is treated differently from defecation and urination – which no creature can avoid. Although menstrual blood is more strongly tabooed than either faeces or urine, it is scarcely used in insult or malediction, although the epithets *bloody*/*bleeding* possibly receive some boost from the fact.[89] All three effluvia give rise to many X-phemisms based on perceptions of, and conceptions about, their denotata (i.e. about faeces, urine, menstrual blood). Children and animals do not find bodily effluvia odious; the repulsion to them as 'dirty' is something learned in the course of toilet training and the like. It is at first paradoxical that bodily effluvia have been used as restorative and curative agents in many, perhaps all, human groups. However, there may be two rational explanations: one is a continuing belief in homoeopathy; the other is that, as compost and manure aid the growth of plants, and because the human is born of a womb whose mysterious functions were marked by menstrual fluid that enabled it to be (wrongly) likened to a compost heap, bodily effluvia must have properties to enhance health and growth in humans.

The importance of language play among human beings has been generally ignored, although see Crystal (1998), Allan and Burridge (1991). We have seen through a handful of examples that to speak of sex or bodily effluvia, self-censoring human beings use figurative language and/or verbal play in generating X-phemisms, many of which show remarkable inventiveness of either figure or form; and some are indubitably playful. In such ways do taboos drive the renewal of language.

8   Food and smell

In this chapter, we examine the language of food and drink. We look both at how we talk about food and also how we use food to talk about ourselves. The chapter concludes with a discussion of smell, because our sense of smell is closely tied in with the appreciation of food and drink. It is also inextricably linked to the most widely tabooed aspects of human life – bodily functions, sex, disease and death.

The significance of food

Everywhere, eating is a culturally transforming – sometimes a magically transforming – act. It has its own alchemy. It transmutes individuals into society and sickness into health. It changes personalities. It can sacralize apparently secular acts. It functions like ritual. It becomes ritual. It can make food divine or diabolic. It can release power. It can create bonds. It can signify revenge or love. It can proclaim identity. A change as revolutionary as any in the history of our species happened when eating stopped being merely practical and became ritual, too. From cannibals to homeopathists and health-foodies, eaters target foods which they think will burnish their characters, extend their powers, prolong their lives. (Fernándes-Armesto 2001: 34)

Before looking at the language of eating and drinking, consider for a moment the nature of these activities and what they mean to us. There is very much more at stake here than simply a means of keeping body and soul together. People choose what to eat and drink for spirituality, for brainpower, for beauty, for sex drive, for well-being, for a longer life. Food products are now often marketed as being health-enhancing or illness-preventing. People turn to food when they are stressed; the comfort foods and nursery foods of childhood memories seem particularly sought after. Risotto is now touted as 'gourmet comfort food' and the menus of fashionable restaurants boast 'sophisticated comfort food' (ravioli filled with truffle-scented mascarpone and peas, braised veal shanks and truffled mash).[1] In fact, there is scientific support for the ability of sweet and fatty foods to calm down anxious brains.[2] Eating and drinking are among the greatest of human pleasures, too. Engaging with the senses of touch, sight, taste and smell, these activities are intensely individualistic and intimately connected to our bodies. What we put in our mouths becomes a part of us. Thus, in many languages, the words for 'hunger' and 'thirst' are treated as inalienable possessions, like body parts and other properties of personal representation such as mind, spirit, soul, shadow and reflection; this is reflected in the grammatical behaviour manifested by them.[3]

The pleasures of eating and drinking are strongly social, forging attachments with family and friends. Food and drink have important symbolic functions when it comes to signalling hospitality and marking significant occasions and rites of passage. Why else would most Australians struggle through their traditional hot mince pies, roast turkey dinners and steaming plum puddings on a Christmas Day in the middle of a stinking hot summer? Some food writers worry about the social impact of fast food technology and the convenience mentality that goes with precooked prepackaged foods, microwave ovens, and dinner in front of the TV, instead of in the context of a discussion around a table. Fernándes-Armesto comments: 'The loneliness of the fast-food eater is uncivilizing. Food is being desocialized.'[4] Widespread condemnation of this has given rise to the Slow Food movement, an international organization with 60,000 members (or *eco-gastronomes*) with the mission 'to protect the pleasures of the table from the homogenization of modern fast food and life'.[5] Slow foodies teach *sensory education* and *gastronomic culture* to young children, and develop a variety of initiatives that promote agricultural biodiversity and the preservation of endangered dishes and cuisines.

If people connect what they eat and drink with what, who and where they are, then – not surprisingly – eating habits and dietary regimens not only bind us, but also strongly divide us. The items that appear on our everyday menus make us feel good about ourselves. We use them to locate ourselves within a social space. Food is a potent indicator of class and lifestyle: they eat meat, we don't; they grill food, we fry; they drink beer, we drink wine; and so forth. As with other social practices, what one group relishes another group spurns. Food also marks ethnicity, of course. Pasta is associated with Italians, baguettes and croissants with the French, stir fry with the Chinese, roast beef with the English, hamburgers with Americans, pavlovas with Australians and New Zealanders. Melbourne chef Marieke Brugman describes the battle lines drawn between olive oil and butter, not just commercially but also culturally, as she was growing up in Anglo-Celtic Australia in the 1950s, 'when olive oil and garlic made people shudder'. She recalls how her mother, a 'new' Australian, could only obtain olive oil in small bottles purchased from a chemist.[6] Now conceitedly multicultural, Australians pride themselves on their enthusiasm for foreign foods and *fusion cooking* (dubbed *gastronomic Lego* by some purists), relishing in combinations such as 'Cajun Salmon on a bed of Udon Noodles',

'Tandoori Pizza', 'Japanese Pizza', 'Thai-style chicken burger', 'Mango Risotto' (with olive oil, garlic, coconut cream, curry paste and lemon grass stock) and the 'McOz Burger' (with Australian beetroot).

Food and drink help to define a group's personality and, at the same time, they are a very public expression of that personality. This symbolic value is sometimes used for political effect. In the 1990s, when the French resumed their nuclear tests in the Pacific, some Australians were tearing up baguettes in protest. A number even baked them into the shape of boomerangs, an action reminiscent of the American patriotic rechristening of *sauerkraut* as *liberty cabbage* during the Second World War. And when France criticized the 2003 invasion of Iraq, Americans renamed French fries *liberty fries* (an event that led one wag to comment 'too bad [President George W.] Bush's parents didn't use a liberty letter'). It is not surprising, therefore, to find that culinary stereotyping underpins much of the malediction that English speakers hurl at other races, and we shall explore some of the abusive potential of gastronomy.

All human groups have food taboos of some sort. Beef is the forbidden food for Hindus, as pork is for many Jews and Muslims. Jewish law forbids the eating of milk products and meat products together in the same meal; shellfish is also out. Apparently, a glass of milk is about as appealing to Chinese consumers as a glass of cow saliva would be to westerners.[7] Protein-packed insects are a gastronomic delight for many who live in Latin America, Africa, Asia and remote parts of Australia, but they are certainly not high on the list of edible foods for most Anglos and Europeans (although one of us has enjoyed scrumptious queen termites in Africa). The whole of the offal repertoire is also off-limits for many in the west. Small or unborn creatures, dogs, cats and other pets are a delicacy for some, and an abomination for others. Vegetarians avoid body parts of any animals and products derived from them, such as lard and gelatine; vegans avoid all animal products, including eggs, milk, cheese and even some non-food products such as leather. For some environmentalists, anything genetically modified is *franken-food*: products that result from the cutting, joining and transferring of genes, especially across species, are viewed by their critics as the gastronomic equivalent of Frankenstein's monster.

Food taboos such as these can be powerful, and inter-cultural menu planning has become big business. Hilka Klinkenberg, founder and managing director of Etiquette International, writes: 'by making the extra effort to accommodate guests and delegates, your event will also receive a five-star rave revue'.[8] An example of the potentially dire consequences of being insensitive to other people's food habits was the Indian Mutiny of 1857. Social unrest probably made the mutiny inevitable, but the final trigger was the British disregard for the Hindu sacred cow and the Muslim execrable pig.[9]

In those days, rifle cartridges had a protective coating of grease, and soldiers were required to bite the cartridge open before loading; the grease was rumoured to be beef and pork fat which are respectively intolerable to Hindus and Muslims.

So where do we derive our notions of what is good to eat and what is bad? How is the line drawn between a delicacy and an abomination? Most of the things that humans find disgusting to eat are, in fact, comestible; so recoiling from them is not instinctive, but something learned. Do these taboos have a logical explanation or are they irrational? There are those who believe it is not possible to seek sensible explanations for food preferences and avoidances because they are totally arbitrary, illogical and beyond reason. It seems to us, however, that most of the gastronomic habits of humans do in fact have a rational basis. Anthropologist Marvin Harris is convincing when he attributes the significant differences in world cuisines to ecological restrictions and opportunities.[10] Cultural anthropologist Mary Douglas' analysis of pollution and taboo also goes some way to offering a rational account of certain food taboos. As Douglas sees it, the distinction between cleanliness and filth is the 'by-product of the creation of order',[11] which stems from the basic human need for categorization. That which is despised does not fit nicely into a society's classification of the world.

Whatsoever parteth the hoof, and is clovenfooted, and cheweth the cud, among the beasts, that shall ye eat. (Leviticus 11: 3)

Prohibited creatures are those which do not meet the criteria of a 'normal' animal. The pig, being a cloven-hoofed non-cud-chewing animal, is anomalous and is therefore despised. Of course, the question remains – why Leviticus classifies edible animals in this manner in the first place. But whatever rationale we may posit for these food habits, today's consumers are clearly following ancient routines here, and for the most part are oblivious to any original reasoning that might underpin their food preferences. Cultural values dictate what is good to eat and what is not. Food preferences are in all senses a matter of taste. Some foodstuffs are tabooed for reasons that are lost in the mists of time; observation of the taboo has become unthinking ritual. Food habits obey our need for ritual, but also fall to gastro-chauvinism: in other words, they are an expression of group belongingness and otherness. Like all taboos, food prohibitions help to maintain a cohesive society. They derive from, and also support, the collective beliefs and behaviour of particular groups; group members are identified and unified by what they do and do not eat.

Because eating and drinking are so connected with the body, food habits are also deeply entwined with the way we think and feel about our bodies. In western societies, food is plentiful and no longer seasonally dependent as it was before the twentieth century. Cultural context is crucial here. After western society had broken away from the voluptuous ideal for the female body, the 'flappers' of the 1920s bound their breasts and lost their curves. As Wallis Simpson (Duchess of York) famously said: 'No woman can be too rich or too thin.' Today's values continue to associate thinness with sexual attractiveness, and this goes some way to account for the dietary restrictions of modern-day eaters; there is a lot of social pressure, particularly on women, to be thin. However, current views about eating also stress the central significance of control.[12] Comparing the significance of food to women during the Middle Ages with the way modern people view food and body, Bynum writes:

> modern people see food and body as resources to be controlled. Thus food and body signify that which threatens human mastery. They signify the untamed, the rebellious, the excessive, the proliferating. (Bynum 1987: 300)

A fear of losing control lurks behind many of our current taboos, in particular those surrounding the body and bodily urges. Technology has intensified this anxiety. Products of modern science – deodorants, pain relief, tranquillisers, the pill, fertility drugs, Viagra, hormone replacement therapy, Botox, hair dyes – have made it possible to control some aspects of bodily experience. Advances in cosmetic surgery – face lifts, tummy tucks, breast enhancements, labial reduction, pectoral and calf implants, penile reconstruction – have meant we can change the way we look and function. Food and drink are just shit and piss waiting to happen. Yet, for the most part, the so-called *calls of nature* are not things over which we have a lot of sway. Because we are human, and our view of animals is fairly negative, we tend to despise those body parts, bodily functions, acts and actions which answer to the call of nature. When we restrict what we eat and drink, there is a sense in which we are trying to take charge of our bodies. Binge eating disorders are characterized by episodes of compulsive, uncontrolled eating. People (overwhelmingly women) who practice binge eating often have difficulties with impulse control in other areas of their lives. Anorexics and bulimics pursue extreme regimens of body control; by starving themselves they assert power over their vile bodies.[13] With fasting, their sex drive diminishes and other bodily functions start shutting down too – for females most notably ovulation and, hence, menstruation. Be they modern-day dieters or the religious aesthetes of the Middle Ages (who drank pus and ate lice and the scabs of lepers), those who deliberately starve themselves are profoundly disparaging of their bodies and bodily sensations.

Culinary camouflage – gastronomic red herrings

In this section, we consider euphemistic aspects of the language that English speakers use in talking about their food. A metaphorical *red herring* is, of course, any sort of misleading distraction; the expression derives from the early practice of drawing a smelly dried red herring across the path of a hunted animal to sharpen up the skill of the hounds. John Ayto[14] extended the term to gastronomy, in order to describe foods such as *Scotch woodcock, Bombay duck* and *Welsh rabbit*, whose names suggest something they are definitely not. *Scotch woodcock* is scrambled eggs on toast, topped with anchovy fillets. *Bombay duck* involves fish, generally dried and eaten with curry; the fish floats near the surface which perhaps explains the description *duck*. *Welsh rabbit* is a mixture of melted cheese, ale or wine and butter or mustard on toast – 'for a rich rabbit, fry the toast in bacon fat'.[15] We extend the term *gastronomic red herring* to include any sort of misleading (and generally euphemistic) language of food; for instance *I can't believe it's not butter*, and the range of fake meat products for vegetarians. It is language that disguises, distorts, deceives, misleads, inflates, obfuscates – language that makes the unpalatable seem palatable, the negative seem positive, the unpleasant seem attractive, the ordinary seem extraordinary.

Most English speakers are distant from the source of much of the food they eat, and this can be a trigger for culinary camouflage. Many of us don't like to think of the living originals of our meat and fish dishes. Butcher shops no longer have a backdrop of hanging carcasses and sawdust to soak up the blood. Cooking now eschews its once close association with the slaughter of animals. Creatures are today seldom served whole; a roasted pig with head, tail and trotters intact is repugnant to some. Most people who still eat meat buy cuts. Many prefer their meat wrapped in neat plastic packs, perhaps already crumbed and marinated or turned into burgers, so that it bears little resemblance to a creature once living. Because they are said to be healthier, some even resort to soy products that imitate the taste and texture of meat. Carving at table has become a rare sight, and the special vocabulary that once accompanied it has disappeared, along with the skills. *The Compleat Housewife or Accomplish'd Gentlewoman's Companion* of 1729 advises on how to *tulk* a barbel, *souce* a capon, *frush* a chicken, *unlace* a coney, *transon* an eel, *barb* a lobster, *splay* a bream, *wing* a partridge, *disfigure* a peacock, *allay* a pheasant, *thigh* a pigeon, *splat* a pike, *mince* a plover, *chine* a salmon, *tranch* a sturgeon, *lift* a swan and *culpon* a trout.[16]

Death is banished from the modern kitchen, and instructions in early cookbooks appear gruesome to modern readers. Here are a few examples from the seventeenth and eighteenth centuries:[17]

> [Recipe for roast duck] Kill and draw your ducks.
> [Dry devils] Dissect a brace of woodcocks . . . split the heads, subdivide the wings . . . crush the trail [entrails] and brains.
> [Jugged hare] Cutt her in small pieces.
> [Stewed prawns] Pick out their tails. Bruise the bodies.
> [Stewed carp] Stirr the blood with a little white wine.
> [Boiled pike] Kill the fish in the head, pierce, take a handful of coarse salt, rub it until the phlegm goes out of the fish, open it at the belly and take out the refete [contents of the stomach] and take out the gall-bladder and strip all the small intestine and . . . save the large gut.

Culinary activities are very different today, and so too is the vocabulary of cooking. Most of us no longer *kill*, *draw*, *gut*, *pluck*, *clean and bone*, *hack*, *hew* or even *mince*. Modern recipe books approach the killing of lobsters humanely:

Put the lobsters in a very large saucepan of cold salted water . . . place pan over a low heat. Bring to the boil very slowly. The lobsters will remain asleep and die without suffering. (Gray and Rogers 1997: 77)

Certain animal parts make people feel squeamish; and when testicles, lungs, kidneys, hearts, livers and cheeks are served at the table, naming them becomes an issue. It is telling that for many English speakers, folk etymology now connects the label *offal* with the word *awful*.

Liver. Try rolling the word around your tongue like a fine red wine. Savour its liquid consonants, the flow of its syllables, the music of its vowels. It doesn't work. It's still offal. (Halligan 1990: 85)

When liver is turned into a dish, it usually acquires a French name; for example, *foie gras* and *paté de foie* sound more appetizing than 'fat liver' and 'liver paste'. (True French *paté de foie* is actually *foie gras* encased in pastry.) Sometimes, we just use the French word for the earthenware or china dish the food is cooked in, such as *terrine* and *casserole*. The French language has been dressing up the language of our food for centuries. No better illustration can be found than in the familiar nomenclature for meat: the name for the animal is Old English: *pig*, *boar*, *swine*, *deer*, *sheep*, *ox*, *cow*, *calf*; when it is served up as a tasty dish it is French: *ham*, *gammon*, *pork*, *venison*, *mutton*, *beef*, *veal*. The names for cuts of meat also tend to be French: *loin*, *chine*, *haunch* or *brawn*; Old English words are used for the inferior cuts. We eat *beef fillet*, *pork tenderloin*, *veal fillet* or *medallions* (round slices cut from it) but *ox tails*, *ox liver*, *pig tails*, *pig's trotters*, *calf's liver* and, in some parts of the world, *calf's-foot-jelly*. Names such as *ox fillet* and *pig tenderloin* sound odd because there is a clash of styles. For some 200 years after the

Norman Conquest in 1066, French was the language used among the upper classes, and the effect on English was enormous. Between 1250 and 1400, some 10,000 words were adopted, and roughly 75 per cent of these are still in use today. The nature of the borrowed items reflects the prestige that the Norman French enjoyed during this time. Interestingly, *dinner* and *supper* are French, but humble *breakfast* is Old English. The Normans controlled the state, the military and cultural and intellectual interests, and French words flooded into these areas. They imported spices, foreign herbs, plants, even animals; and they introduced to the English their tastes in food, their culinary methods – and their expressions for all of these.[18]

Antipodeans are dubious about eating something called *shark* (perhaps it is because they sometimes eat us); so when shark is intended as food, it is called in Australian English *flake*, and in New Zealand English *lemon fish*. Well, why not? Apparently, no one would eat *tuna* either until the name was changed from *horse mackerel* – 'tuna' tastes better than 'horse mackerel', it seems. Now that *mad cow disease* or *BSE* (bovine spongiform encephalopathy) has come to light, it will be interesting to see if a new gastronomic red herring appears for *beef* – there is no sign of one, even though in the mid 1990s, beef and beef products disappeared from many British menus. In fact, the risks of contracting the fatal brain disease euphemistically known as *CJD* (Creutzfeldt-Jakob disease) are lower than they have ever been before; nonetheless, the squeamishness endures.

Often, linguistic disguises are recruited to conceal unmentionable parts of the animal. Our late nineteenth-century forbears avoided terms such as *leg*, *thigh* and *breast*, even when speaking of a cooked fowl, referring instead to its *dark* (or *red) meat* and *white meat*; terms still heard today. Coy Americans resorted to the term *joint* for the leg of a cooked chicken or turkey. The use of *drumstick* in this context is an earlier expression (dating from the mid eighteenth century), and it provided another useful linguistic escape hatch for speakers. The Victorians had an almost pathological dread of speaking about anything below the waist; this was a time when frilled pantalettes hid the *limbs* of the table and the pianoforte.[19] But modern English speakers should not be smug. We employ a variety of linguistic manoeuvres to ensure that when certain animal parts are turned into food, we don't mention them. *Prairie/ mountain oysters* refer to calf's testicles – also referred to as *fry*. In fact, in many English dialects *fry* has become a kind of all-purpose euphemism for any culinary unmentionable. The label refers to the method of cooking and nicely sidesteps the issue as to what bits actually appear in the dish. There was once a noun *plucks*, which meant literally 'that which is plucked out', and covered liver, heart and lung; in other words, the so-called *variety meats* or *organ meats*. In some English dialects, *lamb's fries* are testicles of young sheep; in others *lamb's fry* is *liver and lights* ('lungs'). The name effectively disguises the fact that liver is involved – with repellent thoughts of hydatid cysts, and all the unappetizing associations that offal generally has for us now (even under the name *sweetbread*).[20] In some English-speaking parts of the world, the testicles of the calf or young sheep get transformed via euphemistic magic to *external kidneys* – in French *rognons blancs* or 'white kidneys'. This is reminiscent of the slippery meanings of certain human body part terms (a linguistic phenomenon known by some as 'genital flip-flop'): the slang anatomical expressions *fanny*, *prat* and *tail* have all at some stage in their history meant 'buttocks' and 'female pudendum' – and in the case of *tail*, the 'penis' as well. Such was the trepidation in the Victorian era surrounding the part of the body between the diaphragm and the groin that the word *belly* was metamorphosed linguistically into *stomach*, *chest* and even *viscera*.

The gastronomic superstitions of today taboo heavy consumption of substances such as salt, cooking oil, sugar, caffeine, butter and margarine. Even mineral waters proudly proclaim on their labels '0 calories', '0 carbohydrates', '0 fat', and '0 sodium' (*sodium* avoids mention of salt). Fat is high on the list of banned foods, and terms such as *fried*, *oil*, *butter* and *fat* have become dirty words. Exploiting the notion that fatty foods are sinful, advertisements describe 'guilt-free indulgences' such as '99.9% fat-free skimmed milk yogurt', 'lean 'n' tasty 97% fat-free leg ham' and '97% fat-free fruit swirls'; presumably, many of us would be less inclined to eat them if the label read *0.1% fat* or *3% fat*. When words such as *rich* and *creamy* appear in advertisements, they are typically coupled with *light/lite* and *fat-free* – 'Pauls extra fruit yoghurt and Pauls Extra Lite so thick and creamy you can eat them with a fork' or 'New Sara Lee rich and creamy light Ice Cream'. Visual euphemisms are commonplace; for example, low calorie salad dressing (usually oil-free) is presented in shapely, slender-waisted bottles. The shape, the cleverly altered spelling and reversed colouring on some of the packaging sends out the message *non-fattening* loud and clear – compare the outward appearance of a can of Diet Coke versus (regular) Coke. Even the spelling 'l-i-t-e' looks 'light'! On the other hand, preferred foods now come equipped with all manner of nutritional supplements: *high-fibre* products are thought to be healthy; food and drinks are now enhanced with *vitamins*; yogurt and milk come with added *bioregulating microbic flora*. So the current euphemistic food descriptives are *low fat/cholesterol*, *lite*, *diet*, *added fibre*, *vitamin enriched*, *fortified*, and so on. Food products are often marketed as being health-enhancing or illness-preventing. There are *nutraceutical* foods designed to prevent cardiovascular disease, reduce cholesterol, hypertension or osteoporosis, and to replenish our supplies of the mysterious substances called *free radicals*. We can buy *carbohydrate-electrolyte sports drinks*, *eggs enriched with essential oils*, *chewing gum enhanced with calcium and algae*, *anti-stress mints*. Modern advances in the food-tech industry mean you can now have your cake and eat it too – anxious eaters can now buy *smart meat*, with vegetable oil pumped into cuts of meat to give the effect of marbling, *cheese spread* without fat or diary products (and in a handy spray can) and *guiltless creme anglaise*, guaranteed to contain no eggs or cream. Products such as 'rich creamy Norco Prestige Vanilla and Chocolate Ice-cream wrapped in a generous choc coating' and chocolate desserts that go by names like *Death by Chocolate* and *Decadence* trade on the thrill people experience when they transgress food taboos.

In her account of the rampant sanitizing of textbooks and state education testing services in the USA, Ravitch describes how publishers are expected to include references and illustrations of only nutritious foods, and omit all references to food high in fat, sugar and salt.[21] In a glossary of forbidden words and topics, she includes a hit list of foods, originally compiled in 1981 by the California State Nutrition Unit and adopted by various publishing houses in their guidelines for textbook writing. The banned substances include alcoholic drinks, bacon, salt pork, butter, margarine, lard, cakes, candy, coffee, condiments, corn chips, cream, cream cheese, doughnuts, french fries, fruit punches, gravies, gum, honey, jam, jelly, preserves, ketchup, juice drinks, pickles, pies, potato chips, pretzels, salad dressings, mayonnaise, salad oil, shortening, salt, snack chips, soda pop, sour cream, sugar (all kinds), sweet rolls, tea, water (Italian) ices, whipped cream. Acceptable foods include meat (preferably unfried), fish, poultry (unfried), shellfish, eggs, cooked beans, peas, nuts, nut butters, seeds, milk, cheese, yogurt, cottage cheese, fruits, vegetables, fruit and vegetable juices (100%), bulgar, cornmeal, fish sandwiches and, finally, enriched and wholegrain breads, rolls, muffins, biscuits, cereal, pastas and rice. Small wonder Kentucky Fried Chicken Inc. felt compelled to change its name to *KFC* to hide the 'Fried'. Ravitch reports how one publisher was required to remove an illustration of children clustered around a birthday cake because it is not considered nutritious. She also describes a case of gastronomic bowdlerism. Two texbook publishers had selected a story entitled 'A Perfect Day for Ice Cream'[22] to include in the junior high school literature anthology. Complying with California's ban on junk foods, however, they proceeded to expunge all references to chilli burgers, pizza, and ice cream – even the title was changed to 'A Perfect Day'. As an aside, it is interesting to note that a number of takeaway food products, such as hamburgers and hot dogs, did in fact make it onto the Nutrition Unit's list of acceptable foods – even though the 'photo don'ts' clearly block representations of junk food, including hot dogs. This is the sort of hypocrisy and doublethink that usually accompany taboo avoidance. Of course, in an American book it would be problematic to ban a national gastronomic icon like the hamburger. Presumably, the fast food corporations had a hand in this decision.

Culinary euphemism is often motivated by the need to make something that is intrinsically unappetizing or mundane sound better by giving it a nice name. A scarcity of meat was perhaps the motivation for the description *Welsh rabbit* and also *Welsh rarebit*, a genteel variant of the name of this cheese dish that appeared in the eighteenth century. The name *Alaska strawberries* sounds tastier than the reality of dried beans. *Luncheon meat* sounds mouth watering for *poor man's Spam*™. *Chicken-Ham à la Princesse* was a 1950s combination of canned cream of chicken soup with cubed spam and evaporated milk.[23] Prime examples of this sort of culinary hyperbole can be found on the names of pet foods. On supermarket shelves we find cat food labelled *Tuna Flakes Fusion with Whitebait in Tuna Jus* and *Greek Isle Feast with Calamari, Lamb and Rice*.[24]

Cookbooks, restaurants and cafes sometimes offer fine examples of this kind of inflated language. Much of it is French-inspired vocabulary to connote culinary refinement. How much classier a meal becomes when a *leek tart* is changed to *flamiche aux poireaux*, *oxtail* to *queue de boeuf* and *tossed salad* to *salade composée*. *Soup* versus *potage de* whatever, *stew* versus *casserole*, *slice* versus *tranche*, *aged* versus *affiné*, *swimming* versus *nageant*, *in aspic* versus *en gelée*, *reheated* versus *rechauffé* – all distinguish the mundane from the elegant. Of course, French can capture finer gastronomic distinctions than English: we have no term for 'a chunk of meat or fish that is longer than it is wide' or 'the edible heart of a vegetable' – French *tronçon* and *trognon* plug these gaps. For those in the business of food, it is important whether the vegetables are *chiffonade* 'cut into very thin ribbon-like strips' or *julienne* 'cut into fine matchstick strips'. There is probably a significant difference between vegetables that have been diced into a *brunoise* (tiny cubes) and those that have been diced into a *mirepoix* (not so tiny cubes). And let's face it, there is not a lot of poetry in names like *mushy peas*, *spotted dick* (and *treacle dick*), *toad in the hole*, *Sussex puddle*, *bloated herring* (or *bloater*).[25] 'How-to' books for menu designers in the US advise using foreign languages to 'continentalize your menu'.[26] As the Zwickys illustrate in their glorious account of American restaurant menus, the language of 'restaurantese' can go to extraordinary lengths in the quantities of French dressing applied.[27] Frenchifying a menu might simply involve a dash of token phrases like *du jour* and *au* added onto strings of otherwise English words: *Turtle soup au Sherry* and *Split Filet of Tenderloin au Burgundy*. Other linguistic condiments include *au gratin* and *en casserole*: *Ravioli parmagiana, en casserole*; *Au Gratin Potatoes en Casserole*. (English *gratin* 'topped with grated grilled cheese' has moved a long way from the original French, which referred simply to a crispy baked topping or any crisped surface.) But the examples go beyond the straightforward incorporation of loan words; aspects of French grammar are also used much like pieces of garnish. Just the French definite article is enough to suggest fine food. It doesn't have to be the correct one – typically masculine *le* is the unmarked article of 'menuese' (as it generally is in French borrowings from English): *Le Crabmeat Cocktail*; *Le Peach Melba Sundae*; *Le Coupe aux Marrons Sundae*; *Le Salade*; *Le Crab Meat d'Alaska au Sherry*. Compare the use of masculine *le* with the feminine form *petite* 'small' that commonly appears in examples like *Petite Filet Mignon* – the English word *small* never appears on menus. In fact *small* is avoided at all costs in foodspeak, even for those products that come in more than one size – these often start at *large* and then move to *extra large*, *king-size* or *jumbo*. Extraordinary linguistic hybrids like *Stuffed Tomato aux Herbes, Shoreham Style*; *Café American*; *Broiled Steak Minute*; *Flaming Coffee Diablo, Pre-pared en Vue of Guest* and our favourites *Clams Larry* and *Baked Stuffed Lobster Larry* also have that truly *je ne sais quoi* word order – in the tradition of the culinary greats like *Tournedos Rossini* and *Steak Diane*, the modifiers follow that which is being modified.

Occasionally, you encounter menus that don't go in for this sort of decorative language. The following is a sample of informative and orthophemistic menu entries from a Chinese restaurant in Melbourne. Of course, the fact that the foods listed here would not feature in many Anglo repertoires of edible animal parts adds to the shock value of this menu.

> Pig's Blood and Skin with Carrot Platter
> Soya Yin Yang Large Intestines
> Crispy Skin Large Intestines
> Bone Marrow with Abalone, Mushroom, Sea Cucumber and Shredded
>   Bamboo Shoots
> Sea Cucumber, Shark's Lips with Duck Feet in Clay Pot
> Stir Fried Hakka Cabbage with Small Intestines
> Stir Fried Hakka Cabbage with Large Intestines
> Stir Fried Mixed Chicken Gizzards
> Stewed Head and Stomach of Schnapper with Brown Sauce
> Mixed Offal with Ginger
> Pig's Blood

Cannibalism

Somewhere at the back of our minds, carefully walled off from ordinary consideration and discourse, lies the idea of cannibalism – that human beings might *become* food, and eaters of each other. Violence, after all, is necessary if any organism is to ingest another. Animals are murdered to produce meat; vegetables are torn up, peeled, and chopped; most of what we eat is treated with fire; and chewing is designed remorselessly to finish what killing and cooking began. People naturally prefer that none of this should happen to them. Behind every rule of table etiquette lurks the determination of each person present to be a diner, not a dish. It is one of the chief roles of etiquette to keep the lid on the violence which the meal being eaten presupposes. (Visser 1992: 3–4)

Cannibalism or *anthropophagy*, as it is labelled by anthropologists and historians, is the strongest of all our food taboos, if not society's ultimate taboo. It comes in many forms. There are the well-known cases of *survival cannibalism*, where desperate victims of air disasters and shipwrecks eat their dead comrades, or in extreme cases draw lots and sacrifice the living. Some groups of people eaters, such as the Aztecs and those of Old Polynesia, practised a kind of *ritual cannibalism*. This has a deeply religious significance, usually involving the public killing and eating of an enemy. In other groups, it can be a more private intimate practice; as part of a funerary ritual, for example, whereby people consume parts of their dead kin (in Papua New Guinea and Amazonia) or for medical and nutritional purposes (in parts of China). Then, of course, there are the real-life Hannibal Lecters – 'cannibal killers' who murder other people and eat their flesh. In their history of cannibalism, Korn, Radice and Hawes document the ghoulish tales of some of these psychopaths, from one of the first recorded cases, the sixteenth-century Sawney Beane and his cannibal family, who terrorized the Galloway coast for about twenty-five years, through to the twentieth-century Jeffrey Dahmer, whose murderous tastes turned from sadism and gay necrophilia to cannibalism.[28]

The technical term *anthropophagus* first appeared in English in the early 1500s (from Greek *anthropos* 'man' and *phagein* 'eat'). It has spawned a surprising number of alternative expressions such as *anthropophaginian*, *anthropophagist*, *anthropophagite* and *anthropophagizer* that are rarely encountered. The more familiar word *cannibal* is a Spanish corruption of what was originally one of the forms of the ethnic name for the Caribs from the West Indies, as used by Christopher Columbus in his journal of 1492. They were reputed to be anthropophagi, and the term extended to include all people eaters – probably reinforced by Columbus' association of the term with the Great Khan of the Mongols whom he expected to encounter on his voyage. A later folk etymology that connected *cannibal* with the Latin *canis* 'dog' contributed to the term's wide acceptance.[29]

These days the expression *cannibal,* like *primitive* and *savage,* tends to be avoided because of its racist overtones. The highly coloured cannibal narratives of the early chroniclers were an effective way of justifying the activities of the 'civilized' colonizers – human sacrifice and flesh-eating are 'savage' practices, and people who eat other people are not quite human.[30] European invaders either converted them to Christianity or had few qualms about wiping them out entirely. Perhaps knowing these details makes many guilty westerners reluctant to believe accounts of cannibalism. They are the stuff of folklore, literature and racist jokes. Cartoons of painted natives stewing their victims (missionaries or big game hunters with pith helmets intact) in large pots over open fires persisted into the 1960s. Accounts of cannibalism are generally believed to be bogus, with the exception of desperate survival stories such as the Andes air crash of 1972, or extreme cases of individual cannibal killers like Dahmer and more recently Amin Meiwes (who killed and ate parts of Bernd Jürgen Brandes after posting an advertisement on the Internet for a well-built man for slaughter). But perhaps the behaviour is also so repellent to us as to be unimaginable – to such an extent, in fact, that in places like Britain and Australia, acts of cannibalism are not technically illegal. (The Meiwes case was particularly problematic for German law since Brandes had actually volunteered himself to be killed and butchered for the dinner table.) It is certainly striking that, despite abhorrence of this practice, English lacks euphemisms for 'people eaters'.

From anthropological and archaeological evidence, it is clear that cannibalism comes in a wide variety of different forms and is just one of the many kinds of behaviour that may or may not be practised by human groups. Most of us would presumably baulk at placenta-eating; but in 1998, UK Channel 4's cooking series *TV Dinners* did feature *placenta paté* on one of its programmes.[31] Yet if we think about it, there are a lot of aspects to modern life that smack of cannibalism. Human tissue (including placenta) is used in prescription medicines. Organ transplants and blood transfusions are now standard medical practice. Moreover, many of us chew our finger nails and surrounding skin (*onychophagia*), plunge cut fingers into our mouths, and swallow nasal mucus. Some people regularly drink their own urine and a very few eat their own stools. The Christian doctrine of *transubstantiation* is a type of ritual cannibalism whereby the wine and bread consumed is believed to become the blood and flesh of Christ. Certainly, as we will later explore, the resemblances between our sexual activities and eating are striking and, not surprisingly, metaphorical cannibalism features large in the language of sex. Cannibalism in some form or other is more commonplace than we like to think.

Gastronomic xenophobia

Given the symbolic values we attach to foodstuffs and foodways, it is not surprising to find that these have a significant role to play in the language of nationalism and race. Names of foods are often flavoured with old and new prejudices. Indeed, a number of the gastronomic red herrings mentioned earlier are derogatory to other races. The cheese dish called *Welsh rabbit* is a nice example of linguistic xenophobia. During the seventeenth and eighteenth centuries, *Welsh* was used for anything of an inferior grade: a *Welsh comb* is when one 'combs one's hair with one's fingers'; a *Welsh pearl* is a 'counterfeit pearl or one of inferior quality'; a *Welsh cricket* is a 'louse'. There are many more examples – *French Pie* 'a type of stew', *Jew Butter* 'a dripping made of goose grease' and *German Duck*, which in the late eighteenth and early nineteenth centuries referred to 'half a sheep's head boiled with onions' (or alternatively was slang for 'bed bug'). *Irish grapes, lemons, apples* and *apricots* were all once used for 'potato'; *Irish cherry* was a sneer term for 'carrot'. *Nigger candy* was the name given to a nineteenth-century lolly made of hard black licorice (later renamed *chocolate baby*), and around that same time were also dishes such as *niggers in a snow storm* (stewed prunes and rice) and *nigger-in-a-blanket* (a dessert made of raisins in dough). On the other hand, black waiter's lingo from that same period has terms like *burn the British* ('toasted English muffin'), and in-group names like *nigger steak* ('liver'), *nigger and halitosis* ('liver and onions'). *Pope's/parson's nose* denotes the fatty tail of a cooked chicken and is reputed to have originated as a slur on Catholics during the reign of James II (1685–8).

Increasingly, it seems, food and drink are featuring in racial and ethnic slurs. Whereas early racial abuse displayed strong moral stereotyping (often with religious overtones), in modern times it plays much more on superficial characteristics to do with appearance and dietary habits.[32] Abuse terms show a rich exuberance of racial insults based upon food. Most of the expressions are extensions of the names for the food items stereotypically associated with each group. Here is just a small sample: *frog* and *frog-eater* 'French person'; *kraut* and *krauthead* 'German'; *cabbage-eater* 'German or Russian'; *macaroni, spag, spaghetti, spaghetti-head, spaghetti-bender, spaghetti-eater* 'Italian person' (giving rise to *spaghetti western* 'cowboy films made cheaply in Italy'); *frijole-guzzler, beaner, bean-eater* 'Mexican'; *ricer, rice-eater* 'Chinese' (to which we can add the Australian slang term *RGB* = rice gobbling bastard 'Asian person'); *french fries* or *snow frogs* ('Québecois', in Canada); *potato-head, potato-eater* 'Irish person' (also *potato-fingered Irishman* for 'clumsy person'); *leek* 'Welsh person'. The Scots, like the Dutch, are celebrated for being thrifty, and a *Scotch fillet* is a cheaper cut than other fillets. It seems that the English mind has long connected the Dutch with dairy products, and labels like *butter-mouth, butter-bag* and *butter-box* meaning 'Dutchman' date back to the sixteenth and seventeenth centuries. The Scots have been known to refer to their English neighbours as *pock-puddings* or *poke-puddings*, referring to a kind of boiled pudding (from Scots *poke* 'sack'). There is also the label *limey* for 'English person', which has its origins in the early practice of English sailors eating limes as a protection against scurvy. Related nicknames include *lime-juice, lime-juicer* and *lemon-eater*; also *Limeyland* used by Australians to refer to 'the mother country'.

Food and sex

Looking at the spread I've laid out on the table, I begin to feel wary of the competition. I go back to the bathroom and dab on more perfume and inspect my face for spots with increasing dismay.

But later I'm reassured by the thought of the bite-size filo-pastry pouches filled with camembert and cranberries, the spinach and salmon mousse, the tomato I found almost ready to burst that now reclines in slices, on a bed of fresh marjoram lapped by raspberry vinegar, the apple tarts with slices spread open like legs and the champagne, all left hardly touched as we fuck, bare and forked, on the floor.

He cups my cunt in his hand like a bread-roll, nudges the halves apart, and fills me. (Ellman 1989: 35)

The first bite rises towards the opening mouth. The sentinel nose having anticipated the pie's arrival, a tide of saliva rests in the mouth, pools in the tongue's centre, washes over several thousand taste buds. The teeth bite through flaky, slightly salty crust and then into tart cherries and rhubarb and apple. The fruits' sweet and buttery juices, in a total immersion baptism of the mouth, flood tongue, teeth, cheeks. There is no more outside. Everything is in. (Moore 1994: 6–7)

The beer [Heineken™] that reaches parts others can't touch.

Food is a common source concept for naming parts of the body, particularly the sexual organs and associated acts and actions.[33] But before we look at this vocabulary, we need to consider what gives food its sexy reputation. Food is often the prelude to sex. 'After a perfect meal, we are more susceptible to the ecstasy of love than at any other time.'[34] Eating and love-making go together. It is not just in the condition of euphoria that both activities bring on. The quote above from Lucy Ellman's *Sweet Desserts* is a not-so-subtle reminder of the similarities between our sexual practices and eating habits. Both depend on a tangle of bodily sensations – sight, touch, taste, smell. Their long and intimate association has been made much of by writers like Laura Esquivel (*Like Water for Chocolate*) and film makers like Peter Greenaway (*The Cook, the Thief, his Wife and her Lover*). Who could forget that glorious scene in Tony Richardson's film *Tom Jones* where Tom (Albert Finney) and Mrs Waters (Joyce Redman), frantic for flesh, tear into juicy pieces of chicken. Even basic food writing these days draws heavily from sex, and descriptions like the following seem to ooze erotic possibilities. Chefs are the new rock 'n' roll stars, cookbooks are the new pornography.[35]

At Armstrong's Tables of Toowong fat oysters had been lifted from their shells, and then returned onto a gently spiced cushion of noodles, touched with an olive oil, lemon and saltwater vinaigrette, and topped with a dollop of oscietra caviar. Linguini had been tossed in truffle oil, studded with shards of crisp asparagus, topped with a soft-poached egg and a generous slice of fresh, black truffle. (*Vogue*, Entertaining, February/March 1996 p. 52)

As a **summer treat** homemade ice-creams take some licking. Chins, wrists, elbows – we're up to our ears in **sticky fingers**. Gluttony for **cool sensations** overcomes us. Fruit seduces us into feasting. Salads toss a new leaf. Picnics are the obsession of **long, luscious days:** casual affairs which take breakfast and newspapers to the water's edge; and **elegant settings** from which the dining room walls seem simply to have melted away. (*Vogue*, Entertaining, February/March 1996 p. 59; *sic*)

The juicy waffle of winespeak relies heavily on sex for inspiration. Tasting notes refer to *sex on a forest floor* and *sex in a bottle*. A California Cabernet is 'Naomi Campbell in latex'; an Australian Shiraz 'a Chippendales dancer in leather chaps – tight, full bodied and ready for action'.[36] The following review describes what is claimed to be an outstanding Australian pinot noir:

Purple/red. An alluring nose with coffee and chocolate combined with wild berries and forest floor aromas. Fresh and clean with fleshy fruit, ripe summer berries and cacao bean flavours. Silky smooth and sensuous, this is a wine for seduction, as a symphony of taste sensations saturate the palate. Seamless and integrated, there is a continuity of flavour that lasts from first sip until last drop. Wine so sexy they should attach a birth control warning to the back of the bottle! (Sloane 1999)

The preparation of food seems charged with ardent expectation of sensuous manipulation. Even in these days of microwaves and takeaway, we are advised to 'get floury, sticky, wholly involved'.[37] Think of plunging your hands into a bowl of egg and raw mince, pushing up moist herb-scented stuffing into the open orifice a chicken, rubbing flour into soft dough. The stuffing of courgette (zucchini) flowers is described like a wedding night: getting your hands on fresh, small, plump, creamy-fleshed courgettes with their flowers intact. 'Born limp and languid, the shooting star of the vegetable world, fiori di zucca beg to be dealt with quickly.'[38]

Of course, this style of writing is wonderful fodder for lampooning comedians. BBC Two's *Posh Nosh* is a notable example. Its website informs us that this satirical show teaches you to 'relax an avocado, bamboozle a parsnip and shave a fennel, all on a duvet of rice paper'.[39] Here is Simon Marchant explaining a number of the steps in his recipe for 'Leftover Supper' (as he describes it, 'dinner with its shirt undone . . . relaxed, languid, louche'):

Now for the chicken. **Brando** one-third of the butter in the chicken's world of interior. Then mollify its complexion with the remaining two-thirds. Massage rhythmically and gently. Your aim is to make the dead bird happy. If a chicken feels bitter, it tastes bitter. Aga-sweat at 200, for about 58 minutes, butter-basting often. When your chicken is noblesse oblige, embarrass a leg and some decolletage and twirl some flaked flesh in the pan-sweat. Leave by a south-facing window for an hour, giving the chicken ample time to de-traumatise and **un-heat**.

Place your parsnips in an auction-bought dish. Arrange them centrifugally like the spokes of a wheel in a Brueghel painting. (Brueghel the Elder, of course.) **Twirl** a smattering of leaves from still-beating lettuce hearts. Shower the epicentre with French still mineral watercress. Let almonds fall where'er they may, at five centimetre interludes.

Regard your Parsnip and Watercress Salad with amusement. It's just like the pugliese, isn't it? Or that floppy Tuscan mane. It's all too precise and perfect. So, just imagine you're muzzing that young man's mane. Plunge both hands in and fiddle with your fingers. Turn it from immaculate to **untidy**. It may feel wrong, but it's right. It's natural, it's what happens, he really can't complain. He may tell you you've made him feel 'like something leftover on the side of the plate'. Explain that a leftover is something wonderful. One doesn't want a five-course meal all the time. (http://www.bbc.co.uk/comedy/poshnosh/recipes/leftover.shtml; *sic*. Accessed October 2004)

The link between eating and sex has of course been commercially recognized and is very much exploited in food and wine advertising. Ravishing photographs of plump chorizo sausages speckled with globules of gleaming fat, plump ripe figs split open and nestling in a bed of soft cream cheese, advertisements with luscious lascivious figures selling everything from chocolate to spaghetti sauce – when it comes to promoting food and drink, nothing beats sex.

The long and close association of food and sex is most obvious in aphrodisiacs – those foods that are claimed to have erotic properties and are used to stir up sexual desire. Nowadays – the low-fat fads aside – we tend to base our culinary creations upon our imaginations, upon our fancies and tastes at the time. In early days, however, it was quite different. Culinary creations were placed within a strict system of dietary constraints that carefully balanced hot against cold, dry against moist. The wrong ingredients could provoke certain ailments, conditions, serious injuries – and of course debauchery. One fifteenth-century text warns of the risks of eating eggs: 'All maners of egges waken a man to the worke of lecherie, and specialli sparowes egges.' A later text from the sixteenth century alerts its readers to the danger of figs. 'Fygges . . . they doth stere a man to veneryous actes, for they doth auge and increase the seede of generacion. And also they doth prouoke a man to sweate: wherefore they doth ingendre lyce.'[40]

Years ago, London's 'protein passion man' used to roam the streets around Oxford Circus distributing his pamphlet *Eight Passion Proteins With Care* (in 1983, it cost 12 pence). He advised, 'read this booklet occasionally and in times of need . . . at all changes of life: marriage, expectancy, menopause, retirement, old age, new situations, etc'. His 'Protein Wisdom' was straightforward (typography as in the original):

TOO MUCH protein and passion have afflicted humanity, with much distress and oppression.

Proteins are for body building; for body maintenance; and for reproduction involving the build up of passion for mating.

Most foods contain – some protein; but the eight passion-proteins are foods that have much protein, and that individuals eat frequently. So, how obvious it is that we should regulate passion, by regulating our eating of these eight classes of food.

Those who do not have to work hard with their limbs, and those who are inclined to sit about – will STORE UP their protein for passion, during these spells of easiness. Retirement could be a time of boosted passion and marital discord. – During prolonged extreme inactivity, one's needs of protein, could be very small.

The EIGHT passion-proteins are MEAT, FISH, and BIRD; CHEESE, EGGS; PEAS (incl. lentils), BEANS; and NUTS.

. . .

When protein material is building-up the spent reproductive organs again and gradually, this is – recorded in the sensitive brain, and this is increasingly fascinating – the mind wanting – more and – more of it. This is passion.

Other provokers of passion generally fall into several categories. Most obvious are the sex organs of creatures prized for their procreative prowess. Bull's testicles in a red wine sauce is reputed to be excellent food for lovers. Pies made of testicles of young cockerels were once consumed widely in Europe for their erotic boost. More often, though, it is the appearance of the food that stimulates people's minds to lecherous thought. Perhaps they re-semble human sexual organs – phallic asparagus spears, vulval oysters – and via a kind of sympathetic magic, they are claimed to arouse bodily lust. The mandrake root has always had erotic significance because its forked tuber resembles spread human thighs; but also its skin contains a high concentration of narcotic toxins that produce hallucinations. If nature did not fashion the food into the form of sexual organs, then humans would; venereal breads, cakes and pastries date back to Ancient Greece and Rome. Fish of all kinds have always been famous as aphrodisiacs – one of the earliest food scientists, Brillat-Savarin (1755–1826), was of the opinion that fish were strongly sexual and awakened in both sexes the instinct for reproduction.[41] This is presum-ably on account of their aromatics and their slippery quality (more on this below).

Truffles also have a notoriously sexy reputation. Perhaps it is because they are rare, mysterious, terribly expensive and, of course, delicious. More likely, though, it is the musky fragrance – it turns out that the truffle steroid that causes this smell is a match for the steroid that men secrete though their armpits. An experiment conducted in Birmingham, England exposed one group of volunteers to the truffle steroid and one group to nothing but filtered air. The first group awarded higher scores for attractiveness to photographs of the opposite sex.[42] This is probably the only aphrodisiac that has scientific endorsement. The rest are 'a kiss in the dark'.[43] Nevertheless, from ancient dietetics through to modern times, people have believed in the erotic possi-bilities of certain foods. Now, there are signs that these beliefs are being overshadowed by Viagra and other chemical aids.

Food as a metaphor for the sexes

In earlier chapters, we touched on the linguistic ramifications of the close connection between the alimentary and the sexual, and we now explore it further. Even our ordinary, everyday language reminds us of the link between eating and sex: a good looking person is *a dish* or *dishy*. And look in a thesaurus at the entries under **desire**; the overlap of vocabulary is striking: *appetite, hunger, hungry look, craving, greed*. Both food and bodies *whet the appetite, stimulate the juices, make the mouth water, activate the taste buds, excite, smell good, titillate, allure, seduce*. Mouths are sexual organs, of course; usually the first point of contact in early sexual activity. Comparisons between the mouth and the vagina – images of the *vagina dentata* 'toothed vagina' – are widespread in myth and folklore and implicit in many slang epithets: *box with teeth, nether mouth, snapper, snatch, penis fly trap, mangle, organ grinder* and so forth. In many languages, euphemisms for *copulate* are the equivalent of *eat*, and this is also used occasionally in English for both copulation and oral sex. Certainly, the talk between lovers is sometimes strikingly cannibalistic – *I could eat you up*; *I want to suck you dry*. Women, particularly, are depicted as the carnivores, e.g. in the lyrics of Bob Dylan, 'She's a man-eater, meat-grinder, bad loser' or of Hall and Oates, 'Watch out boys, she'll chew you up . . . She's a man-eater.'

Throughout the history of English slang, we find a strong food/eating metaphor for sex, with both sexes depicted as edible objects – *tasty morsels* or *bonne-bouche* ('pleasant taste', literally 'good mouth'). From early times, the meat metaphor has provided one of the strongest images for these slang expressions. The male sex organs, and the body that goes with them, have for centuries (perhaps millennia) been depicted as *meat*. This image continues to spawn new slang items: *beat one's meat* 'masturbate', *meat injection* 'sexual intercourse' and *meat and two veg* 'penis and testicles'. Many slang epithets play on the meat metaphor, with the penis described as *beef bayonet, mutton dagger, pork (sword), gristle, hambone, tubesteak, white meat, dark meat* (depending on race), *joint, marrowbone, marrowbone and cleaver, marrow pudding, (live) sausage* and older *pud* and *pudding*. The early expression *butcher* 'penis' (the instrument of deflowering) has also given rise to *butcher's shop* and *butcher's window* 'vagina'. Newcomers are British English *lunchbox* 'penis and testicles' (*lunchbox* has also been used for 'vagina'; see below) and Australian English *he's packing a good lunch*. Also striking is the recent flourishing of brawn terms for males, including expressions like *beefcake*,[44] *hunk (of meat), piece of meat* and *dog meat*.

For centuries, women have been described as food objects, and the meat idiom has also featured strongly here. Both the nineteenth-century expression *meat-cleaver* 'penis' and sixteenth century *to flash the meat* use the women-as-meat image. But even as early as the fourteenth century, we find the term *piece*, and new compounds based on this appear regularly in the language, referring both to 'vagina' and 'woman' generally. Of course, other foodstuffs could be intended here, but the meat image has always been the strongest: *piece of stuff* (seventeenth century), *piece of mutton*, *piece of ass*, *piece of tail*, *piece of stray* (twentieth century). From the nineteenth century, *bit of* also started appearing in compounds of various kinds: *bit of mutton*, *bit of meat*, *bit on a fork*, *bit of pork* and *a bit of crackling* (a play on *crack* 'vagina'). *Catsmeat* combines the imagery of meat with women-as-cats; compare twentieth-century American slang *PEEP* (perfectly elegant eating pussy). Since the sixteenth century, expressions for promiscuous men have also employed the meat idiom: *mutton-mongers/muttoner* (sixteenth century, from *mutton* 'prostitute; vagina'; mutton was the commonest meat eaten), *flesh-mongers* (from the seventeenth century, also meaning 'whore'), *meat-mongers* (eighteenth century, from *meat* 'vagina') and even *carrion-hunters*. Pimps were known as *meat merchants*, and brothels as *meat houses* and *meat markets* (as dance clubs and beauty pageants are today).

The image of vagina as fish or fishpond is pervasive. Fishy terms include: *fish*, *tench* (playing also on a common nineteenth-century abbreviation for *penitentiary*, in which the penis was imprisoned), *trout, tuna, bit of fish, bit of skate, shell, whelk, periwinkle, fishery, lobster pot*. Copulation becomes *go fishing, groping for trout* (*in a peculiar river*); promiscuous men are *fish-mongers* and *ling-grapplers*. Presumably, these expressions all play on the slipperiness of vaginal secretions and the fishy aromas evoked by a woman's intimate body parts.

Current expressions for the female pudendum appear to rely less on the meat/fish metaphor (though there is the long-standing *bunny*, and twentieth-century additions like *bacon sandwich, hairburger, fuzzburger* and *furburger* 'vagina' show that the image is not dead). More commonly, though, this body part is described in terms of sweets and desserts: *yum-yum* (also 'penis'), *cake, crumpet, pancake, jelly roll* (the jam-filled sponge cake, known also as *swiss roll*), *muffin, cookie, bit of jam* (link to menstruation) and the recent addition *golden doughnut*. Earlier expressions involved a range of different fruits: *apple* (a backformation from sixteenth-century *apple squire* 'pimp'), *split apricot, fig* and *split fig, plum* and, of course, *cherry*.

There is, in fact, a surprising array of different edible food products covered by these slang expressions. For female genitalia, they include a range of vegetables: *cabbage, cabbage patch, cabbage garden, cabbage field, cauliflower, mushroom* and *sweet potato pie* (also *hair pie, fur pie*).

Food may also be the figure in American *cut yourself a piece of poontang*, which echoes the cutting of pie or cake. Food-related expressions for *vagina* also include *oven* (eighteenth century; compare *bun in the oven* 'pregnant'), *kitchen* (nineteenth century), *lunchbox* (twentieth century), *jelly box, honey pot, jampot, sugar basin* and *saltcellar* (from *salt* 'copulation')[45] that are based on the image of containers for food. The words for testicles draw from a variety of small, roundish and naturally occurring foodstuffs such as eggs, seeds, nuts, fruits, stones, potatoes. A penis is often construed as sweet food (something to suck or lick): *sugarstick, lollipop, (tummy) banana, creamstick, ice-cream machine*, and from recent Australian English *blue-veined junket pumper*. One of the great English stereotypes is the association of the French with sex (*French vice* 'sexual malpractices', *French prints* 'pornographic pictures', *French kiss* 'a tongue kiss', *give French* 'fellate'), and some food expressions play on this: *French dip* 'vaginal fluid' and *French dressing* 'semen'. Additional expressions relating to sexual secretions include *love juice* 'vaginal fluid', *going down for the gravy* 'cunnilingus', *dripping pan, gravy giver, gravy maker* 'vagina'.

If ever there were doubt about this food/eating nexus, peruse (as we did) the Valentine's Day notices in newspapers.[46] The range of food types covered was extraordinarily broad. There were the usual suspects – women as buttered buns and crumpets, men as meaty bites and beefcakes – but many other comestibles besides. Breakfast cereals featured prominently – *You are my Snap and Crackle* from *Lizzy Pops*; *Dearest Honey Smacks*. So did pies and casseroles – *Punkin Pie* from *your Tuna Casserole*; *To My Darling Patti Plumb Poo Pie* from *Snutchums*. Fruit, vegetables and nuts were certainly well represented. Pumpkin doesn't usually feature as a sexy vegetable, [47] and it is difficult to think of mashed potato as a provoker of passion, but references to these two vegetables abound in love notices – *Will you be my Chunky Pumpkin*; *I love you Mashed Potato*. There were cheeses of various kinds, and cheesy scones. The meat metaphor was particularly strong. Pet names included *Sloverinfestedpieceofsloverwurst, Chicken Skin, Plum Chicken, Spunky Chicken, Ham Sandwich, Baby Lamb Chop, Chicken Legs, Succulent Tasty Lamb*. Not surprisingly, women called Rosemary made much of the lamb metaphor. There were lashings of references to cakes, biscuits and sweets generally, with pet names like *Cookie, Chewy, Cherryripe, Baby Cakes, Tart, Cupcake, Little Marshmallow, Muffin-Burger, Fig Jam*. The notices also contained references to an array of items that one would not normally connect with bodily lust, but presumably foodstuffs like pickles, omelettes, cream rice, pizzas and guacamole must have special erotic significance for some lovers. The following are just a handful of the Valentine's Day messages we uncovered:

My succulent tasty lamb, just the smell of you drives me wild! Love Rosemary

PUMPKIN. I'm still so happy that we rock, happy Valentines Day No 2. – Love Pumpkin

ANGEL FACE Tonight chocolate, strawberry and banana, yum. – Kitten

A. The 3 months were worth the wait cause you're a burger. – Love always, A.

BABY PUMPKIN SCONE To my darling wife, I love you more than word can express. Thank you for being the one that keeps me going and loves me. All my love on this first Valentine's Day as husband and wife.– Your Baby Lamb Chop

D. Happy Valentine's Day Love you heaps – Your little 'ham sandwich'

D. (POTATO) 1 year, 1 month and 10 days to go. Luv you heaps. – Your fiancee Jodie (Pumpkin) XX

F.J.W. I'll grab the tim tams, you get the custard.– Love C.

LOLLILOVEPOP MAN You're the sweetest my friend Be my Valentine All day suck, XXX

L'OMELETTE Au fromage est prete – Frenchie

LOVE MUFFIN Happy Valentine's Day I love you – STUD MUFFIN. XX

SNOOKUMS A kilo of spinetingling passion, 3 cups of lust, 1 pint of inspirational desire, 2 cups of incredible stamina, Throw in heaps of spontaneity, laughter and romance, And serve with lashings of friendship, love and honesty, For you are destined to make me. 'YOUR MUFFIN'

STICKY DATE PUDDING GIRL Can't stop thinking about you. Chocolate Cake Guy.

Smell

The fallen angel of the senses . . . a potent wizard that transports us across thousands of miles and all the years we have lived. (Keller 1908: 66)

I believe that the most curious feature of our sense of smell is that while we generally relish the sweet scents of a summer garden, or the bouquet from a fine wine, we do not generally relish the natural scents of our fellows. (Stoddart 1990: 56)

Our sense of smell goes hand in hand with taste and is closely linked with the sensations of hunger and thirst. When we lose our sense of smell, taste goes with it; all that remains is texture and temperature. But more than this, the 'fallen angel of the senses' links together many of the seriously tabooed aspects of human life.

   Most of us have read about, if not experienced first-hand, the unmistakable smell of death. It is sweet and sickly. Even diseases are accompanied by their own distinctive smells – typhoid fever brings to mind freshly baked bread, tuberculosis stale beer, diabetes acetone, yellow fever meat, some mental diseases like schizophrenia have a characteristic sweaty odour.[48] Fear in animals, including humans, emits a distinctive odour. Stress brings on the production of adrenalin, getting the heart beating, the blood pressure rising and the sweat pouring. The German language has a name for it – *Angstgeruch* 'fear-smell'. Not least is the smell of sex. In early times, adulterers were punished by amputation of the nose; it was, of course, a very public advertisement of the sin, and the nose is symbolic of the penis (and perhaps by extension, the clitoris); but it also attests to the importance of smell in sexual arousal. Nowadays, we are preoccupied with washing, douching, depilating and deodorizing our bodies. We certainly don't tend to think of the nose as a sex organ (though, in some people, sexual arousal is accompanied by an itchy nose). Modern science confirms that smell is one of the most sexy and provocative of the senses. Sexual arousal in most species is triggered by olfactory experiences, and humans are no exception. Even when we try to conceal our natural body odour with fragrant disguises, these serve to enhance sexual attraction. (Did the marketing gurus deliberately chose the brand name *Viagra* because the word supposedly has its roots in a verb meaning 'to smell'?) Research shows that women linger longer inside telephone booths that have been treated with a musky smelling androgen, and favour seats in a dentist's waiting room that have been sprayed with male hormones. There is even a possibility that incest taboos are closely linked with smells. From puberty on, we are programmed to disregard the sexual attractions of those who we have grown up with (and therefore those who are most likely to be related to us). If sexual attraction has partly to do with odour then, suggest the experts, the block must also have to do with smelling.[49]

Science confirms (1) that we prefer the smells of our friends over strangers; (2) different diets cause people to smell differently; (3) it is a biological fact that different races have different smells (partly this has to do with the varying sizes of axillary glands; people of Asian origin, for example, have smaller or no armpit glands at all and therefore little or no detectable underarm odour). It is hardly surprising, therefore, to find that words for disagreeable smells feature prominently in our dysphemistic repertoires. In these expressions, we refer explicitly to the unpleasant odour, real or imagined, of those human beings or objects we disapprove of, despise, dislike or plain hate. They might be described as *smelly*, *rotten*, *stinking*, *foul* and so on. All language groups have derogatory expressions available for other groups that they come in contact with, and olfactory xenophobia provides the basis for such linguistic taunts. Often, the expressions invoke the food and diet stereotypically associated with the groups. For example, in the nineteenth century, the Japanese described the European traders they came in contact with as *bata-kusai* (literally 'stinks of butter'). During the First World War, English soldiers claimed that the German soldiers lived on and smelled of Sauerkraut (hence the name *krauts*). The smell of garlic (so distinctive it has its own adjective *alliaceous*) provides the basis for several ethnic and racial insults.[50]

As with our food tastes, very little of the way we react to smells seems to be biological. Typically, it depends on the associations that a smell has for us as to whether we find it agreeable or disagreeable. So why are we so uneasy about smells – why the taboos? Perhaps it is simply that we like to stand aloof from our animal origins, and this sense doesn't let us. We can shut our eyes, we can cover our ears, but we cannot stop breathing and when we breathe we take in odours. More than any other sense, our ability to smell reminds us that, as much as we like to deny it, we are animals. We all have our own odour-producing glands, and when we try to mask their smell with perfumes and deodorants we cannot overcome the fact that each person smells different.

Ambivalence is part of the human condition, unavoidable in a species struggling to reconcile the existence of an advanced brain in the scented body of a naked ape. (Watson 2000: xii)

Distaste for the body and its effluvia goes back a long way. Christian teaching maintained that human life was only a temporary stage in what was seen as a journey towards a much better future existence. Therefore only the soul was worthy of attention, and any attempt to prolong life was deemed irreverent. The body was just too base a thing to be of any importance and was certainly not the affair of the pious, some of whom went to extraordinary lengths to uphold this belief; there are even records of people canonized solely on account of the fact that they did not wash.[51] However, it seems our queasiness about smells and smelling has endured, to the extent that natural body odours are now subject to some of the most stringent of taboos, particularly when it comes to women's procreative organs. So-called *personal hygiene products* explicitly target women – there are no male-oriented sprays to complement the array of *feminine sprays* (vaginal deodorants) currently on the market.

A memorable figure in any discussion of smelling would have to be Patrick Süskind's creation, Jean-Baptiste Grenouille, the grotesque character in his novel *Perfume: The Story Of A Murderer*. Grenouille's remarkable gift was his extraordinary sense of smell. Described as 'the finest nose in Paris', and capable of nuancing hundreds of thousands of different odours, Grenouille could differentiate objects by smell far more keenly and more precisely than others could do by sight. For Grenouille, the mismatch between his rich world of smells and the poverty of his language was particularly acute. The French language proved totally inadequate for his intense olfactory experiences, even those he encountered on a day-to-day basis. 'Why should smoke possess only the name "smoke"', he complained. 'Why should earth, landscape, air – each filled at every step and every breath with yet another odour and thus animated with another identity – still be designated by just those three coarse words.'[52]

For the rest of us, with our more pedestrian protuberances, the sort of lexical richness that Grenouille was seeking might seem totally unnecessary. Yet,

We can diagnose disease, detect danger, and distinguish between good and bad food just with our noses. With a little practice, we can learn to discriminate between hundreds, perhaps even thousands, of different fragrances, using such sensitivity to identify the vintage of a fine wine or the maker of a particular perfume. But our talents don't end there.

It seems that we are also surprisingly adept in the use of odours as a source of social information. We can recognise our relatives by smell alone, picking out a garment worn by someone who shares our genes from a large selection worn by total strangers. We can determine the sex of such outsiders by nothing more than a whiff of breath from the other side of a screen. (Watson 2000: ix)

It is surprising, therefore, to find that when it comes to the language of smells, most of the languages of the world are found wanting. The English lexicon is as impoverished as the French when it tries to put smells into words. Descriptions borrow heavily from taste – unpleasant smells can be *bitter*, *sour*, *rank*, *acrid*, *salty*; pleasant smells *fruity*, *ambrosial*, *spicy*, *herby*, *yummy*, *delicious* and so on. Moreover, pick up any English language thesaurus and peruse the words and phrases associated with smelling. What is immediately striking about these words for those 'substances which excite the membrane of the nose' (*OED*) is the asymmetry: there are many nouns and adjectives to describe bad smells (such as *stink*, *stench*, *reek*, *pong*, *niff*) but very few positive expressions (such as *fragrance* and *perfume*) and curiously few, if any, genuinely neutral ones. Even the term *smell* is rarely inodorous – certainly its derived adjective *smelly* has a distinct whiff about it. There is a social taboo that makes the words for smells unstable and prone to change. The typical path of development is from *good smell*, to *disagreeable smell*, and it is a descent we find repeated across languages.

Take the following eight examples which rank the terms, starting with those that have the most unpleasant connotations and ending with those that have the most pleasing. The dates are based on the first attestations cited in the *OED*:[53]

> *stink* verb eighth century; noun thirteenth century
> *stench* noun ninth century; verb tenth century
> *smell* noun and verb twelfth century
> *odour* noun fourteenth century
> *scent* verb and noun fifteenth century
> *perfume* verb and noun sixteenth century
> *fragrance* noun seventeenth century
> *aroma* noun nineteenth century

The longer the word has been in the language, the more disagreeable the denotation. *Stink* and *stench* have been around the longest. The most fragrant terms listed are French – *odour, scent, perfume, fragrance* and *aroma*. French and Latin have long been sources for English euphemisms. Yet, the deodorizing property of the sweet-smelling euphemism inevitably fades as the taboo sense asserts itself. *Odour*, as the oldest of these five, has already festered.

Forbidden fruit

This chapter has been concerned with the language of food and drink, especially the culinary delicacies and abominations of modern times. Avoidance strategies take the form of gastronomic red herrings – language that disguises, distorts, deceives, misleads, inflates and obfuscates. Current nutritional superstitions and gastronomic fetishes condemn salt, fat, sugar, caffeine, butter and margarine. Food labels and advertisements send out 'healthy' messages, with descriptions such as *fat-free, salt-free, sugar-free, meat-free, guilt-free*, and so forth. One *lite* product advertised itself with 'Nothing added'. Even the *king-size* nomenclature, so popular in food labels generally, has now been dropped from chocolate bars in an effort to promote healthy eating and combat obesity (and its trendy offspring *macbesity, globesity* and *diabesity*).

Food has an intimate association with our bodies. Eating and drinking bind us within a community and differentiate us from others. Eating habits and dietary regimens are deeply entwined with cultural traditions, connecting with things religious, moral, medical and sexual. Food and drink taboos are identity tags for group membership; using Brillat-Savarin's aphorism, 'Tell me what you eat: I will tell you what you are.'[54] The food consumed by one group is despised by another, so that ethnic and racial slurs can play on gastronomy; and they are increasingly common.

The most robust taboo of all is that people should not be turned into food. Somewhat surprising therefore is the dearth of euphemistic expressions for cannibalism. Perhaps the idea of people as food is so repugnant as to be barely mentionable – even if a common response to tension is nail-biting and finger chewing. Metaphorical cannibalism flourishes where the language of food and the language of sex meet. Expressions such as *I could eat you!* capture the similarities between our eating habits and sexual behaviour. This link is exploited in the food metaphors used to describe sexual body parts and associated activities. The image of an edible lover can be found in language as diverse as the poetic diction of elevated literature, through to the amateurish efforts of those who post their St Valentine's Day messages in a local paper. In this tangle of eating and sexual desire we find smell provoking all sorts of appetites, not least sexual attraction. And yet the language of olfaction is surprisingly impoverished. Descriptions of smells rely heavily on taste. There are few positive expressions and perhaps no true orthophemisms. Maybe this reflects the fact that humans are uncomfortable with the smell of their bodily effluvia. Certainly, words to do with smelling are prone to deteriorate as euphemism is undermined by taboo.

9   Disease, death and killing

In this chapter, we examine some of the less happy aspects of human existence: disease, death and killing. We shall focus on the modern western experience of human affliction and the language that speakers use when they have to confront the unnerving reality that, despite miracle cures and ageless bodies, we will not live for ever. This is not a medical textbook; our discussion is about the way people use language when expressing the emotional and social aspects of disease and death.

Unease in talking about disease

Misfortune is taboo. Even though few in our technically advanced and largely secular twenty-first century would admit to the sort of fear and superstition that we associate with the taboos of exotic and unenlightened peoples, there are many who still carry talismans when they travel, avoid walking beneath ladders, and believe in lucky and unlucky numbers. We try to avoid *tempting fate* by not speaking of misfortune. On the other hand, we try to protect good fortune by doing things like *crossing fingers* and *touching wood*. Humans seem to be naturally pessimistic creatures and, with time, words to do with chance typically deteriorate – 'good fortune' becomes 'bad fortune'. The English word *accident* originally had the much wider meaning of Latin *accidens* 'happening' (preserved in the expression *by accident*), but it has now narrowed to 'misfortune'. Diseases are really 'accidents' of the body. From those in antiquity through to today's Christian Scientists and devotees of televangelists, people have regarded such events in providential and supernatural terms – as the result of ill will, sorcery, the workings of malevolent spirits, diabolical or divine intervention. Even the non-religious have plenty of reasons to taboo diseases and speak of them euphemistically, not least the attendant suffering and perhaps a prospect of death.

The verbal taboos surrounding disease and sickness can have other motivations, too. Some euphemisms seem to reflect the cooperative desire not to impose one's troubles on others and not to be seen to whinge. People resort to understatements, often frivolous, such as being *unwell, under the weather*, *off-colour, down in the dumps, indisposed, out of sorts, below par, out of kilter, green around the gills, one degree under, in bad nick, in a bad way, poorly, funny, laid up* and *seedy*. Advertisements for cold remedies these days show the office worker pulling a sachet or bottle out of the office drawer – the emphasis is very much on *soldiering on*. Even when the *complaint* is more serious, the talk can be just as vague. The *problem* or *trouble* might warrant a *procedure* and if there is a *turn for the worse*, expect *complications*. The sick person might then be described as *doing as well as can be expected*. General expressions like *bouts, episodes* and *turns* also treat illness as short term. Doctors use a similar strategy when they ask *Do you experience any discomfort?* instead of *Do you have any pain?* Even the word *disease* was once a euphemism, as its constituent morphemes reveal – *dis-* 'cease to' and *ease* 'be comfortable'. The expression *to be in condition* is the contrary of to *have a condition*, which is used of some fairly serious illnesses, though usually with an appropriate qualifier such as *heart, liver, kidney*. The expression *to be in a delicate condition* was once used of pregnant women but is now rarely heard; perhaps as a result of advances in medicine, the social taboos surrounding pregnancy are no longer strong. Such euphemisms respond to our notions of decency and decorum, and support the already strong taboos against mentioning one's bodily effluvia. *Sick leave* covers every kind of indisposition that keeps one away from work. People talk about *being sick* to describe the condition of *vomiting*; they talk about having *an upset stomach* or *the runs* rather than *diarrhoea*; an advertisement for travel sickness pills refers to *being uncomfortable* while travelling; a woman might say *I'm not feeling too good*, rather than *I've got menstrual cramps*. Nicknames like *the barfs, the trots, Montezuma's revenge* and *Bali Belly* are also commonly used of indecorous illnesses of this sort, which are more humiliating than life-threatening.[1] One way of confronting fear is to make fun of it. Humour is often used as a means of coming to terms with the less happy aspects of our existence. There are jocular names for even serious illnesses: during the last century, the fear of syphilis gave rise to an array of flippant rhyming slang expressions for *pox*, such as *band in the box, jack(-in-the-box), Nervo and Knox* (music hall stars of the 1930s), as well as *bang and biff* [= syph(ilis)] and *hat and cap* [= clap].

The dread of disease

The fear of disease is a happy restraint to men. If men were more healthy, 'tis a great chance they would be less righteous. (Edmund Massey in a sermon, 2 July 1722; quoted by Black 1986: 78)

As any narrative history of medicine reveals, fear and superstition have always attached to disease. It didn't help that early treatments were often fearsome and that there were few effective remedies available. Physicians had little knowledge of physiology and none of today's sophisticated instruments to guide them. It is only relatively recently that the mystery surrounding the aetiology of disease has been lifted. In the past, the dearth of knowledge concerning bodily organs, their processes and their pathological changes produced exotic medical doctrines built upon imagination and superstition. To be fair, in their own context these doctrines did not appear as absurd as they do from today's perspective; in many cases, simple faith in the ritual may well have been enough to effect a cure. Nonetheless, disease was generally thought of as something mysterious and supernatural. Typically, explanations for sickness connected the complaint with the workings of malevolent spirits or with divine punishment for sins committed. Epidemics were believed to be retribution for the indiscretions of entire communities. As often as not, cures took the form of appeals for clemency to those higher powers believed responsible, as people resorted to prayers, incantations, sacrifices and sorcery. Even post-Renaissance, therapeutics in Europe was still showing a curious mixture of Christian theology and the superstitions of pagan antiquity. A common term for an illness or malady was still *evil*; for example, *the foul evil* 'pox', *the falling evil* 'epilepsy', *king's evil* 'scrofula' (a sickness that was thought to be curable by the touch of a king, because a king was invested with God's power on earth).

   In the past, the names of many maladies were favourable appellations (some almost reverential), obviously aimed at placating the unseen powers that caused them. The label *St Vitus' Dance* (chorea), for example, dates back to the medieval period and what became known as the 'cult of saints'. During that time, it was a common practice to invoke the saints and, strange to our eyes, a variety of diseases were called by their names, typically the most horrific.[2] St Vitus' Dance was originally an epidemic of considerable proportion. Known also as *the dancing mania*, it was a kind of mass hysteria that swept through medieval Europe (very different from the symptoms of today's St Vitus' Dance). Thousands of people, believed to be possessed by demons, took to the streets, leaping about in mad frenzy for hours, sometimes for days, until they dropped foaming at the mouth. The description *St. Vitus' Dance* suggests a joyous romp, and conveys nothing of the suffering that attended this particular psychotic disorder. *St Antonius' Fire* (erysipelas) referred to another epidemic that raged successively throughout the Middle Ages, killing and deforming on a huge scale. So great was the terror surrounding the plague, that it masqueraded under a number of different saints' names; St Adrian, St Christopher, St Valentine, St Giles and St Roch were some of the many saints invoked to protect against the disease. St Christopher, when he wasn't called on for plague, also looked after epileptics. St Blaise took care of throat problems, St Lawrence backaches, St Apollonia teeth, and

St Margaret of Antioch was the patron saint of women in labour. St Luke and St Michael were called upon for a variety of illnesses. In all, some 130 saints were invoked to serve as protectors and comforters of the sick and medically distressed.

If ever a euphemistic practice backfired, it was this use of saints' names. The diseases became so associated with the names of the saints that the saints themselves came to be seen, not as comforters and protectors of the faithful, but rather as wrathful tyrants to be feared as perpetrators of contagion. In the minds of sufferers of herpes zoster, it was now St Antonius who was stoking up the fires in their burning blisters. Much to the horror of the church, this change in perspective inspired a dramatic return to pagan worship. The cult of saints was consequently tabooed by the church, and the practice largely disappeared. It is a striking illustration of the pejorative path that euphemism often takes.

The most dreaded of diseases typically went by a number of different labels, as people struggled to find ever sweeter-sounding words for them. Syphilis is a notable example; although syphilographers disagree as to when the disease first appeared, by the late 1400s it was endemic, and dreaded with good reason. Joseph Gruenpeck (1473–1552), a sufferer, describes it thus:

I have seen scourges, horrible sicknesses and many infirmities affect mankind from all corners of the earth. Amongst them has crept in, from the western shores of Gaul, a disease which is so cruel, so distressing, so appalling that until now nothing so horrifying, nothing more terrible or disgusting, has ever been known on this earth. (Cited in Porter 1997: 166)

It was not only on account of its mortality rate that syphilis was so feared; there were many diseases just as deadly. What was most shocking were its immoral sexual origins: the moral depravation that was believed to cause it was made obvious in the physical symptoms of the disease. Beginning with sores in the genital area and progressing rapidly to a general rash, the syphilitic pustules, if not checked, eventually eat into the bone and destroy the nose, lips and genitals.

The taboos surrounding syphilis were so severe that it masqueraded under dozens of names. None of the countries in which the disease raged would admit to being its place of origin, each blaming it on the deviance of foreigners. In sixteenth-century English, it was known as *Spanish needle*, *Spanish pox*, *Spanish pip* and *Spanish gout*, reflecting Spain's status as number one enemy of the day. (Seventeenth-century *scabbado* is a mock-Hispanic version of English *scab*.) These labels were later replaced by *the disease of Naples* and *Naples canker* – Shakespeare referred to the disease as 'Neapolitan bone-ache'.[3] Next, it was the French who featured most prominently in xenophobic epithets for syphilis. In the eighteenth century, the most common names were the *malady of France*, *French pox*, *French disease*, *French aches*, *French fever*, *French malady*, *French gout* and *French marbles* (⇐ French *morbilles* 'small blisters'). Captain Cook was dismayed to discover that the Tahitians called the disease *Apa no Britannia* 'the British disease' because he believed it was introduced by the French.[4] The buboes associated with the disease were known as *French pigs*; those struck by syphilis were *Frenchified*, and someone whose nose had been destroyed by the disease was *knocked with a French faggot*. If we look beyond English, we see the same practice, each country attributing blame elsewhere. The Italians charged the French, and called the epidemic *mal francese* or *morbus gallicus*. The French retaliated, calling it *mal de Naples*. The Germans also blamed it on the French – as we see from the Gruenpeck quote above. To the Dutch, it was *spaensche pokken* 'Spanish pox'. The Russians blamed it on the Poles, who in turn called it the *German disease*. In Turkey, it was known as the *Christian disease*, and in India and Japan, the *Portuguese disease*. The Portuguese called it the *Castilian disease*. There is a parallel today with AIDS: while those in the western world usually locate its origins in Africa, many in Africa attribute it to the west, most notably to the United States.[5] The history of names for nasty diseases offers interesting diachronic evidence for contemporary political antagonisms: the common dysphemistic practice among human groups is to blame an enemy for the spread of diseases that afflict those who engage in vice and immorality.

It was in 1530 that the euphemistic name *syphilis* first appeared. Syphilis, a shepherd suffering from the disease, was the main protagonist in the poem *Syphilis, sive Morbus Gallicus*. The author, Girolamo Fracastoro of Verona, was a doctor who also wrote a treatise on syphilis. These days, it is difficult to appreciate the euphemistic qualities of the label – all pleasing pastoral associations have disappeared. Even doctors now avoid using the word *syphilis* with their patients, resorting instead to labels like *treponemal disease*, *luetic disease* (from Latin *lues* 'contagion, plague'), *spirochaetal disease* and even the general-for-specific euphemism *special disease*. The linguistic taboo is still strong. Despite the fact that most of the mystery of cause and cure is now gone, *social diseases* like syphilis are scarcely more freely named today: general-for-specific abbreviations like *STD* and *VD*, or colloquial labels such as *cupid's measles* (compare *venereal* [Venus'] *disease*) are preferred.[6]

Another example of disease seen as punishment is leprosy. Curiously, there were few euphemisms for it, or few that have survived. Most of the earlier labels were descriptive, such as *leper* and *leprous*. They first appeared in the language some time during the 1200s; they came via French but derive ultimately from the Greek *lepra* 'scaly', describing the scale-like lesions symptomatic of the disease. In the 1300s, the terms *lazar* 'leper' and *lazarous* 'leprous' were also common. These were based on the name of the beggar

Lazarus, who was 'full of sores', assuaged at death in Abraham's bosom.[7] As a description of leprosy, the names began as a general-for-specific euphemism for any deforming disease, but were most commonly applied to leprosy. Their use may also reflect the ignorance surrounding the disease in these early times – many different cutaneous complaints, including psoriasis and syphilis, were confused with true leprosy.[8] The proper name *Lazarus* also gave rise to the term *lazaret(to)*, used of a medieval hospital established and run by the Order of Saint Lazarus (of Bethany)[9] to care for the diseased and poor and, more particularly, lepers. The term later came to be used exclusively of leprosaria, and therefore shows the same pejorative narrowing as the word *asylum*.

Leprosy has always been highly stigmatized, and perhaps the poverty of euphemism simply reflects the despised status of the leper. In the eyes of the rest of the community, leprosy was the punishment for sin and heresy; lepers were viewed as both physically and morally dangerous. The following description (our translation) comes from the fourteenth-century surgery text written by the Brabant physician Thomaes Scellinck. According to contemporary theories of the 'humours', the horrible physical disfigurement of lepers was felt to reflect an inner corruption and mental derangement (and note the common-sense separation of lepers).

Leprosy is corruption of the body externally and internally . . . their complexion [i.e. the lepers' combination of humours] is bad and corrupting and so are their thoughts and their mind is bad and poisoned. And therefore one should separate them from healthy people. (Scellinck 1343: 198)[10]

In particular, leprosy was associated with lust and sexual misdemeanours. Within society, lepers were branded *tanquam mortuus* 'as though dead'. Fear of contagion deprived them of all normal community rights such as marriage and laws of inheritance, and forced them to undergo appalling rites of exclusion. In most places, lepers were made to dress distinctively and to sound a warning bell whenever they approached. Occasionally, they were even expected to undergo a sort of ritual burial before entering the leprosarium – presumably marking their civic death.[11] Their animal-like physical appearance was perceived to be fitting punishment for their transgressions against God. Along with other despised members of the community, lepers were commonly blamed for disasters and epidemics like the plague. An effective means of bringing contumely upon your enemy was to spread a rumour that s/he had leprosy. The social upheaval through terror of contagion that frequently went with epidemic diseases like leprosy encouraged moral judgment of this sort; in the medieval mind, it strengthened the connection between physical and mental corruption.

Despite the fact that there is no longer any mystery surrounding the cause and cure of leprosy, much of the stigma attached to the disease still exists today. It lives on in the idiom *to be treated like a leper* and in other powerful images retained in the metaphorical use of *leper* and *leprosy*. Examples taken from the *OED* demonstrate the persistent dysphemism: *the leprous humour of Popery* (Sanderson, 1632); *When nations are to perish of their sins, 'tis in the church the leprosy begins* (Cowper, 1781); *that leprous stain Nobility* (Coleridge, 1796); *Idleness is a moral leprosy which soon eats its way into the heart* (H. Smith, 1836). Compare also the modern French *lépreuse*, referring to an eroded stone edifice. Given such a stigma, it is not surprising that the preferred term today among the medical profession is *Hansen's disease*,[12] though this term has not spread to the ordinary layman's language. The disease is now rare in western communities, and there is little need to refer to it.

Disease and women's bodies

Because women are much weaker . . . therefore they have many kinds of sickness. And especially in those parts which nature has added for pregnancy and the sickness affects them in secret parts, so that from shame they dare not reveal (them) to any master. Therefore I pity their shame and have prepared a book to help all women. (Daems 1967 [*c*.1300]: 179)

This quote (our translation) comes from a medieval Dutch text that is remarkable for having a section devoted exclusively to women's problems. In eleven other medieval medical treatises between 1300 and 1600,[13] the only ones that freely mentioned the female sex were collected works of recipes and potions; and then always it was in connection with recommendations for testing virginity, pregnancy, the sex of a foetus and sterility – those things also of concern to men. Sterility was viewed as the wife's failing, even though men were believed to make the more significant contribution to reproduction; from the time of Aristotle, women were viewed as mere incubators for the male seed.[14]

Authors of the ancient and medieval medical treatises were all male, and the problem of communication between female patients and male physicians (although often assisted by female attendants) is well documented in their treatises; a number of medical writers discussed the fact that women were inhibited when describing their complaints to men.[15] There was a reciprocal reserve on the part of the male physicians and writers when discussing gynaecological problems. Indeed, ancient and medieval medical works mostly discuss male patients. If women are mentioned at all in the text, it is more often than not as carriers of disease, even though suggested remedies always envisaged male rather than female patients. Physicians used ingenious and imaginative biological arguments to support their contention that women were dangerous purveyors of disease.

Particularly neglectful of women are the surgical treatises of the day; for example, the detailed treatise *Boeck van Surgien* by Meester Thomaes Scellinck (quoted earlier). Such reticence is all the more remarkable, given the importance placed at the time on the different physical characteristics of patients: texts went to great lengths to point out that different treatments were necessary, depending on whether the patient was fat or thin, old or young, bilious or not, and so forth; yet sexual differences were completely ignored. However, the following observation by the famous thirteenth-century physician Arnold of Villanova, in his book on poisons (!), suggests that we are perhaps looking in the wrong place for accounts of women's complaints:

In this book, I propose, with God's help, to consider the diseases of women, since women are poisonous creatures. I shall then treat the bites of venomous snakes. (Guthrie 1945: 113).

The coincidence of periodicities of the moon and a woman's menstrual cycle link her with matters of the occult. Since before the time of Aristotle, women were associated with the left side of the body, regarded as weaker and colder than the right side.[16] Though Aristotle (on empirical evidence from dissections) refuted the claim that male embryos developed on the right side of the uterus and female embryos on the left,[17] it was still widely believed until recent times. Women were seen as the source of magical actions, and when causes had to be found for calamities like a natural disaster or the outbreak of an epidemic, many unfortunate women were accused of witchery (perhaps because their behaviour fell outside of community norms) and found themselves made into scapegoats. Even those who tried to cure lepers could be accused of witchcraft because it was supposed that leprosy was incurable.[18] The depiction of women as dirt bags of disease persisted well into the 1900s, particularly in respect of venereal infection. Despite greater knowledge and public discussion, VD was still widely regarded as a corollary of prostitution. General hostility to female sexuality saw many a public diatribe about the dangers of promiscuous women. Women who fornicated for pleasure were viewed as worse than prostitutes. In 1927, the Venereal Diseases Officer of Salford, in northern England, wrote:

Unlike her regular and professional sister, she is, as a rule, definitely and deliberately immoral. She experiences a thrill of satisfaction from nibbling at forbidden fruit . . . Deliberate wrongdoing gives her immense enjoyment. She is a sexual kleptomaniac. Her conduct is an expression of vicarious criminality. She is a degenerate, an abnormality, the female equivalent of the hooligan and apache. She is equally to be found in the palace and the hovel. She is amenable to little except incarceration in an asylum, and yet but rarely is she a lunatic. She is often extremely difficult to detect although she exists in such large numbers. Such women are . . . very heavily infected, especially with gonorrhoea, and exceedingly few of them ever . . . request treatment. This type of woman reaches her zenith in the nymphomaniac; but every variety is found, from the Madonna-faced maiden who indulges in *flirtage* between dances to Messalina. Her ranks were strongly reinforced during the war, and immediately post-war period. (Davenport-Hines 1990: 255f)

Dr Burke was not an oddball, but a well-respected authority on the subject of venereal disease, and his views met with widespread approval: 'It pleases me to know that you are a man who can see plain facts', responded a Fulham lorry driver. Women infected men with VD: 'It's up to the schools to teach girls to keep themselves clean, as men pick it up from them.'[19]

Cancer too 'is a "female" and a "dirty" disease, whereas heart disease is a "male" and a "clean" one'.[20] One early twentieth-century writer observed that 'want of proper exercise and changed surroundings' was emasculating men and making them prone to 'women's diseases', and this, he believed, explained the rising incidence among men of mortality from cancer.[21]

Ortner has persuasively argued that the secondary status of women in society derives indirectly from their physiology.[22] Because women and not men bear children, and consequently menstruate and lactate, women are perceived to be more closely bound by and to their bodies and body functions than are men. This renders women more like (other) animals, and therefore closer to the dirty reality of nature.[23] Men, not being so physiologically tethered, not only had the opportunity to become politically and economically dominant, but furthermore had the time and energy to expend on things of the mind rather than on the body; that is, to control the intellectual domain that distinguishes humans from animals. The association of women with the animal side of humans, and men with power and cerebral pursuits, produces a cultural and social appraisal in which men are superior to women, and has given rise to the extraordinary sanctions not only on women's bodies, but on their scholarly and artistic accomplishments.[24]

Medical labelling

The very terms for 'leprosy' and 'tuberculosis' are restricted in use, because of the danger of 'contagion'. Especially in dwelling houses, euphemisms or alternative terms must be used; a sequence of these have been employed in recent decades, then discarded as they acquired dangerous power. (Keesing and Fifi?i 1969: 160)

In Chapter 6, we explored some of the beliefs that centre around the potency of naming: the belief that knowing a name gives one power over the named person or object; alternatively, that not uttering a name, or substituting a more favourable appellation, can avert the incursion of something feared. The quotation from Keesing and Fifi?i refers to twentieth-century practices among the Kwaio, an Austronesian people, but the attitudes revealed there are similar to those of early Europe. The superstition attached to disease was great and extremely primitive in nature. Simply uttering the name of a disease could summon it; hence, the most dreaded of diseases went by a number of different names. Many were auspicious, obviously aimed at placating unseen malevolent powers.

Beliefs in verbal sorcery might have waned, but there is plenty of evidence for the powerful magic of names in contemporary society, particularly when it comes to the vocabulary of disease. Few today would allow that our gut reactions have any scientific basis; yet expressions such as *scared to death* or *worried sick* are commonplace in our everyday vocabulary. Even those who acknowledge hocus-pocus or make-believe in such ritual observances may avoid tempting fate by walking under ladders, sleeping in hotel rooms numbered 13,[25] or naming deadly diseases.

Attaching a diagnostic label to someone's suffering is a two-edged sword. There is an enormous sense of relief when an ailment is identified: its name legitimizes one's status as a patient[26] and puts one back in control by allowing for a plan of treatment and a prognosis. The label itself can hasten the rate of recovery. On the negative side, there is plenty of evidence that naming a disease can be enough to induce the apposite physical symptoms.[27] For example, after RSI (repetitive strain injury, tenosynovitis) received a lot of media attention in Australia during the 1980s, the number of cases appeared to mushroom, and astonishingly large numbers of people were suddenly suffering from an affliction which almost no member of the lay public had heard of ten years before. We assume that the overwhelming majority of those who took sick leave and early retirement did have a genuine complaint, given prevailing beliefs; but what is puzzling is why one had not heard of RSI before, and why it did not have such a large incidence in countries where it was given little or no media attention. The conclusion must be that when the condition was virtually unknown, people suffering from what would later be known as RSI attributed it to arthritis, or dismissed it as a non-specific ache or pain. Once the condition is known, people are found to have it.[28] It used to be said that, in so-called 'primitive' societies, people would become ill and die from spells and curses, or if the witch-doctor pointed the bone at them: a lot of baloney, you say? It looks to us as though you can persuade some people that they have a disease simply by talking about it. The *nocebo* (Latin 'I will harm') phenomenon is the power of suggestion or belief to cause the symptoms of ill health; and words, it seems, can be potent nocebos. Medical students are notorious for discovering in themselves the symptoms of whatever disease they happen to be studying. Conversely, words can have a curative force; the medical profession admits that the placebo effect can be powerful; many cited cancer cures, for instance, have no rational explanation.

And whereas just the sight of a physician can make some people feel better, for others it induces *white-coat hypertension*, which causes blood pressure to rise in the doctor's office.[29]

The drawbacks of medical labelling become particularly acute where the disease is a stigmatizing one. Usually, it is one of mystery – of uncertain cause, with no ready cure. Such a disease is quick to become tainted with attitudes of shame and disgrace. Patients may find themselves branded with a label they find impossible to lose, even after treatment is complete. Mental illness carries just such a stigma.

Mental illness

A demonological concept of mental illness prevailed even as late as the 1800s. The idea of insanity as demonic possession meant that people suffering from mental disorders were especially feared. Usually, their symptoms were thought to be the work of malicious devils, so that cruel, often drastic, measures were needed to dislodge the demons. People whose madness manifested itself in the form of religious fervour were more fortunate. If their madness was seen as a gift that was divinely inspired, they were able to escape the brutal treatments normally recommended. But whether *touched* by holiness or by evil, madness was linked with the supernatural world and the insane were feared and shunned, much like lepers in the Middle Ages.

The term *mental illness* covers an enormous assortment of conditions, ranging from mildly eccentric or neurotic behaviour, to severe psychotic disorders where a patient might lose total contact with reality (as in the case of severe schizophrenia, for example). The lay person lumps all these together as *insanity*. When is non-normal behaviour to be considered an illness? When is behavioural deviance considered problematic? '[T]he fear of becoming insane is one of the most common of fears felt by normal people, taking equal place with those of cancer and death.'[30] This fear continues to inspire strong linguistic taboos.

The origins of mental illness are usually mysterious, and because of this, there is great shame attached to having the disease, the burden of responsibility often falling on patients themselves. Even the role of patient is not one that is readily accepted. Mental illness is viewed not so much as a disease but as a moral failure, and onlookers are more judgmental than they are with other illnesses. This disease suggests a deficiency in the person, some sort of weakness of character, even if it results from a tumour or an accident of some sort. Until quite recently, people used to visit an insane asylum for entertainment, much as they nowadays visit the monkey house in a zoo. Bedlam (Bethlehem Royal Hospital for the insane, founded in 1247 and located just outside of London) was open to fee-paying spectators in the seventeenth and eighteenth centuries. With an entry fee of one penny, it had revenue of around £400 per annum in the early eighteenth century – that's 96,000 visits per year![31] There is a long history to the perceived link between madness and funny behaviour, so that many terms for madness are associated with the funny; for example, *funny (in the head), funny farm, w(h)acky, wacko, mad, crazy, bats, nuts*.

As we have seen, euphemisms thrive when humans fear they are losing control over their thoughts and actions. Madness is perceived as a lack of control; hence there are expressions like *out of / losing one's mind*. The loss of control that is a feature of slapstick humour links it with insanity and with historical treatments of the mad as witless clowns. Loss of control is the motivation behind many of the different meanings of the terms *mad* and *crazy* in normal non-clinical usage; for example,

- *I'm going mad/crazy*, indicating forgetfulness, confusion, losing one's grip on sanity;
- *I must be mad/crazy*, said of undertaking something beyond one's capabilities, doing something excessively foolish;
- *He was mad/crazy*, said of someone in frenzied rage;
- *He was quite mad/crazy*, said of someone carried away by excessive enthusiasm.

All these suggest extravagant actions and emotions which are out of control, as do many compounds formed on the words *mad* and *crazy*: *boy-mad, girl-crazy, music mad/crazy, car mad/crazy,* and *madman/crazy man; mad dog/bull,* and so on.

Because the behaviour of mental patients does not conform to morally and socially accepted norms, it is usually viewed as threatening and strange, and is often believed to result from maliciousness of character, particularly if the patient somehow 'looks different'. This perception of mental patients is still firmly tied to the old-fashioned notion linking internal and external corruption. It also shows a lingering fear of 'moral contagion' – that the madness might somehow transmit itself to others.[32] The stereotype of the mental patient is someone who is morally deficient, incurable and potentially dangerous; someone who is best *locked up* or *put away*. Curiously, the word *idiot* has the same origin as words such as *idiom* and *idiosyncratic*: all derive from the Greek *idios* 'peculiar to oneself, private'. In ancient Greek, an *idiōtēs* was a 'private person', so an *idiot* was perhaps perceived as someone locked up in their own private world; compare this with current connotations of *hermit* and *recluse*. Nevertheless, for a long time it was thought (and a lot of people still think) that insane people ought to be locked up by us sane ones. And because of the vagueness of the term *mental illness,* even very minor anxious or depressive disorders tend to carry the same negative stigmata as the severe psychotic cases.

The result of all this is a stigmatized illness, with a long chain of euphemistic labels as impressive as any that might have existed in the middle ages. Society's prejudiced perceptions continue to bubble away, undermining the euphemistic value. The negative connotations reattach themselves and a new euphemism must be found. The word *demented* goes back to the Latin *mens* 'mind' and *de* 'out of'; compare expressions such as *out of one's mind*, *out of one's head*, *out of one's skull* and even *out of one's tree*. None of these terms is polite. *Imbecile* is now a strong term of abuse – it derived from the Latin word *imbecillus* (from *bacillum* 'small staff') and meant literally 'without a stick'; in other words, a mind 'unsupported and feeble'.[33] The word *insanity* derives from Latin *in-sanus* 'not-healthy'. It is now confined to 'mentally unsound' but originally had a much broader domain, encompassing all bodily organs and their functions. Today, even the word *sane* (without the negative prefix) has narrowed under the influence of *insane* to denote only a mental condition. (Compare *sanitorium*, a place for the treatment of invalids and convalescents.) *Lunatic* originally referred to a certain type of madness believed to be caused by the changing phases of the moon (after the Roman goddess of the moon, *Luna*). But the euphemistic motivation is no longer apparent; the word has now become pejorative, as are its shortened versions *loon* and *loony*. Describing someone as *touched* suggests intervention by the hand of God. The innocence of the *holy simpleton* or the *holy fool* was divine and something that set these people above ordinary human beings. There is a similar motivation behind the Swiss French euphemism *chrétin* 'Christian' for the people whose combination of physical deformity and mental retardation (cretinism) was endemic in some valleys of Switzerland during the Renaissance period. *Chrétin* was the source for the English dysphemism *cretin*.

The history of the word *deranged* illustrates a typical path of development. Originally from a verb meaning 'to disturb, disarrange', it could be qualified with the modifier *mentally* to be used of people who were 'disturbed in the mind'. But the context of mental illness contaminated the word and now, without the modifier, it has narrowed to the 'mad' sense alone. Even the adjective *mental* has been affected. Dictionaries still list 'pertaining to the mind' as its central sense, but 'denoting a disorder of the mind' is always given as a secondary meaning, as are colloquial senses 'mad' and 'foolish'. Compare also *be/go mental* and *become a mental patient*. It may well be that *disordered* and *afflicted* are moving in the same direction – *disturbed* has already arrived. Though still requiring a modifier like *mentally* to refer specifically to psychiatric illness, this is now becoming their normal context of use. Similarly, the general-for-specific euphemism *sick* is frequently used to describe someone who is *mentally challenged* or in other words *of an unsound mental condition* (two more euphemisms). Dictionaries continue to define *sick* as 'affected by any disorder of health', but in slang usage the word has already narrowed to 'mental ill health, frequently with overtones of perversion' (compare *sicko* and American *sicknik*). The names for establishments holding mental patients show the same pejoration. Latin *asylum* originally meant 'place of refuge, retreat'; it originally required a qualifier, such as *insane/lunatic asylum*. The ordinary understanding of *asylum* (referring to a building) is now specifically 'institution for the care of the insane'.

The nature of our more colloquial expressions is also telling. *Crazy* (and hence *crazed* and *cracked*) originally meant 'flawed, damaged' (cf. *crazy paving*). It was applicable to all manner of illness, but has also narrowed to 'mental illness'. The stereotypical mental patient as someone 'flawed, deficient' (compare *mentally deficient*) is the basis for many other dysphemistic expressions for madness: *crack-brained, scatter-brained, shatter-brained*; *head-case*; *falling to pieces*; *unhinged*; *having a screw/tile/slate loose*; *kangaroos in the top paddock*; *one brick short of a load*; *not playing with a full deck*; *three cards short of a full deck*; *one sandwich short of a picnic*; *two cans short of a six-pack*; *two bob short of a quid*; *not the full quid*; *a shingle short*; *a shrub short of a herbaceous border*; and perhaps *he's lost his marbles*. This kind of dysphemistic formula appears in a number of languages.

It has required a considerable rejigging of our thinking to persuade us to accept mental illness as an illness like any other – as one with patients able to be treated and cured. Western society no longer believes in a demonological concept of mental illness; yet our linguistic behaviour towards the mentally afflicted reveals attitudes that are still firmly tied to old-fashioned notions of behavioural deviance. The strength of the stigma is also evident in the proliferation of maledictions invoking mental abnormality; for example, *retard, moron, jerk, spas(tic), cretin* and *imbecile*. While it is acceptable to be physically ill, it is much less acceptable to be mentally ill.

AIDS (acquired immunodeficiency syndrome)

44 He is a leprous man, he is unclean: the priest shall pronounce him utterly unclean; his plague is in his head. 45 And the leper in whom the plague is, his clothes shall be rent, and his head bare, and he shall put a covering upon his upper lip, and shall cry, Unclean, unclean. 46 All the days wherein the plague shall be in him he shall be defiled; he is unclean: he shall dwell alone; without the camp shall his habitation be. (Leviticus 13: 44–6)

I wish I had cancer instead of AIDS. I could stand the treatments and the pain and my hair falling out. And I'm going to die anyway. But then, at least, my family wouldn't reject me. I could go home. (A young female, quoted in Fisher 1995: 92)

When AIDS first appeared, the social and linguistic parallels with diseases like leprosy and syphilis were striking. It seemed to have arrived out of the blue, with sensational press reports of young homosexual men dying from rare conditions. All at once, dentists started to wear masks and rubber gloves, and there were 'blood rules' on the sports field to protect players from the blood of the injured. People knew AIDS was *catching* and yet, because its onset is asymptomatic, its onslaught was invisible. The projected deaths were apocalyptic. And, as with leprosy and syphilis in earlier times, AIDS was linked in the minds of many with sin and depravity – with intravenous drug users and unnatural, ungodly sexual practices. The fact that it was unwittingly communicable intensified the fear of contagion. Genteel euphemisms warning against *exchanging bodily fluids* did nothing to stem the fears of a public terrified that the disease could spread via all manner of effluvia, including saliva, sweat and tears. There are many, especially on the powerful Religious Right, who genuinely believe that AIDS has been sent as awful retribution for an epoch of excesses and impiety; hence the acronym *WOGS* (wrath of god syndrome). But even the non-religious believed that AIDS was contracted not by ordinary folk, but by people on the margins of society. Gays and drug users got AIDS because of their perverse and dangerous behaviour. The polluting nature of the disease meant those afflicted were hidden away by their families or even expelled from the community. The social disgrace destroyed the possibility of normal social interaction for AIDS sufferers who, fearing the withdrawal of others, found themselves retreating from contact. Like leprosy and syphilis, AIDS was an accusation.

Before it received the name AIDS, the disease went by a number of different labels: *Gay Cancer*, *Gay Plague* (it was doubtless felt appropriate that it should be associated with such deadly diseases) and *GRID* (gay related immuno-deficiency). These were perhaps abandoned because they linked the disease too specifically with the gay community, thus upsetting heterosexual haemophiliacs and other AIDS-afflicted non-gays. However, there was a notional distinction between those 'who brought it on themselves' and the 'blameless', who acquired it through blood transfusion. The acronym *AIDS* was eventually chosen, presumably because of its optimistic ring – as though it were 'a disease that wanted to help, not hurt. Just a plague whose intentions were good.'[34] In general usage the word *aids* denotes a material means of help, as in *hearing/visual/legal aids*. *AIDS* also fits in with other *s*-final disease names such as *measles*, *mumps*, *rabies* and *shingles*.

There were also a number of examples of dysphemism or verbal flippancy in reference to *AIDS*; for example, *Anally Inserted Death Sentence* or *Toxic Cock Syndrome*. Here, the motivation was as much fear as it was the facetious down-playing of death and the hospitalized. But like so many colloquial expressions for serious illness, there was also a real cruelty. Such labels smack of homophobic antagonism and the rampant moralizing and finger-wagging that went on when AIDS first appeared on the scene. There was also a new acronym *GAY* 'got AIDS yet', which is a sick joke. The high risk groups were also labelled the *4-H Club*. The pun was a triple-whammy: first, it recognized the fact that AIDS sufferers were HIV positive, where the alphabetism for 'human immuno-deficiency virus' is reinterpreted as 'H-four' (roman IV). Second, it alluded to the four groups at greatest risk in those early days – homosexuals, Haitians, haemophiliacs and heroin-users. Moreover, the expression ironically played on the fact that 4-H Clubs in North America are organizations of wholesome young farmers.[35]

In the 1980s, there appeared a new euphemistic vocabulary for AIDS that became known as 'AIDSpeak'. The following is the opening statement of the principles articulated (in 1983) in Denver by the first AIDS activists. They became known as *The Denver Principles*.[36]

We condemn attempts to label us as 'victims', which implies defeat, and we are only occasionally 'patients', which implies passivity, helplessness, and dependence upon the care of others. We are 'People With AIDS'. (The advisory committee of People with AIDS)

In some places, the abbreviation *PWA* was later replaced by *PLWA* or *PLA* (person living with AIDS), and also PWArcs (person with AIDS-related complex).[37] Although no cure or vaccine had been discovered, advances in medical research meant that AIDS could be managed by drugs, and those with the disease now could expect many years of a relatively healthy life. Promoters of such vocabulary emphasized that healing could be achieved by developing perceptions of well-being; the new names avoided the negativity of *patient*, *sufferer* and *victim*, and stressed positive aspects to do with survival and hope. Other fighting acronyms in the AIDSpeak lexicon include PISD (people with immune system disorder), PLUS (positive living for us) and ACT UP (AIDS coalition to unleash power). As is always the case with renaming initiatives, such labels were, and still are, controversial. As we saw in Chapter 4, the battle is often as much about who has the power to name as the naming itself; who decides the identity of a group and its desires and interests.[38] Labels like *victim* and *patient* persist in the media and are still the preferred terms of politicians, health care workers and others involved in campaigning for 'victim rights'.

Recent progress in AIDS research has brought some optimism, but also worries, because AIDS is spreading like wildfire in Africa, and more recently in India and East Asia. Initiatives like the AIDS Memorial Quilt gave the disease positive media coverage, as did the late Diana Princess of Wales' glad-handing of AIDS sufferers. On the down side is the behaviour of people like President Thabo Mbeki of South Africa, who pointedly ignores the AIDS epidemic in his country and discourages practical disease management. And there are still many people (like United States President George W. Bush) who believe that AIDS is an affliction on the sinful. Evidence is that we are a long way from coming to terms with the disease. The prohibitions and social taboos surrounding AIDS remain severe. As the quotation given at the start of this section reveals, discrimination continues against individuals with AIDS, those thought to have it, and even their care-givers. There is evidence that the word *AIDS* is extending to metaphorical use, in much the same way *leprosy* did. An environmentally conscious population labels the phenomenon of *land degradation* in Australia (specifically, the erosion of top-soil and salination caused by irrigation after deforestation) as *AIDS of the earth*; the same metaphor is used in America. AIDS deaths are still not typically reported as such in obituaries and memorial services. Sometimes, the cause of death is not given, or – because HIV allows opportunistic infections such as pneumonia or tuberculosis to attack the defenceless immune system – these sorts of illnesses are listed. Such AIDS-related conditions (ARCs) provide the self-censoring speaker with a verbal escape hatch.

It is telling that even in AIDSpeak, AIDS continues to appear in upper case. Once they've been around for a while, acronyms normally lose their dots and capital letters and enter the language as ordinary words, for example, *laser* and *snafu*. Certainly, the dots were dropped when AIDS became the accepted name for this disease. Yet it is not well enough accepted to become lower-case *aids* (like the French translation equivalent *sida*). British English has gone some way to abandoning the acronym origins, but there is still a preciousness in the naming – *Aids* retains an initial capital, something that is not usual for disease names. The label for the virus responsible for the disease *HIV* (human immunodeficiency virus) is an alphabetism (not an acronym), so unlikely to become an ordinary word. Yet the fact that people commonly refer to the 'HIV virus' shows that its origins have been obscured (compare *ATM machine* 'automatic teller machine machine' and *PIN number* 'personal identification number number').

Cancer

I heard the word cancer, and I didn't hear another word the doctor said to me.
(Patient interviewed in 'Breaking the News', Australian Broadcasting Corporation's *The Health Report*, 22 January 1990)

The figures for cancer in the western world are startling. It seems that around a third of the population will develop some form of cancer in their life-time. And while the medical profession recognizes something like two hundred different varieties of cancerous diseases, each with their own biology, to the lay person the word *cancer* is treated as if it were a single condition. The taboos surrounding it are considerable. In obituaries and death notices, the euphemisms *died after a prolonged illness / a long battle against illness* are still fairly common for someone who has died from cancer. Despite the fact that *died suddenly* should often be interpreted as *died from a heart attack*, the taboos on mentioning heart disease are nothing like so strong as those on naming cancer. The reason for the different linguistic treatment of cancer and heart disease cannot lie in the mortality rate, because heart disease easily outstrips cancer as the commonest cause of death in so-called 'advanced' nations today. Despite its reputation, most cases of cancer are not, in fact, terminal. The reason for the very different linguistic treatment must lie elsewhere.

There is a distinction made between so-called *preventable cancers* – those linked to *lifestyle choices* such as smoking, (unprotected) sun-baking, un-healthy diet, over-eating, lack of exercise – and those which apparently are not, such as breast cancer and mesothelioma. The image of cancer is very much that of a latent malignancy which, even after treatment, is ready to strike again. Of course, there are some cancers that do not remain hidden. Lumps can appear on the body, tissue wasting can become apparent, there may be unpleasant discharges, some cancers distort normal excretory func-tions, therapy can be mutilative. Chemotherapy is toxic and has side effects such as nausea, vomiting, diarrhoea, hair loss, even sepsis and bleeding. All these frightful symptoms and effects serve to strengthen the lay public's view of cancer as a contamination and perhaps, to some minds, the wages of sin – just the kind of evaluation once given to leprosy. We may no longer believe, as the medievals did, that the cancer patient is invaded by a deadly crab-like demon; yet attitudes are reminiscent of the sort of dread and superstition that attended disease during the Middle Ages.

Concealing a cancer diagnosis, particularly if it involves incurable cancer, was once common practice[39] – ostensibly to spare the feelings of the patient, but perhaps also to spare the doctor, who can find these situations as perturb-ing as the patient. The cancer diagnoses of American Presidents Grover Cleveland and Lyndon Johnson were not disclosed to the public; and the mooted malignancies of both George Washington and Franklin D. Roosevelt have never been publicly confirmed nor disconfirmed. Only since the 1970s has it become usual for patients to be told that they have cancer.[40] It is also only relatively recently that authorities have overcome their reticence to use the word *cancer* in the names of hospitals, clinics and special units for cancer patients, preferring something like *oncology* instead (from the Greek *onkos* 'mass'). In 1906, Charles Childe, the leading British expert in the disease at the time, was prevented from using the word *cancer* in a book title, which then became *The Control of a Scourge*. Even as recently as 1987, Patterson writes that publishers tried to persuade him to drop *cancer* from the title of his history of the disease, *The Dread Disease: Cancer and Modern American*

Culture – which is a nice irony, in view of the fact that the book documents the reticence and fear inspired by cancer; he gives many instances of people's unwillingness to use the word.[41]

These days, we see much more frequent use of the word *cancer* in the media, names of hospitals, etc. And there was wide and quite explicit coverage of former US President Ronald Reagan's malignancies. Significantly, however, Reagan himself denied that he had cancer: 'I didn't have cancer. I had something inside of me that had cancer in it and it was removed.'[42] But although there may be greater public acceptance nowadays, there are still many reports of the reluctance among doctors to use the word *cancer* with their patients because of its demoralizing effect on them. The label preferred by many doctors in place of *cancer* is *mitotic disease*. This is a non-specific term that refers generally to multiple cell division, and includes both *malignant* and *benign* cancers. Instead of *cancer*, patients themselves prefer to use words like *tumour* or *growth*, which do not evoke the same unpleasant imagery of decay and corruption. Whereas a cancer diagnosis is equated with malignancy and death, tumours and growths have a more benign image. Growths can be removed, but a cancer continues to lurk in the system. Even technical-sounding expressions such as *melanoma*, *lymphoma*, *neoplasm* and *carcinoma* appear to be less frightening than *cancer*. In some schools in Australia during the 1980s, someone even created the character 'Mr Melanoma' – a large but fairly harmless looking creature who warned school children about the dangers of skin cancer. Mr Melanoma was later replaced by the more fun-sounding *SLIP SLAP SLOP campaign* ('SLIP on a T-shirt, SLAP on a hat and SLOP on sunscreen'), later renamed *Sunsmart*. Other euphemisms include *The Big C* and *CA*; we recall hearing of a seriously ill cancer patient described as someone with *a touch of the c's*. These sorts of euphemism typify mention of cancer, and they are often accompanied by a characteristic set of paralinguistic phenomena such as lowered eyes and hushed tones. There is still a superstitious reluctance to pronounce the word *cancer*, as if some hidden supernatural force were at work.

Censoring the language of death

Ay, but to die, and go we know not where,
To lie in cold obstruction and to rot,
This sensible warm motion to become
A kneaded clod; and the delighted spirit
To bathe in fiery floods, or to reside
In thrilling region of thick-ribbed ice;
To be imprisoned in the viewless winds,
And blown with restless violence round about
The pendent world; or to be worse than worst

Of those that lawless and uncertain thought
Imagine howling – 'tis too horrible!
The weariest and most loathed worldly life
That age, ache, penury, and imprisonment
Can lay on nature is a paradise
To what we fear of death.
(Shakespeare, *Measure for Measure*, III.i.118)

Death is a fear-based taboo. There is fear of the loss of loved ones; fear of the corruption and disintegration of the body; fear of the very finality of death; fear of what follows the end of life (few, and arguably none, have first hand experience of death); fear of malevolent spirits, or of the souls of the dead.

Then, suddenly again Christopher Robin, who was still looking at the world with his chin in his hands, called out 'Pooh!'
    'Yes?' said Pooh.
    'When I'm – when – Pooh!'
    'Yes, Christopher Robin?'
    'I'm not going to do Nothing any more.'
    'Never again?'
    'Well, not so much. They don't let you.'
Pooh waited for him to go on, but he was silent again.
    'Yes, Christopher Robin?' said Pooh helpfully.
    'Pooh, when I'm – *you* know – when I'm *not* doing Nothing, will you come up here sometimes?' . . .
    Still with his eyes on the world Christopher Robin put out a hand and felt for Pooh's paw.
    'Pooh,' said Christopher Robin earnestly, 'if I – if I'm not quite –' he stopped and tried again – 'Pooh, *whatever* happens, you *will* understand, won't you?
    'Understand what?'
    'Oh nothing.' He laughed and jumped to his feet.
    'Come on!'
    'Where?' said Pooh.
    'Anywhere,' said Christopher Robin. (Milne 1948: 77f)

Christopher Robin cannot bring himself to speak explicitly of his own death,[43] and this is common – except perhaps among the very elderly and terminally ill.

Life insurance is insurance against death; *death*'s antonym *life* is utilized to put a value on the life continued. A doctor (or financial planner) may advise a terminally ill patient with the words *I think it's time you got your affairs in order* – prepare for death, with all matters arranged to cause the least inconvenience to family, friends, the law, government officers and the undertaker.[44] Ancient Greek and Latin have exact counterparts to the English *if anything should happen to me*, which demonstrates a very persistent euphemism. Taken literally, the condition in this idiom cannot fail to be true: there can be no doubt that something will happen to the speaker, so such a blatant statement of the obvious implicates the ultimate event: death. There is no 'if' about death, the only uncertainty is when it will happen. This persistent euphemism not only avoids mentioning death, it seemingly pretends that death is uncertain.

Death has become the great taboo subject, smothered in prudery.[45] There is a parallel between the repression of sex, which brought with it a thriving industry in pornography during the Victorian times, and today's taboo on death, which exists alongside the depiction of murder and violent death in fiction and fantasy in print, comic books, and on screen – from *Dr Who* to *Kill Bill*. News stories featuring violent death are just as ubiquitous. (The difference is that Victorian pornography was – at least supposedly – underground, whereas today's depictions of death are publicly acknowledged and often publicly celebrated.) With extraordinary irrationality, some citizens who admitted to allowing their children watch violent death on television petitioned against the building of a church wall which would store the ashes of its congregation, on the grounds that it would be harmful to their children as they walked by.[46] This censorious behaviour contrasts with the Middle Ages, where everyday life was full of symbols to constantly remind people of death; the Ancient Egyptians often placed a miniature mummy on the meal table for a similar reason. Today, this seems macabre. The open acknowledgement of grief and mourning during a wake may still occur, but public carousing at or after the funeral is unusual and silent stoic endurance is considered the proper way of grieving. Private ceremonies, like public ceremonies in memory of the war dead or of assassinated public heroes (like US President John F. Kennedy, the Reverend Martin Luther King Jr, pop star John Lennon, and the untimely death of Diana, Princess of Wales in a car crash) often celebrate the life of the deceased.

People in the Middle Ages confronted their own mortality in a way that now seems quite appalling to us. We catch vicarious glimpses of it from documentaries of human tragedies that result from natural disasters like famine and man-made ones like war and terrorism; yet the majority of people in our society are removed from immediate interaction with death. Life expectancy has increased enormously, infant mortality has dropped to very low levels, and there do not exist anywhere near the same number of life-threatening diseases to confront. We are insulated from death by hospitals and other institutions which care for the sick and dying; and there is a funeral industry to dispose of the dead. Many people reach adulthood without ever having laid eyes on a real corpse, except on film or video. And – in striking contrast with the medieval fascination with corrupting corpses – we now rely on modern embalming techniques to help create for us *the Beautiful Memory Picture*.[47] Today, in our community, cremation has replaced burial as the most usual means for disposing of the dead. For *those left behind*, cremation is the quickest and most final way of removing the remains – particularly if the ashes are then scattered; though some people like to take them home. While people still visit grave sites, visits to the urns which house the ashes of the cremated are less common. And, in general, we go out of our way to avoid death and anyone tainted by it and, in so doing, we largely expel it from our consciousness.

Gradual suppression of direct reference to death is reflected in changes which have occurred to epitaph and gravestone design over the years. A study of colonial New England gravesites between 1680 and 1820 notes basically three designs.[48] The first is that of the winged and grinning death's head, which comes with grim reminders of the transience of life and the inevitability of bodily decay. In the eighteenth century, this gives way to the softer and more optimistic spectacle of a winged cherub, whose accompanying message now stresses not the decay of beauty, but the soul's flight to glory. Towards the end of the eighteenth century, religious symbols give way to secular images in the form of an urn and cascading willow pattern with the words *In Memory of* . . . Today, gravestones have become little more than a commemorative marker – sometimes the body is not even present.

A few years ago, only one out of 536 'Death' and 'In Memoriam' notices[49] we looked at included a use of the verb *die* or noun *death*; all the others used euphemisms of one kind or another. The ultimate euphemism is not mentioning death in any way at all, though it is true that located among death notices, one knows that the subject of the notice has died.

SMITH (Ross), Frances Winifred. – On March 8 at Sherbrooke Private Nursing Home. Upper Ferntree Gully, aged 71 years.

THOMAS, Margot – On March 11 in Adelaide. In affectionate memory of our dear Aunt and good friend.

However, there is usually some mention of the event. Within newspaper announcements of death, the euphemisms fall into four broad categories: death as loss, worries about the soul, death as a journey, and death as beginning a new life.

We begin with death as loss. Both of the euphemisms *losing* and *missing* take the point of view of those left alive – or, to use the metaphor of death as a journey, those *left behind*. In *Our condolences for your tragic loss*, the particular loss is carefully unspecified. *We lost our father last winter* and *Our condolences on the loss of your husband* capture death as malign fate and evoke the misfortunate lack caused by an event over which the bereaved has no control. The deceased, having been lost, is then *missed* by those left alive to mourn their loss, as in the death notice that reads:

Nature's gentleman, sadly missed.

The loss motif is also found in statements about the loved one being *taken* (either by a god or by malevolent fate):

On this day you were taken away . . .

Our darling brother, taken so tragically in New Zealand . . .

In Egypt's Valley of the Kings, a relief showing the birth of King Ameno-phis III depicts two neonates: one is the king's corporeal form, the other is his soul. Belief in this dual character of living things is almost universal. Activity in animals and humans is explained by the presence of a soul in the body; sleep and death indicate its absence – which is why *sleep* is a frequent euphemism for *death*. In sleep, the soul's absence is only temporary but on death, the soul vacates the body forever; and a soul without a body to reside in must be laid to rest somehow, lest it become distressed and trouble the living. The ancient notion of a displaced soul is invoked in such death notices as the following, which reflects orthodox Roman Catholic belief:

Prayers for the repose of the soul of Mr Philip Rowe Parker will be offered in our Chapel.

Our word *cemetery* derives from Ancient Greek *koimōtḗrion* 'dormitory'. The dead are often likened to the sleeping: 'The sleeping and the dead / Are but as pictures.'[50] There is an obvious similarity between a sleeping body and a dead one, and sleep has often been regarded as a temporary death, a period when the soul leaves the body to return when it awakens:

> Now I lay me down to sleep,
> I pray the Lord my soul to keep,
> If I should die before I wake,
> I pray the Lord my soul to take.

To describe death as sleep is to pretend that it, too, is temporary; so death notices often substitute *sleep* for *death*.

Wayne . . . Sleeping peacefully, free from pain.

In loving memory of my darling husband Percival William who fell asleep on May 21, 19—.

The stem of the word *obituary* is Latin *obiter* 'on the journey'. Many peoples have regarded death as the start of the soul's journey into the afterlife, and buried their dead with all sorts of paraphernalia (including sacrificed humans) to help them on the way. Accordingly, death is often represented euphemistically as a journey to a better place for the soul of the dead person. The metaphors that arise from this notion include *part, depart, pass, pass away, pass on, pass over* and *arrival at the final resting place* – perhaps to be *reunited with loved ones* already dead.

One day I went in to see her, and I thought that she'd gone [said of an old lady who was shortly to die].

Kaye Reeves departed suddenly on Mar. 5, 19—.

We knew the time was coming and soon we'd have to part . . .

Maggie, on May 19, aged 94, passed away at DDH. Gran, you slipped away from us peacefully. All your pain has gone, now you're reunited with Grandpa after 53 years.

Somewhat more poetic are the euphemisms *go the way of all flesh* and *go to the happy hunting ground*. The latter is supposedly borrowed from Native American religious mythology; Christian counterparts are *go to meet one's maker, go to a better place, go to heaven* and:

Aunty Em. Reunited in God's kingdom with Nan, Pop . . .

In ever loving memory of my loving husband, who was suddenly called Home to Glory on May 21, 19—.

The Salvation Army often uses *promoted to glory* as a euphemism for *die*. Death is also looked upon as the end of life's journey, and the notion of death as a state of rest from the pains of life gives rise to euphemisms like *was laid to rest*, for example:

A great man gone to rest . . .

We watched you suffer. God knew you had enough. He took you gently with Him and gave you a place at last. Rest in peace . . .

Death is seen as beginning a new life. Euphemistic expressions which have to do with notions of an afterlife are used by both the religious and non-religious alike when dealing with death. For non-believers and agnostics, the conventional language is comforting insurance against the possibility that believers have it right and that the soul might continue to live on after the body is either consumed in fire or committed to the earth to rot. But what about people of religious conviction, for whom expressions demonstrating belief in a better afterlife are statements of simple fact? Are such expressions euphemistic for them, or simply orthophemistic? For all who use them, they are preferred expressions and the image they offer is one of consolation. By glossing over the physical event of death and dying, the image is also a more palatable one. Some examples:

Born into eternal life 10 March 19—.

Called to a higher life on 9th March 19—.

Aubrey John (Bray), passed away after a short illness on Mar. 10, 19—. Beloved husband of Betty. Alive with Jesus.

In the last notice, there is a fiction that the deceased is somehow still alive. Children are often told that a dead parent has gone to become a star in heaven. In many of the notices quoted, the dead are directly addressed.

The death of someone associated with a particular profession or pastime leads to euphemisms with the recurrent theme of a final act, like *went to meet the great golfer in the sky, pulled up the stumps for the last time* [cricketer], or *finally cashed in his chips* [gambler]:

We had to send our little dog to the kennel in the sky at the beginning of the year.

[Below Masonic compasses] GILBERT. – George Richard. Our friend and confidant for thirty years. You lived respected and died regretted. In your promotion to the Grand Lodge above . . .

Joan, aged 60. Passed away Mar. 6, 19— . . . I hope there's a T.A.B. up there.[51]

Every now and then, the death columns reveal a real gem:

The luggage van ahead, making plum pudding, bread and milk for breakfast, exploding spaghetti tins, you have gone, my childhood memories can never. Thank you. – Tracey, Geoff, and Kimberley.

Not so much an example of exquisite euphemism, but stream-of-consciousness eulogy.

The hospital records of deceased patients have described their deaths in terms such as *therapeutic misadventure, substantive negative outcome* and *The patient failed to fulfill his wellness potential.*[52] Such euphemisms gloss over the fact that the death was premature and seek to prevent an action for negligence against hospital staff. It is questionable whether *kick the bucket*, used in banter, can be other than dysphemistic, with its suggestion of kicking the bucket away in order to hang (as suicide or, less likely, execution).[53] *To breathe one's last* is literal and indelicate, but not as bad as *cark it* (possibly derived from Scots *kirkit* 'to be laid out in church'). A dead person can be said to be *pushing up daisies* (the metaphor is also dead, since it can be used of someone cremated). *Snuff it* is from a candle being snuffed out and can be the result of foul play. Unassisted death is referred to in *fall/drop off the perch/*

twig, turn up her toes, park/pop his clogs and the like; these are irreverent and potentially dysphemistic, but more often than not used to challenge the fear of death. Death while on military service is referred to by euphemisms that vary between the solemnly patriotic *do one's bit for one's country, make the ultimate sacrifice* – which glamorize death and help to reinforce for those still surviving the illusory world of a glorious battlefield – and the wryly humorous (if not downright flippant) *come home in a box, X bought it* and, for flyers, *be grounded for good*. In Australia at least, *gone to God* is used flippantly of inanimate objects that are broken or worn out.

Censoring the language of killing

Dangerous pursuits that put life in danger, such as war, mining, hunting and fishing, are often beset with taboos on both language and behaviour, as people seek to avoid defeat and subjugation, mining disasters, dangerous beasts and getting lost at sea. People fear the spirits of dead enemies:

we may with some probability assume that, just as the dread of the spirits of his enemies is the main motive for the seclusion and purification of the warrior who hopes to take or has already taken their lives, so the huntsman or fisherman who complies with similar customs is principally actuated by a fear of the spirits of the beasts, birds, or fish which he has killed or intends to kill. For the savage commonly conceives animals to be endowed with souls and intelligences like his own, and hence he naturally treats them with similar respect. Just as he attempts to appease the ghosts of the men he has slain, so he assays to propitiate the spirits of the animals he has killed. (Frazer 1911: 190)

In many communities therefore, a hunter will conceal his purpose, saying such things as *I'm going to collect rattan, I'm going to climb a betel-nut tree*.[54] And often he will not name the game that he is hunting, even if he sees it. Sometimes, men will not address other hunters by name lest their quarry is monitoring their language. The same is true for fishermen. In addition, many peoples have taboos against mentioning the names of dangerous animals, whether hunting or not. In Chapter 2 we have already referred to the Ukrainian proverb warning against mentioning the wolf's name; there is also the Korean *holangito ceymal hamyen ontayteni* 'Speak of the tiger and it comes'. In a story from central Australia, we find the following:

The child talked on persistently, 'Do they say that cattle are always goring people? How do they talk about cattle? They say they always gore people but they didn't gore us this time.' The man answered the child. 'Don't talk like that! The cattle might hear us, and attack and kill us.' (Hudson and Richards 1978: 15)

This attitude reflects a fear that the souls of animals can understand human language, and if a dangerous creature hears its name, it may attack. So wolves and bears, snakes and other venomous creatures, sharks, rays and saltwater crocodiles are often named by euphemisms. The Zia of south-eastern Papua New Guinea also invoke the names of powerful dead ancestors as a help when hunting. For instance, when throwing his spear at a quarry, a Zia man might yell 'A Omguta!' hoping for that ancestor's aid in scoring a hit. This is a euphemistic use of names of the dead, and can only be successful when employed by mature men, otherwise it will bring misfortune to the hunter.

There are verbal taboos reported for Scottish and Cornish fishermen.[55] Euphemisms are (or were) employed during fishing expeditions when speaking of churches and clergymen, women and land animals, in particular the rabbit and, in Scotland, anadromous fish (such as salmon and trout, which live part of their life in saltwater and part in freshwater). Possibly, this language behaviour is based on a contrast between the insider world of the fishermen and an outsider world which can only be spoken about euphemistically. For instance, the anadromous fish are game fish, traditionally the fare of the laird, not the fisher-folk who observe the taboo. Until recently, there were dreadful hazards attendant on life at sea and great uncertainty in locating fish; but as the catch has become more predictable and the occupation much safer, the taboos have tended to disappear. The taboo on churches and clergymen may guard against the risk of being thought to want to be called to God, or perhaps they are like other topics tabooed by fishermen: things associated with the security and comforts of the land, for which a man at sea might yearn and so cause him to be distracted or his luck to turn against him. There is some evidence for a similar constraint among Malay fishermen.[56] Lest misfortune befall their canoes, Zia fishermen taboo the names of headlands and other shoreline features where accidents have happened in the past.

In most societies, women's sexuality is believed to be a danger to hunters, fishers, warriors and sportsmen.[57] The Zia will not allow women on hunting trips, believing that they frighten animals away; this belief is so strong that if attacked by a wild boar, cassowary or other dangerous creature, a hunter will call out his wife's name, supposing this to be enough to drive the creature away from him. This behaviour is reminiscent of invoking God to frighten away the devil and saying *Bless you!* when someone sneezes. The reason that rabbits have been singled out for taboo in Britain is probably their centuries-old link with women. Does it arise from fear of over-stimulating sexual desire when no heterosexual outlet is available? Yet boats have for centuries been pronominalized by *she/her* and are often given women's names. Nonetheless, when women today do get on board a fishing boat they are likely to be blamed if the catch is bad.[58]

We remarked in Chapter 1 that killing other human beings is normally taboo, unless those others are sentenced to capital punishment by the judiciary or branded enemies by the government. Language is censored so as to reflect the representation of enemies as evil,[59] aggressive, immoral, inhuman and unjust, whereas we and our allies are the exact opposite. Hypocritically, the enemy is dehumanized, as in the infamous Vietnam War photo caption referring to *an oriental human being*, depicted being dropped to his death from a helicopter.[60] As we said in Chapter 2, we are *invited in* as *liberators*, they are *aggressors* and *invaders*; we make a *pre-emptive strike*, theirs is a *blitzkrieg* or an *invasion*; our boys (and girls) are *freedom-fighters*, theirs are *insurgents*, dehumanized as *softskin targets*; civilian deaths caused by our troops are *collateral damage*, whereas theirs are *murderous terrorist acts against civilians*; and whereas we might *disengage from the enemy* or make a *tactical withdrawal*, they *retreat*. Our bombing is *protective reaction* and we make *surgical strikes*; bombs that fall outside the target area are *incontinent ordnance*, and those dropped on one of our own allies are excused as *friendly fire*; they have *concentration camps*, but we have *pacification centres*. When the United States went into tiny defenceless Grenada in 1983, President Ronald Reagan at first referred to the act as an *invasion*; after it was all over, however, he objected to reporters about their 'frequent use of the word invasion. This was a *rescue mission.*'[61] The word *invasion* is typically a dysphemism, with connotations of unwanted interference and enforced domination of others, whereas *rescue mission* is a euphemism, with connotations of humanitarian aid. The United States ousted the dictator of Panama (1989–90) in *Operation Just Cause*. A couple of years later in Somalia was *Operation Restore Hope* – a complete failure. Having abandoned the Kurds to Saddam Hussein's revenge after the first Gulf War, *Operation Provide Comfort* airlifted supplies to the beleaguered Kurds (1991–6). The invasion of Taliban-dominated Afghanistan in 2001 was *Operation Infinite Justice* and later, *Operation Enduring Freedom*: by 2005, there was not much freedom under the powerful warlords and nothing but chaos has endured. But a *Coalition of the Willing*, led by the United States and Britain in defiance of the United Nations, launched *Operation Iraqi Freedom*. This put not only military personnel, but also at least ten (some say 100) times as many Iraqi civilians *in harm's way*. Saddam's military was quickly *softened up* by bombs before being *degraded* and *attrited*. Within a year, Iraq was unstable, unsafe for civilians and seemingly going the way of Afghanistan a couple of years earlier. Iraqis who in 2005 continue to attack the coalition forces and their stooges are branded *terrorists* by their targets, although they use exactly the methods used by the now revered *resistance forces* against Nazi occupation in Europe. The same methods were used by the Zionist gangs to kill British troops and commit acts of sabotage in British-occupied Palestine after the Second World War; the Zionists succeeded in forming the state of Israel, now strongly supported by the *Coalition of the Willing*, who abhor such tactics used against them in Iraq. The language of

Figure 9.1. Squatters 'dispersing' Australian Aborigines; late nineteenth century (from A. J. Vagan, *The Black Police: A Story of Modern Australia*. London: Hutchinson, 1890).

warfare provides a heaven for hypocrisy; it is a kind of political language which, as George Orwell said, 'is designed to make lies sound truthful and murder respectable, and to give an appearance of solidity to pure wind'.[62]

'Militarese' uses euphemisms which are loaded to the point of deception; perhaps *terminate with extreme prejudice* and *take out* [a target] are transparent; but *pacify* means 'be killing (be at war with)'; *neutralize* and *salvage* mean 'kill selected targets'; *mopping up operations* include killing off the remnants of *the resistance*. In nineteenth-century Australia, *disperse* was an officially sanctioned euphemism for Aboriginal killings by the 'native' police force set up in 1848. When a young sub, just new to the police force, used the word 'killed' instead of the official *dispersed* in a report he had submitted, he was severely reprimanded and told to correct his error. The sub, described as 'rather a wag', rewrote the report thus: 'We successfully surrounded the said party of aborigines and dispersed fifteen, the remainder, some half dozen, succeeded in escaping.'[63] So-called *collisions* between Aborigines and the native police force were usually massacres. Individual shootings were described as *self-defence* (like most police shootings are). Reports invariably recorded how the police, *exercising great restraint*, were *forced in the end to shoot*. The few reports that exist are euphemistic cover-ups of the carnage that really took place.

Legal killings are called *executions*: *to execute* was once a euphemism whose literal sense was (as it still is in other contexts) 'to do or perform'.

Otherwise, it is *capital punishment* (from a time when the head – 'capital' – was chopped off). Macbeth spoke of Duncan's *taking-off*,[64] and more modern descriptions of criminal and undercover murders include *it's curtains for X*, *rub X out*, *take care of / terminate / waste / silence X*; from hanging, *be/get strung up*; from lynching, *decorate a cottonwood*. In a funeral oration for someone shot to death in a gangland killing, he was said to have died from *lead poisoning*. The CIA had a *Health Alteration Committee* to decide on *hits*.[65] The verb *liquidate* is a metaphor from the comparatively harmless practice of shutting down a business.

In recent times, names for weapons have been subject to onomastic variation for reasons of secrecy, avoidance, propaganda and play. During the development of the army tank in the First World War, the term *tank* was a deceptive term, suggesting a storage tank for liquids; however the term has stuck. When the first atomic bomb was being developed, it was often referred to by general-for-specific euphemisms like *the gadget*, *the device*, *the thing* and even the all-embracing *it*.[66] Although secrecy was doubtless the main motivation, avoidance (not wanting to face up to the potential horror of its deployment) may have played a part. Propaganda explains Ronald Reagan's naming of a ten-warhead MX missile *Peacekeeper*, and perhaps the naming of the *Daisy Cutter*, used for *shock and awe* (sudden, noisy and devastating bombardment from air and land). During the two twentieth-century world wars, weapons were sometimes given the names of household items; for example, a machine gun was called both *a sewing machine* and *a coffee mill*. Obversely, household items were given the names of weapons, e.g. *hand grenade* was playfully used to mean 'potato'.[67]

During the twentieth century, state-sanctioned deaths resulting from wars, genocide, engineered famines, environmental and social neglect, and other *humanitarian disasters* wiped out well in excess of a hundred million people. The twenty-first century is keeping up the momentum. Money spent on weapons far exceeds the resources committed to health programmes. Bureaucratic terminology tends to dehumanize disaster,[68] such that the 1986 *Challenger* Space Shuttle disaster was described by NASA as an *anomaly*; the remains of those killed were *recovered components* placed not in coffins but in *crew transfer containers*; all of which plays down the loss of human life caused by an inattention to safety measures, motivated by short-term political and financial gain.

The June 1972 Watergate break-in led directly to the resignation of President Richard M. Nixon in 1974. *Watergate* became a byword for any real or suspected hushed-up political scandal, and the suffix *-gate* was adopted by the language to give this interpretation to the noun prefixed to it, e.g. *Billygate*, *Irangate*, *Camillagate* (and *Squidgygate*), *Wine-gate*, and from the 2000 US Presidential election *chadgate*. Similar, though nothing like so prolific, are the names for certain catastrophic war-time or terrorist events, that become standards of comparison for roughly comparable events, or events that are hyperbolically presented that way. A decisive final contest is often referred to as a *waterloo* (after the 1815 battle, in which Napoleon was finally defeated). *Pearl Harbor* is used as a figure for a sudden and unexpected attack (after the December 1941 Japanese destruction of the US fleet in Pearl Harbor, which brought the US into the Second World War). *911* (or *9/11*), pronounced 'nine-eleven', is the term used for a catastrophic terrorist attack (after 11 September 2001, when four passenger planes were hijacked by al-Qaeda members, killing those on board and destroying the World Trade Center and part of the Pentagon, killing 3,030 people and injuring 2,337);[69] a terrorist attack on a school in Beslan, North Ossetia, which resulted in 334 deaths and about 1,000 injured, was described by many sources as *Russia's 9/11*.

Abortion has been legalized in most English-speaking countries for several decades. Before it was legalized, so-called *backyard abortions* often created severe physical trauma to the mother; this, the social cost of the birth of an unwanted child, and the feminist push to give greater freedom of choice to women led to its legalization. Those favouring abortion, people who are *pro-choice*, refer to *the product of conception* as a *foetus*; so-called *right-to-lifers* instead speak of the foetus as a *baby* or a *child* because they argue that there is no distinction between abortion and infanticide. Curiously, a very few right-to-lifers believe that although it is morally wrong to abort a fetus, it is not wrong to murder doctors and others who serve abortion clinics; there have been several convictions for such murders.

Suicide is mostly regarded as a sin and a path to eternal damnation; it is a path that a secular society takes measures to prevent, often against the wishes of the would-be suicide. The excuse seems to be the social cost to the family of a suicide. Most suicides cannot see the advantages of staying alive; some suicides wish to kill others along with themselves. This renders them murderers, and perhaps terrorists, and they are condemned; although if they succeed in their purpose, the only recourse that society has is to punish the family that they leave behind.

Another moral dilemma arises with the question of *euthanasia* (orthophemism). The spectacular leaps in modern medicine have an ironical twist. A new fear has appeared – namely, the fear of *not-dying*. The dread of spending one's last years *bedridden*, alone and attached to some machine is a very real one, as evident in the current debate over *mercy killings*. As in the past, those suffering from chronic illnesses often view death as a welcome relief from their suffering.

Our anxieties about death have shifted from the fact of dying to the methods that medicine will use to keep us alive. 'Don't let me die on a machine,' patients now whisper to their physicians or assert in advance directives. The widespread call for physician-assisted suicide is not simply the result of documented medical failures in pain management, failures that come despite an abundance of powerful opioids that guarantee almost no patient should die in pain. It is a logical extension of the biomedical model. When the biomedical 'continuous repair' job inevitably fails, many people reasonably (but incorrectly) suppose that doctors have nothing left to offer except one last drug or high-tech mechanism that will quickly and painlessly dispatch us. (Morris 2000: 16)

The argument often advanced for euthanasia is that animals in great pain are regularly *put down* or *put to sleep* (euphemisms), and that humans should likewise be *allowed to die with dignity* (euphemism). As with abortion before legalization, a certain amount of covert euthanasia is practised and a blind eye turned when *medical treatment is withheld* from severely disabled or trauma-tized patients, or very infirm persons make *end-of-life decisions*, such as requesting to be included on the *NFR* (not for resuscitation) list. Many religious people and the right-to-life movement believe euthanasia to be morally wrong; and many non-religious voters and medical professionals are worried by possible abuses of the system or legal actions taken when such abuse is perceived, so legislators will not risk legalizing it. It has been legalized (under severe constraints) in the Netherlands, and it was very briefly legal in the Northern Territory of Australia, but before ever being practised, the law was overturned by Australia's Federal Government.

Censoring the language for disease, death and killing

In this chapter, we have reviewed some of the taboos and X-phemisms that occur from the censoring of vocabulary used when speaking about matters of disease, death and killing. As we have seen elsewhere in this book, when human beings use figurative language and/or verbal play in generating X-phemisms, they are responding to their perceptions of and conceptions about the denotata; for the most part, these involve fear or distaste.

In most societies, past and present, references to diseases are censored: they are spoken of euphemistically. It might be because they are thought to result from the actions of a malevolent spirit or person, or in consequence of their connection with death, or just because of their intrinsic unpleasantness. A mild or indirect term for a disease will generally serve to make speaking about the harsh reality more tolerable. Politeness conventions might also require that we censor direct reference to an indecorous and embarrassing complaint, and instead hint. Yet, on other occasions, we may want to play down an illness for the simple reason of not wanting to appear to complain: talking about one's health problems has the reputation for being boring to others.

From the secure position afforded us by twenty-first-century medicine, when each new day seems to bring some new medical breakthrough, our fear of disease is no less acute than in earlier times. Disease is still something of a mystery: there are symptoms and there are sick patients, but there is often nothing tangible in disease itself. It seems mostly to arrive out of the blue and just as mysteriously seems able transmit itself from person to person, affecting some while leaving others curiously untouched. This is particularly true in the case of stigmatizing illnesses, such as AIDS or cancer. Current social attitudes towards these and disorders included under the label *mental illness* still reflect the medieval equation of good with well-being and evil with disease.

Human beings fear losing control of their destinies, and this is at the root of many taboos. Disease is something that afflicts us; we are *patients,* we exercise no control. This adds to the horror of disease, which in the past would have been more acute because diseases were more mysterious and the fear of contagion greater. In normal non-clinical usage, madness is also perceived to result from a lack of control, and the fear of becoming insane has inspired some of the strongest linguistic taboos to be found in the general area of illness and disease. Death is, of course, simply another unavoidable body process; no one gets out alive. We can end our own life, but we have no control over when Nature will rob us of it. Death awaits all of us, and to most of us it is an unknown, something to be avoided and something that it is reasonable to be fearful of. Even those with strong religious beliefs are not usually in a hurry to meet their maker. For those who die after enduring severe pain, death is a haven. For others, death is eternal sleep or the start of a new afterlife. As we have seen, the language of death reflects all such attributes.

Except for enemies, killing of persons is taboo. People we don't like may be told to *drop dead* or *go to hell* (not heaven!); and if annoyed, we may say something like *I'd like to wring his/your neck*, even to persons we are normally fond of. Legally sanctioned killings are set about with euphemism. Acts of war are often cloaked in language that masks the true purpose and nature of acts of killing. By using deodorant language to describe dirty deeds, it is perhaps easier to commit those dirty deeds. Expressions such as *soft skin target*, *surgical strikes*, *collateral damage* and *friendly fire* help to minimize feelings of responsibility. They play down the slaughter of human beings and also create psychological distance between the perpetrators and their actions. And, while it is unlikely anyone is really taken in by such doublespeak – public opinion is not as easily manipulated as George Orwell's Newspeak would suggest – research carried out by people like Elizabeth Loftus shows that loaded language does work to influence memory and perception.[70] Hunting is also characterized by language motivated by fear of dangerous creatures or fear of bad luck befalling the hunter – language that seeks to avoid the retribution of the killer being killed.

Taboos drive the renewal of language. We have seen in the fields of disease, death and killing that self-censoring leads to the creation of X-phemisms, many of which show remarkable inventiveness; and even on these sad topics, some are playful.

10 Taboo, censoring and the human brain

Forbidden words are the most emotionally evocative of all language stimuli. Research in psychology, physiology and neurology corroborate that they are processed differently from ordinary language and are subject to more acute recognition and recall. Taboo language has a special place in our neural anatomy. Before reviewing the evidence for these claims, we look back at what has been said about taboo and censoring.

Revisiting taboo, censoring and X-phemism

The word *taboo* refers to forbidden behaviour, and tabooed behaviour is subject to censoring. We have discussed constraints on the use of jargon, slang, swearing and insult; censoring the way we talk about people who may be perceived or perceive themselves to be disadvantaged or oppressed; notions about correct and incorrect grammar; taboos on naming and addressing people and dangerous animals; injunctions on speaking about the organs of sex, micturition and defecation, their functions and effluvia; censoring the language for foods, and language dealing with diseases, death and killing. The most serious taboos apply to things thought to be ominous, evil or offensive to supernatural powers; to violate such taboos automatically causes harm (even death) to the violator and perhaps his/her fellows. In this context, euphemism can be quite literally a matter of life or death. However, taboos do not always risk physical or metaphysical injury; Old Polynesia had taboos on bad manners such as readers of this book may experience in their everyday lives – taboos that are merely social sanctions placed on behaviour that is regarded as distasteful or impolite within a certain social context. Many taboos of contemporary western society rest ultimately on traditions of etiquette, and are therefore defined by culturally sensitive social parameters such as age, sex, education and social status. Even though some people believe metaphysical harm is still a possibility if religious sensibilities are transgressed, a taboo word in today's English is avoided – that is to say, censored out of use on a particular occasion – not (unless one is a child) because of any fear that

237

physical harm may befall either the speaker or the audience, but lest the speaker lose face by offending the sensibilities of the audience. All normal individuals censor their own language (and other behaviour) constantly: they sometimes consciously, but mostly unconsciously, choose among such alternatives as *micturating, powdering my nose, going to the washroom, taking a leak, a pee* or *a piss*, saying *Holy shit!* or *Gosh!* Such taboos are often observed in private, but they are strongest in the public domain, where euphemism is the polite thing and dysphemism (offensive language) breaks social convention. As social beings, humans can ill afford to violate social conventions without suffering adverse sanctions. People censor their behaviour so as to avoid giving offence, except when deliberately intending to offend.

We distinguished an individual's *censoring* of language from institutional and public *censorship* of language. One of the reasons that political correctness has been so successful in getting people to change their linguistic behaviour is that it has created a climate of tacit censorship. Speakers who use non-PC terms run the risk of being lumped together with true bigots with malevolent motives. The safest course of action is to be PC. Governments and other institutions exercise censorship as a means of regulating the moral and political life of their people, controlling the media and communications between citizens against language deemed to be subversive of the common good. Government censorship flourishes in times of public insecurity, when there is a fear of civil unrest, invasion from outside or risk from acts of terrorism. We argued, as Milton did long ago, that, in the end, censorship is futile. In fact, it is probably only ever effective when it coincides with what individuals would choose to censor for themselves (hence the comparative success of non-discriminatory language guidelines).

In contemporary western society, taboo and euphemism are closely entwined with concepts of politeness and face (basically, a person's self-image). Generally, social interaction is oriented towards behaviour that is courteous and respectful, or at least inoffensive. Participants have to consider whether what they are saying will maintain, enhance or damage their own face, as well as be considerate of, and care for, the face needs of others. We defined euphemism as 'an alternative to a dispreferred expression', namely an expression that is not desired or appropriate on a given occasion. Typically, the dispreferred expression denotes a taboo topic, and so might alternatively be called a *taboo term*. A speaker (or writer) uses a euphemism to escape disapproval and to avoid offending the hearer (or reader) or often some third party (maybe a bystander). Some speakers would claim that the obnoxious nature of taboo terms offends their own sensibilities.

Examples of euphemism we have seen in this book are wide-ranging: medieval Dutch physicians used to write of *figs in the secret passage* to denote 'piles'; the nineteenth-century Victorian moral code created negative words such as *inexpressibles*, *unmentionables* and *unhintables*, so that those in polite society could avoid uttering *legs*, *trousers* and *underclothing*; some people still say *crumbs* instead of *Christ*; many newspapers still print *c**** and *f****; politicians speak of *community charges*, *levies* or even *voluntary contributions* rather than of *taxes* and *tolls*; *prairie oysters*, *mountain oysters* and *fry* sound more appetizing than *calf's testicles*; *lemon fish* and *flake* sound tastier than *shark*; companies *downsize*, *rightsize* or implement an *RIF* (reduction in force) through *targeted voluntary separation* or *involuntary resignation*; the push for non-sexist usage has rendered words like *chairman* and *actress* taboo for some people, and so on. Not all euphemisms are in response to taboo, however. Euphemisms are simply alternatives for expressions speakers prefer not to use on a given occasion. Clause 28 of the Melbourne Metropolitan Planning Scheme makes several references to the *accommodation of stationary vehicles*.[1] The author presumably believed that this phrase has more favourable connotations than either *parking places* or *car spaces* – whose taboo status is not obvious; in fact they are probably dispreferred because they do not have the Latinate ring of bureaucratese. It is comparable with the upgrade of *potholes* to *pavement deficiencies*, *dried beans* to *Alaskan strawberries*: such euphemisms supposedly enhance whatever is being referred to. They exhibit wordplay that may even have been created to amuse. Euphemisms are the product of a human mind confronting the problem of how to talk about something for which there is a dispreferred expression they wish to avoid. They result from the censoring of language, though they only rarely arise from the censorship of language.

From earliest times, themes such as private parts, bodily functions, sex, lust, anger, notions of social status, hate, dishonesty, drunkenness, madness, disease, death, dangerous animals, fear and God have inspired taboos and inhibitions, such that there has been considerable impact from censoring discussion of them. However, notions about what is forbidden vary, sometimes dramatically, across cultures and across time. Since the 1980s, English speakers have shown a growing apprehensiveness of how to talk to and about 'women and minorities'. There has been a gradual establishment of legally recognized sanctions against what we have described as *-IST language*. The new taboos make sexist, racist, ageist, 'religiousist', etc. language not only contextually, but also legally dysphemistic. The -IST taboos have surpassed irreligious profanity, blasphemy and sexual obscenity in significance, against which laws have been relaxed. Individual societies will also differ with respect to the degree of tolerance for taboo-defying behaviour, depending on their values and belief systems at the particular time in history. It was not so long ago that transgressions against some western taboos were very severely punished; for instance, up until the end of the seventeenth century, blasphemy was punishable by burning in Britain. There are still people who would follow such biblical commandments as:

He that blasphemeth the name of the LORD, he shall surely be put to death, and all the congregation shall certainly stone him: as well the stranger, as he that is born in the land, and when he blasphemeth the name of the LORD, shall be put to death. (Leviticus 24: 16)

Whereas the term *euphemism* is well known and has wide currency, *dysphemism* rarely appears in ordinary language; curious, since there's so much dysphemism about. Like euphemism, it is sometimes motivated by fear and distaste, but also by hatred and contempt. Speakers resort to dysphemism to talk about people and things that frustrate and annoy them, that they disapprove of and wish to disparage, humiliate and degrade. Curses, name-calling and any sort of derogatory comment directed towards others in order to insult or to wound them are all examples of dysphemism. Exclamatory swear words that release frustration or anger are dysphemisms. Like euphem-ism, dysphemism interacts with style and has the potential to produce stylistic discord; if someone at a formal dinner party were to publicly announce *I'm off for a piss*, rather than saying *Excuse me for a moment*, the effect would be dysphemistic.

The concepts of euphemism and dysphemism imply the presence of direct terms that are neither sweet-sounding, evasive, overly polite (euphemistic) nor harsh, blunt or offensive (dysphemistic); such expressions we call *ortho-phemisms*. As alternatives to offensive expressions, orthophemisms, like euphemisms, will typically be preferred as desirable or appropriate terms. Examples of all three kinds of language expressions would be *pass away* (typically a euphemism), *snuff it* (typically a dysphemism) and *die* (typically an orthophemism). However, these descriptions are problematic, since what determines them is a set of social attitudes or conventions that may vary considerably between dialect groups and even between individual members of the same community. Because there is such complexity and variety of opin-ions and attitudes, we are unlikely ever to find uniformity of judgment between speakers of even very similar social backgrounds. There can be no such thing as 'Everyman's euphemism' or 'Everyman's dysphemism'. X-phemisms (members of the union set of euphemisms, orthophemisms and dysphemisms) are primarily determined by evaluating an expression within the particular context in which is it uttered. For example, the verb *die* is direct, and in some contexts might well be the neutral and mundane orthophemism. However, it would be offensive and dysphemistic in a more personal context where it conjures up an image that is just too blunt. On the other hand, an expression like *snuff it* or *croak* can also be euphemistic between certain individuals; its flippancy detracts from the seriousness of death, and can make it preferable to *die*. A jocular approach to death is offensive only if it can be expected that the hearer would regard it as such.

Even though the choice between alternative expressions will always depend upon context, it would be true to say that ordinary people do perceive expressions to be somehow intrinsically either orthophemistic, euphemistic or dysphemistic. For example, terms for 'die' such as *pass away* and *sleep* are euphemistic, whereas *croak*, *snuff it* and *peg out* are not. We mentioned a British survey where participants were asked to respond to the perceived 'strength' of twenty-eight swear words;[2] no context was provided, yet participants were clear about the severity of such words, and the researchers were able to put together a broad topography of swear words across all groups. We therefore link the default evaluation of expressions as euphemistic, dysphemistic or orthophemistic – the kind of evaluation made in some dictionaries – to the middle-class politeness criterion (MCPC): that which would be considered the polite form when addressing a casual acquaintance of the opposite sex, in a formal situation, in a middle-class environment. The MCPC is presupposed in the X-phemistic evaluations and degrees of offensiveness ascribed to words in dictionaries and collections of euphemisms and dysphemisms (such as Ayto 1993, Green 1996). The MCPC is automatically assumed in the public domain, where the exact composition of an audience is not known; etiquette demands that language is chosen carefully and consciously for a respectable, gender-mixed, middle-class audience.

The X-phemism mill: word taboo and the naturalist hypothesis

Words are symbolic. Despite the fact that every language has some vocabulary based on sound symbolism (e.g. *clang*, *jangle*, *woosh*),[3] the correlation between the form and the meaning of a language expression is arbitrary – there is no natural or necessary connection between the physical shape of a word and what it denotes. Individual sounds (e.g. /e/, /p/, /n/) do not have meaning, and Shakespeare was correct to write that 'that which we call a rose, by any other name would smell as sweet'.[4] Most language users, however, are constantly on the look out for a meaningful connection between the sound of a word and its denotatum. Meaning may shift because of the way the word sounds. For some people, the word *flagrant* now describes 'the way flowers smell' as the result of a blend of *fl[ower]* and *[fr]agrant*. Speakers might also perceive a similarity between forms on the basis of meaning, and then change the forms so that they are pronounced alike. For example, the regular processes of sound change would have shifted Modern English *groin* to something like *grine*; but the word was altered to *groin* to be more like *loin*. The sounds used to denote certain phenomena start off being arbitrary, but over time this arbitrariness can fall away.[5] In the case of taboo words, the link made between sound and sense is particularly strong; speakers really do behave as if somehow the form of the expression communicates the essential nature of whatever it represents (*'Cunt' is such a horrible word!*).

More generally, the belief in the potency of words has been dubbed the 'naturalist hypothesis';[6] to quote Sir James Frazer, 'the link between a name and the person or thing denominated by it is not a mere arbitrary and ideal association, but a real and substantial bond which unites the two'.[7] The naturalist hypothesis forms the very basis for the distinction between the mentionable euphemism on the one hand, and an unmentionable taboo alternative on the other. Why would orthophemistic expressions such as *vagina* and *excrement* have fewer unpleasant connotations than their taboo synonyms *cunt* and *shit*? The taboo terms have been contaminated by the taboo concepts they represent. Yet the obscenity lies in the actual words themselves – what they connote – and not in what they denote. This is why taboo words are often described as unpleasant or ugly-sounding and why they are miscalled *dirty words*. These words are felt to be intrinsically nasty, and that makes them disturbing. In fact, the ability of forbidden words to 'chill the blood and raise gooseflesh'[8] is now scientifically confirmed. Recent physiological studies demonstrate that they elicit far stronger skin conductance responses than any other kinds of words.

Such is the potency of taboo terms that innocent vocabulary may also be affected through spurious association. *Regina* makes some people feel uncomfortable because of its phonetic similarity to *vagina*, and they avoid it. Phonetic proximity to *fuck* puts a constraint on the use of *suck* in polite society. However, the censoring of *suck* is strengthened by the fact that, since the 1920s, it has been used for 'fellatio' and, since the 1970s, in homophobic-inspired expressions for 'something contemptible or disgusting', as in *School sucks!* The word *coney* (rhymes with *honey*) 'rabbit' dropped out of use when it took on unmentionable anatomical significance. Similarly, when *arse* collided with *ass*, this caused problems for *ass* 'donkey', which is now avoided by many English speakers. Some still use *cock* to mean 'rooster', but its identity with the name of the tabooed body part is killing off the 'rooster' sense. Gender, sexuality, disability and especially race are now so highly charged that speakers will shun anything that may be interpreted as discriminatory or pejorative – and this includes blameless bystanders who get in the way. The word *niggardly* has no etymological connections with the taboo term *nigger*, yet many Americans now censor out the expression. The effects of taboo often cross language boundaries, too. In the Nootka language of Vancouver Island, British Columbia, the English word *such* so closely resembles the Nootka word meaning 'cunt' that teachers find it very difficult to convince their students to utter the English word in class. Thai–English bilinguals are apprehensive about using their word *fuk* 'gourd, pumpkin' in the hearing of English speakers; they also avoid the English word *yet* because of its phonetic resemblance to the dysphemistic Thai verb 'fuck'. Many other peoples practise similar self-censoring under multilingual conditions.

The English words *titivate* and *titillate* illustrate another effect of taboo. The two similar-sounding words are currently in the process of coalescing. *Titivate* originally meant 'to tidy up', but some dictionaries give the additional meaning (usually labelled 'incorrect') 'tickle, excite agreeably'.[9] *Titivate* is taking on the meaning of similar-sounding *titillate* meaning 'to excite pleasantly', with a strong association to lust. The fact the first syllable is *tit-* may also play a part. We should not be surprised that *titillate* wins out over *titivate*; risqué meanings will always come to dominate. Economics has Gresham's Law: 'Bad money drives out good'.[10] Sociology now has Knight's Law: 'Bad talk drives out good'. Linguistics has the Allan–Burridge Law of Semantic Change: 'Bad connotations drive out good.'[11] The effect of this law is that many euphemisms become tainted over time, as the negative associations reassert themselves and undermine the euphemistic quality of the word. Such is the shame surrounding mental illness that any euphemism for the condition will quickly degenerate into a taboo term. As society's prejudiced perceptions foment, the euphemistic value is diluted and the negative connotations reattach themselves, requiring a new euphemism to be found. The word *insanity* derives from Latin *in-sanus* 'not-healthy' and originally had a much broader domain, encompassing all bodily organs and their functions; but once pressed into euphemistic service, it quickly narrowed to 'mentally unsound'. Today, even the word *sane* (without the negative prefix) has narrowed under the influence of *insane* to denote only a mental condition.

Taboo areas of the lexicon perpetually generate this sort of narrowing and deterioration of meaning. The result is a constant turnover of vocabulary for words denoting taboo concepts. Very few euphemisms that have degraded into taboo terms in this way ever come back from the abyss, even after they have lost their taboo sense. This promotes X-phemistic recycling. And the more severe the taboo, the more rapid the turnover. For example, the vocabulary for bodily effluvia, sex and tabooed body parts manifests significantly more synonymy than one encounters anywhere else in the English lexicon; there are literally thousands of X-phemisms. Lexical richness is always a key to understanding society's preoccupations, and it is striking that over the years, English has accumulated more than 1,000 expressions for 'penis', 1,200 for 'vulva/vagina', 800 for 'copulation' and an extraordinary 2,000 expressions for 'wanton woman'.[12] Given these figures, it does seem curious that people are always so fascinated by the myth that Eskimo languages have hundreds of different words for 'snow' (in fact they don't).[13] English speakers myopically overlook the lexical abundance of their own sexual vocabulary.

Raising gooseflesh: extra-linguistic evidence

Obscenities . . . are fighting words, gross words, dirty words, words charged with power; they are hurled like insults, heaped up to contaminate and defile, to incite or inflame, or just to let off steam. They leap out before we can stop them. They draw attention, they get us into trouble. The emotion and the obscenity proceed together, as if fused, overriding cortical inhibitions in a quick, involuntary burst. (Morris 2000: 174)

We have presented plenty of linguistic evidence for the emotional quality of taboo expressions. Even across languages they can contaminate other words, bringing down innocent expressions that just happen to sound similar. More-over, taboo senses seem to have a saliency that will dominate and suppress other senses of a language expression recruited as a euphemism. In this next section, we examine the psychological, physiological and neurological studies that all corroborate the fact that forbidden words are more arousing, more shocking, more memorable and more evocative than all other language stimuli.[14]

In 1957, Charles Osgood and his colleagues outlined a technique, the 'semantic differential', for systematically (though subjectively) quantifying connotative meaning; and the results provide psycholinguistic evidence for the Allan–Burridge Law of Semantic Change and the X-phemism mill.[15] People were asked to evaluate words and phrases on a series of seven-point bipolar rating scales, intended to locate a concept in semantic space within three dimensions of attitude: evaluation (is the word good or bad?); activity (is the word active or passive?); potency (is the word strong or weak?). The research confirms what we know from the behaviour of words over time: that there is a general tendency for any derogatory or unfavourable denotation or connotation within a language expression to dominate, whatever the context.

A number of experiments measure the emotional impact of words using techniques such as electrodermal monitoring, which records skin conductance responses (galvanic skin responses). Research overwhelmingly supports what every native speaker knows: compared to other words, 'dirty' words cause bigger goosebumps; that is, they evoke stronger skin conductance re-sponses.[16] There has been a lot of research into the effects of arousal on memory. The findings are always the same: taboo words, are more stimulat-ing than non-taboo words and we appear to store them differently in our memory.[17] Using natural conversation, researchers found excellent recogni-tion memory for the surface structure and content of profane and sexually suggestive language.

The results showed that those 12 high interactional content sentences with profane and sexually suggestive language elicited responses quite different from those elicited by the remaining 44 high interactional content sentences . . . Sentences with off-color language possess a memorability that is quite independent of their role in a conversation. (MacWhinney et al. 1982: 315)

Unfortunately, the study was bowdlerized: although we learn a lot about people's memory and awareness of this 'off-color' language, we never actually see examples of the 'high interactional content sentences' that served as stimuli – a sad example of euphemistic omission.

A 2004 report describes the effects of emotion on memory and attention, using what is known as a Stroop task.[18] Taboo words were displayed in a salient colour, and participants were asked to name the colour and ignore the word. There were three significant effects. Participants were slower in naming the colour of the taboo words than the colour of the 'neutral' words; we infer that they were distracted by the disturbing nature of taboo words. Interestingly, this effect diminished with word repetition – which is consistent with the fact that the affective power of frequently encountered words wears out. The second effect was superior recall of taboo words in surprise memory tests following colour naming. The third effect was better recognition memory for those colours consistently associated with taboo words, rather than with neutral words. Other experiments have demonstrated that taboo words impair immediate recall of the preceding and succeeding words, in rapidly presented lists. All these findings are consistent with the strong emotional reactions triggered by culturally potent taboo expressions.

A slightly different perspective is provided by experiments that examine the emotional responsiveness of bilingual speakers. For example, a study of thirty-two English–Turkish bilinguals used fingertip electrodes to measure the emotional responses of participants to taboo and other kinds of highly charged words.[19] Researchers found that the greatest emotional reactivity was to taboo words in both languages. Consistent with earlier studies using only monolingual speakers, taboo words (curses, bawdy sexual and body-part terms) generated far stronger responses, measured by amplitude of skin conductance, than other kinds of emotional words such as reprimands (*Don't do that!*), aversive words (*cancer, kill, death*), positive words (*bride, joy, kind*) and neutral words. In fact, the amplitude was almost double that of neutral words. The responses were even stronger for the speaker's first language. These findings support what second-language speakers have often reported anecdotally; namely, that they find it easier to utter taboo words in their second language than their first. Moreover, they are far less self-conscious when discussing taboo topics in their second- language. This study also recorded that the auditory stimuli elicited greater emotional arousal than the visual stimuli in the first, but not in the second, language. In other words, the sound of taboo words was found to be more disturbing than their appearance in print, once more confirming the subjective reports of language users generally: dirty words sound awful and are much harder to say than to write.

These findings are consistent with earlier work on bilingual speakers.[20] But why would the language learned early in life, especially emotive expressions such as dirty words, elicit stronger physiological responses than language learned later in life? When we learn taboo words at a young, impressionable age, they are presumably coded with the equivalent of a linguistic health warning: DANGEROUS – USE ONLY WITH EXTREME CAUTION. Children acquire the emotive components of the meaning of these words very early on, before they have knowledge of the social and cultural pressures that require us to censor them.[21] Taboo words come with social rewards (maximum attention) and penalties (reprimands, banishments). Here is someone recalling her childhood experience, a startlingly literal enactment of the dirt metaphor for taboo:[22]

When my brother Roy was a little boy – on this occasion I was undressing him to put him to bed – and I said, 'I'm a duffer, I didn't take your bodice off before I put your pyjamas top on,' and he said, 'Well, take my bloody bodice off.' And mother went into the bathroom and she came out with a cake of soap, and pulled his tongue out and slithered it up and down his tongue. The poor kid. He was like someone having a fit. The soap was foaming all over the place.

As our brain systems mature and we develop discretion about what we say, we learn to censor taboo words via the usual neurological processes of inhibition.[23] Taboo words and phrases acquired by late bilinguals lack the cultural imprint of the forbidden and have different neurological representations. In fact, a number of subjects report feeling nothing when they hear and even utter taboo expressions in their second language.[24]

The processing of the emotional components of language, such as taboo words, belongs to the limbic system. This is an older, deeper part of the mammalian midbrain (about the size of a walnut) that adds emotional spice to the surrounding cerebral cortex – the part of the brain that is responsible for verbal reasoning, calculation, analytical thinking and rational thought. Bilingual studies suggest that first-language acquisition may involve the subcortical limbic area, while second-language acquisition, at least for late bilinguals, may depend more on the later-developing cortical area. Interesting in this regard is that fact that cerebral imaging using Magnetic Resonance Imaging and Positron Emission Tomography has demonstrated that second languages are stored in different places in the brain, depending on the age at which the languages have been acquired. MRI scanning techniques have revealed that native and second languages acquired during the early acquisition period are represented in common frontal cortical areas, whereas second languages acquired as an adult are spatially separated from native languages.[25] This explains why most people who acquire a second language never attain native-like fluency; such research is cited as evidence for something now known as 'the critical period hypothesis', which is shared with other animals.

For instance, if finches are not exposed to song within the first fifteen months, they never acquire a normal song. Humans are similar: there exists in our early lives a window of opportunity during which language must be acquired. Our brain gets set in its ways, and if linguistic skills have not been acquired, they remain deficient.[26] Bilingual studies of taboo and arousal add further support to the hypothesis of a critical learning period for language acquisition.

Neurological and psychiatric disorders shed additional light on the neural architecture that underpins the production and control of taboo expressions. People with certain kinds of dementia and/or aphasia lose all language ability, except the ability to produce dirty words.[27] The technical term for the involuntary utterance of obscene language is *coprolalia* (from Greek *kopros* 'dung' and *lalia* 'talk'). It is related to the variety of highly emotional language that we automatically produce when we are angry and frustrated, under pressure, or in sudden pain. People who manifest this kind of disorder curse profusely, producing what sound like exclamatory interjections as an emotional reaction. However, if called upon to repeat the performance, they are unable to do so because they have lost the capacity to construct ordinary language. Dirty words, abusive words and slurs pour forth from the victims of these particular mental disorders, just because these expressions are stored separately from other language.

Further evidence linking taboo language to the limbic system (the emotional processing areas) comes from people manifesting *Tourette's Syndrome* (TS), a neurological disorder associated with frequent and repetitive involuntary vocal tics (utterances of noises or words) and motor tics (muscle movements). The range of symptoms that can be seen in TS includes *copropraxia* (the compulsion to make obscene gestures), *coprolalia* (the compulsion to vocalize obscene or other socially unacceptable words or phrases), even *coprographia* (the compulsion to write obscene expressions), as well as *echolalia* and *echopraxia* (the mimicking of other people's language and movements). These tics are a type of spasm that can be more or less controlled (much like an urge to scratch an itch or to sneeze). Some people seem able to hold back their tics for hours at a time, although suppressing them can sometimes lead to more severe outbursts later. The tics increase with stress and decrease when the person is relaxed or concentrating on an absorbing task. We quote from some responses to a web forum on coprolalia, maintained by the Department of Neurology at Massachusetts General Hospital; they have been written either by sufferers of TS (*Touretters*) or close relatives.[28] (The typos and typography are in the originals.)

[1] Coprolalia, in my experience, seems to be the expression of maximal socially inappropriate noise. In my case, coprolalia consists of loud belching, often saying a

word or phrase; and expression of ethnic slurs as words, phrases or little songs. All quite complex, and definitely socially inappropriate! (12 May 1999)

[2] Uttering unacceptable words causes a delicious reaction in others which makes the utterer the centre of attention. Perhaps this is initially an attention seeking device which becomes habit and part of normal speech when the person doesn't notice the difference between acceptable and unacceptable. My son went through a phase of muttering 's—t' all the time which passed after a while when we ceased to show that we were outraged. Of course another tic took over . . . (25 May 1999)

[3] My 5 yr old daughter sufffers from coprolalia. She has no idea what the words mean. In fact, I believe coprolalia has almost nothing to do with linguistics or language. It has to do with socially inapproriate noises – some of which happen to be words. My daughter's tics started as grunts and other noises whilst eating. (and I would say that in my household it was less acceptable to make noises while eating than it was to swear), and so this is how her tics started. In someone with corpolalia, the need to perform the tic is proportional to the inappropriateness of the situation. Everybody in the world suffers from this to a certain degree. Remember how hard it is to hold back laughter when it is forbidden, but how easy it is to hold back once it is allowed? (there must be clue in the control of TS in the chemical pathways of laughter stimulation and inhibition). My daughter suffers from that feeling og being 'unable to hold it baks' almost all of the time. Corpolalia is just a socially inapropriate noise – like barking in a lecture hall. It is really no different. If whistling the national anthem were considered the most appaling aural insult in western society my daugher would be doing that as a tic and not swearing. Society shapes the noise that is made, and at this end of the 20th century, it shapes it into swearing. A couple of centuries ago there was more religious profanity and blasphemy than swearing because that was an immensely strong social taboo at that time. Where I live (in the UK) blasphemy is only slightly frowned upon by the majority, so my daughter has not really picked up on its (former) social significance.
  An example of coprolalia:
  On putting my daughter to bed at night:
  'I love you, Dad. F**K! Sorry'
  Rather naively I once urged her to try to say 'fun' instead. The result:
  'Fun -F**K', Fun-F**k'. (11 May 1999)

It seems that the obscenities associated with this behavioural disorder involve whatever is most socially inappropriate for the time. [2] is interesting, in that the young boy stopped saying *shit* when he failed to get any sort of reaction. There is one case of a nine-year-old boy who lost his coprolalia entirely when he was told the words he was uttering were not obscene. A bilingual English–Spanish speaker reportedly switched the language of his outbursts depending on the language being spoken around him.[29] The parent in [3] nails a trigger: if whistling the national anthem were considered shocking, their Touretter daughter would be doing it as a tic. It is not surprising, therefore, to find that the symptoms of TS also vary widely from culture to culture.[30] Presumably, too, in earlier times, people manifesting forms of madness attributed to diabolical possession or sorcery were often people with TS. These days, religious profanity and blasphemy have given way to sexually obscene words and, commonly, racial epithets. One woman married to a man with TS felt that coprolalia was specifically something that affected an area of the brain designed to store hostile reactions toward some perceived group of 'others'; she concluded, 'I think that is why racial epithets are so sadly a part of coprolalia for many people.'[31]

A number of researchers have characterized TS as a breakdown of the brain's inhibitory mechanisms: 'a "disinhibition syndrome" due to release of the inhibiting neuronal pathways'.[32] In other words, the characteristic tic disorders are understood to be conditions in which there is a failure to inhibit bits of 'normal' behavior. There is a substantial body of data based on post-mortem and neuro-imaging studies that implicates the basal ganglia (the interconnected areas located deep below the cerebral cortex) both in TS and related neurological disorders.[33] These basal ganglia are the hidden pathways that contribute to the multiple circuits involved in the different cognitive and limbic processes that regulate emotions, thoughts and movement; neurologists suggest that the outbursts of foul language would be associated with a failure to inhibit portions of the limbic mini-circuits.[34] There may not yet be any laboratory or neuro-imaging studies that have conclusively identified the exact neuro-anatomical sites where taboo expressions are stored, or that have evaluated specifically the neurological processing of obscenities, but the evidence seems overwhelming: taboo language is rooted deeply in human neural anatomy; it is inbuilt, hard-wired into the limbic systems of our brains. The socio-cultural setting then provides the expression. 'Society shapes the noise that is made', to quote the mother of the five-year-old Touretter.

Both taboo and censoring represent aspects of the enduring conflict in humans between animal and intellect. Taboo is identified with emotional release, aggression, lack of control, intemperance and intolerance. The pleasurable effect of an expletive employed to release pent-up anger against a person, or to insult and wound someone, reveals the animal (deep subcortical) part of human beings that our inhibitory mechanisms strive to suppress. Censorship on the other hand, whether in the form of legal controls or simple social taste constraints, reflects the intellectual (higher cortical) part of being human that is associated with emotional control, rational thought and tolerance.

An end on't

We know our will is free, and there's an end on't. (Samuel Johnson, 16 October 1769; Boswell 1791)

This book has explored the ins and outs of many words and phrases that have, for a variety of reasons, been subject to cultural and social proscription. They are expressions that we usually censor from our utterances when we wish to present ourselves as being polite. However, for most people there are contexts where the censoring is relaxed and we speak freely. The tabooed expressions include sexual and scatological obscenities, ethnic–racial slurs, insults, name-calling, profanity, blasphemy, slang, jargon and vulgarities of all kinds, including the forbidden words of non-standard grammar. They range along scales of offensiveness, potency and wounding capacity, but they are all of them emotionally powerful in some way.

It would be interesting to measure (using, say, electrodermal monitoring) the emotional impact of a wider range of forbidden language forms, beyond the kinds of obscenity so far investigated; we have in mind slipshod pronunciations, 'mistakes' in grammar, newfangled meanings, colloquialisms, jargon, clichés, new coinages and PC expressions. Early in 2004, the Plain English Campaign asked its five thousand supporters to nominate the phrases in the English language that most enraged them.[35] The expression *at the end of the day* led the field. In equal second place was *at this moment in time* and the recurrent use of *like*. These were followed by the phrase *with all due respect*. We guess that psycho-physiological testing would show that an encounter with one of these irritating phrases not only activates their meaning, but also leads to emotional arousal. Speakers often describe expressions as *getting up their nose, getting under their skin, getting on their nerves/wick, turning their stomach, sticking in their throat, making their hair curl / flesh creep / blood run cold*. Irritating words, phrases and grammatical constructions figuratively touch many parts of the anatomy, and presumably this would be reflected in larger skin conductance amplitudes of a polygraph tracing.

Verbal taboos serve human interests by setting apart those things that threaten to cause distress and offence. Many of them have a rational basis: prohibitions against incest do help to prevent weakened progeny; sensible explanations can be found for most food preferences and avoidances; the bad smell theories of disease that held sway until the nineteenth century may have been built on fantasy, yet we know that communities are far healthier if human waste is kept at a distance. In the case of avoidance speech styles, such as the so-called 'mother-in-law' languages once used extensively in Aboriginal Australia, conflict is prevented where relationships are sensitive and threaten discord to the family unit. Along with appropriate strategies for naming and addressing others, they arise from the need to maintain social harmony in human communities. In today's diverse democratic societies, the practical problems of maintaining dialogue keep attention to face as critical as ever.

Many taboos are tied in with our fears. Government censorship, and the self-censorship of the media in response to government and community attitudes, exploit such fears to extend their power base among the populus. The crusading Religious Right administration of US President George W. Bush censors news about so-called terrorist actions and, in the name of freedom, denies human rights to people in the prison camp at Guantanamo Bay and other institutions; it is strongly backed by the Australian government (also controlled by the Religious Right) which, while loudly propagating a *fair go* for all, holds asylum seekers in Australian prisons indefinitely without trial. As we write, these repressive measures are directed against perceived foes in the manner reminiscent of the authorities in Orwell's *Nineteen Eighty-four*.[36] But the cancer of oppression, and the attendant censorship, is spreading into our communities. The power base of the crusading Religious Right has led television networks in the United States to ban films such as *Saving Private Ryan* because soldiers in it use the kind of language that soldiers are wont to use; the networks have even banned an advert from a church that explicitly welcomes gays and lesbians because the government and its supporters believe such people to be irredeemable sinners. It is the same kind of intolerance that fired the Salem witch trials of 1692 and McCarthyism in the early 1950s. Old taboos are applied to new demons, and hate and fear are whipped up to the detriment of everyone except those wielding power.

Other fear-based taboos seem more benign by comparison. We tend to despise those body parts, bodily functions, acts and actions that remind us that we are part of nature. We live within a fragile temporal frame, and disease and death are natural processes. Our minds dream of immortality, but we are at the same time painfully aware of the inevitable extinction of both body and consciousness.[37] In an attempt to cope with this dilemma, and perhaps even to overcome it, we have created religion and philosophy, science and medicine; and we have screened off the calls of nature with taboos and prohibitions. It helps us disregard our natural mortal condition. Nonetheless, we should not ignore Jonathan Swift's warning against immortality: on the island of Luggnagg, Lemuel Gulliver learns of the immortal Struldbrugs. He fancies that they must have the opportunity to accumulate vast wealth and extensive learning, and so wield great power. He is disabused by learning that the Struldbrugs keep on aging and growing more decrepit so that, from the age of eighty, they are no longer allowed property or other legal and civil rights. They lead an utterly dismal existence and envy the escape that death brings to mortals.[38] Surely the Dean of St Patrick's was absolutely right: immortality would be hell on earth.

Taboos will persist, even when people are unaware of reasons that might have led to their establishment. We know that the repulsion we feel for bodily effluvia is not instinctive, because children and animals do not find them so odious; so the notion that they are dirty is learned. By the twenty-first century, original motivations have become lost to unthinking ritual; fear is accompanied by distaste. A lot of the time, routine ensures the continuance of linguistic sanctions. Yet taboos strengthen group identity and social fabric through feelings of distinctiveness, while the rites and rituals that accompany them give us a sense of control in a chaotic and hostile environment. We have adopted Mary Douglas' hypothesis that the distinction between cleanliness and filth stems from the basic human need to structure the world around us and render it understandable.[39] When old taboos are jettisoned, people grow anxious that disorder is setting in.

Sometimes we happily defy taboos and their purifying impetus. We have seen socio-cultural and psychological benefits in using forbidden words and phrases. For a start, there is the thrill of transgression: it is liberating to defy prohibition by violating linguistic taboos. There is a psychological gain in letting off steam and expressing extreme emotion through cascading expletives and forbidden words. Many societies have public acts of ceremonial misbehaviour to function as a social safety valve: flyting, the dozens, celebrity roasts and other kinds of competitive ritual insulting are examples. In medieval society, carnivals gave licence to publicly debunk the secular and religious hierarchies that ruled people's lives. During the Feast of Fools, for example, minor clergy ran riot in the church and shockingly mocked Christian rites. University *Rag Week* is the mild modern counterpart. There is the obvious link between hostility and the use of forbidden words in curses, name-calling and terms of insult. On the other hand, taboo words can display in-group solidarity (especially when speaking against out-groupers). Like the 'incorrect' language of non-standard grammar, taboo words fall outside what is good and proper, and they help to define the gang; they can be a sign of endearment (*G'day you old bastard*) and part of steamy pillow talk. Taboo terms are also an important component in joke telling:

Jokes . . . are appalling. Almost without exception they deal in bigotry, sexism, racism, ageism and all the other politically incorrect isms. They clearly help people deal with their deep distaste for their own sexuality, their excremental functions, their foreign neighbours, their political masters and an infinite variety of things that go bump in the night. (Adams and Newell 1994: 12)

And now we discover that taboo words are located in a special place within our brains. This may account for the fact that attempts to stamp them out meet with little or no success. Bad language is not just some nasty habit that we can be broken of, like smoking in restaurants or nail-biting. Forbidden words flourish all the more vigorously on a diet of individual censoring and public disapproval. Linguistic prohibition, like other kinds of prohibition and censorship, is doomed to failure in the longer term. Like the worm in the bud, forbidden words feed on censoring imposed by hypocritical decorum. But when we look at the exuberance of expressions that proliferate around the forbidden, it is also clear that we are having a lot of fun. These expressions range from the exquisitely lyrical to the downright crass; yet many demonstrate an expressiveness and poetic ingenuity worthy of William Shakespeare. But that's a topic for another book.

Notes

1 TABOOS AND THEIR ORIGINS

1 17 July 1777: 'Taboo in general signifies forbidden' (Cook 1967: 176).
2 Steiner 1967.
3 Wundt 1927.
4 Cf. Freud 1950: 21–4.
5 Mead 1937.
6 Frazer 1875: 17.
7 People who commit crimes under severe stress or provocation can seek to ameli-
   orate condemnation by pleading extreme provocation, diminished responsibility or
   temporary insanity; but they do not escape condemnation.
8 *Hlonipha* achieves phonetic deformation through consonant substitution, e.g. Zulu
   ulucha for *ulunya* 'cruelty', *xabuka* for *qabuka* 'wake up' (*x* is a lateral click [‖], *q*
   a palatal click [ǂ]), *umugca* for *umuhla* 'day'; consonant deletion, e.g. Xhosa *eka*
   from *hleka* 'laugh', *umenze* from *umlenze* 'leg'. There is also transfer of a noun
   from one class (gender) to another: e.g. Xhosa *intsana* (class 9) from *usana* 'baby'
   (class 2) or *intsapho* from *usapho* 'family'. In addition to phonetic deformation,
   there is lexical substitution e.g. Swati *imphitsa* 'dog' for *inja* 'dog', *kutinta* 'sit at
   ease' for *kuhlala* 'sit', *inkhuleko* 'thing to be tethered' for *imbuti* 'goat', and
   obscure ones like Zulu *ebhodwe* 'in the cooking pot' for *enzansi* 'at the coast'.
   There is also neologism, e.g. Zulu *inhlendla* for *isizense* 'scissors', *ukukathula* for
   ukuxosha 'to drive away'; and borrowing from another language, e.g. Xhosa
   umilisi 'maize' from Afrikaans *mielies*, *ukupeya* 'money' from English *pay*, and
   izambane 'potato' from Zulu (Herbert 1990: 460, 468).
9 In the 1820s, a convict from the particularly vicious penal settlement at Macquarie
   Harbour in Tasmania stabbed a fellow convict in order to be hanged as means of
   escape. Asked by the chaplain why he didn't just commit suicide: 'Oh,' he replied,
   'the case is quite different. If I kill myself I shall immediately descend to the
   bottomless pit, but if I kill another I would be sent to Hobart Town and tried for my
   life; if found guilty, the parson would attend me, and then I would be sure of going
   to Heaven' (Hughes 1987: 379).
10 Steiner 1967: 42f.
11 Steiner 1967: 43.
12 Cf. Turner 1884: 185–7, cited in Steiner 1967: 44f.
13 Freud 1950: 18. The context is 'Taboo restrictions are distinct from religious or
   moral prohibitions. They are not based upon any divine ordinance but may be said

to impose themselves on their own account. They differ from moral prohibitions in that they fall into no system that declares quite generally that certain abstinences must be observed and gives reasons for their necessity. Taboo prohibitions have no grounds and are of unknown origin. Though they are unintelligible to us, to those who are dominated by them they are taken as a matter of course.'

14 Douglas 1966.
15 In 1667, 43-year-old Margaret Cavendish Duchess of Newcastle (whom diarist Samuel Pepys described as 'a very comely woman') went to the theatre in Lincoln's Inn Fields with her husband to see his (but at the time anonymous) play *Humorous Lovers*.

> For the occasion Margaret donned a special outfit of her own designing – 'an antique dress' in classical style, which bared her breasts, revealing 'scarlet trimmed nipples.' Intended to suggest the heroic women of antiquity and contemporary romances, this costume . . . would not have been out of place in the semiprivate, aristocratic contexts of court masques or portrait painting, where loose classical drapes and naked breast (complete with nipples reddened with cochineal and veins painted blue, to emphasize the whiteness of the flesh) were not uncommon, though frequently denounced by moralists. But in a public playhouse Margaret's breasts, 'all laid out to view,' called to mind not so much ancient heroism as the licentious dress of contemporary actresses and prostitutes, and London's gossip filled at once with stories of the occasion. (Whitaker 2002: 294f)

16 Besterman 1957, Letter 4856 from Strasbourg 3 September 1753 (our translation). Elsewhere (Letter 4946) he spoke of kissing her beautiful thighs.
17 Cf. Comings and Comings 1985; Van Lancker and Cummings 1999; Jay 2000.
18 Gildersleeve 1961: 7.
19 Deuteronomy 5: 11 'Thou shalt not take the name of the LORD thy God in vain: for the LORD will not hold him guiltless that taketh his name in vain.'
20 Cf. Montagu 1968: 139. Elizabeth I was a feisty woman. One cannot imagine her successor Elizabeth II chiding her parliament with 'If I had been born crested not cloven, your Lordships would not treat me so.'
21 All three forms occur in Ben Jonson's *Bartholomew Fair* of 1614 (Jonson 1981). The sequence A $\Rightarrow$ B symbolizes 'A is the source of B, or B derives from A'; and C $\Leftarrow$ D 'D is the source for C, or C derives from D'.
22 Fielding 1749.
23 French Connection United Kingdom.
24 Cf. Gildersleeve 1961: 128f.
25 This is obviously not primarily an example of linguistic blasphemy, although some hold the phrase *Piss Christ* blasphemous. As of August 2002 there is a reproduction at http://www.renewal.org.au/artcrime/pages/serrano.html. Serrano does not regard the image as sacrilegious and has said, 'The best place for *Piss Christ* is in a church' ('Shooting the Klan: an interview with Andres Serrano' by Coco Fusco, http://www.communityarts.net/readingroom/archive/ca/fusco-serrano. php). Serrano is also reported as saying that 'his goal all along had been to increase the devotion of his fellow Christians by helping them identify better with Christ in his pain, suffering and humiliation' (Anthony Fisher and Hayden Ramsey, 'The bishop, the artist, the curator and the crucifix (Andres Serrano's "Piss Christ")' *Quadrant* 41 no. 12, 1997: 48).

26 Cf. http://www.csulb.edu/~jvancamp/361_r7.html. Accessed August 2002. D'Amato was adverted to the Serrano work by Donald Wildmon, a religious activist in the American Family Association.

27 Cf. http://www.shootthemessenger.com.au/u_jan_98/life/l_pisschrist.htm, and http://www.dsystems.net/eds_place/Serrano9.4.htm. Both accessed August 2002. The motivation for removal is ambiguous: it was probably to both protect the artwork (although the photograph would be reproducible) and avoid further bigoted condemnation of the gallery.

28 Cf. Gildersleeve 1961: 98f.

29 This is ironical, given the last clause of a 1999 speech by NRA President Charlton Heston: 'The majesty of the Second Amendment, that our Founders so divinely captured and crafted into your birthright, guarantees that no government despot, no renegade faction of armed forces, no roving gangs of criminals, no breakdown of law and order, no massive anarchy, no force of evil or crime or oppression from within or from without, can ever rob you of the liberties that define your Americanism . . . Let me be absolutely clear. The Founding Fathers guaranteed this freedom because they knew no tyranny can ever arise among a people endowed with the right to keep and bear arms. That's why you and your descendants need never fear fascism, state-run faith, refugee camps, brainwashing, ethnic cleansing, or especially, submission to the wanton will of criminals.'

30 Censors sold licenses for profit; cf. Gildersleeve 1961: 44, 82.

31 St Paul, 1 Thessalonians 5: 21.

32 Titus 1: 15: 'Unto the pure all things are pure; but unto them that are defiled and unbelieving is nothing pure; but even their mind and conscience is defiled.'

33 Ernest Pinard, the Imperial Advocate who prosecuted Flaubert's *Madame Bovary* (29 January 1857) took the view that censorship improves art: 'Art without rules is no longer art; it is like a woman who has shed all her clothes. If one imposes on art the sole rule of public decency, it is not to shackle it. It is proof that one holds it in high esteem' (Flaubert 1930: 578, our translation).

34 In January 1843, Karl Marx wrote: 'In Rome, publication of the Koran is prohibited. A wily Italian knew how to get round it. He published a *refutation* of the Koran, that is, a book which bore on its title page *Refutation of the Koran*, but the content was simply the text of the Koran' (Marx 1974: 63).

35 Donatien Alphonse François, Comte de Sade, 1740–1814.

36 Sade 1966–7.

37 Sade 1965: 344.

38 Sade 1968: 765.

39 Sade 1966–7, vol. 9: 580f.

40 Shattuck 1996. Brady and Hindley abducted, sexually abused, tortured and murdered children, keeping audio-recordings of their screams and pornographic photographs of them. Bundy is thought to have abducted, sexually abused, mutilated and throttled at least forty and perhaps twice that number of women.

41 Ernst and Seagle (1928: 239ff) report on 1,200 (anonymous) responses to a questionnaire sent out to unmarried American women college graduates during the 1920s asking about their introduction to information on sex, their sexual practices, reveries, etc.: 570 learned about sex from peers, 351 from parents or guardians, only 72 learned from reading and the prime source was not pornography

but the Bible, followed by dictionaries, encyclopedias and literary works by such as Dickens, Henry James and Shakespeare, then medical books and pamphlets. Authors such as Boccaccio, Baudelaire, Chaucer, or Flaubert did not rate a mention. Given that respondents were willing to report on masturbatory practices and what they found sexually stimulating (men, dancing, art), we may assume that they were being honest. One must conclude that the power of written texts to subvert the morality of young women lacks proof.

42 *The Annals*, book XIV: 50 (Tacitus 1908: 444).

43 Jansen 1991: 46.

44 Robert Mapplethorpe is a rather indifferent photographer by comparison with say Horst, Ansel Adams, Edward Weston or Dorothea Lange. However his photos of gays, fisting, sado-masochism, a man pissing into another's mouth, himself dressed as Satan with a bull-whip in his arse for a tail, and the fact that he was to die of AIDS led to a notoriety that increased his saleability. See Hughes 1993: 163.

45 Quoted in James Hall, 'Kids' author in the bad books', *Weekend Australian*, 25 September 2004.

46 As Karl Marx wrote: 'The real, *radical cure of the censorship* is its *abolition*. For it is a bad institution' (Marx 1974: xii).

2 SWEET TALKING AND OFFENSIVE LANGUAGE

1 Another way to interpret the term *X-phemism* is to imagine that X ϵ {ortho-, eupho-, dys-}.

2 We do not distinguish between 'tact' and 'social politeness' as do Janney and Arndt 1992; it seems to us that 'social politeness' is communalized 'tact' (a similar view to Blum-Kulka 1992: 258).

3 This psycho-emotive characterization of the preferred–dispreferred dichotomy is at odds with its use by conversational analysts like Atkinson and Drew 1979, Bilmes 1988, Toolan 1989 or Boyle 2000.

4 These two aspects of face; are respectively *positive* and *negative* face; see Brown and Levinson 1987; Watts, Ide et al. 1992; Scollon and Scollon 1995; Lee-Wong 2000.

5 These expressions were used in defining the meaning of *a reasonable man* by Lord Justice Greer in *Hall* v. *Brookside Club* (*Law reports, King's Bench Division*, vol. I, 1933: 224), but they serve our purpose well. This despite Lord Justice Greer displaying his prejudice against the ordinary man by saying, 'God forbid that the standard of manners should be taken from the man on the Clapham omnibus.' Today, we have a more demotic notion of the standard of polite manners.

6 Jenkinson 1979: 12.

7 The law in the state of New South Wales, Australia.

8 The first time *fuck* was used in a film was either in 1967 in *Ulysses* or in 1968 in *I'll Never Forget Whatshisname* . . . The first use of *fuck* in a hit was in *M*A*S*H* 1970. Its first use in a PG rated film was in 1976 in *All the President's Men* and also *The Front*. In 1970, on Britain's live-to-air *Frost Programme*, Felix Dennis described Jerry Rubin as 'the most unreasonable cunt I've ever known in my life!' A *Monty Python* sketch 'The Travel Agent' was about a man who replaces the letter c with a b, and who chides himself with being *a silly bunt*. The word *cunt* was scripted in a 1979 drama *No Mama No*. John Lydon (Johnny Rotten) caused

national outrage when he used *fuck* on British television in 1976; when he used *cunt* in 2004 there were only 73 complaints from an audience of 10.5 million (http://members.lycos.co.uk/mathunt/disstertation.html [sic]. Accessed July 2004). The first use of *cunt* in a mainstream film may be in Mike Nichols' *Carnal Knowledge* of 1971. The phrase *fucking, cheating cunt* (quoting a cricket umpire) was printed in *The Independent* newspaper in 1988, though both *fuck* and *cunt* appeared in a quote from Tony Harrison's poem *V* in *The Times* (London) in 1987.

9 Cf. Maines 1999.
10 Cf. Rosten 1968.
11 The Hebrew letters יהוה read from right to left are Yod Heh Vav Heh.
12 This dates from the first half of the twentieth century but may not be anachronistic. In the 1990s, *have my rag(s)* was still being used in a girls' boarding school in Adelaide, Australia.
13 Frazer 1911: 318.
14 See Aristotle, *On Interpretation* 16a, 19.
15 Also *blue*.
16 Cicero 1959, *Epistulae ad Familiares* IX, xxii.
17 See Grose 1811.
18 See Arbeitman 1980: 78f. Perhaps *gay* kept its dark side hidden for a long time; see below.
19 *Epistulae ad Familiares* IX, xxii.
20 *Donkey* was originally pronounced to rhyme with modern *monkey*; the word was a sort of diminutive of *dun*, which for centuries had been a name for a horse and is also an appropriate colour term for an ass
21 Bloomfield 1927: 228.
22 Hock 1986: 295.
23 Ana Deumert, p.c. 2002. A British gardening magazine uses the old spelling *Caffre lime* for Citrus hystrix, perhaps euphemistically (*Gardens Illustrated*, September 2004: 80). Another example of dissimilation is that in Christchurch, New Zealand, the synagogue is not *Christchurch Synagogue*, but *Canterbury Synagogue*.
24 We have already referred to the comments of Read 1977, Osgood et al. 1957, and MacWhinney et al. 1982.
25 This is further discussed later in this book. Cf. Valenstein and Heilman 1979: 431; Jay 2000: chs. 1, 5, 8.
26 Kobjitti 1983.
27 Farb 1974: 82.
28 Cicero 1959, *Epistulae ad Familiares* IX, xxii.
29 Cf. Ernster 1975; Hays 1987.
30 BBC Brains Trust session of 26 April 1948. Blackwell and Ruja 1994: 494; Metcalf 1986: 179.
31 Winston Churchill delivered his 'iron curtain' speech given at Westminster College, Fulton, Missouri, 5 March 1946. The end was marked by the fall of the Berlin Wall on Thursday 9 November 1989.
32 http://www.globeandmail.com/servlet/ArticleNews/TPPrint/LAC/20030416/RVRUSS_2/TPColumnists/. Accessed April 2004.
33 Strom 1984: 7, quoted by Clyne 1987: 38.

34 *OED*, Fryer 1963: 46. There was Gropecuntelane in London, also in Oxford (where it became Grove Street), York (where it became Grape Lane) and Northampton.
35 McDonald 1988: 36.
36 Directed by Terry Jones, 1979.
37 http://members.lycos.co.uk/mathunt/disstertation.html; *sic.* Accessed July 2004. Incidentally, *channel, canell, canal* and *kennel* are variants of the 'same' word.
38 Jonson 1981.

3 BAD LANGUAGE? JARGON, SLANG, SWEARING AND INSULT

1 See Lutz 1989.
2 The asterisked form **garg-* is a reconstructed, not an attested, form.
3 This definition employs the term *jargon* to include what some scholars call 'specialist' or 'technical' language, 'restricted' language (Firth 1968: 98), 'sub-language' (Kittredge and Lehrberger 1982), and others 'register' (e.g. Zwicky and Zwicky 1982; Wardhaugh 1986).
4 This excerpt from Peter Finch's *N Wst Brdg* was found at http://education.guardian. co.uk/higher/artsandhumanities/story/0,12241,785819,00.html. Accessed September 2002.
5 Saussure 1974.
6 Danat 1980: 479.
7 The writer is perceived to have violated the cooperative maxim of manner; cf. Grice 1975.
8 Benson 1985: 530ff.
9 Danat 1980: 451f.
10 Hudson 1978: 1.
11 They remain prestigious even to an out-grouper who finds the jargon obnoxious.
12 Pia Herbert, p.c.
13 1895–1954.
14 Partridge 1952: 16. Also http://www.merriam-webster.com/cgi-bin/wftwarch. pl081104. Accessed November 2004.
15 Inkhorn terms were often neologisms, such as *abequitate* 'to ride away', *commotrix* 'a maid that makes ready and unready her mistress', *dentiloquent* 'speaking through the teeth', *doctiloquent* 'one who speaks learnedly' (Locke 1690: III.iv.9).
16 Burridge and Allan 1998.
17 *Macquarie Dictionary* 2003.
18 *Macquarie Dictionary* 2003.
19 A skeuomorph (thanks to J. C. Smith for this useful piece of jargon) describes features which once had a function, but over time have become decorative. For example, the buttons on the cuffs of jackets and running boards on early cars no longer serve a utilitarian function.
20 Nunberg 1990: 467.
21 Bolinger 1980: 136.
22 Gowers 1987.
23 Burridge 2000: 4.
24 Cf. Householder 1971: 3.

25 Partridge 1984.
26 Cf. Dauzat 1917.
27 Halliday 1978: 171.
28 Andersson and Trudgill 1990: 79.
29 Jay 2000: 178.
30 Bybee 2003.
31 Cf. Cameron 1995.
32 *Oxford Companion to the English Language* 1992: 940.
33 Hughes 1991.
34 Grose 1811, first published in 1783.
35 *Mort* and *mott* (or *mot*) are cognates. The origin of the term is unknown, but the meaning was often 'piece of arse, bit of cunt', since *mot* (or *motte*) is a euphemism for 'cunt' by borrowing the French *mot* 'word'. It may not be irrelevant that a *mort* was a young but mature fish (more precisely a salmon): the terms *fish(tail)* and *ling* were slang for 'vagina', a fishy odour being commonly attributed to this organ – especially when not so frequently washed as is today's practice.
36 Crystal 1998: 183.
37 Cf. Aman 1984–5: 106.
38 Cockney rhyming slang was perhaps best publicized by Thames Television's *Minder* series, 1979–94. However, there is also rhyming slang in Australia and in naval yards in America. *Wear the fox hat* = where the fuck's that.
39 The Oxford University vs Cambridge University row boat race, held annually in March since 1829 (except for war years), on the River Thames between Putney and Mortlake.
40 Notice that *hampsteads*, like *teeth*, is plural; this is common pattern, cf. *minces*, *bristols*, *thrupnies*.
41 When you are scared, you lose your arse (bottle) and you shit yourself.
42 *Gaff* is twentieth-century slang (and is no euphemism). It may derive from Romani *gao* 'town, village', but possibly derives from *gaffer*, in that it is the place over which a *gaffer* (a word that goes back at least to the sixteenth century) dominates – namely his home.
43 *Oxford Dictionary of Modern Slang*. Indeed, *fish* is surely quicker and easier to process that *Lillian Gish*.
44 Joos: 1961.
45 There is a reference to them in the 'First Grammatical Treatise', written in Icelandic around 1135; cf. Haugen 1972.
46 The same text is found in Miles Coverdale's Bible of 1535.
47 Shakespeare, *Romeo and Juliet*, III.i.92.
48 Jay 1992: 68; Jay 2000: 91, 137.
49 For instance, seven-year-old-and-under stories include 'spitting, shitting, pants down, naked girls, pee fights, biting weeners, sucking buggars, pinching asses, and fucking. From 8 onward there are references to having a boner, farting, tits, being horney, a dickey, animalism, having babies, throwing up, massages, cunts, eating shit, leaping on girls, sexual assaults, being pregnant, whores, vaginas, and incest' (Sutton-Smith and Abrams 1978: 524, quoted in Jay 1992: 28).
50 Jay 1992: 60–70.
51 Jay 1992: 123.

52 Goffmann 1978.
53 Most people are right-hand dominant, and their left brain processes language. This is not true for every right-hander, and left-handers are not necessarily right-brain dominant.
54 Jay 2000: 36–43.
55 Jay 2000: 84.
56 Among American children, *bitch* is the favourite insult from girl to girl and used proportionately more often than by boys (who also target girls with it, of course); cf. Jay 1992: 60–7.
57 Jay 1992: 78.
58 *You pussy!* is used, as already mentioned.
59 A *pisshead* is a drunk, so it doesn't fall in with this category of insult.
60 *Nun's Priest's Tale*, line 4565.
61 This leaves one suspicious of those British sports fans who dub themselves *The Barmy Army*, though they have hitherto been well enough behaved.
62 Jay 1992: 25. George W. Bush is often mockingly called *Shrub* (a negative comparison with his father).
63 Clyne 1987. Disease metaphors are common as racist slurs; cf. Dawidowicz 1975: 54; Sontag 1979.
64 Kennedy 2003.
65 Dan Burley, 'The Dirty Dozen', *The Citizen Call*, 30 July 1960.
66 Many are taken from 'Rules for ritual insults', Labov 1972: 297–353.
67 Jay 2000: 59.
68 Grosser and Walsh reported that men recall taboo words more readily than women; however this could in part be an artefact of the experimenter being male (1966: 226). The experiment also predated the feminist movement, which has given women more freedom to speak and act.
69 According to Montagu 1968: 55, 'American Indians do not swear, nor do the Japanese, nor do Malayans and most Polynesians.'

4 THE LANGUAGE OF POLITICAL CORRECTNESS

1 Cited on the *Australian Financial Review* wire services, 6 May 1991.
2 *The Age* 18 June 1991.
3 Dickstein 1993: 554; Goodheart 1993: 551.
4 Perry 1992: 71.
5 Lakoff 2000: 94–5.
6 Perry 1992 offers a short account of the history of the term 'political correctness'.
7 See Wilson 1995: 3 and also Baron's discussion in *The Linguist List*, 9 June 1996.
8 See accounts in Perry 1992 and Cameron 1995.
9 Cf. Peter Jeans, 'So Correct and So Funny', *The West Australian*, 26 December 1998, p. 7.
10 Cameron 1995: 82–4 discusses moral panic, in relation to the public concerns about the teaching of English grammar that broke out in Britain at the end of the 1980s. We look at this in the next chapter.
11 Kramer 1993: 573 is one who expresses the view that political correctness is a serious threat to the well-being of language and in the same breath argues that it

trivializes important issues precisely because it pays attention to trifling facts of language. In an account of anti-sexist language reforms in her own institution, Cameron 1995: 139–40 describes how many of the responses to the leaflet on 'gender-free language' also put forward the same contradiction: 'How can intervening in language be both a trivial diversion from politics and a threat to our most fundamental liberties?'

12 Wendy Harmer, 'Wounded by a Glance', *The Age*, Good Weekend, 29 April 1995, p. 16.

13 What in Australian English could be dubbed a 'claytons' political movement. The label *claytons* derives from the name of a non-alcoholic whisky, advertised as 'the drink you're having when you're not having a drink'. The term has since extended to refer generally to 'something which is illusory or exists in name only'.

14 *The Age*, 1 February 1995, p. 16.

15 These examples were contributed by Fritz Newmeyer, *Linguist List*, 8 June 1996; and Dennis Baron, *Linguist List*, 9 June 1996.

16 E.g. Banks and Mulder 1996.

17 Gay, Lesbian, Bisexual, Transvestite, Intersex, Queer.

18 Bolinger 1980: 96.

19 Cameron 1995: 145.

20 Allan and Burridge 1991: ch. 10 provides an account of 'euphemism as art'.

21 Banks and Mulder 1996: 34.

22 Hughes 1993.

23 Cameron 1995: 146

24 Eagleson 1982: 157.

25 The label 'natural cover' is used by Loury 1993: 615.

26 This example is given in Crystal 1995: 177.

27 Ayto 1993: 288.

28 *Australian Financial Review*, 22 February 1999, p. 8.

29 Hughes 1991: ch. 5 describes the ingenious circumvention that such repression encourages. Ch. 7 also offers a splendid account of the schizoid behaviour of the Victorians – a rich exuberance of swearing went hand in hand with the decorum and censorship of the time.

30 Green 1996: 13.

31 Noonan 1998: 369.

32 'So Correct and So Funny', *The West Australian*, 26 December 1998, p. 7.

33 Lakoff 2000: ch. 3 discusses the difficulty of imposing speech codes.

34 Loury 1993.

35 Cf. discussions in Osgood et al. 1957, MacWhinney et al. 1982, also Allan and Burridge 1991: 21–4.

36 Jacobsen 2002.

37 Hughes 1993: 18–19.

38 Chair of the Human Rights Council of Australia, Morris 1997: 158.

39 Adams 1997: 19.

40 Appignanesi 1994: 156.

41 But not yet the Federal Government.

42 Hughes 1991 offers a full account of the changes to English swearing patterns.

43 Adjudication No. 479, February 1991 on J. D. Purvey's complaint against the *Weekend Australian*, 4 August 1990. Cited in *Police* v. *Butler*, 2003: 4.

44 Legal Court of New South Wales, citation *Police* v. *Butler*, 2003: 2–4. In his summary of the case, Justice Heilpern cites twelve court cases where charges of offensive language have been dismissed. This case was discussed in Chapter 1. Allan and Burridge 1991: ch. 10 gives additional cases in Australia from the 1980s.

45 Scutt 2002.

46 Millwood-Hargrave 2000.

47 Rhyming slang: *Berk*[*ely Hunt*].

48 Burchfield 1989.

49 Lakoff 2000: 39–40, discussing an article by Torri Minton in the *San Francisco Chronicle*, 17 October 1997.

50 Isaacson 1999.

51 Perrin 1992: ch. 11. Hughes also describes various crusades of these self-appointed arbiters of linguistic goodness (1991: ch. 11).

5 LINGUISTIC PURISM AND VERBAL HYGIENE

1 The comments we make in this chapter have been inspired by published letters to the editor, and personal letters and emails we have received over the years. They are also informed by more than twelve years of Kate Burridge's involvement in talkback radio. During regular language segments, members of the public phone in to the radio station and put their observations on language and queries about usage directly on air. Very often, these calls involve complaints about change and the language use of others.

2 Preface to Johnson 1755.

3 The first edition of the *Encyclopaedia Britannica* (1775), identifies it thus: 'The genius of a language is "the particular set of ideas which the words . . . either from their formation or multiplicity, are apt to excite in the mind of anyone who hears it properly uttered."' Quoted in Leonard 1962: 29.

4 Cameron 1995.

5 Truss 2004.

6 'Inner sticklers', as Lynne Truss describes them.

7 Cameron 1995.

8 There are many instances in Allen 1987 of Aboriginal Australians adopting African American speech and whites with speech mannerisms adopted from American film, TV and music sources.

9 Cf. discussion Burridge and Mulder 1998: ch. 12; Burridge 2005.

10 Letter to *The Age* (Melbourne), 9 October 1969.

11 Jones 1948; Jones 2003.

12 See Milroy 2002 on the legitimization of the Standard.

13 See McCrum et al. 1992, also Watts and Trudgill 2002 for alternative histories.

14 Leonard 1962: 13.

15 Preface to Farro 1754.

16 Leonard 1962: 169.

17 Preface to Johnson 1755.

18 Locke 1690.

19 Campbell 1776: 351–3, 366.
20 Cf. Leonard 1962: 154–60.
21 Lowth 1763.
22 Murray 1795; Murray 1799 .
23 Harris 1751: 148. This was a belief that stemmed from Ancient Rome.
24 Buchanan 1767: ix.
25 Cf. Leonard 1962: 189.
26 Lowth 1763.
27 Lowth 1763: 85–9.
28 Cf. Tieken-Boon van Ostade 2002: 463.
29 Lass 1999.
30 Burchfield 1985: 173.
31 Burridge and Florey 2002.
32 E.g. *Funk and Wagnalls*; cf. Stockwell and Minkova 2001: 191f.
33 See Wolfram and Fasold 1974 for a discussion of 'superstandard forms' of language.
34 Lowth 1763: v–vi.
35 Burridge 2005: 162–4.
36 Bolinger 1980; Cameron 1995.
37 *The Washington Post*, 13 January 1992, p. D5 and reprinted in *The Age*.
38 Wardhaugh 1999: 182.
39 Cf. Burridge and Florey 2002.
40 Malcolm Whiffin, letter to the ABC, 21 March 1996.
41 Douglas 1966: 189.
42 Douglas 1966: 193.

6 TABOO, NAMING AND ADDRESSING

1 Keesing and Fifiʔi 1969: 159, writing of Kwaio culture (Kwaio is an Austronesian language spoken in Malaita).
2 *National Geographic*: 172, no. 6, December 1987. Today there are many non-Gullah incomers.
3 Frazer 1911: 389.
4 Also known in Cornwall as *Terry Top*, in Suffolk as *Tom Tit Tot*, in Ireland as *Trit-a-Trot*, in Scotland as *Whuppity Stoorie*, and as *Ricdin-Ricdon* in France.
5 Kinship terminology: *ego* is a given individual designated as the starting point in genealogical reckoning; *lineal kin* those in the same line of descent as *ego*; *collateral kin* are of the same generation; *consanguineal kin* are blood relations; *affinal kin* are related by marriage; *parallel cousins* are traced through a related parent of the same sex (father's brother, mother's sister); *cross cousins* are offspring of father's sister or mother's brother.
6 Ernest W. Lee, speaking of Roglai (an Austronesian language spoken in Vietnam), quoted in Simons 1982: 195.
7 *Macbeth*.
8 Dixon 1980: 28f, 98f.
9 Keesing and Fifiʔi 1969: 157.
10 Simons 1982: 158.

11 Strictly speaking, we discuss *isihlonipho sabafazi* 'wives' avoidance language'; the discussion is based on Herbert 1990.

12 From the traditional point of view.

13 Kripke 1972.

14 See Kripke 1972; Allan 2001: ch.3.

15 We are grateful to Adrienne Lehrer for this snippet of information.

16 Sanders and Bat-Ireedui 1999: 247.

17 We are grateful to Lee-Wong Song Mei, Chen Yan and Hilary Chappell for help with the data on Chinese (the superscript numbers in the transliterated Chinese refer to tone). Hilary Chappell tells us (p.c.) that other popular characters for women are *fang¹* 芳 'fragrant', *feng⁴* 凤 'phoenix', *xiu⁴* 秀 'elegant', *shu¹* 淑 'gentle' and *hui⁴* 惠 'kind'. Various words for kinds of jade too, *yu⁴* 玉 and *bi⁴* 碧. The ones for men can also include metaphors for intelligence (light, brightness) including *xiao³* 晓 'dawn', *hui¹* 辉 'brilliance', in addition to 'talent and virtue': *yan⁴* 彦. It is also possible to gauge a person's age by their given names: e.g. if it includes *hong²* 红 'red' or *dong¹* 东 'east', or something like *jian⁴ guo²* 建国 'establish country' then he (usually a male) was born in the 1950s or 1960s. Furthermore, the preference for flowers in female names is corroborated semi-iconically in the written form, since flowers are often written with characters which belong to the so-called 'grass radical' ⻗ group (*cao³ zi⁴ tou²* 草字头), the one used for the semantic category of plants, flowers, shrubs, etc. (but not for trees). In other words, just glancing at the character in a person's name can reveal his/her gender e.g. 芳 'fragrant', 莲 'lotus'; *lei³* 蕾 'budlet'. Furthermore, where girls are unwanted in rural families, homophonous characters for given names meaning 'just have to (put up with the fact of) raising her' or 'just have to feed' are often chosen.

18 See Lehrer 1992; Allan 2001. For instance, among car models there are Firebirds, Thunderbirds, Falcons and Hawks, but no Chicken, Crow, Goose or Pigeon.

19 There are cognates in other Algonquian languages, e.g. Cree *iskweːw*, Unami Delaware *xkweː*. The information on *squaw* is drawn from Bright 2000. See also http://www.tomjonas.com/squawpeak/squaw.htm. Accessed October 2004.

20 For example, UN Secretary General Kofi Annan was born Friday 8 April 1938.

21 Sanders and Bat-Ireedui 1999: 132.

22 Bering 1992: 187.

23 This discussion of the naming of German Jews is based on Bering 1992.

24 *Kohn*, *Cohn* and *Cohen* all derive from Hebrew *Kohen*, the name for a hereditary caste of priests.

25 Bering 1992: 215.

26 For 'speaker' understand speaker or writer, for 'hearer' understand addressee, whether hearer or reader.

27 See Chapter 3, and especially Figure 3.1, to be reminded of the five-point scale for style.

28 Intimate + casual styles.

29 See, e.g., Taavitsainen and Jucker 2003.

30 Cf. Haiman 1980: 530.

31 We are grateful to Jun Yano for help with the facts about Japanese. There is an interesting discussion of the history of Japanese addressing and referring forms in Traugott and Dasher 2002: 228–52, 258–78.

32 15 July 1976.

33 Hickey 2003: 23.

34 Ana Deumert (p.c.) says that if she met 'someone in the eco-shop in Heidelberg who wears jeans, sandals and long hair, I would say *du* irrespective of his/her age'.

35 See Hickey 2003.

36 See Chapter 2.

37 Cf. Brown and Levinson 1987.

38 On the connotations of names and terms of address, see Brown and Ford 1961; Brown and Gilman 1960; Brown and Gilman 1989; Ervin-Tripp 1969; Ervin-Tripp 1984; Wierzbicka 1992.

39 Cf. Simons 1982: 177–9.

40 For instance, Dyirbal has an unmarked dialect Guwal, for everyday use, and the 'mother-in-law language' Jalŋuy, which is used (reciprocally) whenever a taboo relative is in earshot, e.g. in the presence of a classificatory parent-in-law of the opposite sex, a child-in-law of the opposite sex, and/or a cross-cousin of the opposite sex. Except for just four words, Guwal and Jalŋuy have no nouns, verbs, adjectives or adverbs in common. Jalŋuy *dayubin* 'climb' is used in place of all of Guwal *waynyjin* 'motion up (uphill)', *bilinya* 'climb a tree unaided', *bumirranyu* 'climb a tree aided by a length of vine'. More precise meanings can be expressed in Jalŋuy by circumlocution, with *bilinya* replaced by *dayubin danduŋga* 'climb tree', *bumirranyu* by *dayubin juyibila* 'climb [with] vine'. Similarly, the single Jalŋuy word *jamuy* 'grub' can be further specified to identify with one of five Guwal nouns: *jumbun* 'long wood grub', *bugulum* 'small round bark grub', *mandija* 'milky pine grub', *gija* 'candlenut tree grub', and *gaban* 'acacia tree grub'.

41 These matters were examined in Chapter 4.

42 There is an excellent comprehensive survey in Henley 1989: 65. She wrote: '*in no referential studies known to me has the masculine been found to reference females as readily as males*' (her italics).

43 There is a nice example in Cleese and Booth, *The Psychiatrist* (1988: 191f).

7 SEX AND BODILY EFFLUVIA

1 Cameron and Kulick 2003: 5.

2 Blackledge 2003.

3 Figures given in Stengers and Neck 2001 suggest that about 90 per cent of men and at least 25 per cent of women have masturbated. The latter figure strikes us as low – certainly if partner masturbation is taken into account.

4 Oraison 1972: 87, cited in Stengers and Neck 2001: 166.

5 There was doublethink here: blood-letting was rife as a curative from the sixteenth to the nineteenth centuries; not for nothing were doctors known as *leeches*.

6 Baden-Powell's euphemism in *Scouting for Boys*.

7 See Stengers and Neck 2001 for detailed discussion of *Onania*.

8 Aman 1984–5: 106.

9 Partridge 1955 reckons that *dildo* derives from *diddle-o*; McDonald (1988) favours Italian *diletto* 'darling' as the source.

10 It is notable that the name *Jack* seems to have many dysphemistic associations. In addition to this one, there is its use in *I've got Jack* to mean 'I've got my period'; *I've go the jack* 'VD'; in the past, the use of *jack* meant 'lavatory' (still around in the forms *jakes* and *john*); *I'm jack of it* means 'I'm fed up with it'; and Grose 1811 lists *Jack Adams* 'a fool', *Jack at a pinch* 'a poor hackney parson', *Jack in a box* 'a sharper or cheat', *Jack in an office* 'an insolent fellow in authority', *Jack Ketch* 'the hangman'. *Jack* is often an alias for *John*, and Grose contains the following: 'Johnny Bum. A he or jack ass: so called by a lady that affected to be extremely polite and modest, who would not say Jack because it was vulgar, nor ass because it was indecent.' It is clear that *Jack* has a long history of dysphemistic association.

11 Maines 1999: 5. The onsets to *hysteria*, *hysterectomy*, etc. come from the Greek *hystera* 'womb'.

12 Cf. Wallian 1906: 56, 67.

13 Maines 1999: x.

14 Maines 1999.

15 Kinsey 1953: 362.

16 17 January 1998.

17 Sanders and Reinsich 1999.

18 Said to be derived from Yiddish and propagated by Philip Roth's *Portnoy's Complaint* (1967).

19 Haze 1994 reported 69 per cent of women surveyed claimed to have faked orgasm at least once.

20 Crompton 1980–1: 12 suggests that Judaic intolerance to male homosexuality may derive from rivalry with a Canaanite cult which practised male homosexuality, whereas the women did not.

21 Towards the end of the fourth century CE, St Ambrose wrote of Romans 1: 26, 'a woman would desire a woman for the use of foul lust'; on the same verse, St Anselm of Canterbury (*c*.1080) wrote 'women committed shameful deeds with women', and Peter Abelard (*c*.1125) 'against the order of nature, which created women's genitals for the use of men, and conversely, not so women could cohabit with women' (Crompton 1980–1: 14). The relevant part of Law 20 of the *lex Iulia de adulteriis* (287 CE) was known as the *lex foedissimam* (law of the most foul); it was interpreted by Cino da Pistoia in 1314 as, inter alia, 'a woman suffers defilement by surrendering to another woman'. For this crime later commentators decreed the death penalty and there were a handful of executions of lesbians in France, Germany, Italy, Spain and Switzerland, but not Britain. By contrast, about 400 male homosexuals were executed during the same period; cf. Crompton 1980–1.

22 Under **sodomite**, the *OED* cites William Caxton, *The Game and Play of the Chesse* (1474), the 'vnnaturell synne of lecherye of the sodamites'.

23 Crompton 1980–1: 11.

24 The voice, which is characteristic of many queens, is typically concentrated towards the high end of a speaker's pitch range, though there is frequent fluctuation within a wide pitch range, marked by large fast falls at the ends of phrases, breathiness, lengthening of sibilants and, to a lesser extent, other fricatives, affrication of /t/, /d/, and perhaps dentalization of alveolar phonemes. Sometimes,

there are hypercorrect unreduced vowels and extended vowel lengthening as in *faaabulous* (cf. Zwicky 1997).

25 Morrish 1997: 340.

26 His best quips are well known. Some examples: 'There is no such thing as a moral or an immoral book. Books are well written or badly written', 'There is only one thing in the world worse than being talked about, and that is not being talked about', 'The only way to get rid of a temptation is to yield to it' (*Picture of Dorian Gray*, 1891); 'What is a cynic? A man who knows the price of everything and the value of nothing' (Act 3 of *Lady Windermere's Fan*, 1893); 'The English country gentleman galloping after a fox – the unspeakable in full pursuit of the inedible' (Act 1 of *A Woman of No Importance*, 1894); 'The truth is rarely pure and never simple', 'In married life three is company and two is none' (Act 1 of *The Importance of Being Earnest*, 1899).

27 Lord Darlington in Act 1 of *Lady Windermere's Fan*.

28 'The Decay of Lying', 1889.

29 Pop singer George Michael claimed entrapment by plain-clothed policeman Marcelo Rodriguez in Will Rogers Memorial Park, Beverly Hills on 7 April 1998. Michael was charged with committing a lewd act.

30 Morrish 1997: 337f.

31 London *Times*, 21 February 1994, p. 15.

32 Chauncey 1994.

33 Chauncey 1994: 64.

34 Chauncey 1994: 273, 276.

35 The Stonewall riot, 27–29 June 1969, began at the Stonewall Inn in Greenwich Village, on the night of Judy Garland's funeral. The gay bar was raided and for once the queers (gays, lesbians and drag queens) rioted, throwing whatever they could lay their hands on at the police; there was also a chorus line of queens singing 'We are the Stonewall girls.' The next day there were placards and graffiti calling for gay liberation, gay power and the legalization of gay bars. The 'hairpin drop heard around the world' led to the formation of the Gay Liberation Front and similar organizations. See Stewart 1995.

36 We have also heard *GLBTIQ* – gay, lesbian, bisexual, transsexual, intersexual, queer!

37 Chauncey 1994: 280.

38 Gay icon Judy Garland played Dorothy Gale in *The Wizard of Oz* (MGM, 1939), directed by Victor Fleming.

39 Zwicky 1997: 23.

40 In the 1994 Stephen Elliott film *The Adventures of Priscilla Queen of the Desert*, the boys were Mitzi (Hugo Weaving) and Felicia (Guy Pearce). In prison communities, it is common for gays to be addressed by women's names, cf. http://www.nytimes.com/2004/10/16/national/16rape.html. Accessed October 2004.

41 The vagina is also known as a *snapper*, *clam* and *oyster* – the fishy associations arising from the fishy odour being commonly attributed to this organ; we therefore find terms like *fish(tail)* and *ling* for 'vagina' (and *hook* for 'penis'); *mermaid* was a euphemism for 'whore'. The plant *Chenopodium vulvaria*, also known as stinking goosefoot, was 'readily told by its repulsive smell of decaying fish' (Fitter 1971). The noun and verb *fishfinger* denote 'digital stimulation of a woman'; and

fishing or *angling* 'digital stimulation of the vagina; copulation', and *fishbreath* arises from 'oral sex' (Allen 1987).

42 Murray 1979.

43 We assume that a drugged or drunken victim, or one who is asleep when penetrated, is the less powerful.

44 Ehrlich 2001: 87. The same man was convicted of sexual assault of another woman in a related case.

45 Cameron and Kulick 2003: 40.

46 On 30 September 2004, the Australian Police announced that 'Hundreds of people [around 400] across Australia will be prosecuted for child sex offences, following the nation's largest ever crackdown on internet child pornography . . . Some people involved in this type of activity don't see that viewing and disseminating photographs is a crime, but every child pornographic image portrays a real victim and records an act of abuse against a child' (http://www.afp.gov.au. Accessed November 2004). Within days, two of the people investigated had committed suicide.

47 See Chapter 6. It is a moot point whether sex between a woman and her son-in-law or her father-in-law is strictly speaking incestuous.

48 Simons 1982: 206

49 See Ellis 1963.

50 http://www/luckymojo.com/bodyfluids.html. Accessed May 2005.

51 March 1926.

52 Frazer 1911.

53 Montagu 1968: 39.

54 Allan and Burridge 1991: 52–4, 69–74.

55 Frazer 1911: 250.

56 The Navajo are Native Americans who mostly live in Arizona and New Mexico. The following account of Navajo practices is based on Schwarz 2001.

57 Agyekum 2002. Akan is spoken in southern Ghana.

58 Allan and Burridge 1991. Whether there are different attitudes between gay and straight men is unknown.

59 Bataille 1992: 54 writes: 'These discharges are thought of as manifestations of internal violence.' We doubt the truth of this for a majority of the population.

60 Leviticus 12: 1–8, 15: 25–30.

61 Douglas 1966: 96.

62 Blackledge 2003: 257.

63 On women's attitudes to menstruation, see Hays 1987.

64 Thanks to Ludmilla Antepenko A'Beckett (p.c.).

65 This, and some of the other examples, are taken from Joffe 1948: 185.

66 *Menses* is the plural of *mensis*.

67 Agyekum 2002.

68 Akan *way ɛ asakyima* 'she has flowered' is used of menarche, Agyekum 2002.

69 In one Middle Dutch text, every mention of a remedy to bring on *bloeme* had prompted one early scholar to resolutely supply in the margin the Latin *provocat menstrua* or *producit menstrua*.

70 E.g. by Neaman and Silver 1983: 57.

71 One kind of folk etymology is re-analysis of the nouns that are today *apron, adder, orange* (and, if you are Australian, *ocker*) from *napron, nadder* and *naranj*;

nickname from *ekename*, and *pea* from *pease*. The assumption is that, e.g. *a nadder* pronounced /ənædə/ got reanalyzed into *an adder*, same pronunciation. A *nickname* is a reanalysis of *an ekename* ('eke' = 'also'). If you know the nursery rhyme that begins *Pease pudding hot*, you have met the pre-1600 singular and plural form for 'pea'. *Peas(e)* was then reanalysed as a regular plural of *pea*. Another kind of example is *I could **of** done it*. Much of the time, both *of* and many instances of *have* (particularly following a modal) have exactly the same pronunciation /əv/ , /v/ , or /ə/ (cf. the written forms *cuppa* and *coulda*). They become confused, and *of* usually replaces *have*, in both writing and pronunciation, e.g. /kʊd ɒv/. A third kind is exemplified by the distress call *Mayday*, from French *M'aidez* 'help me'; the score *love* in tennis, from French *l'oeuf* 'the egg', shape of 0; the phrase *checkmate* in chess, from Persian *Shah māt(a)* 'the king is dead'; and the compound (Australian) noun *chaise-lounge* is a sort of metathesis from French *[chaise] longue*, being confused in this context with *lounge [chair]*. In the jargon of nursing, folk etymology has led to the substitution of *carative* from *curative* because nurses *care* for patients, whereas doctors *cure* them.

72 Dauzat 1938.
73 Enright 1985: 10; Aman and Sardo 1982; Ernster 1975.
74 Cf. Allan 2001: 166ff.
75 Cleland 1985: 77, 143.
76 Grose 1811.
77 1647–80.
78 Burr 1766: 86. The poem was probably written in 1674.
79 'Steel waters' from the chalybeate springs at Tunbridge; 'A back of steel' = vigorous copulation.
80 Keesing 1982: 31.
81 *New Idea*, 21 March 1962, p. 39.
82 Arango 1989: 49, 46.
83 See the recipes and remedies collected in Cockayne 1865. Camporesi (1988: 154) describes the importance of dung-based health programmes in early Europe.
84 Durkheim 1963: 94f.
85 Meigs 1978.
86 William McGregor, p.c.
87 Meigs 1978: 312.
88 Aristotle 1984, *Generation of Animals* 728a28–9.
89 See Allan and Burridge 1991: 130f.

8 FOOD AND SMELL

1 See, for example, http://www.restaurant.org/rusa/ and http://www.concierge.com for restaurant reviews featuring comfort foods. Accessed May 2005.
2 See Dallman et al. 2003 for a new view of 'comfort food'.
3 On inalienable possession, see Chapter 6 and Chappell and McGregor 1995.
4 Fernándes-Armesto 2001: 22.
5 Mission statement of the Slow Food Movement; http://www.slowfood.com. Accessed November 2004.

6 Brugman and Burridge 2000. Halligan, in her essay, 'From Castor to Olive in One Generation' (1990: 1–28) also reminisces about Anglo-Australia's discovery of garlic and olive oil.

7 See Harris 1986: ch. 7.

8 Hilka Klinkenberg, 'Taboo Table Offerings: The intricacies of intercultural menu planning' http://www.salesvantage.com/article/view.php?w=239.

9 Cf. Tannahill 1988: 108.

10 Harris 1986.

11 Douglas 1966: 190.

12 In Germov and Williams 1999, chs. 11–15 deal with different aspects of body management by regulating food intake.

13 Bynum 1987: 202.

14 Ayto 1993.

15 Hartley 1999: 492.

16 For the complete list, see Halligan 1990: 107.

17 Recipes come from Black 1977; Chafin 1979; Hodgett et al. n.d.

18 Burridge and Mulder 1998: 129–31.

19 It would seem that this sort of queasiness was always more acute in the USA, some even having a problem with the word *feet*; cf. Discussion in Fryer 1963: 35.

20 Pancreas or thymus gland.

21 Ravitch 2004: 109–13; see also appendices.

22 By Patricia Zettner.

23 Marieke Brugman suggests (p.c.) that a splash of sherry would have made this dish 'truly continental'.

24 See also Lehrer 1990: 395.

25 On the other hand, there are *Angel cake*, *Angels on horseback*, *Maids of honour* and *Queen Mab's pudding*.

26 Seaberg 1973: 144.

27 Zwicky and Zwicky 1981: 88–91.

28 Korn et al. 2001: chs. 9, 10.

29 *OED*.

30 Korn et al. 2001: 14–23.

31 Korn et al. 2001: 188.

32 Hughes 1991: 138. The Australian rightwing dysphemistically dismisses its more intellectual opponents as *the chardonnay set* and *latte drinkers*, implying that they are effete and 'unAustralian', i.e. rough-as-guts drinkers of beer and billy-tea.

33 See Allan and Burridge 1991: ch. 7; Grose 1811; Partridge 1984; Ayto 1993; Green 1993, 1996.

34 German nutritionist Hans Balzli, quoted in Pullar 1970: 236.

35 Harmer 1998: 26.

36 Maclean 2004.

37 Probyn 2000: 59–60.

38 http://www.deliciousitaly.com/carolmalzone.htm. Accessed November 2004.

39 http://www.bbc.co.uk/comedy/poshnosh/. Accessed October 2004.

40 Furnivall 1868: 200 (for figs), 222 (for eggs).

41 Brillat-Savarin 1970.

42 Cited in Watson 2000: 62.

43 Fernándes-Armesto 2001: 37.
44 Counterpart to *cheesecake* for a woman.
45 Not only was salt a valuable commodity, it is also the taste of sweat and sexual excitement.
46 We examined Valentine's Day notices from the Melbourne *Age* and *Herald Sun*, 14 February 2000.
47 This may be inaccurate: breasts are often compared to pumpkins and a half pumpkin is not un-vulva-like. Furthermore, *pumping* is one of the many slang terms for copulating.
48 Watson 2000: 114, 133f.
49 Watson 2000: ch. 4 describes a number of these experiments.
50 See Green 1996 for other examples.
51 Gordon 1959: 19.
52 Süskind 1986: 27.
53 Inspiration for this exercise came from Algeo 1966.
54 Brillat-Savarin 1970: 13.

9 DISEASE, DEATH AND KILLING

1 See further examples in Johnson and Murray 1985: 153.
2 Gordon 1959: 33–40, Huizinga 1924: 173–7 and Porter 1997: 111–12 for various accounts of the cult of saints.
3 *Troilus and Cressida*, II.iii.19.
4 Captain James Cook, 1728–79. Porter 1997: 166.
5 Morris 2000: 241.
6 See Green 1993 for more slang expressions for syphilis.
7 Luke 16: 20–5; this is not Lazarus of Bethany, whom Jesus resurrected from the dead.
8 Cf. Shakespeare, *Timon of Athens*, IV.i.30 and Partridge 1955: 75, 141.
9 John 11.
10 Lepora is corrupcio corporis exterius et interius . . . haer complexie is quaet ende ghecorumpeert also siin haer ghedachten ende haer ghepens is quaet ende ghevenniint. Ende daerom salmense sceiden uut den ghesonden luijden.
11 Cf. Richards 1977 and Gottfried 1983: 13–15.
12 Physician Armauer Hansen (1841–1912) discovered the bacillus (*Mycobacterium leprae*) responsible for leprosy.
13 Details of all twelve texts can be found in Burridge 1991.
14 Cf. Aristotle 1984, *Generation of Animals* 716–28; Lloyd 1983: 86–111.
15 Lloyd 1983: 58–111.
16 See Aristotle 1984, *Generation of Animals* 728a 18–21.
17 765a 5–21.
18 Richards 1977: 71–3.
19 A comment made in a survey conducted in the early 1970s on methods to prevent the spread of STDs; reported in Davenport-Hines 1990: 281.
20 Meigs 1978: 318.
21 F. B. Smith, *The People's Health*; cited in Patterson 1987: 43.
22 Ortner 1974.

23 With the exception, of course, that men's genitalia, like the genitalia of women, are frequently likened to animals in the vocabulary people use to talk about these 'unmentionables.'

24 Margaret Cavendish (née Lucas), Duchess of Newcastle (1623–73), was so unusual in writing about philosophy and many other topics that in the nineteenth century she was nicknamed Mad Madge (Whitaker 2002: 347–59). In her lifetime she published prolifically, which was very unusual for the period, and only possible because of her exalted position among the Restoration nobility, her supportive husband and, not least, her own very strong character.

25 In the west, many buildings have no thirteenth floor, in Japan no fourth floor (for the same reason).

26 Field 1976: 355.

27 Field 1976: 358; Sontag 1979: 6.

28 The same is true for Chronic Fatigue Syndrome.

29 Morse 1999.

30 Gillis 1972: 177.

31 The practice ended in 1770.

32 Gillis 1972: 175–9.

33 Ayto 1993: 213.

34 Black 1986: 40; see also Callen 1990: 172. In the 1970s, AIDS happened to be homophonous with the name of an American brand of diet-candy, *AYDS*, now withdrawn from the market, at least under that name.

35 http://www.4-h-canada.ca/what_is_4-h.html. Accessed October 2004.

36 http://www.actupny.org/documents/Denver.html. Accessed October 2004.

37 Grover 1990: 56.

38 '[T]he question of who has the power to name is an on-going turf battle between people with AIDS and those who insist on defining us as victims' (AIDS activist in Callen 1990: 177).

39 Hinton 1976: 303–14.

40 Stephenson 1985: 103–9.

41 Patterson 1987: 329, n7.

42 Quoted in Sontag 1989: 66. Reagan acting the Gipper, perhaps.

43 Some readers believe Christopher Robin is speaking of growing up, not dying.

44 Cf. Peterson 1986: 48.

45 Cf. Gorer 1965; Brain 1979; Gross 1985.

46 Stephenson 1985: 41.

47 Baird 1976: 87.

48 Deetz 1977.

49 The Melbourne *Sun*, Saturday 21 May 1988.

50 Shakespeare, *Macbeth*, II.ii.52f.

51 A T[otalizator] A[gency] B[oard] outlet is a betting shop.

52 *Medical Observer*, 19 January 1990.

53 This, at least, is the folk belief; some etymologists dispute it and claim (among other things) that *bucket* denotes the 'beam, yoke' where a pig was hung for slaughter – the dying pig would presumably kick the bucket.

54 See Douglas 1966: ch. 5; Simons 1982: 194, 206.

55 Cf. Frazer 1911: 394ff; Cove 1978; Knipe 1984; Knipe and Bromley 1984.

56 Simons 1982: 193.

57 Brain 1979.

58 Cynthia Read once ruefully reported this to us.

59 US President Reagan's *evil empire* (USSR); US President George W. Bush's *axis of evil* – Iraq, Iran, North Korea in 2002.

60 The charges laid against First Lieutenant William L. Calley, Jr for the 16 April 1968 My Lai massacre in Vietnam in his Court Martial (CM426402) refer four times to 'Oriental human being(s)'.

61 *Time*, 9 January 1984, p. 56; our italics.

62 Orwell 1946.

63 Vogan 1890: 142; see also p. 113. Another report on p. 129 includes the following chilling remark: 'The prisoners were marched off in an iligent line or tied to a line, it don't much matter, and three miles outside the town they were neatly dispatched, and left to amuse the crows and ants' [*sic*].

64 Shakespeare, *Macbeth*, I.ii.20.

65 May 1985: 128.

66 Lifton and Olson 1976: 104.

67 Anttila 1972: 139f.

68 Does our own academic turn of phrase do the same when we talk about humanitarian disasters *wiping out* more than a hundred million people?

69 http://vikingphoenix.com/news/stn/2003/911casualties.htm. Accessed September 2004.

70 Loftus 1979.

10 TABOO, CENSORING AND THE HUMAN BRAIN

1 Many thanks to Pia Herbert for supplying us with the relevant passages from the Melbourne Metropolitan Planning Scheme; cf. Börjars and Burridge (2001) for further discussion.

2 Millwood-Hargrave 2000.

3 Cf. Allan 2001: 132ff.

4 Shakespeare, *Romeo and Juliet*, II.i.85f.

5 For more examples of these sorts of sound symbolic changes, see Burridge 2004: 142–53.

6 Allan 1986, Allan 2001.

7 Frazer 1911: 318.

8 Wyld 1936: 387.

9 For example, the *Macquarie Dictionary* 2003.

10 The expression 'Gresham's law' is named after Sir Thomas Gresham, a sixteenth-century English financier who worked for King Edward VI. The law dates back to the 1850s, when it was first used by economist Henry Dunning Macleod to refer to the tendency (when there is more than one form of money in circulation) for bad money to drive out good money.

11 Allan 1986 I: 207f; Allan and Burridge 1991: 22ff.

12 Allan and Burridge 1991; Farmer and Henley 1890–1904; Fryer 1963; Healey 1980.

13 Pullum 1991.
14 Cf. McGinnies 1949; Nothman 1962; Gray et al. 1982; Van Lancker and Cummings 1999; Jay 1992, 2000.
15 Osgood et al. 1957
16 McGinnies 1949; Zajonc 1962; Gray et al. 1982; Dinn and Harris 2000.
17 Jay 2000: 102–5 outlines a battery of laboratory experiments from the 1960s through to the 1990s that look at the recall of taboo words.
18 MacKay et al. 2004.
19 Harris et al. 2003.
20 For example, in Gonzalez-Regiosa 1976 Spanish–English bilinguals were required to read lists of ten Spanish taboo words and ten English taboo words. Participants were then asked to rate themselves on their degree of anxiety. Both high- and low-anxiety participants rated themselves as more anxious after reading the taboo words in their first language. Other studies (for example, Anooshian and Hertel 1994) that have looked at recall also support the fact that words in a speaker's first language have stronger emotional effects. Here is a true story: an Australian woman was speaking German to a native German speaker during a plane flight. After some time, the man revealed that he was a manufacturer of women's sanitary products and whenever he had to name items such as *sanitary pad* and *tampon*, he consistently switched to English; even though he knew the woman was a native English speaker, it was less embarrassing for him to utter such words in his second language.
21 Though see Jay 1992.
22 Miss A. M. Miller (born 1906), interviewed in 1978 by Moya Gunn, of La Trobe University.
23 On children's use of dirty words, see Hartmann 1973; Jay 1992; 2000; Morris 2000: 173.
24 Harris et al. 2003: 12.
25 Kim et al. 1997.
26 This has been linked to brain development. At birth, there is relatively little difference between the functioning of the two brain hemispheres; but around the age of two there begins the process of lateralization, whereby the right and left hemispheres each take over a dominant role for certain mental functions. In most right-handers, the left hemisphere is dominant for language – left-handers are a more complicated bunch. However, the relationship between language and lateralization is an extremely complex one and is the subject of continuing neuro-linguistic research. While the development of this neural one-sidedness would appear to overlap with the main period when first-language acquisition takes place, the hypothesis of a critical learning period is still a controversial one. Smith 2002 summarizes the various pieces of evidence for the critical learning hypothesis but declares the matter controversial.
27 Jay 2000 offers a comprehensive account of the mental disorders associated with coprolalia and other coprophenomena.
28 http://neuro-www.mgh.harvard.edu/forum_2/TouretteSyndromeF/5.7.997.16PM Causesforcopr.html. Accessed October 2004.
29 These last two cases are discussed in Berecz 1992.
30 Jay 2000: 235–41.
31 Posted 18 May 1999.

32 Comings and Comings 1985: 440.
33 Cf. neurolinguistic research by LaBar and Phelps 1998, and Anderson and Phelps 2001 on the working of the brain's emotional systems.
34 Cf. Leckman, James F., Bradley S. Peterson and David L. Pauls 2000. *Tic Disorders*. http://www.acnp.org/g4/GN401000161/CH.html. Jay 2000: 74 offers convincing evidence from a number of spheres for a 'cursing module' that is situated in the right hemisphere of the brain, with interconnections to the amygdala and basal ganglia.
35 Burridge 2005: 42–4.
36 Orwell 1987.
37 Cf. Becker 1973 on the 'terrifying dilemma' that humans have to live with.
38 Swift 1958: 166–71.
39 Douglas 1966.

References

Abbey, Edward. 1968. *Desert Solitaire*. New York: Ballantine.
  1975. *The Monkey Wrench Gang*. New York: Avon Books.
Adams, Phillip (ed.). 1997. *The Retreat from Tolerance*. Sydney: ABC Books.
Adams, Phillip and Patrice Newell. 1994. *The Penguin Book of Australian Jokes*. Ringwood: Penguin.
Adams, Robert M. 1985. Soft soap and nitty gritty. In *Fair of Speech: The Uses of Euphemism*, ed. D. J. Enright. Oxford: Oxford University Press, pp. 44–55.
Adler, Max K. 1978. *Naming and Addressing: A Sociolinguistic Study*. Hamburg: Helmut Buske Verlag.
Agyekum, Kofi. 2002. Menstruation as verbal taboo among the Akan of Ghana. *Journal of Anthropological Research* 58: 367–87.
Algeo, John. 1966. *Problems in the Origins and Development of the English Language*. 3rd edn. San Diego: Harcourt Brace Jovanovich.
Allan, Keith. 1986. *Linguistic Meaning*, vols. 1 and 2. London: Routledge & Kegan Paul [Reprint edn: World Publishing Corporation, Beijing, 1991].
  2001. *Natural Language Semantics*. Oxford and Malden, MA: Blackwell.
Allan, Keith and Kate Burridge. 1991. *Euphemism and Dysphemism: Language Used as Shield and Weapon*. New York: Oxford University Press.
Allen, Wendy F. 1987. Teenage Speech: The Social Dialects of Melbourne Teenagers. BA Honours Thesis. Linguistics Department, La Trobe University.
Aman, Reinhold. 1984–5. Offensive language via computer. *Maledicta* 8: 105f.
Aman, Reinhold and Grace Sardo. 1982. Canadian sexual terms. *Maledicta* 6: 21–8.
Anderson, Adam K. and Elizabeth A. Phelps. 2001. Lesions of the human amygdala impair enhanced perception of emotionally salient events. *Nature* 411: 305–9.
Andersson, Lars-Gunnar and Peter Trudgill. 1990. *Bad Language*. Harmondsworth: Penguin.
Anooshian, Linda J. and T. P. Hertel. 1994. Emotionality in free recall: language specificity in bilingual memory. *Cognition and Emotion* 8: 503–14.
Anttila, Raimo. 1972. *An Introduction to Historical and Comparative Linguistics*. New York: Macmillan.
Appignanesi, Lisa. 1994. Liberté, égalité and fraternité: PC and the French. In *The War of the Words*, ed. Sarah Dunant. London: Virago, pp. 145–63.
Arango, Ariel C. 1989. *Dirty Words: Psychoanalytic Insights*. Northvale, NJ: Jason Aronson.
Arbeitman, Yoël. 1980. Look ma, what's become of the sacred tongues. *Maledicta* 4: 71–88.

Aristotle. 1984. *The Complete Works of Aristotle. The revised Oxford translation*, ed. Jonathan Barnes. Bollingen Series 71. Princeton: Princeton University Press.

Atkinson, John M. and Paul Drew. 1979. *Order in Court: The Organisation of Verbal Interaction in Judicial Settings*. London: Macmillan.

Atkinson, Martin, David Kilby and Iggy Roca. 1988. *Foundations of General Linguistics*. 2nd edn. London: Unwin Hyman.

Austen, Jane. 1983. *The Complete Novels of Jane Austen*. Harmondsworth: Penguin.

Ayto, John. 1993. *A Dictionary of Euphemism*. London: Bloomsbury.

Baird, Jonathan. 1976. The funeral industry in Boston. In *Death: Current Perspectives*, ed. Edwin S. Schneidman. Palo Alto: Mayfield, pp. 82–91.

Baker, Robert. 1779. *Reflections on the English Language*. n.p.

Banks, Julie and Jean Mulder. 1996. *What Did I Say? Using Non-Discriminatory Language*. Melbourne: Equal Opportunity Unit, University of Melbourne.

Barker, Ronnie. 1979. *Fletcher's Book of Rhyming Slang*. London: Pan.

Bataille, Georges. 1992. *Death and Sensuality: A Study of Eroticism and the Taboo*. New York: Walker [Reprint of 1962 edition].

Becker, Ernest. 1973. *The Denial of Death*. New York: The Free Press.

Benson, Robert W. 1985. The end of legalese: the game is over. *Review of Law and Social Change* 13: 519–73.

Berecz, John M. 1992. *Understanding Tourette Syndrome, Obsessive Compulsive Disorder, and Related Problems*. New York: Springer.

Bering, Dietz. 1992. *The Stigma of Names: Antisemitism in German Daily Life, 1812–1933*, trans. Neville Plaice. Ann Arbor: University of Michigan Press [First published as *Der Name als Stigma*. Stuttgart: Ernst Klett Verlag. 1987].

Besterman, Theodore (ed.). 1957. *Voltaire's Correspondence*, vol. 23. Geneva: Institut et Musée Voltaire.

Bilmes, Jack. 1988. The concept of preference in conversation analysis. *Language in Society* 17: 161–81.

Black, David. 1986. *The Plague Years: A Chronicle of AIDS*. London: Picador.

Black, Maggie. 1977. *A Heritage of British Cooking*. London: Charles Letts.

Blackledge, Catherine. 2003. *The Story of V: Opening Pandora's Box*. London: Weidenfeld & Nicolson.

Blackwell, Kenneth and Harry Ruja. 1994. *A Bibliography of Bertrand Russell*, vol. 2. London and New York: Routledge.

Bloomfield, Leonard. 1927. On recent work in general linguistics. *Modern Philology* 25: 211–30.

Blum-Kulka, Shoshana. 1992. The metapragmatics of politeness in Israeli society. In *Politeness in Language: Studies in its History, Theory and Practice*, ed. Richard J. Watts, Sachiko Ide and Konrad Ehlich. Berlin: Mouton de Gruyter, pp. 255–80.

Bolinger, Dwight. 1980. *Language: The Loaded Weapon*. London: Longman.

Börjars, Kersti and Kate Burridge. 2001. *Introducing English Grammar*. London: Edward Arnold.

Boswell, James. 1791. *The Life of Samuel Johnson, LLD*. London: Henry Baldwin for Charles Dilly.

Boyle, Ronald. 2000. Whatever happened to preference organization? *Journal of Pragmatics* 32: 583–604.

Brain, James L. 1979. *The Last Taboo: Sex and the Fear of Death*. New York: Anchor/ Doubleday.

Bright, William. 2000. The sociolinguistics of the 's-word': 'squaw' in American place names. http://www.ncidc.org/bright/Squaw_revised.doc. Accessed October 2004.

Brillat-Savarin, Jean-Anthelme. 1970. *The Physiology of Taste*, trans. A. Drayton. Harmondsworth: Penguin [First published 1825].

Brown, Penelope and Stephen Levinson. 1987. *Politeness: Some Universals in Language Usage*. Cambridge: Cambridge University Press.

Brown, Roger W. and M. Ford. 1961. Address in American English. *Journal of Abnormal and Social Psychology* 62: 375–85.

Brown, Roger W. and Albert Gilman. 1960. The pronouns of power and solidarity. In *Style in Language*, ed. Thomas A. Sebeok. Cambridge, MA: MIT Press, pp. 253–76 [Reprinted in *Language and Social Context*, ed. Pier P. Giglioli Harmondsworth: Penguin, pp. 252–82].

1989. Politeness theory and Shakespeare's four major tragedies. *Language in Society* 18: 159–212.

Brugman, Marieke and Kate Burridge. 2000. Gastronomic Red Herrings. The Age Epicure Master Class, as part of the Melbourne Food and Wine Festival (the Grand Hyatt).

Bryson, Bill. 1984. *The Penguin Dictionary of Troublesome Words*. London: Allen Lane.

Buchanan, James. 1767. *A Regular English Syntax: wherein is exhibited the whole variety of English construction, properly exemplified*. London: J. Wren.

Burchfield, Robert. 1985. An outline history of euphemism in English. In *Fair of Speech: The Uses of Euphemism*, ed. D. J. Enright. Oxford: Oxford University Press, pp. 13–31.

1989. *Unlocking the English Language*. London: Faber & Faber.

Burke, Peter. 1995. Introduction. In *Languages and Jargons: Contributions to the Social History of Language*, ed. Peter Burke and Roy Porter. Cambridge: Polity Press, pp. 1–21.

Burr, Thomas B. 1766. *The History of Tunbridge-Wells*. London.

Burridge, Kate. 1991. *Syntactic Change in Germanic*. Amsterdam: John Benjamins.

2000. *The Power of Language: Proceedings of the Insurance Enquiries and Complaints 4th Annual Conference* (13–14 November, Sheraton Hotel, Melbourne). In-house publication.

2004. *Blooming English: Observations on the Roots, Cultivation and Hybrids of the English Language*. Cambridge: Cambridge University Press.

2005. *Weeds in the Garden of Words: Further Observations on the Tangled History of the English Language*. Cambridge: Cambridge University Press.

Burridge, Kate and Keith Allan. 1998. The X-phemistic value of Romani in nonstandard speech. In *The Romani Element in Non-Standard Speech*, ed. Yaron Matras. Wiesbaden: Harrassowitz Verlag, pp. 29–50.

Burridge, Kate and Margaret Florey. 2002. 'Yeah-no he's a good kid': a discourse analysis of *yeah-no* in Australian English. *Australian Journal of Linguistics* 22: 149–71.

Burridge, Kate and Jean Mulder. 1998. *English in Australia and New Zealand: An Introduction to its Structure, History and Use*. Melbourne: Oxford University Press.

Bybee, Joan L. 2003. Mechanisms of change in grammaticalization: the role of frequency. In *The Handbook of Historical Linguistics*, ed. Brian D. Joseph and Richard D. Janda. Oxford and Malden, MA: Blackwell, pp. 602–23.

Bynum, Caroline Walker. 1987. *Holy Feast and Holy Fast: The Religious Significance of Food to Medieval Women*. Berkeley: University of California Press.

Callen, Michael. 1990. AIDS: The linguistic battlefield. In *The State of the Language*, ed. Christopher Ricks and Leonard Michaels. London: Faber, pp. 171–84.

Cameron, Deborah. 1995. *Verbal Hygiene*. London: Routledge.

Cameron, Deborah and Don Kulick. 2003. *Language and Sexuality*. Cambridge: Cambridge University Press.

Campbell, George. 1776. *Philosophy of Rhetoric*, 2 vols. London: W. Strahan, T. Cadell.

Camporesi, Piero. 1988. *The Incorruptible Flesh: Bodily Mutation and Mortification in Religion and Folklore*. Cambridge: Cambridge University Press.

Cassileth, Barrie R. and Jane Hamilton. 1979. The family with cancer. In *The Cancer Patient: Social and Medical Aspects of Care*, ed. Peter A. Cassileth. Philadelphia: Lea & Febiger, pp. 233–49.

Chafin, Mary. 1979. *Mary Chafin's Original Country Recipes from a Dorset Family Cookery Book of the 17th Century*. London: Macmillan.

Chappell, Hilary and William McGregor (eds.). 1995. *Body Parts in Grammar*. Amsterdam: John Benjamins.

Chaucer, Geoffrey. 1898 [1396]. *The Works of Geoffrey Chaucer*. Globe edition, ed. Alfred W. Pollard, H. Frank Heath, Mark H. Liddell and W. S. McCormick. London: Macmillan & Co.

Chauncey, George. 1994. *Gay New York: Gender, Urban cultures, and the Making of the Gay Male World 1890–1940*. New York: BasicBooks.

Cicero. 1959. *Letters to His Friends (Epistulae ad Familiares)*, trans. W. Glynn Williams. London: Heineman.

Cleese, John and Connie Booth. 1988. *The Complete Fawlty Towers*. London: Methuen.

Cleland, John. 1985. *Fanny Hill or Memoirs of a Woman of Pleasure*, ed. Peter Wagner. Harmondsworth: Penguin [First published 1748–9].

Clinton, Bill [William J.]. 2004. *My Life*. London: Hutchinson.

Clyne, Michael. 1987. Language and Racism. In *Prejudice in the Public Arena: Racism*, ed. Andrew Markus and Radha Rasmussen. Melbourne: Centre for Migrant and Intercultural Studies, Monash University, pp. 35–44.

Cockayne, Oswald (ed.). 1865. *Leechdoms, Wortcunning, and Starcraft of Early England*. London: Longman, Roberts & Green.

Comings, David E. and Brenda G. Comings. 1985. Tourette Syndrome: clinical and psychological aspects of 250 cases. *American Journal of Human Genetics* 37: 435–50.

Cook, James. 1893. *Captain Cook's Journal During his First Voyage round the World made in H. M. Bark Endeavour, 1768–71*. A literal transcription of the original MSS ed. Captain W. J. L. Wharton. London: Elliot Stock.

   1967. *The Journals of Captain James Cook*, vol. 3: *The Voyage of the Resolution and Discovery 1776–1780*, ed. from the original MSS by J. C. Beaglehole. Cambridge: Cambridge University Press for the Hakluyt Society.

Cove, John J. 1978. Ecology, structuralism, and fishing taboos. In *Adaptation and Symbolism: Essays on Social Organization*, ed. Karen A. Watson-Gegeo and S. Lee Seaton. Hawaii: East–West Center, University of Hawaii, pp. 143–54.

Crawley, Ernest. 1960. *The Mystic Rose: A Study of Primitive Marriage and of Primitive Thought in its Bearing on Marriage*. 2nd edn. New York: Meridian Books [First published 1927].

Crompton, Louis. 1980–1. The myth of lesbian impunity: capital laws from 1270 to 1791. *Journal of Homosexuality* 6 (1/2): 11–25.

Crystal, David. 1995. *Encyclopedia of the English Language*. Cambridge: Cambridge University Press.

1998. *Language Play*. Harmondsworth: Penguin.

Cutts, Martin and Chrissie Maher. 1984. *Gobbledygook*. London: George Allen & Unwin.

Daems, W. F. (ed.). 1967. *Boec van medicinen in Dietsche* [c. 1300]. Een Middel-nederlandse compilatie van medisch-farmaceutische literatuur. Thesis. Leiden.

Dallman, M. F., N. Pecoraro and others. 2003. Chronic stress and obesity: a new view of 'comfort food'. *Proceedings of the National Academy of Science USA* (September issue), pp. 1696–701.

Danat, Brenda. 1980. Language in the legal process. *Law and Society Review* 14: 445–564.

Dauzat, Albert. 1917. *Les argots des métiers franco-provençaux*. Paris: Champion.

1938. *Dictionnaire étymologique de la langue française*. Paris: Librairie Larousse.

Davenport-Hines, Richard. 1990. *Sex, Death and Punishment: Attitudes to Sex and Sexuality in Britain since the Renaissance*. London: Collins.

Dawidowicz, Lucy. 1975. *The War Against the Jews, 1939–1945*. New York: Bantam.

De Klerk, Vivian. 1992. How taboo are taboo words for girls? *Language in Society* 21: 277–89.

Deetz, James. 1977. *Small Things Forgotten: The Archeology of Early American Life*. New York: Anchor Press.

Dickstein, Morris. 1993. Correcting PC. *Partisan Review* 60: 542–9.

Dinn, W. M. and C. L. Harris. 2000. Neurocognitive function in antisocial personality disorder. *Psychiatry Research* 97: 173–90.

Dixon, Robert M. W. 1980. *Languages of Australia*. Cambridge: Cambridge University Press.

Douglas, Mary. 1966. *Purity and Danger: An Analysis of Concepts of Pollution and Taboo*. London: Routledge & Kegan Paul.

Durkheim, Emile. 1963. *Incest: The Nature and Origin of the Taboo*. New York: Lyle Stuart [First published 1897].

Eagleson, Robert D. 1982. Aboriginal English in an urban setting. In *English and the Aboriginal Child*, ed. Robert D. Eagleson, Susan Kaldor and Ian G. Malcolm. Canberra: Curriculum Development Centre.

Ehrlich, Susan. 2001. *Representing Rape*. London and New York: Routledge.

Ellis, Albert. 1963. *The Origins and the Development of the Incest Taboo*. New York: Lyle Stuart.

Ellman, Lucy. 1989. *Sweet Desserts*. Harmondsworth: Penguin.

Ellmann, Richard. 1988. *Oscar Wilde*. Harmondsworth: Penguin.

Emerson, Ralph W. 1856. *Aristocracy. Works of Ralph Waldo Emerson*. London: George Routledge & Sons.

Enright, D. J. (ed.). 1985. *Fair of Speech: The Uses of Euphemism*. Oxford: Oxford University Press.

Ernst, Morris L. and William Seagle. 1928. *To the Pure: A Study of Obscenity and the Censor*. New York: Viking.

Ernster, Virginia L. 1975. American menstrual expressions. *Sex Roles* 1: 3–13.

Ervin-Tripp, Susan. 1969. Sociolinguistics. In *Advances in Experimental Social Psychology*, vol. 4, ed. Leon Berkowitz, pp. 93–107.

Ervin-Tripp, Susan et al. 1984. Language and power in the family. In *Language and Power*, ed. Cheris Kramarae, Muriel Schulz and William M. O'Barr. Beverly Hills: Sage Publications, pp. 116–35.

Farb, Peter. 1974. *Word Play: What Happens When People Talk*. New York: Knopf.

Farmer, John S. and W. E. Henley. 1890–1904. *Slang and Its Analogues*. 7 Vols. London [Reprint edn: Arno Press, New York, 1970].

Farro, D. 1754. *Royal Universal British Grammar and Vocabulary*. London.

Fernándes-Armesto, Felipe. 2001. *Food: A History*. London: Macmillan.

Field, David. 1976. The social definition of illness. In *An Introduction to Medical Sociology*, ed. David Tuckett. London: Tavistock Publications, pp. 334–66.

Fielding, Henry. 1749. *The History of Tom Jones, a Foundling*. London: printed for A. Millar.

Firth, John R. 1968. Descriptive linguistics and the study of English. In *Selected Papers of J. R. Firth, 1952–59*, ed. Frank R. Palmer. Bloomington: Indiana University Press, pp. 96–113 [First published 1956].

Fisher, Mary. 1995. *I'll Not Go Quietly: Mary Fisher Speaks Out*. New York: Scribner.

Fitter, R. S. R. 1971. *Finding Wild Flowers*. London: Collins.

Flaubert, Gustave. 1930. *Œuvres complètes de Gustave Flaubert. Madame Bovary: mœurs de province*. Paris: Louis Conard.

Folb, Edith. 1980. *Runnin' Down Some Lines: The Language and Culture of Black Teenagers*. Cambridge, MA: Harvard University Press.

Forestus, Alemarianus Petrus [Pieter van Foreest]. 1653. *Observationem et Curiatonem Medicinalium ac Chirurgicarum Opera Omnia*. Rouen: Berthelin.

Frantz, David O. 1989. *Festum Voluptatis: A Study of Renaissance Erotica*. Columbus: Ohio State University Press.

Frazer, Sir James G. 1875. Taboo. *Encyclopaedia Britannica*. 9th edn.
    1911. *The Golden Bough Part II: Taboo and The Perils of the Soul*. 3rd edn. London: Macmillan.

Freud, Sigmund. 1950. *Totem and Taboo*, trans. James Strachey. London: Routledge & Kegan Paul [First published 1913].

Fryer, Peter. 1963. *Mrs Grundy: Studies in English Prudery*. London: Dennis Dobson.

Furnivall, Frederick (ed.). 1868. *The Babees Book, The Bokes of Nurture of Hugh Rhodes and John Russel*. Published for the Early English Text Society. London: Trübner and Co.

Garner, James Finn. 1994. *Politically Correct Bedtime Stories*. New York: Macmillan Publishing Company, pp. 1–2.

Germov, John and Lauren Williams. 1999. *A Sociology of Food and Nutrition: The Social Appetite*. Oxford: Oxford University Press.

Gildersleeve, Virginia C. 1961. *Government Regulation of the Elizabethan Drama.* New York: Burt Franklin [First published 1908].

Gillis, Lynn. 1972. *Human Behaviour in Illness: Psychology and Interpersonal Relationships.* London: Faber & Faber.

Goffman, Erving. 1978. Response cries. *Language* 54: 787–815.

Gonzalez-Regiosa, F. 1976. The anxiety arousing effect of taboo words in bilinguals. In *Cross-Cultural Anxiety*, ed. C. D. Spielberger and Regiosa Diaz-Guerrero. Washington, DC: Hemisphere, pp. 89–105.

Goodheart, Eugene. 1993. PC or not PC. *Partisan Review* 60: 550–5.

Gordon, Benjamin L. 1959. *Medieval and Renaissance Medicine.* New York: Philosophical Library.

Gorer, Geoffrey. 1965. *Death, Grief and Mourning in Contemporary Britain.* London: Cresset Press.

Gottfried, Robert S. 1983. *The Black Death: Natural and Human Disaster in Medieval Europe.* New York: The Free Press.

Gowers, Sir Ernest. 1987. *The Complete Plain Words.* Revised by Sidney Greenbaum and Janet Whitcut. Harmondsworth: Penguin.

Gray, Rose and Ruth Rogers. 1997. *River Cafe Cook Book Two.* London: Ebury Press.

Gray, S. G., H. H. Hughes and L. J. Schneider. 1982. Physiological responsivity to a socially stressful situation: the effect of level of moral development. *Psychological Record* 32: 29–34.

Green, Jonathon. 1993. *Slang Down the Ages: The Historical Development of Slang.* London: Kyle Cathie.

  1996. *Words Apart.* London: Kyle Cathie Ltd.

Grice, H. Paul. 1975. Logic and conversation. In *Syntax and Semantics 3: Speech Acts*, ed. Peter Cole and Jerry L. Morgan. New York: Academic Press, pp. 41–58 [Reprinted in Grice. *Studies in the Way of Words.* Cambridge, MA: Harvard University Press. 1986].

Griffiths, Andy. 2004. *The Bad Book.* Illustrations by Terry Denton. Sydney: Pan Macmillan Australia.

Grose, (Captain) Francis. 1811. *Dictionary of the Vulgar Tongue.* London [First published 1783].

Gross, John. 1985. Intimations of mortality. In *Fair of Speech: The Uses of Euphemism*, ed. D. J. Enright. Oxford: Oxford University Press, pp. 203–19.

Grosser, George S. and Anthony A. Walsh. 1966. Sex differences in the differential recall of taboo and neutral words. *Journal of Psychology* 63: 219–27.

Grover, Jan Zita. 1990. AIDS: keywords. In *The State of the Language*, ed. Christopher Ricks and Leonard Michaels. London: Faber, pp. 142–62.

Guthrie, Douglas. 1945. *A History of Medicine.* London: Thomas Nelson.

Haiman, John. 1980. The iconicity of grammar: isomorphism and motivation. *Language* 56: 515–40.

Halliday, Michael A. K. 1978. *Language as a Social Semiotic.* London: Edward Arnold.

Halligan, Marion. 1990. *Eat My Words.* North Ryde, NSW: Angus and Robertson.

Harmer, Wendy. 1998. Are cookbooks the new pornography? *HQ* 57: 26–9.

Harris, Catherine L., Ayse Ayçiçegi and Jean B. Gleason. 2003. Taboo words and reprimands elicit greater autonomic reactivity in a first language than in a second language. *Applied Psycholinguistics* 24: 561–79.

Harris, James. 1751. *Hermes: or, A Philosophical Enquiry Concerning Language and Universal Grammar*. London: H. Woodfall for J. Nourse et al.

Harris, Marvin. 1986. *Good to Eat: The Riddles of Food and Culture*. London: Macmillan.

Hartley, Dorothy. 1999. *Food in English*. London: Little, Brown and Company. [First published 1954].

Hartmann, Lawrence. 1973. Some uses of dirty words by children. *Journal of the American Academy of Child and Adolescent Psychiatry* 12: 108–22.

Haugen, Einar. 1972. *The First Grammatical Treatise: The Earliest Germanic Phonology*. London: Longman.

Hays, Terence E. 1987. Menstrual expressions and menstrual attitudes. *Sex Roles* 16: 605–14.

Haze, Dolores. 1994. Faking it. *Mademoiselle* 100 (1): 125.

Healey, Tim. 1980. A new erotic vocabulary. *Maledicta* 4: 181–201.

Henley, Nancy M. 1989. Molehill or mountain? What we know and don't know about sex bias in language. In *Gender and Thought: Psychological Perspectives*, ed. Mary Crawford and Margaret Gentry. New York: Springer Verlag, pp. 59–78.

Herbert, Robert K. 1990. *Hlonipha* and the ambiguous woman. *Anthropos* 85: 455–73.

Hickey, Raymond. 2003. The German address system: binary and scalar at once. In *Diachronic Perspectives on Address Term Systems*, ed. Irma Taavitsainen and Andreas H. Jucker. Amsterdam and Philadelphia: John Benjamins, pp. 401–25.

Hinton, John. 1976. Speaking of death with the dying. In *Death: Current Perspectives*, ed. Edwin S. Schneidman. Palo Alto: Mayfield, pp. 303–14.

Hobley, C. W. 1910. British East Africa: Kikuyu customs and belief. Thahu and its connection with circumcision rites. *Journal of the Royal Anthropological Institute of Great Britain and Ireland* 40: 428–52.

Hock, Hans H. 1986. *Principles of Historical Linguistics*. Berlin: Mouton.

Hodgett, Gerald, A. J. Hodgett and Delia Smith. n.d. *Stere Htt Well: Medieval Recipes and Remedies from Samuel Pepys's Library*. Adelaide: Mary Martin Books.

Holzknecht, Susanne. 1988. Word taboo and its implications for language change in the Markham family of languages, PNG. *Language and Linguistics in Melanesia* 18: 43–69.

Householder, Fred W. 1971. *Linguistic Speculations*. Cambridge: Cambridge University Press.

Hudson, Joyce and Eirlys Richards. 1978. *The Walmatjari: An Introduction to the Language and Culture*. Darwin: Summer Institute of Linguistics.

Hudson, Keith. 1978. *The Jargon of the Professions*. London: Macmillan.

Hughes, Geoffrey. 1991. *Swearing: A Social History of Foul Language, Oaths and Profanity in English*. Oxford: Blackwell.

Hughes, Robert. 1987. *The Fatal Shore: A History of the Transportation of Convicts to Australia 1787–1868*. London: Collins Harvill.

   1993. *Culture of Complaint: The Fraying of America*. New York: Oxford University Press.

Hughes, Susan E. 1992. Expletives of lower working-class women. *Language in Society* 21: 291–303.

Huizinga, Johan. 1924. *The Waning of the Middle Ages*. New York: Doubleday Anchor.

Isaacson, David. 1999. Review of Encarta World English Dictionary. http:// www. wmich.edu/library/bookreviews/1999/encarta-dictionary.php.

Jacobsen, Anders. 2002. American political correctness the word niggardly. http:// www.jacobsen.no/anders/blog/archives/2002/09/03/americanpoliticalcorrectness thewordniggardly.html. Accessed October 2004.

Janney, Richard W. and Horst Arndt. 1992. Intracultural tact versus intercultural tact. In *Politeness in Language: Studies in its History, Theory and Practice*, ed. Richard J. Watts, Sachiko Ide and Konrad Ehlich. Berlin: Mouton de Gruyter, pp. 21–41.

Jansen, Sue Curry. 1991. *Censorship: The Knot that Binds Power and Knowledge*. New York: Oxford University Press.

Jay, Timothy. 1992. *Cursing in America*. Philadelphia: John Benjamins.

　　2000. *Why We Curse: A Neuro-Psycho-Social Theory of Speech*. Philadelphia: John Benjamins.

Jenkinson, Edward B. 1979. How to keep dictionaries out of the public schools. *Verbatim* 5 (4): 12–13.

Joffe, Natalie F. 1948. The vernacular of menstruation. *Word* 4: 181–6.

Johnson, Diane and John F. Murray. 1985. Do doctors mean what they say? In *Fair of Speech: The Uses of Euphemism*, ed. D. J. Enright. Oxford: Oxford University Press, pp. 151–8.

Johnson, Samuel. 1755. *A Dictionary of the English Language: in which the words are deduced from their originals, and illustrated by examples from the best writers. To which are prefixed, a history of the language, and an English grammar*. 2 vols. London: W. Strahan.

Jones, Daniel. 1948. *An English Pronouncing Dictionary containing 56,300 words in International Phonetic Transcription*. 9th edn, revised with supplement. London: Dent.

　　2003. *English Pronouncing Dictionary*. 16th edn, ed. Peter Roach, James Hartman and Jane Setter. Cambridge: Cambridge University Press.

Jonson, Ben. 1981. *The Complete Plays of Ben Jonson*, ed. G. A. Wilkes. Oxford: Clarendon Press.

Joos, Martin. 1961. *The Five Clocks*. New York: Harcourt, Brace & World.

Kachru, Braj. 1984. The alchemy of English: social and functional power of non-native varieties. In *Language and Power*, ed. Cheris Kramarae, Muriel Schulz and William M. O'Barr. Beverly Hills: Sage Publications, pp. 176–93.

Keesing, Nancy. 1982. *Lily on the Dustbin: Slang of Australian Women and Families*. Ringwood: Penguin.

Keesing, Roger M. and Jonathan Fifiʔi. 1969. Kwaio word tabooing in its cultural context. *Journal of the Polynesian Society* 78: 154–77.

Keller, Helen. 1908. Sense and sensibility. *The Century Magazine* (February issue).

Kennedy, Randall. 2003. *Nigger: The Strange Career of a Troublesome Word*. New York: Vintage Books.

Kim, Karl H., Norman R. Relkin, Kyoung-Min Lee et al. 1997. Distinct cortical areas associated with native and second languages. *Nature* 388: 171–4.

Kinsey, Alfred. 1953. *Sexual Behavior in the Human Female*. Philadelphia: W. B. Saunders.

Kittredge, Richard and John Lehrberger (eds.). 1982. *Sublanguage: Studies of Language in Restricted Semantic Domains*. Berlin: De Gruyter.

Knipe, Edward E. 1984. *Gamrie: An Exploration in Cultural Ecology*. Lanham, New York and London: University Press of America.

Knipe, Edward E. and David G. Bromley. 1984. Speak no evil: word taboos among Scottish fishermen. In *Forbidden Fruits: Taboos and Tabooism in Culture*, ed. Ray B. Browne. Bowling Green: University of Ohio Popular Press, pp. 183–92.

Kobjitti, Chart. 1983. *The Judgement*, trans. Laurie Maund. Bangkok: Laurie Maund.

Korn, Daniel, Mark Radice and Charlie Hawes. 2001. *Cannibal: The History of People Eaters*. London: Channel 4 Books.

Kramer, Hilton. 1993. Confronting the monolith. *Partisan Review* 60: 569–73.

Kripke, Saul. 1972. Naming and necessity. In *Semantics of Natural Language*, ed. Donald Davidson and Gilbert Harman. Dordrecht: Reidel, pp. 253–355 [Republished separately as *Naming and Necessity*. Oxford: Blackwell 1980].

LaBar, Kevin S. and Elizabeth A. Phelps. 1998. Arousal-mediated memory consolidation: role of the medial temporal lobe in humans. *Psychological Science* 9: 490–3.

Labov, William. 1972. *Language in the Inner City*. Philadelphia: University of Pennsylvania.

Lakoff, Robin T. 2000. *The Language War*. Berkeley: University of California Press.

Lass, Roger. 1999. *The English Language Volume 111 (1476–1776)*. Cambridge: Cambridge University Press.

Leap, William L. 1996. *Word's Out: Gay Men's English*. Minneapolis: University of Minnesota Press.

Lee-Wong, Song Mei. 2000. *Politeness and Face in Chinese Culture*. Frankfurt-am-Main: Peter Lang.

Lehrer, Adrienne. 1990. As American as apple pie – and sushi and bagels: the semiotics of food and drink. In *Recent Developments in Theory and History: The Semiotic Web*, ed. Thomas A. Sebeok and Jean Umiker-Sebeok. New York: Mouton de Gruyter, pp. 359–402.

  1992. Names and naming: why we need fields and frames. In *Frames, Fields, and Contrasts*, ed. Adrienne Lehrer and Eva F. Kittay. Hillsdale: Lawrence Erlbaum, pp. 123–42.

Leonard, Sterling A. 1962. *The Doctrine of Correctness in English Usage 1700–1800*. New York: Russell and Russell [First published 1929].

Lifton, Robert J. and Eric Olson. 1976. The nuclear age. In *Death: Current Perspectives*, ed. Edwin S. Schneidman. Palo Alto: Mayfield, pp. 99–109.

Lindau, Sidney I. 2001. *Dictionaries: The Art and Craft of Lexicography*. 2nd edn. New York: Cambridge University Press.

Lloyd, Geoffrey E. R. 1983. *Science, Folklore and Ideology – Studies in the Life Sciences in Ancient Greece*. Cambridge: Cambridge University Press.

Locke, John. 1690. *Essay Concerning Human Understanding*, 4 vols. London: Tho. Basset.

Loftus, Elizabeth F. 1979. *Eyewitness Testimony*. Cambridge, MA: Harvard University Press.

Loury, Glen C. 1993. Self-censorship. *Partisan Review* 60: 608–18.

Lowth, Rev. Dr Robert. 1763. *A Short Introduction to English Grammar. With critical notes*. 2nd edn, corrected, to which are added observations on style by Joseph Priestley. Dublin: H. Saunders [First edn 1762].

Lutz, William. 1989. *Doublespeak: From 'Revenue Enhancement' to 'Terminal Living'. How Government, Business, Advertisers, and Others Use Language to Deceive You*. New York: Harper and Row.

Lynn, Jonathan and Anthony Jay. 1989. *The Complete Yes Prime Minister*. London: BBC Books.

MacKay, Donald G., Meredith Shafto, Jennifer K. Taylor et al. 2004. Relations between emotion, memory, and attention: evidence from taboo Stroop, lexical decision, and immediate memory tasks. *Memory and Cognition* 32: 474–88.

Maclean, Natalie. 2004. The last word. In *The Australian Wine Selector*. Australian Wine Selectors Pty Ltd. 114.

Macquarie Dictionary. 2003. 3rd edn, revised. North Ryde, NSW: Macquarie Library.

MacWhinney, Brian, Janice M. Keenan and Peter Reinke. 1982. The role of arousal in memory for conversation. *Memory and Cognition* 10: 308–17.

Maines, Rachel P. 1999. *The Technology of Orgasm: 'Hysteria', the Vibrator, and Women's Sexual Satisfaction*. Baltimore: Johns Hopkins University Press.

Marshall, L. 1957. N!ow. *Africa* 27: 232–40.

Marx, Karl. 1974. *On Freedom of the Press and Censorship*, ed. and trans. Saul K. Padover. The Karl Marx Library 4. New York: McGraw-Hill.

May, Derwent. 1985. Euphemisms and the media. In *Fair of Speech: The Uses of Euphemism*, ed. D. J. Enright. Oxford: Oxford University Press, pp. 122–34.

McCrum, Robert, William Cran and Robert MacNeil. 1992. *The Story of English*. Revised edn. London: Faber & Faber.

McDonald, James. 1988. *A Dictionary of Obscenity, Taboo and Euphemism*. London: Sphere Books.

McGinnies, Elliott. 1949. Emotionality of perceptual defense. *Psychological Review* 56: 244–51.

Mead, Margaret. 1937. Tabu. *Encyclopaedia of Social Sciences*. London: Macmillan, vol. 7: 502–5.

Meigs, Anna S. 1978. A Papuan perspective on pollution. *Man* 13: 304–18.

Metcalf, Fred. 1986. *The Penguin Dictionary of Modern Humorous Quotations*. Harmondsworth: Penguin.

Millwood-Hargrave, Andrea. 2000. *Delete expletives?* London: Advertising Standards Authority, British Broadcasting Corporation, Broadcasting Standards Commission, Independent Television Commission.

Milne, A. A. 1948. *The House at Pooh Corner*. London: Methuen.

Milroy, Jim. 2002. The legitimate language: giving a history to English. In *Alternative Histories of English*, ed. Richard Watts and Peter Trudgill. London: Routledge, pp. 7–26.

Milton, John. 1644. *Areopagitica; a Speech of Mr. John Milton For the Liberty of Vnlicenc'd Printing, To the Parlament of England*. London.

Montagu, Ashley. 1968. *The Anatomy of Swearing*. New York: Macmillan.

Montaigne, Michel de. 1948. *The Complete Works of Montaigne: Essays, Travel Journal, Letters*, trans. Donald M. Frame. Stanford: Stanford University Press.

Moore, Judith. 1994. *Never Eat Your Heart Out*. New York: Farrar, Straus & Giroux.

Morris, David B. 2000. *Illness and Culture in the Postmodern Age*. Berkeley: University of California Press.

Morris, Meaghan. 1997. Sticks and stones and stereotypes. In *The Retreat from Tolerance*, ed. Phillip Adams. Sydney: ABC Books.

Morrish, Elizabeth. 1997. Falling short of God's ideal: public discourse about lesbians and gays. In *Queerly Phrased: Language, Gender, and Sexuality*, ed. Anna Livia and Kira Hall. New York: Oxford University Press, pp. 335–45.

Morse, Gardiner. 1999. The nocebo effect. *Hippocrates*. Published on-line by the New England Journal of Medicine, http://www.hippocrates.com/archive/November1999/11departments/1integrative.html.

Moses, Peter. 1993. Non-consent in rape: a critique of the 'no means yes' controversy. *Alternative Law Journal* 18 (6): 290–2.

Muehlenhard, Charlene L. and Lisa C. Hollabaugh. 1988. Do women sometimes say no when they mean yes? The prevalence and correlates of women's token resistance to sex. *Journal of Personality and Social Psychology* 54: 872–9.

Murray, Lindley. 1795. *English Grammar, adapted to the different classes of learners. With an appendix, containing rules and observations for promoting perspicuity in speaking and writing*. York: Wilson, Spence and Mawman.

1799. *English exercises, adapted to the grammar lately published by L. Murray. Designed for the benefit of private learners, as well as for the use of schools*. 4th edn, corrected. London: T. N. Longman & O. Rees.

1824. *English Grammar*. 5th edn. London [First published 1795].

Murray, Stephen O. 1979. The art of gay insulting. *Anthropological Linguistics* 21: 211–23.

Neaman, Judith S. and Carole G. Silver. 1983. *Kind Words: A Thesaurus of Euphemisms*. New York: Facts on File.

Noonan, Peggy. 1998. Toward candor and courage in speech. In *Essays from Contemporary Culture*, ed. Katherine Anne Ackley. Fort Worth: Harcourt Brace, pp. 368–76.

Nothman, Fred H. 1962. The influence of response conditions on recognition thresholds for taboo words. *Journal of Abnormal and Social Psychology* 51: 427–33.

Nunberg, Geoffrey. 1990. What the usage panel thinks. In *The State of the Language*, ed. Christopher Ricks and Leonard Michaels. London: Faber, pp. 467–82.

Oraison, Marc. 1972. *Vie chrétienne et problèmes de la sexualité*. Paris: Lethielleux-Fayard, Centre d'études Laennec [First published 1952].

Ortner, Sherry B. 1974. Is female to male as nature is to culture? In *Woman, Culture, and Society*, ed. Michelle Z. Rosaldo and Louise Lamphere. Stanford: Stanford University Press, pp. 67–87.

Orwell, George. 1946. *Politics and the English Language. Shooting an Elephant and Other Essays*. New York: Harcourt, Brace & World.

1987. *Nineteen Eighty-Four*. London: Secker & Warburg [First published 1949].

Osgood, Charles E., George J. Suci and Percy H. Tannenbaum. 1957. *The Measurement of Meaning*. Urbana: University of Illinois Press.

Oxford Companion to the English Language. 1992. Ed. Tom McArthur. Oxford: Oxford University Press.

Oxford English Dictionary. 1989. 2nd edn. Oxford Clarendon Press [Abbreviated to *OED*]. Also available on compact disc.

Paget, Sir James. 1879. Sexual hypochondriasis (1870). In *Clinical Lectures and Essays by Sir James Paget*, ed. Howard Marsh. 2nd edn. London: Longmans Green & Co., pp. 275–98.

Partridge, Eric. 1952. *Introduction to Chamber of Horrors: A Glossary of Official Jargon both English and American*, ed. 'Vigilans'. London: André Deutsch.

1955. *Shakespeare's Bawdy.* London: Routledge & Kegan Paul.

1984. *A Dictionary of Slang and Unconventional English*, ed. Paul Beale. 8th edn. London: Routledge & Kegan Paul.

Patterson, James T. 1987. *The Dread Disease: Cancer and Modern American Culture.* Cambridge, MA: Harvard University Press.

Pauwels, Anne. 1993. Gender and language reform in Australia. In *Style on the Move: Proceedings of Style Council 92*, ed. Pam Peters, pp. 105–19.

Perrin, Noel. 1992. *Dr. Bowdler's Legacy: A History of Expurgated Books in English and America.* Boston: David R. Godine.

Perry, Ruth. 1992. A short history of the term *politically correct*. In *Beyond PC: Toward a Politics of Understanding*, ed. P. Aufderheide. St Pauls, MN: Graywolf Press, pp. 71–9.

Peterson, Alan. 1986. *Word Words Words: The Use and Misuse of English in Australia Today.* Sydney: The Fairfax Library.

Porter, Roy. 1995. 'Perplex't with tough names': the uses of medical jargon. In *Languages and Jargons: Contributions to the Social History of Language*, ed. Peter Burke and Roy Porter. Cambridge: Polity Press, pp. 42–63.

1997. *The Greatest Benefit to Mankind: A Medical History of Humanity from Antiquity to the Present.* London: HarperCollins.

Preston, Dennis R. 2002. The story of good and bad English in the United States. In *Alternative Histories of English*, ed. Richard Watts and Peter Trudgill. London: Routledge, pp. 134–152.

Probyn, Elspeth. 2000. *Carnal Appetites: FoodSexIdentities.* London: Routledge.

Pullar, Phillippa. 1970. *Consuming Passions: A History of English Food and Appetite.* London: Hamish Hamilton.

Pullum, Geoffrey K. 1991. *The Great Eskimo Vocabulary Hoax and Other Irreverent Essays on the Study of Language.* Berkeley: University of Chicago Press.

Quinion, Michael. 1999. Review of Encarta World English Dictionary. http://www. worldwidewords.org/reviews/encarta/htm.

Quintilian. 1920–22. *The Institutio Oratoria of Quintilian*, 4 vols., trans. H. E. Butler. Loeb Classical Library. London: William Heinemann.

Radcliffe-Brown, A. R. 1939. *Taboo.* Cambridge: Cambridge University Press.

Ravitch, Diane. 2004. *The Language Police: How Pressure Groups Restrict what Students Learn.* New York: Vintage Books.

Read, Allen W. 1977. *Classic American Graffiti: Lexical Evidence from Folk Epigraphy in Western North America.* Waukesha, WI: Maledicta Press [First published 1935].

Richards, Peter. 1977. *The Medieval Leper.* Cambridge: D. S. Brewer.

Risch, Barbara. 1987. Women's derogatory terms for men: That's right, 'dirty' words. *Language in Society* 16: 353–8.

Rochester, John Wilmot, 2nd Earl of. 1968. *The Works of the Earl of Rochester*, ed. David M. Vieth. New Haven: Yale University Press.

Rosten, Leo. 1968. *The Joys of Yiddish*. New York: McGraw-Hill.

Sade, Marquis de. 1965. *Justine, Philosophy in the Bedroom, and Other Writings*, trans. Richard Seaver and Austryn Wainhouse. New York: Grove Press.

   1966–7. *Œuvres complètes du Marquis de Sade. Édition définitive*. Paris: Cercle du livre précieux.

   1968. *Juliette*, trans. Austryn Wainhouse. New York: Grove Weidenfeld [First published as *La Nouvelle Justine, ou les Malheurs de la Vertu, suivie de l'Histoire de Juliette, sa sœur ou les Prospérités du vice*. Paris. 1797].

Sanders, Alan J. and Jantsangiin Bat-Ireedui. 1999. *Colloquial Mongolian: The Complete Course for Beginners*. London: Routledge.

Sanders, Stephanie A. and Julie M. Reinsich. 1999. Would you say you had 'sex' if? *Journal of the American Medical Association* 281: 275–7.

Saussure, Ferdinand de. 1974. *A Course in General Linguistics*, ed. Charles Bally and Albert Sechehaye, trans. Wade Baskin. Glasgow: Fontana/Collins [First published 1915].

Scellinck, Thomaes. 1343. *Het 'Boeck van Surgien' van Meester Thomaes Scellinck van Thienen*. Opuscula Selecta Neerlandicorum de Arte Medica, ed. E. D. Leersum. Amsterdam. 1928.

Schwarz, Maureen T. 2001. Allusions to ancestral impropriety: understandings of arthritis and rheumatism in the contemporary Navajo world. *American Ethnologist* 28: 650–78.

Scollon, Ronald and Suzanne Wong Scollon. 1995. *Intercultural Communication: A Discourse Approach*. Oxford and Malden, MA: Blackwell.

Scutt, Jocelynne A. 2002. Vilifying Women on the Football Field. http://www. philcleary.com.au/afl_racism_football_scutt.htm. Accessed October 2004.

Seaberg, Alvin G. 1973. *Menu Design-merchandising and Marketing*. Boston: Chaners' Books International.

Shakespeare, William. 1951. *The Complete Works*, ed. Peter Alexander. London and Glasgow: Collins.

Shattuck, Roger. 1996. *Forbidden Knowledge: From Prometheus to Pornography*. New York: St Martin's Press.

Shaw, George B. 1946. *Pygmalion*. Harmondsworth: Penguin.

Shem, Samuel. 1978. *The House of God*. New York: Dell.

Simons, Gary F. 1982. Word taboo and comparative Austronesian linguistics. In *Papers from the Third International Conference on Austronesian Linguistics*, vol. 3: *Accent on Variety*, ed. Amran Halim, Lois Carrington and Stephen A. Wurm. Canberra: Pacific Linguistics, pp. 157–226.

Sloane, Patrick. 1999. Taste of the Vine. *Melbourne Palate* 15: 7.

Smith, Neil V. 2002. *Language, Banana sand Bonobos: Linguistic Problems, Puzzles and Polemics*. Oxford: Blackwell.

Sontag, Susan. 1979. *Illness as Metaphor*. New York: Vintage.

   1989. *AIDS and Its Metaphors*. New York: Farrar, Strauss, Giroux.

Spender, Dale. 1984. Defining reality: a powerful tool. In *Language and Power*, ed. Cheris Kramarae, Muriel Schulz and William M. O'Barr. Beverly Hills: Sage Publications, pp. 194–205.

Steiner, Franz B. 1967. *Taboo*, ed. Laura Bohannan. Harmondsworth: Penguin [First published 1956].

Stengers, Jean and Anne van Neck. 2001. *Masturbation: The History of a Great Terror*, trans. Kathryn A. Hoffmann. New York: Palgrave [First published 1998 as *Histoire d'une grande peur, la masturbation*].

Stephenson, John S. 1985. *Death, Grief, and Mourning: Individual and Social Relations*. New York: The Free Press.

Stern, Gustaf. 1965. *Meaning and Change of Meaning (with Special Reference to the English Language)*. Bloomington: Indiana University Press [First published 1931].

Stewart, William. 1995. *Cassell's Queer Companion*. London: Cassell.

Stockwell, Robert and Donka Minkova. 2001. *English Words: History and Structure*. Cambridge: Cambridge University Press.

Stoddart, D. Michael. 1990. *The Scented Ape: The Biology and Culture of Human Odour*. Cambridge: Cambridge University Press.

Strom, K. A. (ed.). 1984. *The Best of Attack! and National Vanguard Tabloid*. Arlington: National Alliance.

Süskind, Patrick. 1986. *Perfume: The Story of a Murderer*. Harmondsworth: Penguin.

Sutton-Smith, B. and D. M. Abrams. 1978. Psychosexual material in stories told by children: the fucker. *Archives of Sexual Behavior* 7: 521–43.

Swift, Jonathan. 1712. *A Proposal for Correcting, Improving, and Ascertaining the English tongue: in a letter to the most honourable Robert Earl of Oxford and Mortimer, Lord High Treasurer of Great Britain*. London: Benj. Tooke [Facsimile. Menston: Scolar Press. 1969].

  1958. *Gulliver's Travels and Other Writings by Jonathan Swift*, ed. Ricardo Quintana. New York: Random House [First published 1735].

Taavitsainen, Irma and Andreas H. Jucker, (eds.). 2003. *Diachronic Perspectives on Address Term Systems*. Amsterdam and Philadelphia: John Benjamins.

Tacitus, Publius Cornelius. 1908. *Tacitus, Historical Works*, vol. 1: *The Annals*, trans. Arthur Murphy. London: J. M. Dent.

Tannahill, Reah. 1988. *Food in History*. Harmondsworth: Penguin.

Tieken-Boon van Ostade, Ingrid. 2002. Robert Lowth and the strong verb system. *Language Sciences* 24: 459–70.

Toolan, Michael. 1989. Ruling out rules in the analysis of conversation. *Journal of Pragmatics* 13: 251–74.

Traugott, Elizabeth C. and Richard B. Dasher. 2002. *Regularity in Semantic Change*. Cambridge: Cambridge University Press.

Truss, Lynne. 2004. *Eats, Shoots and Leaves: The Zero Tolerance Approach to Punctuation*. Harmondsworth: Penguin.

Turner, G. 1884. *Samoa a Hundred Years Ago and Long Before*. London: Macmillan.

Twain, Mark. 1981. *Roughing It*. Harmondsworth: Penguin [Set from the first edition published by the American Publishing Company, Hartford, 1872].

Valenstein, Edward and Kenneth M. Heilman. 1979. Emotional disorders resulting from lesions of the central nervous system. In *Clinical Neuropsychology*, ed. Kenneth M. Heilman and Edward Valenstein. New York: Oxford University Press, pp. 413–38.

Van Lancker, D. and J. Cummings. 1999. Expletives: Neurolinguistics and neuro-behavioral perspectives on swearing. *Brain Research Reviews* 31: 83–104.

Vining, Donald. 1986. *How Can You Come Out If You've Never Been In?* Trumans-burg, NY: Crossing Press.

Visser, Margaret. 1992. *The Rituals of Dinner: The Origins, Evolution, Eccentricities and Meaning of Table Manners.* London: Viking.

Vogan, A. J. 1890. *The Black Police: A Story of Modern Australia.* London: Hutch-inson.

Wallian, Samuel S. 1906. *Rhythmotherapy: A Discussion of the Physiologic Basis and Therapeutic Potency of Mechano-Vital Vibration, to Which is Added a Dictionary of Diseases and Suggestions as to the Technic of Vibratory Therapeutics.* Chicago: Ouellette Press.

Wardhaugh, Ronald. 1986. *An Introduction to Sociolinguistics.* Oxford: Basil Black-well.

1999. *Proper English: Myths and Misunderstandings about Language.* Malden, MA: Blackwell.

Watson, Lyall. 2000. *Jacobson's Organ and the Remarkable Nature of Smell.* New York: W. W. Norton & Company.

Watts, Richard J., Sachiko Ide and Konrad Ehlich (eds.). 1992. *Politeness in Lan-guage: Studies in its History, Theory, and Practice.* Berlin: Mouton de Gruyter.

Watts, Richard and Peter Trudgill (eds.). 2002. *Alternative Histories of English.* London: Routledge.

Whitaker, Katie. 2002. *Mad Madge: The Extraordinary Life of Margaret Cavendish, Duchess of Newcastle, the First Woman to Live by her Pen.* New York: Basic Books.

Wierzbicka, Anna. 1992. *Semantics, Culture, and Cognition: Universal Human Con-cepts in Culture-specific Configurations.* New York: Oxford University Press.

Wilson, J. K. 1995. *The Myth of Political Correctness: the Conservative Attack on Higher Education.* Durham, NC: Duke University Press.

Wolfram, W. and Ralph W. Fasold. 1974. *Social Dialects and American English.* Englewood Cliffs, NJ: Prentice-Hall.

Wundt, Wilhelm. 1927. *Völkerpsychologie.* 10 vols. 4th edn. Leipzig: Kröner.

Wyld, Henry C. 1936. *A History of Modern Colloquial English.* Oxford: Blackwell [First published 1920].

Yeats, William B. 1965. *The Collected Poems of W. B. Yeats.* London: Macmillan.

Zajonc, R. B. 1962. Response suppression in perceptual defense. *Journal of Experi-mental Psychology* 64: 206–14.

Zilbergeld, Bernard. 1978. *Male Sexuality: A Guide to Sexual Fulfillment.* New York: Bantam Books.

Zwicky, Ann and Arnold Zwicky. 1981. America's national dish: the style of restaur-ant menus. *American Speech* 56: 83–92.

Zwicky, Arnold. 1997. Two lavendar issues for linguists. In *Queerly Phrased: Lan-guage, Gender, and Sexuality,* ed. Anna Livia and Kira Hall. New York: Oxford University Press, pp. 21–34.

Zwicky, Arnold and Ann Zwicky. 1982. Register as a dimension of linguistic vari-ation. In *Sublanguage: Studies of Language in Restricted Semantic Domains,* ed. Richard Kittredge and John Lehrberger. Berlin: De Gruyter, pp. 213–18.

Index